A M O N G
FRIENDS

Princess Pale Moon
American Indian Heritage Foundation
6051 Arlington Blvd.
Falls Church, Va. 22044

AMONG
FRIENDS

*Who We Like,
Why We Like Them,
and
What We Do with Them*

LETTY COTTIN POGREBIN

McGRAW-HILL BOOK COMPANY

New York   St. Louis   San Francisco
Toronto   Hamburg   Mexico

1 2 3 4 5 6 7 8 9   DOCDOC   8 7 6

ISBN 0-07-050404-0

LIBRARY OF CONGRESS CATALOGING-IN-PUBLICATION-DATA

Pogrebin, Letty Cottin.
  Among friends.
  1. Friendship.   I. Title.
BF575.F66P64   1987   302.3'4   86-10290
ISBN 0-07-050404-0

BOOK DESIGN BY PATRICE FODERO

For Alan Alda,
who asked the first questions
and for
all the friends who answered

Contents

Author's Note

The friendship patterns described in this book are derived from both published research and interviews with nearly 150 people over the course of twenty-two months during 1984 and 1985. Although not scientifically selected, the sample provides a full variety of cultural, economic, and geographic backgrounds with subjects ranging in age from early adolescence to 82 years.

People who were willing to speak for attribution are quoted under their own first and last names. The names of those who requested anonymity have been changed and their privacy has been further protected by using a first name only and altering the details of their identity and experience.

Psychology Today's "The Friendship Bond" and Claude Fischer's *To Dwell Among Friends: Personal Networks in Town and City,* two exhaustive friendship surveys, have been most helpful. The former is cited as "*PT*'s survey" and the latter is recalled by Fischer's name.

Although this book concentrates on the friendship patterns experienced in the United States today, interviews with a number of non-Americans indicate that the findings are, if not universally applicable, of great interest elsewhere as well.

Acknowledgments

Warmest thanks—for their forthrightness, their time, and their trust—to all the strangers, acquaintances, and friends who were willing to share intimate thoughts and feelings and thus provide the substance of this book. Special gratitude goes to:

- My children, Abigail, Robin, and David, who each contributed anecdotes, quotes, ideas, critiques, and that which is most precious: loving tolerance for a mother who writes.
- My husband, Bert, who validated my own fascination with this subject, read drafts of the manuscript, cheered me out of countless funks, and made it possible for me to obsess about friendship for two full years without ever feeling guilty.
- My agent, Wendy Weil, for her spirited enthusiasm and unflagging support.
- My colleagues at *Ms.* magazine for once again allowing me to leave them in the lurch, drop out, write a book, and come back to the office without hearing a single recrimination—truly an act of friendship.
- My editor at McGraw-Hill, Leslie Meredith, who gives strong guidance with a light touch.
- My research assistants, Evelyn Israel, Sharon Portnoy, Linda Bennett, Naomi Bernstein, and Pat Bear, for delivering facts,

documents, books, and photocopies with a smile on unconscionably short notice.

- My personal computer gurus, Cindi Carbine, J. B. Blunck, and Lindsy Van Gelder, for launching me, however reluctantly, into the world of word processing and modem data banks without which the preparation of this book would have taken four years not two.

- Two writers' colonies, The Cummington Community and School of the Arts in Cummington, Massachusetts, and The Millay Colony for the Arts in Austerlitz, New York, for granting me residencies that permitted undisturbed contemplation, unprecedented productivity, and unbelievable peace and quiet.

Part One

Definitions and Passages

Chapter 1

❧   ❧

The Dinner Party

Five years ago at my house a well-known actor-screenwriter asked the others gathered around the dinner table to give him some ideas for a script in progress.[1]

"The movie is about friendship," he explained. "I need to know what role friendship plays in the average person's life. What do you look for in a friend? How many really good friends do you have and how often do you see them? What do you do together? Could you live without them? Can you stay friends after a serious fight? Did you ever lose a meaningful friend? Do you keep making new ones? Is there such a thing as having too many friends? Are *you* a good friend to the friends in your life?"

The minute he stopped to take a sip of wine, the other seven of us started talking at once—unlike nuclear arms and Central America, friendship was a subject on which each of us was an expert. What's more, how often did we get the opportunity to contribute to an artist's conceptual formulations, especially when our pearls of wisdom might one day be repeated by a star on the silver screen?

An hour later, long after finishing dessert, we were still at the table, mining friendship for all it was worth. At first, I chalked it up to good conversation. But when two hours had passed and the discussion was becoming more animated by the minute—and my friends had moved beyond glib anecdotes to astonishing revelations about themselves and their friends—I realized that this was far more than just talk. The screenwriter had touched a nerve.

With all the variations and idiosyncrasies represented among those eight people, one theme in particular seemed to drive the engine of personal disclosure: Everyone at the table felt inadequate in regard to some aspect of friendship. Nobody was entirely satisfied with the friendships in his or her life, and each of us assumed everyone else was a better friend or had better friends than we did ourselves.

"I have a lot of friends," mused a certifiable Nice Guy, who had just turned 40. "But lately some of them bore me. I'm tired of them. Maybe it's mid-life crisis that's making me reassess the people in my life. All I know is, not one is quite like the best friend I had when I was 12. Come to think of it, I can't say I've ever had a really close friendship as an adult."

A normally self-confident woman looked down at her plate. "Most of you are better at maintaining friendships than I am," she said quietly, arranging her leftover cake crumbs into neat rows. "It takes work, and with my job and family, I never seem to have enough time. I'm in a constant state of guilt about the people I haven't called in ages or the ones I owe a dinner or a letter or a birthday card. I feel like a real failure as a friend."

"When I'm with one of my close friends I feel totally comfortable," said a cheerful man in his early thirties. "I know I can say anything. I'm also genuinely interested in their lives and I think I'm a good listener. But after we've spent one nice warm evening together, the truth is I have no impulse to see them again for a while. Is that weird? I mean, I really like my friends and I even love two or three of them, but I don't *need* them."

"I'm afraid I need my friends *too* much—so much that I'm a burden to them," said a woman with intense, dark eyes, who was drinking her third cup of coffee. "I'm afraid my idea of intimacy is most people's idea of suffocation."

"It's the inevitability of problems that gets me down," offered a man I'd known for years and never known to admit to a problem. "Eventually something goes wrong. A friend doesn't come through for me, or I disappoint him without realizing it, or a friendship with a woman gets complicated by sex, or my wife is best friends with a woman whose husband bores me, or friends do something horrible and I can never feel the same about them . . ."

"All right, already," interrupted the screenwriter, "we get the point."

"The point is," the man pushed on, "why does everything have to turn to crap?"

"Maybe it's different because I'm single," said an intellectual feminist who had been especially pensive. "For me, friends are family. I need them, I enjoy them, I give a lot and get a lot in return. But I have to admit, with all my friendships, I'm still lonely."

A man in his fifties with a great sense of humor was uncharacteristically serious. "It's not loneliness that I feel; it's envy," he said. "I envy the friendship my wife has with her women friends. They seem so much more *connected* to each other than I've ever felt with a man. When I'm around my wife and her friends I know I'm missing something. Something that would make my friendships deeper or more vivid. Something that would help me be a better friend. What do you think I'm missing?"

"What am I missing?"

The question resonated. Until that moment I had been watching and listening with the rakishly remote participant-observer posture common to writers. I had been remarking to myself about the man who seemed unusually emotional, and the man whom I had never before heard admit weakness, and the woman whose praise of friendship was almost poetic. I had been sitting there in what felt like full consciousness, watching, listening, observing how the screenwriter orchestrated the discussion, noticing my husband become reflective, nodding my head as each person confessed or commiserated.

But when that one friend asked "What am I missing?" I felt suddenly as if he were asking it for me. "Me too," I put in, "I think I might be missing something too. Friendship is like sex: You always suspect there's some secret technique you don't know about. How can I know if I'm a good friend? How can I be better? Do I really have good friends? Do other people have more friends, closer friendships, different ways of being friends?" The hostess-writer vanished and I began searching for answers.

Here was this exposed nerve—something deeply important to all of us and yet we had never before said a word to each other about it—never even let it be named. Now it throbbed openly: None of us felt sure of ourselves or fully contented with our friendships. Underneath our casual social style, we weren't at all confident and our relationships were far from effortless. We wondered if we were inadequate to the people we cared about; we wondered if we cared about enough people. We worried about time, about emotional commitment, about the logistics of our lives.

Clearly, if this group was at all typical, being friends is not an instinct; it doesn't come naturally. What's more, *being* friends was not enough. We wanted to understand the meaning of friendship, the expectations friends have of each other, other people's ideas of "too little" or "enough." We wanted to hear about friendship's avoidable pitfalls and ultimate possibilities.

Were we typical? If so, millions of people are quietly doubting themselves and worrying about their friendships. Are we all missing something?

My friends left at 2 a.m. but their words and feelings stayed with me.

That is where this book began.

Chapter 2

≈   ≈

Contradictions

I went looking for the truth about friendship at other people's dinner tables, in offices, nursing homes, barrios, and factories; on street corners and college campuses; at conferences and co-op meetings; in prisons, powder rooms, military bases, union halls, housing projects, and high school gyms. What couldn't be learned from observation and interviews, I found in books, studies, surveys, movies, public polls, and private diaries. I found friendship in Aristotle, Cicero and Seneca, Montaigne, Bacon and Emerson, Elizabeth Cady Stanton, Virginia Woolf and Alice Walker. I found it in fiction and history, in futurists' projections and in the here and now—and wherever there was friendship, there were contradictions.

Contradiction #1. In earlier times, friendship was a haven from stress; today our friendships (or lack of them) are frequently a *source* of stress, another arena in which to fail.

After reviewing European art, literature, and iconography from the Middle Ages until 1800, Philippe Ariès concluded that friendship occupied "a great place" in the life of people of every age and class. They socialized in cafés, pubs, and manor houses. They prided themselves on cordial relationships. They met in the streets "for gossiping, conversation, entertainments and games." There was constant visiting. By the late eighteenth century, however, family life slowly became more dominant and privatized. Soon, it was no longer considered good form to call on a friend unannounced. Since then, in a remarkable shift of emphasis, says Ariès, "professional and family life have stifled that other activity which once invaded the whole of life: the activity of social relations."[1]

To this day, the competing pressures of friendship and family have not lessened but have been further strained by the demands of modern life. From 1974 to 1984 the average American lost six leisure hours per week. Now our time is taken up with commuting, consumerism, housework, child care, second jobs, second families, single parent responsibilities, and a compulsive commitment to television and physical fitness.[2] With all this, people want to give themselves to friendship too. Asked what aspects of life gave them the most satisfaction, most Americans ranked their friends relatively high on the list: spouse/lover, family, friends, religion, recreation, work, and community activity.[3]

Many of us feel incompetent to manage the third most important relationship in our lives, the one that's supposed to be the icing on the cake. Seven out of ten people say they feel "rushed"—they don't have enough time for the things that give them pleasure. So our high-pressured lives give us less time to devote to friends even as we need friends more to help us relax from our high-pressured lives. But we rarely talk about it. We don't go into friendship therapy. We just continue feeling inadequate and believing everyone else must be doing it better.

Contradiction #2.   Almost everyone has a different definition of friendship, yet we all use the word as if it had a universal meaning. Friendship is a category each of us invents. The criteria for admission into my friendship Hall of Fame might not pass muster in yours. In essence, a friend is a friend because we say so. The label is the fact. The astounding thing is, regardless of amorphous definitions and a lack of objective criteria, each of us is absolutely certain of what *we* require in a friend.

When you think about it, this paradox is an endearing symbol of the democratic spirit. Americans seem to be saying, okay, marriage is a legal arrangement, child-rearing and employment are subject to state-controlled standards, but friendship is our turf; here, we make the rules.

Contradiction #3.   Our generation has the most sophisticated understanding of the psychodynamics of personal relations—but no
greater gift for the practice of friendship. We idealize friendship but
are unduly critical of friends. We expect more perfection from friends
than from families because friends are voluntary intimates. We chose
them, so they must be whom we want and need. Yet in a crisis,
most of us still favor blood over friendship.

Contradiction #4.   We are torn between a desire for freedom and
a need for love. Yankee individualism plus recent ideologies of personal fulfillment have made us fierce guardians of our own independence. When asked to put their values in order of priority,
Americans ranked "freedom" well ahead of "true friendship" and
"mature love."[4] At the same time, the need for love—both sexual
liaisons and the fusion of friendship—keeps driving us toward other
people. This contradiction speaks to humanity's deepest dilemma:
In the primacy of the self we find our voice and identity; but in
relationships with friends and lovers, we are nurtured and made safe.
The tension between these coequal but conflicting needs describes
the most fundamental paradox of all: *We are lonely, but we fear intimacy*.
We cherish our privacy but dread being alone in the world. We want
the comfort of an embrace but we fear confinement.

   Balancing love and freedom is especially challenging in friendship
where it is so easy to walk away from the struggle. Unlike marriage
and family, friends have no legal bonds, vows, or sexual magnetism
to keep them cleaving. Friendship is answerable to its own unwritten
laws, a phenomenon of pure choice and delicate moderation. Extremes don't just complicate a friendship, they negate it: Extreme
attachment negates friendship by transforming it into dependency,
and extreme detachment is, of course, no friendship at all.

But Who's Counting

   Behind these contradictions are some arresting facts. Today's city
dweller comes into contact with more people in a week than the
seventeenth-century villager did in a year or even a lifetime. When
asked to keep track of those with whom they interacted during a
100-day period, the average person was found to have an acquaint-

ance pool of from 500 to 2500 people, including relatives, neighbors, service people, officials, teachers, classmates, clients and customers, tradespeople and coworkers. Of these, how many would you guess might be considered real "friends"? According to a great variety of studies of children and adults, whites and people of color, homosexuals and heterosexuals, city and rural dwellers, the answer is between three and seven.

Although numbers reveal only a small part of the truth about friendship, at least we know that most Americans are not isolates. With an average of five friends per person, we are quantitatively if not qualitatively involved with others. Even lonely people have as many best friends as non-lonely people. Therefore, when we say we are not sure we have enough friends, what we invariably mean is we are not sure that the friendships we have are giving us enough.

The feelings of inadequacy expressed at my dinner table match a key finding reported by sociologist Claude Fischer in *To Dwell Among Friends,* his exhaustive studies of more than 1000 people and their relationships with 20,000 others. Fischer found that people with the richest, most supportive personal networks were as likely or more likely to say they "wished they knew more people" as were those who had marginal or sparse friendships.[5] It seems the more companionship we have, the more we want—a contradiction that dooms even the most sociable of us to feel that "something's missing."

Rather than suffering from a real lack of friends, we may be suffering from a perceived discrepancy between the kind of friendships we have and what we think we *should* have. As Ben Jonson wrote, "True happiness consists not in the multitude of friends but in their worth and choice." In that case, the something missing is the Ideal Friendship—the perfect unions that we are sure "other people" must be having while we are making do with our three to seven ordinary friends.

What if the something missing is just another vague desire for more, more of whatever is valued or sought after by others? What if we've been trained or trapped into viewing friendship as an "asset"— something to have a lot of, like money, sex, or possessions? What if the fault lies not in our friends but in our idealized *expectations* of friendship?

Hold those questions on your screen while we dip into another body of research: studies of loneliness.[6] Psychologists define loneliness as either a disturbing lack of social companions or a feeling of being misunderstood, rejected, or "different." By that measure, on any given day, more than a quarter of all Americans say they feel lonely. Robert Weiss, author of *Loneliness: The Experience of Emotional and Social Isolation,* believes that every human being has the simultaneous need for *community* (connection to friends) and *attachment* (intimacy with a spouse or lover).[7] He says that the absence of either kind of relationship causes loneliness, and that one area of satisfaction cannot substitute for the other. Thus, someone with friends but no lover can be as unhappy as someone with a lover but no friends.

That's logical as far as it goes, but it doesn't go far enough. It makes loneliness into an entirely personal problem, a psychological state of mind that people bring upon themselves because of their private inadequacies. It leaves us counting our attachments and connections as though having enough of each should make us happy. In theory, maybe it should, just as in theory the "personal" problem of loneliness should appear randomly throughout the population. But loneliness has a funny habit of selectively striking those who are weak or powerless. The loneliest people in America tend to be either young, single, unemployed, female, or poor. It is highly implausible that these groups share one psychological trait that would account for their disproportionate loneliness. More likely it has something to do with what they obviously do have in common: a paucity of real assets, a lack of autonomy, status, or economic resources.

We know that friends can occasionally work miracles to cheer and inspire us, but friends cannot compensate for all the financial and structural deficiencies in a person's life. Friends may help us with a loan or a gift when the unemployment insurance runs out, but a friend is not a job. Friends can comfort us after an attack by an abusive parent, but a friend is not a loving mother or a caring father. Youngsters and single people might be less lonely if there were more social activities and decent gathering places where they could meet each other. Poor people might be less lonely if they could afford to invite a friend to their supper tables. And women might be less lonely if they didn't still have to wait to be taken to certain places by men, or if they could safely go visiting alone at certain hours, or if they could leave their children in adequate child care centers and thus "escape" the house. It's too much to ask of private friendships that they fill the gaps created by large social problems, or to suggest that people who are poor and powerless would be happy if only they knew how to run their personal lives.

As the contradictions mount up, so do the questions:

- What if our problems with friendship originate not with ourselves and our friends but with our having false and idealized expectations of friendship?

- What if these expectations stem from a sort of personal capitalism that views friends as human assets of which we have learned to want *more* and *better* regardless of whether our present friendships are satisfactory?

- What if we've been brainwashed to believe that oppression can be alleviated by the right kind of friends—and these friends are supposed to distract us from the concrete problems inherent in our circumstances?

- What if our circumstances are the reason we have no energy to put into friends, so that the *causes* of our friendship problems are also the *symptoms* of what's wrong with our lives?

- What if, rather than relieve the symptoms, we are jollied into trying to fix the friendships? And what if we accept the assignment because we are taught that "everyone" is responsible for his or her own problems and, since we can't solve poverty or divorce or child abuse or sex discrimination, at least we should be able to have some of those magical human assets "everyone" else has.

- What if it is to society's advantage to keep us busy working on relationships that—on their own merits without inadequacy brainwashing—are really quite satisfactory?

- If friendship is basically in good shape in America and yet we're not encouraged to see it and enjoy it, who, or what interests, are benefitting from our discontent?

Why a Friendship Problem?

According to pollster Daniel Yankelovich, 70 percent of Americans say that they have many acquaintances but few close friends and that they experience this as a serious void in their lives.[8] We've seen that "few" amounts to about five for most people, and we've suggested how and why people might have come to believe that five close friends are not enough. Nevertheless, since a "void" is felt, we ought to discuss the factors that supposedly cause it.

Depersonalization

Depersonalization is usually cited first. Human relations are diminished by big cities and organizations, seemingly insoluble social problems, international tensions, and of course the looming possibility of nuclear destruction. Do friendships matter in the face of all that?

More than ever. The same global and immense problems that dwarf the individual also make human affiliation all the more precious. Depersonalization doesn't destroy friendship; rather, it makes it even clearer that friends are needed to affirm our values and to help us retain our sanity in the shadow of the bomb. Ironically, we sometimes have to sacrifice a social life to gain the time for lobbying and educational activities that argue for planetary survival. But building relationships and repairing the world (as the Talmud puts it) are not always mutually exclusive activities. As we will see in Chapter 8, social activism is a well-traveled route to friendship.

Social Mobility

A measure of each American's freedom and independence, social mobility is also blamed for the void in friendship. Psychologists worry because people on the move may be hesitant to put down roots and form relationships. From other quarters, the worry is not so well-intentioned. More than thirty-five years ago, David Riesman warned that complaints about "too much mobility" often mask reactionaries' objections to the average person's sudden access to as much freedom as the privileged. Whereas wealthy people have always been able to move around and make friends in a variety of places, reactionaries want to "freeze" lower-level people into communities where their friendships and progress are limited. Said Riesman, "here we have the classes attempting to root down the masses," an observation that remains applicable today.[9]

Conservatives who find rewards in the status quo do not like anything that upsets the economic order. Yet, every twenty-four

hours, more than 100,000 people change residences, many of them
in pursuit of education and better jobs.[10] Workers who earn between
$25,000 and $65,000 a year move to another firm once every thirty-
one months. Electronics engineers, computer scientists, and M.B.A.'s
change jobs about four times a decade. Even the least active job-
changers—civil service executives—change jobs every eight years.

"All this moving is not quite as debilitating as we might think,"
wrote psychologists Carin Rubenstein and Phillip Shaver in their
book *In Search of Intimacy*. Citing national studies showing that most
people tend to move to places where they already have friends or
relatives, the co-authors found that "people who moved often were
no lonelier than those who didn't." What's more, after a year in a
new place, whether it's a big city like New York or a town of 31,000,
most people say they have established satisfying new friendships as
well as retained some of their old ones.[11]

The Ethic of Competition

Another reason, some say, for the decline in friendship is the ethic
of competition. Indeed, many people are highly competitive in love
and in work, the two areas Americans cite most when asked to define
success. Rarely do we mention the word friendship. Yet none of us
can be a success as a human being *without* friends. Here, then, is
another paradox: The higher we rise in occupational status, the greater
our stresses. The greater our stresses, the more we need the support
of friends—but the more barriers we erect against revealing any
vulnerability that might contradict a strong, confident image. So
we're conned into "winning by intimidation" and "looking out for
Number One." Cool detachment frees us to shaft the next person.
A hard shell protects us when we are the one being shafted, and
social distance keeps us from an elbow in the ribs when a "friend"
passes us in the fast track. (More on competition in Chapter 12,
"Friends at Work.")

Obviously, none of these competitive strategies is conducive to
friendship, but who's to blame for this no-win situation? Why are
we sucked into competing on every front? And in competing, why
do we let others force us to choose between job and family, between
family and friends, between career and friendship? Isn't there something wrong with a system that makes such untenable choices necessary?

The Fragmentation of Modern Life

Another popular reason for the alleged social void is the fragmentation of modern life. Sentimentalists say people were friendlier in the old days when all our needs were satisfied in the family and immediate community. Today we turn to specialists, to far-flung agencies and bureaucracies. We get different strokes from different folks and rarely enough contact in any one place to forge a shared history. Transactions have replaced relationships. Supposedly, specialization obviates common knowledge. What can we talk about if your world never overlaps mine?

We can talk about each other's worlds. We can stop romanticizing the familiar and start relishing variety and learning from our differences. Then, this thing called "fragmentation" might be recast as "diversity" and experienced as "enrichment."

Changing Patterns of Marriage and Sexual Behavior

Some people's need to get more from friendship is attributed to changing patterns of marriage and sexual behavior, a claim that is true in some ways but distorted in others. It's true that Americans are staying single longer; the median age for first marriage is now 23 for women and 24 for men.[12] Add the divorced and widowed to the never-married and there are 70 million single people in this country. How does being single affect friendship? Research tells us what common sense predicts: Friends who are single see each other much more often than friends who are married, but singles with family responsibilities have little time for friends.

Beyond this, we know about how being single affects living arrangements, which in turn may affect friendships. At least one person in four now lives alone or with nonrelatives, an astounding increase of 88 percent since 1970.[13] Those who cannot afford to live alone seek another single to share the rent. When they join forces, they tend to worry more about each other's mental health, honesty, and financial reliability than about a perfect personality fit. Because of such practical considerations, single people sometimes wonder if their lives are too full of compromises. Roommates become part of their lives, nice or not. There are incompatibilities, inconveniences, arguments.

Here again, we are not talking about a failure of *friendship* but rather a shortage of choices. Just as marriages made for financial advantage usually disappoint one's dreams, so roommate unions inspired by economic necessity are frequently less than ideal. Plenty of single people who can afford to live alone prefer to do so and are happy in their living situation and in their friendships. And plenty of single people who want company and are not forced to make an economically motivated alliance have been able to team up with chosen friends and enjoy a convivial roommate relationship.

As for the purported connections between friendship and marriage, they are confusing to say the least. One psychologist asserts that people are less likely to have a happy marriage if their spouse is their best friend than if they have a best friend of their own; others say strong friendships outside marriage threaten the primacy of the spouse.[14] Some people get married because they can't achieve intimacy in friendship. And some people with cheerless marriages are famous for being great at friendship because they have so much love left over.

I have trouble discussing love and friendship as if they were Siamese twins, joined at the hip and competing for one head and heart. Obviously, each day is finite and the time we devote to a romantic or sexual partner is time unavailable to friends and vice versa. But rather than get caught up in ranking the competing priorities of lover and friend or blaming one because we're short-changing the other, we need to honor both according to the needs of each.

Parents of multiple children do it by giving one child *all* their attention *some* of the time. It's not possible to satisfy equal priorities any other way. The same is true of the important adults in our lives. There is room for each one to be *most* important *some* of the time. But people need flexibility to apportion their hours appropriately. A too-demanding friendship or a jealous lover undermines our ability to make serious commitments in both spheres. As flattering as possessiveness may seem at first, the friend or spouse who insists on all of you all the time is expressing selfishness not love.

When die-hard traditionalists object to friendship on the ground that "it comes between husband and wife," I suspect it is because they want to prevent those cross-checks between friends that help us assess the quality of our marriages. This is healthy. For example, the women's movement and its paradigms of sisterhood have set a standard for female commitments that many women have translated into higher expectations from a husband. Cross-checking between relationships helps us to determine which imperfections we should be prepared to tolerate and which are simply intolerable.

A good marriage may put a friendship in a dim light. By the same token, an especially satisfying friendship may cover for an empty marriage. But when we ask each relationship to consistently compensate for the deficiencies of the other, we are asking too much.

While love and friendship are not distinctly separate emotional categories, the markers on the continuum on which they lie can be ignored only at our peril. One of the most misguided claims about friendship is that it is "only natural" for it to overlap romance or sex. I am aware that this can happen, but I am strongly convinced that it shouldn't. Or rather, that once it does, the relationship is no longer "just" a friendship, and no amount of theory or rhetoric will make it so. Even though I will return to this subject later in the book, I want to make some careful distinctions here to avoid mixing apples and oranges.

First, although romance or sex is enlarged and enlightened by friendship, in most cases, friendship is diminished by romance and sex. True friendship *requires* intimacy. In contrast, sex is an intimate act that people often perform in the absence of intimacy— or as a substitute for it. Many lovers are not good friends, and some people manage to have great sex without knowing each other at all.

Second, romance and sex often involve titillating artifice, while with any trace of trickery, friendship becomes its own fraud.

Third, since friendship's intimacy is harder to achieve and more solid than the capriciousness of romance and sex, we need to know we can count on it, like an anchor in those other stormy seas. We need friendship to remain pure. By that I do not mean morally pure; rather, I mean immune to the whiplashes of the libido. The sight of a friend should warm the heart; when it quickens the loins, the rules change.

In short, once a friendship crosses the line, it is a love affair. We may resist acknowledging it. We may try to create a third class of feelings somewhere between friendship and sexual love, but we are only playing games with the language. Virtually everyone who lets sex into their friendship believes "it won't change anything." But it always does. Protestations to the contrary, it introduces the possibility of inequality—unequal intensity and unequal commitment. Love can coexist with inequality, friendship cannot. Sexual partners have the right to demand exclusivity; friends do not.

The sexual revolution has been blamed for devaluing friendship, and friendship has been blamed for not withstanding the sexual revolution. Neither conclusion is correct because you cannot blame an orange when the apples go bad.

Changing Sex Roles

Another trend people cluck about in connection with friendship is the transformation in sex roles. Some say the "new woman" has not only deserted her family but also left her old friends behind. Maybe she's hungry for stimulation and new faces. Maybe she's bored with the old crowd. Maybe she is developing new interests and her taste in people is following suit. Or maybe she hasn't left her old friends but, rather, has added new ones. Undoubtedly, she is meeting a greater variety of people. If she has a nontraditional job, she is also allegedly meeting men on equal ground. In any event, changes in a woman's social relationships would naturally accompany changes in her social role because both are organic symptoms of personal growth.

Role changes among men are less dramatic but still noteworthy as some men have made a parallel move into formerly women-only jobs and some are consciously trying to cultivate a more open emotional life.

Where common sense might predict that these streams of social change would swell the rivers of friendship, in many cases they only muddy the waters. Working women meet more potential friends, yes, but they also have more responsibilities and less time for friendship. As sex roles blur, nontraditional workers meet members of the opposite sex, yes, but the men often greet female newcomers with resentment, ridicule, or even sabotage, and the cultural habit of eroticizing every male-female relationship is as hard to break in the workplace as anywhere else.[15] And yes, some men are becoming more open, but other men feel threatened by openness and thus give wide berth to those who display such behavior, and most women are so unaccustomed to male sensitivity that they read it as weakness. So we learn that adding new people and new roles may increase our expectations about friendship but not necessarily their fulfillment.

All these factors—depersonalization, social mobility, competition, fragmentation, changing marital/sexual patterns, and changing sex roles—seem to explain the "something missing" expressed at my dinner table and the felt "void" found in the Yankelovich study. What I am suggesting, however, is that we look at the same set of facts in a different way. I have critiqued each claim separately. Now I want to go further. Rather than accept the view that these vast social developments have weakened friendship, I contend that they have turned us *toward* friendship. Friendship seems more manageable than vast social forces, so friendship gets our attention. Actually, feeling inadequate gets our attention. In fact, we may be undervaluing the friendships we have and demanding more because we are *supposed* to feel inadequate; we are supposed to put the pressure on our friends and keep it off other sources of discomfort. We are supposed to busy ourselves with the management of private relationships, to blame ourselves for fundamental societal failures, and to call our malaise personal. I take issue with that.

While subsequent chapters will discuss many aspects of friendship that are ripe for improvement, my research leads me to conclude that we are basically doing fine; we are reaching out, coming together, and seeking *more* togetherness despite the appalling emphasis on competitive individualism in the public sphere. I am moved and encouraged by this friendship fervor. Yankelovich called it the "Search for Community": "an intense need to compensate for the impersonal and threatening aspects of modern life by seeking mutual identification with others based on close ethnic ties or ties of shared interests, needs, backgrounds, age or values."

In 1973, in the aftermath of Woodstock and during the era of be-ins, marches, communes, and other visible collective events, only 32 percent of Americans said they were committed to this Search for Community. But in the 1980s, about half the population is involved in an effort to make connections.

This book will not further the fiction that our society is in trouble because of interpersonal aphasia. But it may help you to understand the friendships you have and why you feel about them as you do. It may help you to rethink the meaning of friendship in your life. It may allow you to sort out your particular friendship contradictions and appreciate yourself as a complex social being. And it may help you to become more relaxed and comfortable about the friend you are and the friends you have.

Chapter 3

❧ ❧

Soul-searching

Or How to Tell the Difference between an Acquaintance, Neighbor, Confederate, Pal, Close Kin, Coworker, and Friend

Audacious as it may seem to use the word "soul" in connection with friendship, I take my cue from the many thinkers who have already done so. As recorded in the Bible: "The soul of Jonathan was knit with the soul of David, and Jonathan loved him as his own soul." Aristotle called friendship "a single soul dwelling in two bodies." Cicero declared, "Whoever is in possession of a true friend sees the exact counterpart of his own soul." Montaigne wrote of himself and his friend, "Our souls travelled so unitedly together." Voltaire said, "Friendship is the marriage of the soul." And Mahatma Gandhi described true friendship as "an identity of souls rarely to be found in this world."

Thus far we have identified the "search for community" as a generalized yearning. Now we have to penetrate the soul of friendship to understand what it is, if we have it, or why we want more of it.

I thought I might begin my probe by studying one pair of friends, peeling their relationship layer by layer like an onion—to see how they met, what they do together, what they talk about, how they handle conflict—until I could expose the core of friendship. Then, I would evaluate it against classical principles to see if it fulfilled Aristotle's three purposes of friendship: utility, pleasure, and virtue. Or embodied Emerson's vital "two elements": Truth and Tenderness.

Or reaped Francis Bacon's three "fruits of friendship": someone to confide in, get counsel from, and count on to do for you what you cannot do for yourself.

But choosing one pair of friends to represent all of contemporary friendship seemed presumptuous and risky. So I thought of another strategy: Instead of asking one friendship to stand for many, I would analyze the many relationships of one person. This method, building on Georg Simmel's concept of "differentiated friendship,"[1] might bring to light how various friends fulfill different functions in the life of one individual.

I turned first to my own relationships but the words that came to mind to describe them were either corny or vague. It was impossible to say where I drew the line between an acquaintance and a casual friend, a casual friend and a good friend, a good friend and a best friend. The yardstick that measured one dimension of friendship seemed ill-suited for another. There are people I see often but don't talk to about intimate things and people I talk to a lot but don't see often. I have office friends, old friends from school or former jobs, my husband and grown children whom I count as friends, friends who came into my life through family activities, friends from the women's movement and other group affiliations, friends from the Jewish community, friends made during vacations or business travel, and some neighbors and relatives I consider close. Are these "friends" all really my *friends?* How precise is the word if I can apply it to so many relationships? What other words might distinguish my feelings about them? Without an organizing framework I was stuck. So I turned to social science to help me stalk the soul of friendship more systematically.

Exchange vs. Communal Friendship

The researchers are divided roughly into two camps: One group supports the "social exchange" theory, which argues that friendship requires an exchange of resources such as love, status, services, goods, money, and information. According to Graham Allan, a British sociologist, relationships are not threatened when friends make use of one another, "provided it is clear that they are being used because they are friends and not friends because they are useful."[2]

"Exchange is a basic human need," wrote anthropologist Robert

Brain. "Reciprocity expresses a principle of equity based on the recognition of the moral equality of persons."[3]

To apply the exchange (also called "equity") model to real life, let's use its perspective to describe your hypothetical friendship with Kay. Kay asks advice from you, you borrow money from her; she helped you move across town, you took care of her dog while she was away. Being your friend makes her feel important because you are prominent in the community; you have been helpful to her career, you know many interesting people, and you include her in your social activities. Being Kay's friend makes you feel good because she is playful, has a cheerful personality and a great sense of humor, includes you in her recreational adventures, and is generous with all her material possessions.

In social science terms, your give-and-get exchanges with Kay provide three levels of satisfaction:

- *Instrumental* rewards (advice, money, or joint work)
- *Emotional* rewards (discussing problems or just being together)
- *Shared interests* (joint leisure activities or common values)

Because the exchange theory of friendship ignores the more inchoate, mystical aspects of human interaction, I was not surprised to find another school of thought taking a more holistic approach. Rather than accept that relationships are founded solely on extrinsic rewards, the holistic thinkers identify a kind of intrinsic *person qua person* rewardingness: This is when a friend is so pleasing to us that he or she *is* the reward.

One holistic theorist, Paul Wright, argues that we tend to like people who, just by being the way they are, make us feel good about ourselves.[4] These friends don't have to *do* anything to win us. When their inherent qualities complement our positive evaluations of ourselves, just being with them gives us ego support, stimulation, self-affirmation, and security.

Margaret Clark also disagrees with exchange theory but she calls the alternative "communal" friendship.[5] Under that rubric, she says real friends give to one another not to get something back but simply because they want to benefit the other person. They act on the assumption that each "is concerned about the welfare of the other." They may alternate roles, depending on what each person needs from the other at any given moment. Their acts are unselfish. The benefits they enjoy from one another are often noncomparable and neither *expects* the benefits to be reciprocal. The communal theory reminds me of the man who said "simultaneous satisfaction in friendship is as unnecessary as simultaneous orgasm in sex. If you make your friend happy, you'll get yours eventually."

Let's look at your friendship with Kay from *this* perspective. Materially, it appears Kay does more for you than you do for her, but you don't feel over-indulged and she doesn't feel put upon. Neither of you is keeping tabs. You are unaware of the "rewards" each of you brings to the other. Both of you would be surprised to see your relationship reduced to Give and Take columns on a sheet of paper. You just get pleasure out of knowing each other, helping each other, and being together.

In sum, exchange theory says friends aren't happy unless they feel they're getting equal benefits from the friendship. (You like Kay when Kay fulfills your needs.) Communal theory says the well-being of one friend is *connected* to and *contingent* upon the well-being of the other. (You can't be happy unless Kay is happy, so making her happy becomes your reward as much as hers.)

While it may seem silly to resort to academic terms to describe the nuances of human interaction and especially these two very different attitudes toward friendship, everyday English offers little alternative. That's why the people I interviewed had so much trouble explaining why one person was a friend and another wasn't quite. I got used to hearing otherwise eloquent people resort to such flat-footed words as "close," "good," "true," "real," or "best" to distinguish one friend from another. But after sorting through the most frequently cited distinctions, and putting them in the context of basic friendship research, I organized the muddle of relationships into seven categories, which contain varying degrees of exchange and communal qualities.

Seven Degrees of Friendship

Acquaintances

Other than family, everyone in your life starts as an acquaintance. If they all remained acquaintances, your social life would be shallow and bland, but having an array of acquaintances along with more substantive relationships adds spice and vitality to your social world. Acquaintances are the passersby, coworkers, schoolmates, or hometowners you see periodically simply because of where you live or what you do. Like "landsmen" from the old country, they are bound to you by loose accidental ties of place or time. You have not *chosen* them.

Acquaintances are the people you know by name or face, the "familiar strangers" with whom you exchange smiles and amenities on the streets or in the corridors, the people you deal with year after year in local stores and service relationships: the letter carrier and gas station attendant, butcher and barber, shoemaker, and newspaper deliverer. If acquaintances are anything more than "nodding," they are exchange relations.

Acquaintances are the bit players in the movie of your life; they needn't be cast with care, but they must be noticed and treated with dignity because they are the stars of their own movie.

This comment from a woman who runs a laundromat describes how significant even the most fleeting acquaintances can be:

> I meet all kinds of interesting people at work, and they depend on me to keep the place nice. When I don't go in sometimes, the place gets to be a mess. Nobody sweeps up, and sometimes they don't even call to have a machine fixed. It makes me feel good—you know, important—when I come back and everybody is glad to see me because they know everything will be nice again.[6]

A somewhat different type of acquaintance is the friend of a friend. You and this person meet year after year at Butch's Christmas party or Sue's barbecue where you recognize one another as recurrent co-guests but never fully "click" as friends. Distant relatives fit into the acquaintance category as do the people you see occasionally through your job but would not call a coworker or colleague. Finally, some people like to consider a prominent figure an acquaintance after a single meeting. "I knew Albert Schweitzer," says the typical namedropper who was once favored with a handshake from the great man. We ooh and aah as we were meant to do, but we do not mistake the dropped name for a friend.

Neighbors

Neighbors are a special breed of acquaintance. In "The Friendship Bond," a *Psychology Today (PT)* survey of friendship in America, neighborhoods ranked fifth as a place where friendships start. But there are endless permutations of neighboring. You and your neighbors may be the kind who merely call greetings across a fence, borrow sugar, or chat in the elevator of your apartment building. Or you may be heart-to-heart intimates who are fortunate enough to live on the same block.

According to sociologist Lois Verbrugge, up to 45 percent of us name one or more neighbors among our three closest friends.[7] Social psychologists Carin Rubenstein and Phillip Shaver wrote: "Most of us know seven out of ten neighbors by name and have visited, on the average, about five of them. Only five percent of Americans know none of their neighbors."[8]

Even when neighbors are not dear to one another they often are important for mutual help and protection; that is, some kind of mutually agreeable "exchange" relationship exists. The thing people most often count on their neighbors for is taking care of their homes when they're away.

While only 37 percent of us frequently visit with our neighbors, fully 60 percent of us feel we can frequently "rely on our neighbors."[9] Neighbors to rely on are invaluable but interchangeable. When you need somebody, *anybody,* you value whoever is nearby and willing to help.

When my three children were all under age 3 and I was home alone with them, I accidentally injured myself so severely that I had to rush out of the house to get medical attention. "Once in every ten years a man needs his neighbor," asserts an English proverb, and 1968 was the year I needed mine. The old man across the way, to whom I'd never said more than hello, instantly agreed to come over. I returned about two hours later, deeply grateful for his attention to the children. We did not, however, become friends.

As Thoreau put it, "Even the utmost good will and harmony and practical kindness are not sufficient for Friendship. We do not wish for Friends to feed and clothe our bodies—neighbors are kind enough for that—but to do the like office to our spirits." That's a fair distinction: Neighbors are for the body—for physical safety and comfort—friends are for the spirit. It is enough for neighbors to be reliable, to be there when you need them, to mind your children, to be willing to watch your house when you're away. It is enough to treasure them for that.

Confederates

Confederates may seem an odd label for a significant relationship, but according to the dictionary definition—those "combined in support of each other in some act or enterprise; a league, compact, alliance"—it fits my meaning. Confederates are the epitome of exchange friends; confederates get together because each suits the other's purposes. They are a symbiotic pair, like Don Quixote and Sancho Panza or the Lone Ranger and Tonto. They are mutually dependent but rarely symmetrical in power. Robert Brain cites dozens of examples of such "lopsided friendships" in underdeveloped societies where "clientage"—alliances of lower-caste people with those in superior castes and spheres of influence—is legitimated by the economic and political system. While acknowledging that clientage perpetuates social inequalities, Brain insists these asymmetrical relationships are formed for mutual advantage and are considered friendships.

In our society confederates may or may not be social, economic, or educational equals, but they are *equalized* by their need for one another. Typically, the pair is composed of a leader and a follower or two people who need each other whether they like it or not. For example, the most popular teenager and his or her sidekick, one needing a deferential underling, the other gaining protection and status from association with the top dog. Or the painter who wants money and exposure and the patron-collector who wants to rub up against the glamour of the art world. Or the lesbian and the gay man who each need a "socially acceptable" opposite sex escort for formal occasions. Or any number of relationships that go by the name of "business contacts." These associations may look and feel like the real thing, but at best they are functional pseudo friendships, and they are often temporary. When the weaker member gets strong— when the sidekick becomes a star, the artist commands high prices, or the homosexual comes out of the closet and no longer needs a cover—the confederacy collapses.

Alvin Toffler described another recognizable pair of temporary confederates: "The neighborhood integrator . . . derives pleasure from serving as a 'bridge' for newcomers. She takes the initiative by inviting them to parties and other gatherings. The newcomers are duly flattered that an 'oldtime' resident is willing to invite them. The newcomers alas quickly learn that the integrator is herself an 'outsider' whereupon, more often than not, they promptly disassociate themselves from her." But by the time she is abandoned, there are *new* newcomers to play their part in the revolving duet.[10]

The most fertile and long-lasting confederate relationships have been those of certain professional friend-makers combined in an enterprise with their chosen targets. "I married the world," wrote Elsa Maxwell, the legendary party-giver. "Age cannot wither nor custom stale the infinite variety of my friends."[11]

This passion for collecting people, special people, was fully realized in the literary salons of such catalytic personalities as Natalie Clifford Barney and Mable Dodge. In New York or Italy, Dodge brought together the likes of Emma Goldman and Margaret Sanger, poets Edwin Arlington Robinson and Amy Lowell, photographer Alfred Stieglitz and writers Walter Lippmann, Lincoln Steffens, and Max Eastman. Although Dodge herself was a philanthropist, writer, and political radical, she was better known for whom she knew than for what she did.

Sylvia Beach of Shakespeare and Company, the American salon-bookshop in Paris, and Frances Steloff of the Gotham Book Mart in New York were also legendary people-collectors. Each in her way created a literary oasis for writers, artists, and expatriates that left an impact on the intellectual life of her time. Steloff supported, promoted, helped, hyped, and subsidized James Joyce, Henry Miller, Gertrude Stein, Anaïs Nin, and a host of other avant-garde talents whom she called her friends while holding them in absolute awe. She believed it was a privilege to stock and sell their books and give parties for them. Her writers needed her for loans, praise, a home away from home. She needed the magic they brought into her life. The perfect confederacy.

Pals

Pals are people who have something in common besides living in the same neighborhood or having matching ambitions. Usually they feel that what they have in common is bigger than both of them—a sports team, sorority, fraternity, stamp collecting, or the

Green Berets. Pals are political cronies or weekend falconers. Pals can be spectators or participants but whatever they are, they are together. Or as one research team put it, "those who play together stay together."[12]

Pals are most comfortable with friendship that accrues to mutual activity not conversation—unless it is conversation about their mutual activity.

Unlike confederates, people who become pals are usually fundamentally equal in ability. In fact, one of the nicest things about palship is the way shared interests or equal skills can overpower age and class (and racial) differences and yield an otherwise unlikely pair of friends. For instance, after playing basketball together in a few pickup games at the YMCA, a high school kid who had perfected his bull's-eye jump shot in city school yards became pals with a college senior who plays varsity ball for his Ivy League school. An irascible white man and a contentious Black man are never so close as when they face each other across a chessboard in the park. Two single mothers, one 40 and divorced, the other 28 and never married, who met at a PTA meeting, discovered a mutual love for old movies and now travel the film circuit together. An immigrant man in his sixties and a teenage girl found each other while playing in the violin section of a summer festival orchestra.

Yet not all pals are friends and not all friends are pals. The intimacy of pals is usually too shallow to withstand what true friends can weather: competition and inactivity. Nor are all friends playmates; many of us are united by talk or togetherness rather than by action. When *Psychology Today* asked people what they and their friends had done together during the past month, about half said they had participated in sports and two-thirds reported going to a movie, play, or concert. But 90 percent of the women and 75 percent of the men had "had an intimate talk." Friends but not pals would agree with my friend Martin Edelston who says, "I'm tired of *doing* things with people. What I want is someone to do nothing with."

Pals may consider each other to be intense lifesaving buddies who jointly defy the elements and manage to survive in the wilds against all odds. For the survival of their relationship, however, the danger lies not in the risks they pursue but in the possibility that their natural competitiveness will turn them against one another. That's what happened with Larry and Paula, who put their lives in jeopardy together—climbing mountains.

"It got too tense," Paula recalls, talking about how their climbing expeditions turned from cooperative to competitive. "We started making bets and timing each other. We cut corners on safety. It got so that at the end of a climb, I didn't feel good, even if I won. When you check the energy flow and it's all negative, there's something wrong." Paula doesn't agree that the palship wasn't a real friendship in the first place. "We used to have a lot to say to one another," she insists. "It's just that once I decided to stop climbing with him, he sort of drifted away."

Pals are unable to withstand inactivity. Len and Roger who play indoor tennis every Tuesday night are a good example of this. A year and a half ago, the pro paired them for a singles game and the match stuck. To watch the two of them in action was to witness the warm camaraderie and easygoing banter of partners with amazingly compatible talent and temperaments. Both are advanced players. Each was serious about the game but confident and gracious enough to laugh off his mistakes and give the questionable calls to the other guy. Although they rarely kept in touch from one week to the next, after each game they lingered over a beer, reviewed their shots, and made small talk. If you'd asked either one to describe their relationship, undoubtedly each would have called the other his "friend."

Last winter Roger broke his leg skiing. He got someone else to play in his place and didn't see Len for ten weeks. "When my cast came off and I showed up one Tuesday night, Len burst into a big smile and said, 'Hey old buddy, welcome back. The game hasn't been the same without you,' " Roger recalls. "He was genuinely glad to see me, even though he had called me only once and had never come to visit when I was laid up. If I'd been permanently crippled or couldn't afford to pay for an hour of tennis every week, I don't think he and I would have seen each other again for the rest of our lives."

Pals too are exchange friendships. There's not much *person qua person* appreciation when the person is always attached to an activity. Like Hasidic couples who dance holding two ends of a handkerchief to keep from touching, pals need something between them—tennis, music, mountain climbing—to be comfortable with their friendship. In the absence of a connecting activity, some learn to take each other's hands and just sit still, but many back away looking for a new partner who will grab the other end of the handkerchief and keep on dancing.

Close Kin

As we'll see later on, many people use the idiom of kinship to describe friends—whether they are part of a *compadrazgo,* or godparent relationship, in ethnic groups, the fictive kin of poor and working-class communities, or the friends middle-class people make into their "chosen" family. All these practices reflect a desire to honor friendship by giving it the imprimatur of what is thought to be the closest of all relationships. In fact, however, our relatives—who are supposedly the closest—are the people most of us forget to mention when we talk about friendship. We may say friends are "like family," but rarely do we think of our family as our friends. We act as if friends and family are two separate species. Relatives come with the territory. We take them for granted. Family just *is.*

"It is chance that makes brothers but hearts that make friends." So goes the proverb and so goes the popular wisdom on the subject. Since we choose our friends and we don't choose our relatives, many people assume we also *can't* choose our relatives as friends.

"What amazes me is that my relatives are someone else's friends," says Sam, one of those who think family should be seen at weddings and funerals but not heard from otherwise. For millions of others, relatives are almost the only people they see. The question is, are they friends?

Rubenstein and Shaver report that six out of ten Americans see at least one relative at least once a week, which suggests more than the obligatory holiday visit. Verbrugge says up to 18 percent of us name a family member in the list of our top three friends. Close kin seem to be most prevalent in "social groups which need frequent economic assistance"—laborers, production workers, "people of low prestige," the self-employed, old folks, Catholics, and immigrants from Southern Europe. Despite the stereotype of Black communities rife with "broken homes and family disorganization," anthropologist Carol Stack found many poor Blacks "immersed in a domestic web of a large number of kinfolk who can be called upon for help and who can bring others into the network."[13]

It is only logical that poor or powerless populations would turn to their close kin for their most intimate needs. But while this pattern has been noted by experts, on its way from the experts to us, this pattern has been distorted to: "The poor and working class have

kinship and everyone else has friendship." When people understand
that friendship can exist *within* any kind of relationship, the finding
is restated as: "The poor and working class have mostly kin-friends
and everyone else has mostly nonkin-friends." Any other construct
denies that less affluent people have the same friendship *feelings* as
everyone else.

What comes across in my interviews with people who have close-
kin friends is the great security they feel when friendship is kept
within the family and the way they trust in the stability and permanence of relationships with those who are related to them by blood
or marriage.

"Barry got divorced from my daughter but in my mind he'll
always be my son-in-law," says an Arizona man. "We had twelve
years together and I like the guy. I'm not gonna stop being his friend
just because he and my daughter couldn't get along."

Whether or not economic utility figures into the close-kin relationship, it is the sharing of memories, cultural traditions, and family
history that accounts for much of the warmth between relatives.
Two sisters who live 500 miles apart say they have a lot of friends
but each is still the other's *best* friend. "No one knows me like she
does," says one sister. "Who else is going to remember my eighth-
grade teacher or understand why I need a psychiatrist to sort out my
relationship with my mother."

Claude Fischer found those least likely to have close-kin friends
were urbanites, the nontraditional, educated, and affluent. Nina is
all those things and yet when I ask who her best friend is, she answers
without hesitation, "My cousin Dee." Nina, a stockbroker, is four
years younger than Dee, a writer. They grew up together and have
lived near each other as adults. As close as they are, the two cousins
are also very different, Nina says, citing this incident: "In her upstairs
hallway, Dee has a painting of a girl reaching for a bunch of balloons
in the sky above her head. Once I said, 'Why don't you hang that
happy picture where more people can see it?' Dee looked at me like
I was crazy. 'How can you call that picture happy?' she said. 'The
poor girl has lost her balloons.' Well, I didn't see it that way. I saw
the balloons floating down from the sky and the girl reaching up to
grab them."

The two women talk on the phone at least twice a day. The
weekend before our interview, they took a long drive in the country.
"And we still had plenty to say to each other," Nina said, laughing.

Like what? I ask. "Well, as usual, we talked about our kids. One of mine just went away to college so there was a lot to say about him. Then we talked about generators and alternators, and how we roast a turkey, and I recommended a book for her to read. Then we talked about her husband who's in Italy. And my mother who's been sick. We can say anything about anyone in our family without it being gossip because we both know we love them."

Is there anything you and she can't talk about? I ask. "Not a thing," says Nina. "Dee knows my soul."

Another close-kin friendship that defies the working-class stereotype is that of Gaye Tuchman, a professor of sociology, and a male cousin, who is six weeks younger than she is. "We were raised in the same house," Gaye says. "Our mothers are sisters; they gave us quarters to go to the movies together when we were kids. Other than my college roommate, my cousin is my closest friend in the world. I like his wife too and picked out her engagement ring. The two of them will raise my son, Ethan, if anything happens to me. We shared a vacation house on Martha's Vineyard—my cousin, his wife, 2-year-old Ethan, and I. We had only one car and when we went to the beach they'd drive us back for Ethan's nap. At night they baby-sat so I could visit another sociologist. They say it's no favor, because we're not just cousins, we're friends."

Perhaps the least recognized close-kin friendships are the very closest: those between a parent and an adult child or between spouses (more on that in Chapter 15). Ann-Marie talks about both situations: "My mother is my best friend and my husband, Dick, is a close second. I can count on Mom for anything, no matter what's happening in her own life. She would die for me; Dick would live through anything for me. Mom's love is unconditional; Dick's conditions are his own health and sanity. If I cost him those, he withdraws. My six kids come next as my best friends. I ask their advice about everything except sex. Often the best advice comes from the youngest people in the house because you have to simplify your questions to yourself first. How can anything match giving birth to your own friends and raising them to be people you can respect and enjoy for the rest of your life? It's like homegrown vegetables—they're the best."

Her husband concurs: "Ann-Marie and I got married because there was no one we wanted to spend more time with besides each other and we're still best friends. The surprise is how we've grown to prefer our children to so many of our other friends. The people who've become most interesting to me are my children—and they're the only ones I'm willing to screw up my schedule for."

Coworkers

In terms of time, the people you work with every day probably see more of you than anyone else does. Emotionally, a coworker can be anything from a casual acquaintance to a friend for life. Structurally, colleagueships can be categorized as exchange or communal or a combination of the two, which is why work friends will be discussed separately (see Chapter 12). At this point, however, it's important to make one distinction that may clarify some of the borderline feelings in this category: *You can have coworkers who happen to be friends or friends who happen to be coworkers.* Your attitude determines the primary identity of the person, not where you meet or socialize.

Let's assume that you and Barbara, the checkout clerk at the next cash register, have worked in the same supermarket for more than a year. The two of you enjoy shooting the breeze while packing grocery bags. Sometimes you eat lunch together or go shopping before you ride the bus home. In other words, when you talk about this woman, she's "Barbara, my friend at work."

But what if she moved to the meat department or to another store or another city? How much would you miss her and for how long? Would you make time to see each other? Or spend the money to call her long distance? Would you invite her to your house? Choose her as a companion if you won a weekend for two in Jamaica? Remember her birthday two years later?

If you answered Yes to all these questions, then Barbara is a friend who just happens to be, at this time, your coworker.

If you answered No, she is your coworker who happens to be, at this time, your friend.

Coworkers come and go. Friends, we hope, are forever.

Friends

Superficially, each of the preceding six categories—acquaintances, neighbors, confederates, pals, close kin, and coworkers—seems to be distinctly different and differentially rewarding in hierarchical order. But beneath each label, at any time, any of these relationships can undergo a sea change and be transformed into the seventh category: true friends.

True friendship describes a feeling, not a situation. It is a feeling best captured by the word "soulmate" in Aristotle's sense of "a single soul dwelling in two bodies." Coworkers often turn into soulmates; but so can a boss, grandparent, neighbor, teacher, hairdresser, or Ping-Pong partner. Friendship is a heart-flooding feeling that can happen to any two people who are caught up in the act of being themselves, together, and who like what they see. The feeling is deeper than companionship; one can hire a companion. It is more than affection; affection can be as false as a stage kiss. It is never onesided. It elevates biology into full humanity. Friendship. We know it when we feel it but we can spend years trying to put it into words.

Chapter 4

≈   ≈

A Friend Is Someone Who . . .

The idea for a litmus test to separate the chums from the chaff was prompted by the ever-popular children's book *A Friend Is Someone Who Likes You.*[1]

I asked people, "Suppose you had to complete this sentence in twenty-five words or less: *A friend is someone who* . . . What would you say? With what image would you summarize a soulmate? How would you encapsulate the meaning of a friend?"

"A friend is someone who would hide me from the Nazis"
—Gerald, whose parents survived the Holocaust.

Gerald's answer is understandable, but I went on to ask other people if his definition seemed a fair albeit apocalyptic test of true friendship. Many agreed. Others insisted that hiding someone from Nazi barbarism was an act of humanity, not friendship.

Samuel Oliner, a sociologist, has been studying Germans who saved Jews from Hitler to learn what traits differentiate altruists from people who "chose to look the other way."[2] His preliminary findings suggest that great altruists operated from a solid sense of personal security and self-worth, which permitted them to use their strength in the interests of others. However, other theorists attribute extraordinary life-endangering altruism variously to masochism, unconscious guilt or shame, the reinforcement one gets from doing good and being rewarded, or just a biological predisposition to ensure the survival of one's own species.[3]

The Litmus Test

The appeal of the altruistic friend is undeniable, but the formula for altruism remains confounding and the need for it too exceptional. More commonly, people completed the sentence with "a friend is someone who is loyal." Almost everyone asks for that.

Loyalty and Trust

"A friend is someone you can call in the middle of the night when your man is gone, or you wish he would go, or you suspect your cellulite is winning—or even just to prove to yourself that there is someone you can call in the middle of the night"—Anne Beatts, a writer.[4]
"A friend is someone who walks in when the rest of the world walks out"—Walter Winchell, gossip columnist.
"A friend is someone who warns you"—Eastern proverb.
"To be a real friend, a person would have to stick by me no matter what everyone else was saying"—Joanne, once the target of considerable trashing in the women's movement.
"A friend is someone who would take a great risk for me, someone I could call at four in the morning and say, 'I need you to help me bury a body,' and he'd come out with a shovel, no questions asked"—Mark, a man who is rarely given to overstatement.

People who have experienced ostracism, fear, or personal attacks often want a friend who agrees to be an implacable ally. The rest of us might simply describe loyalty as some of the great thinkers have done.
Socrates wrote, "There is no possession more valuable than that of a good and faithful friend."
Montaigne suggests just *how* good and faithful in the story of two friends in ancient Greece. Blossius was asked how much he was willing to do for his friend Gracchus.
"Everything," he replied.

"How everything?" demanded the interrogator. "And what if he had ordered you to set fire to our temples?"

"He would never have told me to do that," answered Blossius in a first defense of his friend.

"But if he had?" the interrogator insisted.

"Then I should have obeyed him," said Blossius, redoubling his loyalty though it cast doubt on his friend's law-abiding nature. Montaigne's commentary: "They were friends before they were citizens, friends to one another before they were either friends or enemies to their country, or friends to ambition and revolt."

C. S. Lewis detailed why the loyalty of friendship is a potential threat to the state:

> It is easy to see why Authority frowns on Friendship. Every real friendship is a sort of secession, even a rebellion. . . . Each therefore is a pocket of potential resistance. Men who have real Friends are less easy to manage or "get at"; harder for good Authorities to correct or for bad Authorities to corrupt. Hence, if our masters, by force or by propaganda about "togetherness" or by unobtrusively making privacy and unplanned leisure impossible, ever succeed in producing a world in which all are Companions and none are Friends, they will have removed certain dangers, and will also have taken from us what is almost our strongest safeguard against complete servitude.[5]

I talked earlier about the danger of *friendship romanticized*—how it can be made into a diversion or a supposed solution to oppressive life circumstances. The other side of the coin is the danger of *friendship prevented*. Loyal friends—especially those who are aware and active in society—can appear subversive to authoritarian rulers whose power depends on obedience. E. M. Forster put it plainly: "If I had to choose between betraying my country and betraying my friend, I hope I should have the guts to betray my country."[6] As unpatriotic as that may sound, it is precisely this sort of steadfast interpersonal loyalty that most dictators fear and most people want from their friends.

Respondents to the *Psychology Today* friendship survey said loyalty and the ability to keep confidences were more important in friendship than warmth, affection, supportiveness, frankness, a sense of humor, availability, independence, good conversation, intelligence, social conscience, or shared interests. Presumably, those latter attributes are readily attainable, while loyalty is the elixir that transmogrifies a friendship from the enjoyable to the sublime.

Psychologist Irwin Sandler makes the point that we need both "buffers" and "boosters" in our lives: buffers to reduce the pain of negative events and boosters to enhance the pleasure of positive experiences.[7] Yet some friends' notion of loyalty is to stand beside us in adversity when we are weak and they can be strong, but not when we are flush with good fortune and all we ask of them is joy.

"After my wife left me for another man I had a thousand comforting friends, but when I won a prestigious fellowship I got only two phone calls," says a physicist. And in sad, defeated tones, a high school girl advises, "If you want other girls to like you, you have to have problems because problems are what we talk about and help each other with. No one wants a friend who's pretty and has a boyfriend and gets A's and has it all together."

"A friend in need is a friend indeed" is a misguided axiom. A friend in triumph is harder to find. It's easy to be the big savior when people are needy and weak, but when they're flying high, it takes real loyalty for us to soar alongside our happy friends rather than pull them down to earth.

Most people mention trust in the same breath as loyalty. A character in Athol Fugard's play *The Road to Mecca* asserts that trust is more important than love. In a police state such as Fugard's South Africa that may be true. But where physical safety is not an issue, it might be enough to say that trust is a prerequisite for friendship.

People have as much trouble defining trust as achieving it. "Distrust is not just the opposite of trust; it is also a *functional equivalent* for trust. For this reason only, is a choice between trust and distrust possible (and necessary)," insisted Niklas Luhmann.[8] "Trust is never wholly realized in social relationships," Bernard Barber wrote. "Maintaining it is a reciprocal and endless task for all."[9]

In new or ordinary friendships, perhaps trust is something we have to keep proving to one another, choosing between trusting and distrusting, whether consciously or not. But at a certain point, friends cross the line into a kind of permanent state of trustingness where mutual confidence no longer need be learned. It simply exists. George

Eliot had this point in mind when she wrote, "Friendship is the inexpressible comfort of feeling safe with a person, having neither to weigh thoughts nor measure words."

That quality of "feeling safe" explains why Karen Lindsey trusted her friends to pull her through a nervous breakdown.[10] In all, some thirty men and women made themselves available for Lindsey's support and care: brought soup, shopped, cleaned, listened, kept her company while she cried or stared at the TV or tried to work and subdued her when she became violent or self-destructive. "Trust and alternatives were equally important," she says of that period. "My friends had promised never to have me involuntarily committed to a mental hospital, no matter how bad things got." Eventually, things got better and "I learned—as did my friends—that all the clichés about tender-loving-care are true."

"The glory of friendship is not the outstretched hand, the kindly smile nor the joy of companionship," wrote Emerson. Rather, "it is the spirited inspiration that comes to one when he discovers that someone else believes in him and is willing to trust him" (like all wise writers of the past, Emerson, too, must be forgiven his male pronouns).

Behavioral research has documented a strong connection between trusting and being trustworthy. "Trusters" tend to be happier, better adjusted, and no more gullible than distrusters, and trusters are perceived by others as more likable, ethical, attractive, and "desirable as a close friend."[11] Shakespeare's Iago is not to be trusted because he trusts no one including himself. Cynical people lose faith in humanity and their gloom makes them friendless. But people who trust are themselves less likely to lie and more likely to act morally, to respect the rights of others, and to give a friend a second chance.

Generosity

"A friend is someone who will take the baby for a week"
—Dorothy, an overwrought new mother.

Practical acts of generosity—the giving of one's time, effort, or money—are indisputably essential to friendship. The trouble is, friendship isn't necessarily essential to those acts. We've all known people who have ulterior motives for every kindness they bestow and keep careful account of favors given and received. Authentically generous friends do not relish having others beholden to them. They don't charge interest in guilt. They are willing to take the baby for a week because you're a wreck, not to store up points so they can later ask you to mortgage your house for them.

In a nationwide survey of American values, many more people said going out of one's way to *help* a friend is more important than *being* with friends.[12] This expression of the preponderance of "exchange" over "communal" relations, this insistence that friends prove themselves through large gestures rather than day to day availability, means either that we need help we are not getting or that we're afraid we won't be able to give help when others need it. Generosity, after all, requires more than just good intentions; it requires strength and resources that many of us do not have.

Consider the humbling example of Virginia Woolf, whose generosity was catalogued in a letter to her from Vita Sackville-West:

> You are one perpetual Achievement; yet you give the impression of having infinite leisure. One comes to see you: you are prepared to spend two hours of Time in talk. One may not, for reasons of health, come to see you: you write divine letters, four pages long. You support mothers, vicariously. You produce books which occupy a permanent place on one's bedside shelf next to Gerard MANLY Hopkins and the Bible. You cast a beam across the dingy landscape of the Times Literary Supplement. You change people's lives. You set up type. You offer to read and criticise one's poems . . . How is it done?[13]

The answer is, it isn't done very often. Or it's done in new ways. Nina says of her husband: "People love George because he carries his friends around in his head. If someone asks 'Do you know someone who . . .' George always does." He puts friends together with other friends; he remembers who is looking for a better job, an orthopedist, a new love. His willingness to share his friends with others is another form of generosity.

"A friend is someone who will give up a free ticket to the Doors concert if I need him to be with me"—Tony, age 15.

Tony's answer suggests still another kind of generosity: self-sacrifice. Victor, a dentist twice Tony's age, cites almost the same example with himself as hero. "I have a friend who just split with his wife. He was a basket case, so I took him out to dinner even though I had to give up the Superbowl to do it; now that's what I call friendship."

I call it friendship too, but my experience with too much self-sacrifice among friends is that, no matter how well-intentioned and voluntary, it can't help but leave a residue of resentment in the sacrificer. While valuing people who would give up something they want for the sake of our needs, it is probably healthier for our friend-ships if generosity is mutual and founded not on giving *up* but on just plain giving.

Acceptance

> "The friend I can trust is the one who will let
>   me have my death.
> The rest are actors who want me to stay
>   and further the plot."—Adrienne Rich. [14]

Thus, Rich appears to be completing the test sentence in one of her poems. Taken literally, she seems to be asserting that to be a friend you have to be willing to stand by while your friends kill themselves, a fatal contradiction that defines friendship right out of existence. Of course, were I suffering from a grave injury or incurable disease, I would not only expect a friend to "let me have my death"; I might also expect her or him to aid me in the act. (In *PT*'s friendship survey, only one person in ten felt a friend should assist another to commit suicide, but this was due more to a moral objection to suicide than to the role of a friend in it.) On the other hand, were I contemplating suicide as a route out of depression, I would expect my friends to behave as Karen Lindsey's did—to go to all lengths to help me find an alternative solution and a sense of hope.

If the poet's meaning is metaphoric—that is, if she is suggesting that the friend "who will let me have my death" is the friend who will let me have my life exactly as I wish it rather than as part of "the plot"—then few would disagree with her.

> "A friend is someone who takes me as I am"—Bruce, an appliance repairman.
> "A friend is someone who knows all about me and still likes me"—Betty Miller, a librarian.

"A friend is someone who makes me feel totally acceptable"
—Ene Riisna, a television producer.

With the rest of the world, we must wear our public faces and proper roles, but with friends, we feel comfortable and safe enough to be ourselves, however idiosyncratic and quirky our "selves" may be. Two behavioral scientists put it this way: "One does not put a rose between his teeth and dance the fandango at a supermarket. He does not sit at the bar and recite 'The Shooting of Dan McGrew' in a strange neighborhood. He does not offer profound wisdom to passing strangers. He does not sing the obscene version of 'On Top of Old Smoky' during the office coffee break. The license for such performances and a great many others can only be issued by friends."[15]

But a caveat is necessary. As Woodrow Wilson put it, "Loyalty may be blind but friendship must not be." In other words, acceptance without love is slavish sycophancy and no favor to a friend. What most of us mean by acceptance is not blind adoration but constructive *support*. We don't mean the uncritical tolerance recommended by the novelist Henry Fielding who advised that friends "take persons and things as they are, without complaining of their imperfections or attempting to amend them." Fielding's view has been brought up to date by the "anything goes, nothing human is alien to me, let it all hang out" gurus of laid-back acceptance. While it sounds virtuous, this approach subverts another vital tenet of friendship: honesty.

Honesty

"A friend is a person with whom I may be sincere. Before him I may think aloud"—Ralph Waldo Emerson.
"Friendship is by its very nature freer of deceit than any other kind of relationship, because it is the bond least affected by striving for power, physical pleasure or material profit" —Francine du Plessix Gray.

Sincerity—freedom from deceit—is the moral imperative of friendship. It is also the primary feature of reciprocal "self-disclosure"— otherwise known as talking intimately to a friend about yourself. Sincerity and caring honesty are not universally available among people who call themselves friends. Yet unless we open ourselves

and speak freely to at least one other person in our lives, psychologists
say we will end up feeling lonely.[16]

Just as loneliness has been linked to an increase in emotional
disorders, confiding in friends is known to improve the immune
system and reduce our vulnerability to illness and stress-related disorders.[17] Dr. Robert Taylor, who organized California's educational
campaign Friends Can Be Good Medicine, and two Yale researchers
have published independent evidence correlating warm social ties
with low mortality rates.[18] A psychologist at Southern Methodist
University found that people who confided in others about the trau-
matic events of their lives—a woman who blamed herself for her
grandmother's death, a man who remembered his father saying that
the boy's birth had destroyed the parents' marriage, women who
revealed childhood experiences of sexual abuse—all made fewer visits
to doctors during the months following their confessions to their
friends than did a group of nonconfessing counterparts.[19] Experts and
ordinary people alike have found that confiding in a friend can be as
therapeutic as psychotherapy.

> "A friend is someone who tells me the truth about me. I want
> to know when my work stinks or I'm being hurtful or stupid.
> I expect my friends to save me from myself"
> —Bill, a carpenter.

Along with the right to be sincere, most of us want sincerity in
return—even if it means hearing about our own faults. People who
repress criticism for the sake of harmony may be protecting their
friendships at the expense of their friends.

One task of a close friend is to be a mirror. But, as Jean Cocteau
wrote, "Mirrors should reflect a little before throwing back images."
Reflective, sensitive, honest criticism is "the highest duty we owe
our friends, the noblest, the most sacred," wrote Harriet Beecher
Stowe. "If we let our friend become cold and selfish and exacting
without a remonstrance, we are no true lover, no true friend."

My Friend Is Someone Who . . .

At last I had all the measures I needed: the philosophers' concepts,
the framework of exchange and communal friendship, the seven basic

relationship categories, and now the baseline criteria for true friendship. Returning to the muddle of my own friendships, I was better able to sort things out. I thought about the people who belong in my soulmate category.

One woman, a family therapist, is intuitive, caring, and incredibly wise about human behavior. She is the person I talk to when I'm upset about any of my other relationships. While her advice is often brilliant, just her presence is calming. We have fun antiquing together, but more important, she is one of the people with whom I feel comfortable debating the root causes of social problems. Although she deals in individual and family dynamics, and I think in terms of society, patriarchy, and changing the world, in the twenty-three years we have known each other, the differences in our world views have enlarged rather than interfered with our friendship.

I have another friend, an editor I've known for nearly twenty years, who reads my manuscripts, is reassuring and encouraging, cares about what I care about, and always has an interesting perspective on interpersonal relations. She knows how much I admire her clear thinking, her judgment, and her way with people. But although we talk about issues, events, and personalities, we share relatively little emotional information. For instance, during the many years when I had children and she didn't, we hardly ever talked about kids. When she and her husband went through the procedures necessary to adopt a baby, she barely spoke of it. When she finally got pregnant, I was told no sooner than anyone else. When her brother was dying, she kept her sorrow to herself. I used to feel her resistance to deeper intimacy was my fault. Now I just accept that in certain areas she wants her privacy.

Another friend of nearly twenty years, a social and political activist, will do anything for me: go anywhere, include me in whatever she is doing, let me borrow anything she owns, introduce me to everyone she knows, promote and defend me, contribute to any cause I care about, give my guests a bed in her house or a seat at her table, water all my plants—you name it. I'm not nearly as generous and she doesn't seem to care. She is the furthest thing from an exchange-type friend. She gives not to get favors back but because that's who she is. She also wears better than almost anyone. My husband and I can see her and her husband five times a week and never tire of each other's company. My friend and I have talked about everything, from international affairs to gardening; we've trav-

eled together, fallen asleep at each other's house after too much wine.
Yet, despite thousands of intimate hours, she would never come to
me and say, "I'm miserable." I have to ask about her hard knocks,
read her feelings nonverbally; she's not much for putting emotions
in words, but between us a hug goes a long way.

The fourth friend, a filmmaker, is exactly my age but otherwise
quite unlike me. She's an insomniac; I can sleep anytime, anywhere.
We have diametrically opposite reactions to most books, movies,
plays, mutual friends, vacation places, and red nail polish. Her clothes
are the latest fashions, while my style is recycled preppie, country,
or hippie. She wears spike heels, I wear flats. When we meet new
people, I'll analyze what they're thinking, she'll tell me what they're
feeling. But none of these differences has mattered much in the ten
years we've known each other, because I find her so warm, so easy
to be with, so open and loving. And on important things—like
enjoying the company of teenagers and the pursuit of new restaurants—we're in total agreement.

Then there's the friend, now a literary agent, whom I've known
for twenty-five years, since we were struggling young "career girls."
We met because we both worked for book publishers in New York.
We traveled together in Europe. She is guileless but smart, and she
underrates herself. I grew to love her gentleness, her insights, her
moral conscience. We share ambiguities. Seneca wrote, "One of the
most beautiful qualities of true friendship is to understand and to be
understood." That is what I feel with her when we talk on the phone
or meet for lunch or spend evenings or weekends together. Whether
we're with our husbands and our combined five children—whether
it is concertgoing in summer or cross-country skiing in winter—I
have that unmistakable "family feeling" when we're together. I remember her at my wedding; she remembers me at the hospital after
she had her first baby. I'm always surprised our memories don't go
back to our childhoods because I feel she's always been in my life.
Yet when I reviewed my recent datebooks, I discovered that we've
seen each other only four or five times a year. At first, it bothered
me. Now I understand that intimacy is more important than frequency. (According to *PT*'s survey, 97 percent of Americans have
close friends they do not see often; 72 percent keep in touch by phone,
70 percent by letter, and 33 percent have reunions only once or twice
a year.)

I could go on. I could choose a number of other women and a

few men and describe the strengths and deficiencies of each friendship. However, the epiphanies I've gained from this process have not come from rating my friends but from recognizing that *all* friendships have both strengths and deficiencies. I've also learned a lot by hearing my own sense of social inadequacy expressed over and over again by people who, in general, are pleased with their friends but worried about themselves *as* friends. I am not talking about depressed or pathologically shy people or those whose friendships are distorted by unresolved childhood psychodynamics. I am talking about ordinary women and men who see themselves failing to measure up to their own expectations of intimacy. I am talking about people who have been made to think relationships should be idyllic, people who view the state of their friendships as a character trait and being alone as a mark of shame, a failure of desirability in a society where human beings compete to feel wanted.

I've come to see how it benefits the status quo for us to think about friendship in terms of "success or failure." Most of us do not understand that the amount of time, money, and children one has, or where one lives and works, or whether one works at all, can be *structural determinants* of "success" in friendship. We do not understand how much our social life depends on factors that are inherent in our circumstances and not in ourselves. We do not see that the malaise—the doubts, the recurring void, the nagging feeling that something is missing—may not be located in flawed friendships but in flawed belief systems and specifically in what I call "the culture of calibration." This is the ethic that asks how big, how much, how many, about everything from cars to clothes to sex to friends. In the culture of calibration, social status is contingent not just on having more-better-best in education and income but in achieving certain relationships. Having more-better-best *friends* is as crucial as having a mentor or a husband or 2.1 children. In the culture of calibration, where the quest for the best is a social correlate of economic acquisitiveness and success has become like a sexual fetish, people determine their worth not through self-evaluation but by comparing themselves with others.

During interviews for this book, Westerners asked me if Easterners' friendships are more intellectual; those in big cities wanted to know if small town friendships are more genuine; and virtually everyone assumed friendships were more *something* somewhere else. Some people described friends as if they were brand-name possessions, with pedigrees and credentials, as if without important friends they might be less valuable themselves. Others mentioned knowing people who hoard *their* friends like children hoard toys, refusing to share them. Someone knew someone who seduces new people into friendship the way a Don Juan leads women to bed; and someone else complained about people who go through friends like comparison shoppers testing one product against another, judging, discarding, never satisfied.

In a way it's all very predictable: If "human potential" is infinite, then the potential of human friendship must be limitless too. If having intimate relationships is the goal of the fully "potentialized," self-actualized person, naturally the movers and shakers are going to amass more and better friends in pursuit of that paragon with whom they can create The Perfect Bond.

To resist the culture of calibration in friendship, we have to learn to deepen our appreciation of the friends we have, enjoy them for what they are, be available to new friendships but stop yearning for an idealized, perfectly matched alter ego or a utopian alliance. We have to accept that there is no ultimate definition of a "true friend," no single standard of "real friendship," and no divining rod for finding more, better, or best friends. Cicero said "a friend is a second self" and claimed to have found it in his friend Scipio. Montaigne insisted that he and Étienne de la Boétie had "a friendship so complete and perfect that its like has seldom been read of and nothing comparable is to be seen among the men of our day." But even Cicero admitted "that genuine and perfect friendships . . . are so extremely rare as to be rendered memorable by their singularity." And Montaigne said, "So many circumstances are needed to build it up that it is something if fate achieves it once in three centuries."

More than four centuries have passed since that was written and if another "genuine and perfect friendship" exists by now, I have not found it. I told you about a few of my friendships not because they are perfect but to make the point that *each one is imperfect and yet precious and irreplaceable.*

I told you about some of my own friends because the search for the soul of friendship leads finally to ourselves, to the organic, one-of-a-kind covenant that you and I make with each person we love. Perhaps the sentence completion that says it best is from the writer Robert Louis Stevenson: "A friend is a present you give yourself."

Chapter 5

The Passage to Intimacy

An actor friend of mine thinks about the passage to intimacy in theatrical terms. "People audition for closeness," he says. "A few get the part, most don't."

But when do we know if we're even in the running? What conditions facilitate the growth of intimacy and which deter it? In other words how do we make friends?

The notion of "making" friends is an odd construct to begin with. What do we mean by *make* friends? Make them what? Make as in *force?* As in "on the make"? Dale Carnegie once said, "To make a friend simply *be* one." But it's no linguistic accident that we say to our children "go out and make friends," rather than "go out and *be* friends." Being is not an act of creation; *making* is. When you make an acquaintance into a friend, you create something new—the two of you, a unit that never before existed in this world.

In the *Pirke Avot* (Sayings of the Fathers), 1:6, a compendium of ancient Jewish thought compiled around the second century, one of the sages instructs: "Make for yourself a teacher; acquire for yourself a friend." Judaic scholar Adin Steinsaltz says the verbs differ because "a teacher can give you information but a friend can influence you." I see the two sentences as one continuous thought: When we acquire friends, we make them our teachers—that is, we allow our friends to influence us.

The unwritten, unspoken pact to take one another seriously, to influence and be influenced, moves two people over the line from casual interaction to commitment and engagement to one another's lives. Taking someone seriously (even in a relationship that is filled with laughter) is a giant step beyond helping and being helped or giving and being given. It differentiates exchange from communal relations and "just a friend" from the friend who really matters.

This process of transformation is nine parts magic and one part cognition. "We cannot tell the precise moment when friendship is formed," said Samuel Johnson. "As in filling a vessel drop by drop, there is at last a drop which makes it run over, so in a series of kindnesses there is at last one that makes the heart run over." While many scholars have constructed models that divide this magical process into a dizzying array of stages, phases, levels, and sequences, the anatomy of friendship reveals itself best in personal stories. What made him your friend, I asked the people I interviewed. Why was she the one you decided to trust? How did this relationship become special?

Every friendship has its story.

We Became Friends Because . . .

Laura and Rosemary

"I'd just turned 40. The kids were into their terrible teens, my business was growing, my husband's business made many demands, and I couldn't fit another friend into my schedule unless one died and opened up a place," says Laura, a career counselor.

"Then in came this new client named Rosemary. She had many talents—writing, art, photography—and a wild wit, but wow, was she scattered. She had no idea what she wanted to be when she grew up—and she was already 35 years old."

Professionally, Laura helped Rosemary evaluate her strengths and narrow her career choice to photography. During this process, the two women became involved on a personal level too, Laura recalls. "I liked her self-mockery. But I also got an earful of her miseries and her money problems. She complained, I reassured. She cried, I comforted. After awhile I got fed up. I was drowning in her depressions. Our relationship had become a one-way street. She made me feel guilty if I didn't see her every day. Since she was single and a free-lancer, she made her own schedule, but I couldn't provide round-the-clock support. One night I told her I had to pull out. I wanted to be her friend, not her savior. She said she had no one else to turn to. I suggested she go into therapy and she did. It made a big difference. After awhile her sense of humor returned. She devoted a lot more time to her photography. She hustled jobs and worked on her technique and got very good at it. She also became a mensch as a friend."

Laura and Rosemary's friendship survived and deepened not just because Laura cared enough to be honest but because Rosemary was able to get the kind of help that no friendship could possibly provide.

"I think of our friendship as one of those graphs with a big downward dip at the beginning and then a straight line all the way up. In the years since that dip we've grown not just close but equal. She's still single, so she has different social needs than I, but she's made a lot of other friends apart from me, including each member of my family. She and my husband have dinner together every now and then and she often goes to the movies with my kids. I think it's rare for a single woman to be so much a part of a married friend's family."

Stephen and Jenny

Students at a large urban university, Stephen and Jenny had seen each other at the Black Students Union but they didn't become friends until they found themselves in the same philosophy course.

"Usually when you talk to people, it's like there's this gauze between you, and all the conversation filters through it," says Stephen. "But with Jenny, from the first we hung out together after philosophy class, there was no filter and no phoniness. We started talking about free will and that got us into the subject of destiny and then somehow we were discussing our whole lives. I never connected with someone else in such an intense way before. I really *heard* her and she really *heard* me.

"Now we meet after class three times a week to talk or do our readings. We've had some incredible conversations about philosophy, about being Black at a white university, about love and sex. Both of us are going with other people. Naturally I've thought about sex with Jenny, but I'm sure it would spoil our friendship and that wouldn't be worth it."

The Team

If it's hard for two people to achieve true friendship, imagine the
feat when eight people do it. That nonetheless is the case with The
Team, four married couples who have been together in collective
(nonsexual) intimacy for ten years—seeing each other en masse at
least once a month and in smaller subgroups in between. One member of The Team remembers the night it all began:

"It was the end of an evening at which we'd all had so much to
say and everyone had been so interesting that we couldn't tear ourselves away from each other. We realized that we had the best times
whenever the eight of us were together, so we decided to meet again
a month later. Someone suggested we assign ourselves a subject for
discussion—the first subject was Our Mothers. That meeting was
such a great success that we started having monthly dinners with a
different subject each time at a different house, and each couple
brought one course for dinner so it wasn't a lot of work.

"After a few years we agreed we didn't need a subject; it was too
confining. We just let people's ideas and problems guide us, which
sounds like ordinary conversation but it was never ordinary because
it was never superficial. I remember the night one of the men talked
about being unhappy in his work and not feeling in control of his
life. He was afraid he might botch a new project. He wasn't even
sure he was in the right field. It was painful to hear so much indecision
and self-doubt from a friend, but we helped him think it through
and he did fine at the project and regained his confidence. Another
night, I remember dealing with the subject of our aging parents.
And several couples have made The Team a conduit for saying things
to their spouses indirectly or using the other couples as a reality
check. A few years back, one of the marriages went through a very
touchy period. We not only worried about the couple, we worried
that if they divorced The Team might break up. The Team is like
the fifth marriage.

"We try not to be therapeutic but it's hard to avoid it because
one member is a psychiatrist and another is a minister. The other
members are a commercial artist, a personnel administrator, two
teachers, a doctor, and a lawyer. This year we're all between the
ages of 46 and 58. It's a pretty middle-class group, so we get middle-
class problems. We're at the stage where we're losing our parents,
one woman has cancer, the men have been through their mid-life

crises, the women have reentered, the children are leaving home. It's lucky we have each other.

"Our only problem is other people, the 'outside' friends who want *in*. We speak of them as Group B—and I know they feel second class. Periodically we talk about taking in new people, but we know each other's friends and when one says 'I'll bring Brenda and Stu,' another says 'Oh, if you're going to bring them, I'll bring Arthur and Honey' and it ends in a big joke. I try not to talk about The Team to my outside friends, but every now and then when I'm having an intense conversation with one of them, she'll ask me, 'Is this what it's like in The Team?' I know the Group B people feel excluded. But I could never sacrifice The Team for anyone else. The eight of us will be together in a nursing home, mark my words."

Ken and Charlie

Although many relatives are dear friends from childhood onward, Ken and Charlie discovered each other late.

"When Charlie found out his wife was cheating on him, it almost killed him," says Ken, 42, about his brother who is two years younger. "He was devastated. He had nightmares in the daytime. I thought he should get away for a while and by chance we'd both been invited to the wedding of a son of a mutual friend down in Memphis. I suggested we drive south together and that car trip changed our relationship.

"In the process of comforting him, I told him my wife had also had an affair—but ten years ago and I never had felt threatened by it. I had a million other reasons to be pretty confused about my own marriage, which I'd recently left after twenty-one years. Charlie wasn't sure he could forgive his wife, but at least he still loved her. I didn't love anyone. I was afraid to live alone, afraid of what my kids thought of me, and generally down on myself. I told Charlie he was lucky; all he felt was angry. I guess my misery took his mind off his. He came out of his depression enough to be very understanding and helpful to me. And it was a great relief for me to get all my unhappiness off my chest.

"I also told him about the affair I'd been having in New Orleans with a woman who was nearly half my age. He suggested that after the wedding we drive on to New Orleans so he could meet her. The three of us had dinner together. Later, over a nightcap, Charlie said to me, 'She's wonderful but there's an awful lot of father-daughter shit going on here.' He said maybe my wife had scared me off grown-up women but a romance with a kid wasn't the answer. The way he said it, I knew he really cared about me.

"Since that trip, he's back with his wife, I'm still separated but I did stop seeing the girl, and Charlie and I have something we didn't have before. We're friends."

Deborah and Cassie

"We met when we were both working for a catering company," begins Deborah. "Cassie and I spotted each other as lesbians—I guess it takes one to know one. There was no sexual attraction between us but knowing that we shared a life-style created an immediate bond.

"She and I each had a lover of long-standing and the four of us got along real well together. Then Cassie opened her own restaurant and asked me to come work for her. She was 23 and I was 38 at the time, but the age thing didn't get in the way of my being her employee or her friend. She amazes me. She's energetic and bright and she has a super-awareness that makes her ageless. She could just look at me and know what I was thinking.

"That's what got us through our crisis. The restaurant was in trouble and Cassie was trying to cut costs. She told me I'd have to work one less day. I felt she was blurring the lines between a friend and an employer. I couldn't afford to give up a day's pay. To me, it was an issue of mutual respect.

"We had a huge fight, with lots of yelling and screaming. In the middle of it, I suddenly realized how important this friend was to me. I didn't want to lose her over this. I got totally silent. She must have known what I was thinking because she gave me that deep look of hers and then she agreed to keep me working full time. We never had another problem. I worked for her for two years, until she closed the restaurant. It's harder to stay in touch now but we're still best friends."

Pete and Justin . . . and Jack . . . and Stan

"In every relationship, there is one who kisses and one who gets kissed," says Pete, a political leader who is well-respected in progressive circles.

"It's very distorting," he says, of his position. "I'm always getting kissed. Zillions of people want contact with me and all I have to do is respond. For a long time, I didn't choose my friends, they chose me. Then about three years ago, I attended a conference where this young musician named Justin entertained, and one of his original songs had a line almost identical to one in a poem I had written months before. It gave me the chills. After the show, I introduced myself. He was 22. He had no idea who I was. I told him I was an amateur pianist and would love to jam with him sometime. He took me into the jazz world and became my friend and my teacher. Through music, we've gotten to know each other from the inside out, not the other way around, the way it usually is in politics.

"My two other best friends are both my age—fortyish. Jack always describes our first meeting this way: 'I took Pete to a cheap Chinese restaurant and several thousand dumplings later, we were friends.' In his political arena, Jack is like me; we're both Big Daddy to our constituents, so neither of us can get support from the people around us. We can collapse and be ourselves only with each other. When I burned out, Jack took care of me and put me back together. I helped him through his divorce. He's also my clothing consultant. Once I admired a sweater of his and he gave it to me. He said I need more class in my wardrobe.

"My third friend, Stan, works for one of the advocacy groups that often lobbies me. We met because he needed my vote. He was so passionate about his issues, and they're things I cared about too, so I spent a lot of time with him. Then I realized I really enjoyed him. To be perfectly honest, Stan made me his friend by sheer positive reinforcement. I love his enthusiasm. He really thinks we can make the world a better place."

Mariagnese and Ursala

"Ursala and I grew up in the same building in the same village in Switzerland," says Mariagnese, an artist, whose story attests to the strength of childhood and cultural bonds. "I was 10 when we met; she was 10 years and 10 months. To this day, we still kid around about her being the older one. When a friendship dates back that far, you cannot say when it actually began. Ursala and I shared everything: school, family, village happenings. We were friends through the teens and at 21 we married men who knew each other from the same crew team. Then my husband and I moved to Peru and Ursala settled in the United States. She became a high school coach. We wrote to one another as if we were still speaking in our childhood bedrooms. Then, in 1975 I came to America too.

"In Switzerland one gets to know one's friends because it's such a small place and we meet the same people year after year again and again. America is so large and people pass each other like ships and they tell me their secrets after one day, but none of my new friends are like Ursala. She and I have our friendship inside us. When I am 80 and she is 80 and 10 months, we will still be close."

Ingredients to Make a Friend

Although these people made the passage to intimacy organically and unconsciously, their relationships fulfill the criteria defined by research as the preconditions for true friendship: *proximity, similarity, reciprocal liking,* and *self-disclosure.* Let's get beneath these abstract terms to better understand how we make strangers into friends.

Proximity

Although friends, unlike lovers, do not require frequent physical contact and many friendships survive long separations, at some point there has to have been physical proximity for the seeds of intimacy to germinate.

One of the "structural" determinants of friendship, proximity depends on your circumstances, on the way your life is set up. Proximity does not mean you must be roommates or next-door neighbors in order to be friends; it means you must have had the *opportunity* to meet each other. Stephen and Jenny happened to go to the same college and register for the same class. Rosemary and Laura met through a formalized counselor-client relationship. For Ken and Charlie, an automobile trip made possible the proximity that changed kinship into friendship. Although the members of The Team organized their monthly get-togethers, they were friends in the first place because of their socioeconomic proximity. Deborah and Cassie were prototypical coworkers who met on the job and remained friends after the job folded. Pete's three best friends came into his life by circuitous routes but all three meetings were connected to his career. For Mariagnese and Ursula, the sisterly bond originated in a childhood spent under the same roof. And many *PT* survey respondents said their closest friendships dated back to their youth, where togetherness is constant and routinized by classes, child's play, or sports.

Every friendship has some physical-factual causation and some way to locate its genesis in place and time, but only recently have analysts begun to understand the key role of these structural determinants in foretelling the pool of strangers from which we make acquaintances and friends.

For example, you pick a workplace because of the job, not the coworkers, but you get the coworkers with the job. Or you pick a neighborhood because you can afford the house, but your kids get a particular school group as part of the bargain. In school, the way classrooms are arranged determines children's opportunities for friendship. Are the grades segregated by age or are there "open" classrooms? How large is each class and how is it set up? A traditional classroom with fixed rows of seats facing forward where students are expected to remain in one place establishes an atmosphere different from that in a nontraditional classroom in which free-standing chairs identify an educational policy that encourages freedom of movement and peer interaction. All these structural characteristics affect children's friendliness and popularity, the incidence of cross-sex friendships, and the number and size of cliques.[1]

College living arrangements have similar effects. Freshmen who live in a dormitory make more new friends than those who live at home or in off-campus housing;[2] and suites, rather than rooms off a common corridor, provide the very best opportunities for dormitory friendship.[3] You have a better chance of striking up a conversation with a schoolmate if you're sharing a hot plate or brushing your teeth at the same sink.

In cities, towns, and neighborhoods, other structural factors promote or inhibit the social proximity that can lead to friendship. Obviously, race or age-segregated neighborhoods limit your choice of potential friends. Less obviously, the more you do in your community, the greater your chance of making friends, and how much you do in your community depends partly on what the community provides. If a wide variety of stores, bars, restaurants, clubs, and parks are within a few blocks of your home you're more apt to participate in neighborhood life—and thus to make friends.

What kind of stores and parks matter too.[4] For instance, disabled and nondisabled children are less likely to meet and interact in a conventional children's playground than in an experimental play area where the swings, seesaws, slides, playing courts, and craft and horticultural activities are especially adapted for use by kids who are disabled and the program staffed by trained recreation workers.[5] A bookstore that serves coffee and donuts and has sofas for browsers is more conducive to friendliness than a supermarket-style chain store. Office buildings surrounded by benches and plantings invite colleagues to sit and chat in the lunchtime sun, while sterile granite plazas keep people moving. Single-room-occupancy hotels in crimeridden areas keep the elderly in their rooms as surely as if they were locked up, but a planned retirement community pulsates with activity and spontaneous friendships.[6]

People can't achieve intimacy if friendship's beginnings are constrained by physical barriers or inhospitable circumstances. Those who feel lonely might ask themselves whether structural inhibitions are to blame, and if so, where to find more friendship-enhancing environments.

Similarity

What draws us to one person as opposed to another person? Those who study behavior seem to agree that friendship thrives on similarity. Thus, although "opposites attract" (heterophily) some of the time, "birds of a feather flock together" (homophily) most of the time.

It is clear that a degree of homophily—a preference for people of similar age, gender, marital status, education, class, race, background, politics, religion, interests, attitudes, and values—characterizes most friendships.[7] But does it actually result from personal *preference*? Or do we choose to associate with similar others because so many structural factors have influenced that "preference"? If we don't live near people of another race or ethnic group, if we don't go to school with anyone who's disabled, if we live in a housing development that bars children, then we are not likely to "prefer" these dissimilar people as friends. *Opportunity predicts preference.* To become mates, we first must meet.[8] At the same time, since the search for a friend represents a search for a soulmate—someone who can understand us from the inside out and support our personality—the attraction to homogeneous traits facilitates the passage to intimacy.[9]

I'm saying that both things are true: We prefer friends who are "like us" and people who are "like us" tend to live, work, and learn where we do. But I'm also saying that if a greater variety of people lived, worked, and learned where we do, then we might perceive them to be "like us," too. Meanwhile, as much as we'd like to believe that Americans enjoy heterogeneous social relations, no alert observer can deny the basic homogeneity of intimate friends.

Consider age homophily. Of the pairs discussed in this chapter, only Deborah and Cassie and Pete and Justin made a leap across the age barrier. And their friendships may be explained by other similarities: The age difference was bridged by the lesbian sexual orientation of the women and by the musical interests of the men. (The Team's twelve-year age span is misleading because men tend to marry younger women, which widens the age range between the oldest man and the youngest woman.)

Given the way life is organized, many of us simply do not have the opportunity to get to know people who are ten or more years younger or older than we are. (See Chapter 11 for more on intergenerational friendship.) The cost of housing separates younger families from more established older families. On the job, age segregation is common because occupational hierarchies usually parallel years of working experience. In one factory, for instance, despite a range in age from 17 to 74 for the total factory population, friendship pairs were found to be the same age because each department included workers of comparable experience and, consequently, the same general age, and people tended to make friends *within* departments.[10]

In addition to age homogeneity, as we've noted, Americans generally prefer friends of the same marital and socioeconomic status, race, ethnic culture, and gender. There is much more to the story than simple "like-self" preference, but in terms of the passage to intimacy, the key point to remember is this: Most adult relationships develop through verbal communication, and verbal communication requires some commonality to bridge the silence between strangers. Thus people who perceive themselves as having the "right type" of similarity are more apt to talk to each other than those who see themselves as unalike.

What is the right type of similarity? While research shows that *status similarity* may be a basis for some attraction, *value similarity* almost invariably is a more powerful magnet:

- It reduces our level of uncertainty in any situation.
- It increases the likelihood that the other person will validate our beliefs.
- It makes us feel safe and unthreatened.[11]

However, the distinction between status and values is often artificial because—through education and social conditioning—people of similar status usually also share the same attitudes and values.

Perhaps the more salient point is that shared values allow friends to eclipse differences in personalities and backgrounds. This explains why I love my insomniac filmmaker friend despite our many conflicting tastes and habits, and my therapist friend despite our divergent analyses of social ills, and my editor and activist friends despite our different emotional styles. Underneath those differences, our value system and our basic attitudes toward life are the same.

Here's another way to conceptualize the power of values similarity: A 30-year-old, single, white, gay man and a 50-year-old, married, black, heterosexual woman might become very good friends if they both belong to the same union and passionately oppose the death penalty. On the other hand, two 30-year-old, married, heterosexual, Irish-Catholic women who live next door to each other might never become friends if one believes reproductive choice is every woman's right and the other believes abortion is murder.

Reciprocal Liking

It hurts me to admit this, but one of the first things people like or don't like about a prospective friend is her or his physical appearance.[12] If you deplore the superficial Miss America-Hollywood-Fashion Model standard of Caucasian beauty, you too would be disturbed to find so much research data that prove looks count or, more precisely, that people respond to whatever is considered beautiful in their society.

Our mothers taught us that beauty is only skin deep, but psychologists have identified a much more widely held belief that "what is beautiful is good."[13] By age 3 or 4, children show a greater liking for more attractive playmates (those children that adults also considered attractive) and call their unattractive peers scary, aggressive, and unfriendly.[14] College students rated attractiveness one of the most important attributes of a friend.[15] People of all ages gravitate toward more attractive job applicants, courtroom defendants, lovers, and friends.[16] All of which suggests that, despite our preference for people who are similar to us, when it comes to appearance, we try to "trade up."

Although researchers disagree about whether looks become less important as people deepen their relationship, it's common for friends we once thought plain to appear attractive as we know them better. Furthermore, while surface attraction may figure into the first phase of friendship, as it does in the beginnings of love, no one I interviewed mentioned looks as a factor in their eventual passage to intimacy. In contrast, a good number of people mentioned "liking" as a conscious and ongoing process in a developing friendship. It may be tautological to say friends make the transition to intimacy because they *like* each other but that's where it begins.

Reciprocal liking brings the rush, the first "high" of friendship that Emerson evoked so lavishly in connection with the "two or three persons as have given me delicious hours." In the beginning, he wrote, "A new person is to me always a great event, and hinders me from sleep." But this ecstasy is a far cry from true friendship and the complicated reality of one's friends: "I shall not fear to know them for what they are," he wrote. "Their essence is not less beautiful than their appearance, though it needs finer organs for its apprehension."[17]

However fine our organs of apprehension, few of us are aware of when we progress from liking the appearance to liking the "essence" of a friend. Pete consciously observed himself warming toward Justin, Jack, and Stan. Each member of The Team recognized his or her fondness for one another at that long-ago dinner and acted to solidify it. Deborah had her "liking epiphany" during her fight with Cassie. But most people I asked said that they had never stopped to think about when or how they knew something special had happened and a friendship had been "made."

Phyllis Theroux, a writer, is the only person I've met who seems to skip that step altogether. She sees herself as part of a wide-open cosmic continuum of friendship. Everyone she meets, she likes. Wherever she goes, she creates "instant intimacy," a phrase my friend Gale Goldberg calls an oxymoron; but for Theroux, it is the rule. The transition from stranger to intimate does not exist for her.

"I don't make a huge distinction between myself and others, so I have very little sense of distance when I meet a new person," she confides one sunny morning over coffee and muffins. "No one seems strange to me. I like everyone right away and I feel I'm the one who has something to prove.

"A well-known author told me there was a three-month period in her life when she saw the sweetness in everyone, but I feel that way most of the time. I like each person for what is genuinely there to like. And the very few times in my life when I haven't liked someone, I've been proven wrong."

The rest of us are considerably more guarded. We go from a who-are-you phase to a maybe-you're-nice phase to a show-me-I-can-trust-you phase before something "clicks" and we really *like* a person. Friends can be said to "fall in like" with as profound a thud as romantic partners fall in love. Yet, we either don't notice the drop that makes the cup runneth over, or we take that magic moment for granted.

Friendship's "falling in like" may seem to be the bastard child in the family of love but its importance has been recognized throughout the centuries. Many writers have tried to distinguish Amicitia, friendship's nonphysical love, from Eros, its sexual counterpart, and today's thinkers are as taken with the parallels between the two relationships as with the differences.

Psychologists Keith Davis and Michael Todd have discovered that a spouse/lover provides more than a friend does in the area of "depth of caring . . . fascination, exclusiveness, sexual intimacy, enjoyment, and giving-the-utmost." On the other hand, a friend outranks a lover in providing acceptance, trust, confidentiality, understanding, and spontaneity and is nearly equal to a lover in providing respect and mutual assistance. Friends experience less conflict and fewer problems in maintaining their relationship than do spouses or lovers. And most people consider best friendships more stable than romantic relationships.[18] (I'll bet you have more ex-lovers than ex-best friends.)

Paul Wright and Paula Berghoff found only four characteristics that applied to love but not to friendship: Love requires exclusivity, is considered more permanent, is regulated by more social standards, and elicits higher levels of emotional expression. Otherwise, friendship and love are neck and neck.[19]

Robert Sternburg is another psychologist who insists that friendship holds its own when compared to love.[20] Both relationships, he says, satisfy the same *core* needs in each of us: to be able to count on the other person, to feel mutual understanding, to get emotional support, to value one another, to want the best for each other, and to feel happy in each other's company. Sternburg's study made head-lines because he found that women love their best female friend about as much as they love their male lover and like their best female friend *more* than their lover. (This will make sense when you read about styles of male and female intimacy in Chapters 13 and 14.)

While the experts are busy equating friendship and love, we who would never be oblivious to falling in love typically remain unaware of when we fall in like. Maybe this is because to like is not enough. As George Eliot wrote in *Daniel Deronda*, "Friendships begin with liking or gratitude—roots that can be pulled up." Unless liking is linked with mutual understanding, friendship does not graduate into intimacy. It is *knowing* and *being known* that gives friends roots in each other's lives.

Self-disclosure

Most of those surveyed by *Psychology Today* said they were com-fortable in talking to their closest friends about their "failure at work," "sexual activities," "a terminal illness," and "their intimate feelings about each other." But subject matter doesn't tell us enough; that is, it doesn't tell *me* enough. My consuming interest in friendship was inspired in large part by my own ambivalence about self-dis-closure and my conflicting desires for both attachment and freedom. Being *able* to talk about personal subjects is one thing; being *willing* to get deeply involved is something else.

William K. Rawlins has formulated a dialectical perspective that accounts for just such "internal oppositions and antagonistic ten-dencies."[21] From his studies, Rawlins learned that it is normal for friends to negotiate a balance between the *freedom to be independent* (to pursue separate goals and interests) and the *freedom to be dependent* (to call on one another for assistance), between the impulse to be open and the impulse to protect against too much candor. "The dialectic of expressiveness and protectiveness regulates the decisions of the self to reveal and conceal personal information," he says.

Just knowing that others experience tension between these two impulses makes the struggle to grapple with them easier. I was sim-ilarly reassured by sociologists Joseph Bensman and Robert Lilienfeld who state "that not all potential friends have equal needs for deeper friendships. Some may already have such friendships. Others may not be burdened by their private or public lives."[22] In other words, getting closer is an option, not an obligation. Friendships that feel comfortable at a certain level are not necessarily stagnant. They may be just right for you, for the moment or for always. You may feel you have enough friends—or too many, perhaps, to do justice to your affection for each. As long as you have one or two close relationships in your life, there is no reason to feel guilty or inadequate for resisting intimacy with others. Although you wouldn't want to rudely dismiss friends who need more from you, you have every right to feel reluctant to become further intertwined with yet another person's life or to unlock yet another layer of your soul.

But if you do want something deeper, don't be surprised if you nonetheless keep teetering on the brink of self-disclosure, wondering: "Am I willing to open up?" "Is this the right person?" "Is this the right moment?" Bensman and Lilienfeld say that the teetering feeling is very common:

> Having established common bonds for casual friendship, we often would like to express to a friend those thoughts, emotions and experiences, the aspects of our inner selves that we have had to keep secret from casual friends. We hope that the existing level of friendship will allow another to accept our revelation of the weakness we have heretofore concealed. We can never be sure of the response. Some of the thoughts and behavior we reveal may horrify the other and cause him or her to withdraw even from the level of friendship previously attained. We cannot be sure of the probable response because the other has not yet revealed enough to make his or her response predictable, perhaps for the same reasons that we hesitate.[23]

When deciding whether or not to "risk" self-disclosure, you might remember Francis Bacon's claim that communicating deeply and honestly with a friend "works two contrary effects; for it redoubleth joys, and cutteth griefs in halves."[24]

Certainly that is true of the friends profiled earlier: They doubled each other's pleasure and lightened each other's burdens. Each friendship was climaxed by an opening up, a presentation of the inner self to the friend. Each achieved the sense of trust, honesty, and being accepted that are the bedrock foundations of friendship. Stephen and Jenny felt *known*. Rosemary and Laura's friendship was cleansed and reborn after a truth-telling. By exposing their fears to one another, the two brothers tore off the masks of a lifetime. The Team is thriving after a decade of collective self-disclosure. Deborah and Cassie let it all out and became enriched in the process. Pete and his friends keep discovering new resources in one another. Mariagnese and Ursala stored up enough closeness to sustain them across continents and years. For each, opening up did not cause the self to leak away—it let friendship's love pour in.

Once again, these aren't perfect friends. Not one friendship may precisely suit your style or mine. But each shows how convoluted are the passages to intimacy—and how earnestly we work at finding our way.

Chapter 6

❧ ❧

Flashpoints

What Friends Fight About

"True friendship," George Washington said, "must undergo and withstand the shocks of adversity before it is entitled to the appellation of friendship."

Centuries later I heard the same message repeatedly: Friendship takes work. You can't know a friend until you've come through a crisis together. Don't expect smooth sailing. Sometimes you just explode—it's normal.

What causes those normal explosions? What are the most frequent flashpoints of friendships, the areas of strain that smolder and burst into flames?

Researchers have found that friends experience less conflict than virtually every other unit of relations—less than spouses, kin, siblings, coworkers, or parents and children.[1] That may be because, rather than stick around feeling bad or mad, friends simply dissolve their bonds—friendships are easier to dissolve than most other relationships. Or it may be because most friends worthy of the name get beyond their sparks, not by threats or coercion but by letting the troublesome issue resolve itself or by empathizing, avoiding, hinting, joking, yielding, persuading, or, most effectively, discussing feelings and spending time on problem solving.[2] Since we can assume two people would not have become friends if they had some basic personality clash or incompatible disposition, the cause of their conflicts *as friends* probably lies in some aspect of their situation. Although almost anything can spark a dispute or spoil a relationship, the following ten causes seem to be the most common:

- Love and marriage
- Children
- Separation and divorce
- Competition and envy
- Money
- Favors
- Dependency
- Illness
- Seeing someone in a new light
- Betrayal

If that sounds like a cross between the seven deadly sins and The Story of Your Life, it's because it is.

The Crises of Friendship

Love and Marriage

When one of two friends falls in love or marries, the change almost always registers on the friendship. Orinda, a poet of the Renaissance, called "the marriage of friends the funeral of friendship."[3]

Current studies confirm that the more involved a couple is the fewer friends they have, the less they confide in their friends, and the less important are the friends' opinions.[4] (Engaged and newlywed couples have the fewest friends of all.) "The more two people are in love," wrote Sigmund Freud, "the more completely they suffice for each other." As a result, some friends feel so painfully displaced by their friend's sweetheart that they act like jilted lovers; many are resentful; a few retreat altogether.

"She trashed our friendship," says one man of a former woman friend. "You'd think I never existed. I didn't ask her to choose between me and him. I never wanted *all,* but she didn't have to give me *nothing* either."

A woman who happens to be blind puts a finer point on it: "Now that most of my close friends are couples, they have less time for me. They're so involved with their spouses that when I'm with them I've become more aware of my singleness than my blindness."

As understandable as the single friend's position may be, so is the point of view of the friend in the love relationship. "Irma and I had been united in our misery," says Pam about a sister reporter on a city newspaper. "We were both working stiffs who never had enough time or money to enjoy ourselves. We bitched and moaned to each other about our lousy lives, or one of us was always mothering the other out of a depression. When I met Tom and became a happy person, I guess I broke the pact. My friendship with Irma went downhill fast. She needs to find another malcontent to be friends with. I'm happy now. I'm in love."

While some people complain that the closeness of couples often makes them insufficiently available to friendship, others understand the time crunch because they too are people with love affairs, families, and time frustrations of their own. As we've seen, friends gravitate to those who are most like themselves and marital status is one of the strongest areas of homophily, or similarity, in friendship. Maybe we have to accept that being in love changes who we are sufficiently to change the kind of friends we seek. It certainly changes the time we have to devote to the care and cultivation of our friendships.

Another source of conflict is friend-lover incompatibility. In *Break of Day,* Colette wrote: "My true friends have always given me that supreme proof of devotion, a spontaneous aversion for the man I loved." Many people admit to being hypercritical of a friend's romantic partner. Perhaps that is how we displace the anger that would otherwise be directed at the friend who has allowed the newcomer to upstage us.

Linda feels especially justified in her aversion to a friend's lover: "When Julie's boyfriend was putting her through the wringer, I was her sounding board, so I got this one-sided awful picture of him. Eventually, she forgave him because she loves him, but I've never gotten over my distaste. Now they're engaged and I'm having trouble pretending that I like him. If I told Julie what I really think, she'd never want to see me again."

When you disapprove of your friend's beloved, not only does it drive a wedge into the friendship, it also casts doubt on your friend's judgment.

"I'm glad he's in love, but frankly I don't understand what he sees in her," says Eric about Richard and his fiancée. "He practically slobbers over her and she is just as idiotic with him. When the three of us are together, I feel like a coaxial cable. They don't speak to me, they speak *through* me."

Witnessing lovers' affection can make an onlooker feel both extraneous and unpleasantly aware of his or her own solitude. Richard's engagement underscores Eric's "oneness." It also signals the end of the friendship as both men have known it. Single people confronting a friend's marriage "may experience a kind of happy rage," says Janet Barkas, a sociologist. "Happy at the friend's good fortune, rage at being left behind."[5] Richard's "good fortune" has discomposed the equality of bachelorhood and dyadic intimacy. Before, each was the other's principal confidant; now Richard's wife-to-be has taken that role.

Although men are much more likely to forsake their male friends and make their wives or lovers their confidantes, the media give the impression that it is women who need lessons in loyalty. It is not men's but women's magazines that frequently run features with such titles as "How to Keep Marriage from Spoiling Friendships with Single Friends." Men are assumed to have no trouble with friendship. Look at all the pals they have. When men's media cover the subject of male friendship at all, they give us the reminiscence of wartime buddies or a profile of a prominent man written by his childhood pal. These paeans to brotherhood can leave the average man feeling prosaic in his attachments and ill-equipped for the ups and downs of getting along with another person.

Few of us, men or women, are forewarned in particular about what happens when love comes between friends. A change in the marital status of one member of a friendship can disconcert *both* members. Singles feel closed out; married friends feel stereotyped and misjudged. Singles sometimes view marrieds as bourgeois bores and exclude married friends from their activities. Marrieds are capable of treating singles as if they were victims of arrested development because their turbulent boy-meets-girl scenarios continue, while the marrieds have "settled down."

Formerly simpatico friends have new reasons for dispute: Singles still have open-ended weekends, but married friends reserve their free time for their spouse. The married one won't linger on the phone anymore. The single one won't come over if the spouse is home. The single one wants to talk about sex and the married one wants to talk about family planning.

Eventually, if they care enough, friends make adjustments and enter a new phase. They alter their expectations of the friendship. They try to anticipate one another's changed needs and new sensitivities. They talk things out when feelings are hurt or words misunderstood. Then there comes a day when the single one gets married. The friends expect this happy event to even out their relationship. Instead, they are stunned when it exacerbates their conflicts or creates fresh turmoil. There's unspoken competition for the Most Happy Couple award. The new bride or groom is more starry-eyed and spouse-oriented than the friend who has been married for a while. The veterans want to play marriage counselors, while the newlyweds feel diminished by their all-knowing advice. Or the friends' respective spouses don't like each other. All in all, it's a minefield and the only way to get through it is to get through it. The alternative is to change friends, and for real friends that is no alternative at all.

Blair Sabol has some commonsense suggestions for the single whose friend is now in a couple: "Avoid any hint of ménage à trois. . . . don't expect your married pals to fix you up. . . . don't intervene in their argument. . . . [and] don't judge each other's lifestyle."[6]

Comparable advice for the married friend might be: Don't treat your single friends as if they are half-a-human because they're unmated. If your spouse flirts with your single friend, don't dump the friend, deal with the spouse (or it's only a matter of time before another friend catches his or her wandering eye). Don't impose on singles by assuming they have nothing to do. A friend of mine brought me up short when I made that mistake. "I have *less* free time than you do," she insisted. "Married women can combine love and work; you can wash your hair, do your taxes and still be with your husband. I need a separate night for each activity. If I asked a date to sit around while I added up my charitable deductions, he'd head straight for the door."

Children

Becoming a parent is another major personal change that is potentially disruptive to friendship. To put it bluntly, one friend's blessed event may be the other friend's curse.

"I didn't used to think shared circumstances mattered in a friendship until a few of my friends started having children," says a florist in her early thirties. Now their babies keep them up until 2 a.m., so they're too tired for a movie or it has to be an early night so they can go home to release the baby-sitter. Some don't go out at night at all. Maybe they don't want to or maybe they can't afford to, I'm not sure. But when I visit them, their kids crawl all over me, so who wants to come again? And after five telephone conversations are interrupted by a baby's screams, the sixth time, I don't call."

A married man who has no desire to have children comments, "To be honest, I couldn't care less whether a baby can eat steak at 4 months of age or how much a stroller costs. But my friend is so wrapped up in those issues he can't talk about anything else."

A single businesswoman finds parent and nonparent life-styles logistically incompatible: "Since Joy had children and moved to the suburbs, we've hardly seen each other. She'll call me at nine in the morning to tell me she has no sick kids at home so she's coming into town and wants to have lunch. I can't go because my lunches are booked up three weeks ahead, but she won't make a date three weeks ahead because her life revolves around her children."

Some single women say it's up to the friend who's a mother to decide whether she wants to keep the friendship active since hers is the life that's changed. Maybe so. But first she must belong enough to herself to be able to make decisions at all. Young children—and strained economic circumstances—do not always give mothers that luxury.

While nonparents bemoan the domestication of their formerly carefree pals, new mothers and fathers resent the disinterest of their childless friends. One father asks, "Why do my buddies tune out when I tell the story of my son's playground accident if they can listen politely to their own medical anecdotes?" Another man complains that his childless friends show little understanding of what his life is really like. "They have no idea of the fatigue, the strain on my bank account, or the fun of it all."

Those friends who do make it through unsynchronized parent-hood seem to do it by practicing a concerned empathy from both directions and keeping in mind that this too shall pass. Eventually, either the nonparents become parents and fall into the same patterns, or the parents become more casual about their kids, or the kids grow up—sometimes to become friends of their parents' friends.

In other cases, it isn't the timing of parenthood that causes discord but conflicting child-rearing styles. Jo had a blowup with her week-end guests because their indulgence of their 2-year-old was so disruptive. They had let Chuckie run around on the tennis court, making a shambles of the adults' doubles game, not to mention the endangerment to the child. The baby-sitter for Jo's two kids could have watched Chuckie too, but the parents wanted him in sight. Nor did they intervene that evening when the little boy decimated a tray of hors d'oeuvres, leaving a half-eaten mess for the other dinner guests. Finally, it was bedtime. Jo reiterated the house rule against eating in bed to discourage the infiltration of ants, field mice, and crumbs in the sheets. Nonetheless, Chuckie brought a cookie upstairs, precipitating a round of "me-toos" from Jo's children, a wrathful outburst from Jo, and indignation from the parents who would not have their Chuckie yelled at by anyone!

"Things between us have never been the same. Since my friends see nothing wrong with their permissive methods, they probably will always feel I was the crazy one," says Jo. "But I learned an important lesson: When you love your friends, you keep your mouth shut about their kids, no matter what."

Separation and Divorce

If love, marriage, and children can shake up a friendship, divorce can cause an earthquake. The tremors are familiar.

THE TREMORS OF DIVORCE

What divorced persons say

"I need some time just to vent my spleen. I wish my friends would be better listeners and not try to respond to everything I say."

"It's a great responsibility to suddenly be a single parent. My married friends don't realize why I need to spend extra time with my kids during this period."

"My women friends don't invite me over anymore. They assume all divorcées are after their husbands."

"It's like Noah's ark in my neighborhood. If you're not a couple, you can't come aboard."

"The woman I date gets the cold shoulder from my ex-wife's friends. They think being nice to her would be disloyal to my ex-wife."

"A few people I met through my ex-lover won't have anything to do with me since we broke up even though I always thought of them as *our* friends."

What their friends say

"After the divorce, he drove me up the wall with his angst. Now he doesn't stop telling me how great it is to be single. Either he's trying to justify himself or he wants me to leave home too."

"He expects his friends to worship him because he's raising his kid by himself. Meanwhile, millions of women—including me—have been doing the same thing and no one's applauding."

"She's a basket case. At first I thought, okay, she's upset, but she's still refusing to take responsibility for herself as a single person."

"He's too moody. She's no fun anymore."

"I'm sick of the young chippies he's dating. I think he parades them around to make us jealous or to make us all feel old."

"They've made it impossible to stay friends with both of them. Either they pump me for information about their ex, or they recite every atrocity the ex has committed since birth."

"Just because her ex-husband is still my friend, she blames me for his leaving her."

How their friends can help

Give your divorced friends room to express their rage, but don't let them wallow in hatred of the former spouse; it becomes addictive to the sufferer and deadening to the friendship.

Offer to babysit for your divorced friend's children to give her or him time to reconnect socially. Invite the single parent family to family events as usual.

Until your friend gets used to not being a couple, leave your own wife or husband at home and see your divorced friend one to one.

Try not to create situations where the divorced friend is the odd man or woman in a group.

Don't reminisce about old times; they arouse painful memories. Or they make your friend's new companion feel awkward.

If possible, keep your divorced friend busy on his or her birthday, former wedding anniversary, and major holidays—and don't stop inviting him or her to major events, even if you have to insist that both ex-es be welcome at your house.

The problem with divorce and friendship is not bad people but a bad situation. If you are divorced, remember that some marrieds think divorce is catching. Don't flaunt your social life once you start dating. Our culture views marriage as unromantic in contrast to courtship and many married people have inferiority complexes.

The loss of friends you made through your ex is another common experience. Even if everyone involved makes an effort, people often remain unconsciously loyal to the person who originated the friendship. Pat Walsh had the opposite experience. She and her best friend, Anne Keegan, met through their husbands, who were cohorts in the Knights of Columbus. When Pat's marriage broke up, the women's friendship survived. Divorced and childless, Pat feels she lost a husband but gained a family. "Anne, Tom, and their five children have made me a part of the Keegan household."

Competition and Envy

I find small comfort in the fact that competition, friendship's ugliest ringworm, has been around so long and infected so many. The seventeenth-century French philosopher La Rochefoucauld said: "It is not enough to succeed, your best friends must also fail." He also advised: "If you want enemies, excel your friends, but if you want friends, let your friends excel you." Sigmund Freud was competitive with his mentor Josef Breuer, his early disciples Carl Jung and Sándor Ferenczi, and with Wilhelm Fliess, the German doctor who was his closest friend for fourteen years.[7] After studying the Freud correspondence, Freud scholar Patrick Mahony concluded: "Freud felt distinctly oppressed by Fliess' superiority" and his theory of bisexuality "evoked some jealousy and envy on Freud's part."[8]

Virginia Woolf was both bewildered by her rivalry with her friend Katherine Mansfield and goaded into doing her best work because of it. When Mansfield died, Woolf wrote in her diary:

Katherine has been dead a week. . . . At that one feels—what? A shock of relief?—a rival the less? Then confusion at feeling so little—then gradually, blankness and disappointment; then a depression which I could not rouse myself from all that day. When I began to write, it seemed to me there was no point in writing. Katherine won't read it. Katherine's my rival no longer.[9]

It is normal to feel jealous, occasionally, of someone else's talents or possessions, especially when we feel underendowed ourselves, but most friends try to rise above this reaction. Those who don't, do not remain friends long. Chapter 12 explores how friends compete in the working world and Chapters 13 and 14 cover each gender's different styles of competition. Right now, I want to make a more general point: It is not objective success but success *discrepancies* that leave an imprint—or a bruise—on friendship.

A New Jersey homemaker says she finds it prudent not to discuss her master of fine arts studies with her neighbors. "My friends don't think *they're* the best," she laughs, "but they don't like you to think *you're* the best either." Many older women who went back to school said they found it easier to move into new relationships than to hold on to old ones because upgrading themselves had caused a perceptible rift between them and their long-term friends.[10]

A writer who won a $15,000 prize says: "My friends didn't exactly turn handsprings for me. I think they're afraid I'm going somewhere without them, that my success will change me and I'll leave them behind. If I do, it will be because they couldn't share my happiness without getting caught in their own envy."

Learning to live with the love-envy dynamic is a continuing task for people whose lives are publicly chronicled and coveted. I'm thinking of a prominent real estate developer who also sits on the boards of some prestigious cultural institutions. As a visible money-maker and achiever, he says he has had to accept that envy comes with the territory. "For instance, the other night when I finished chairing an important budget meeting, a friend of mine good-naturedly slapped me on the back and said, 'Big shot, you think you're so great.' I have a hunch he was really saying *he* thinks I'm great and it pisses him off."

Groucho Marx once confessed that people who envied him treated him as more than human and that made him feel less than human. Some friends thought he was too important to be bothered by spontaneous phone calls and invitations to do nothing together, so he missed out on ordinary pleasures. Others were jealous of his success and unconsciously wanted to punish him by excluding him from friendship activities. That was the only way they could psychologically even the score. Thus, despite their glamorous lives, the greats of any generation can be confined by envy and jealousy to gilded isolation or a cold pantheon populated solely by other deities. As someone once said, a pedestal is a prison like any small space.

Famous or not, *fear* of their friends' jealousy causes some people to hold back from achieving too much and others to censor their accomplishments. Such censorship tempers the red-hot thrill of success and diminishes happiness. It clouds achievement in a furtiveness and offers a reproach to the less accomplished. It enlarges success, making it more real to the friend who suffers on hearing about it than to the one to whom it happened.

If jealousy, envy, and competition do not poison the well of friendship, rivalry for the title "best friend" may do the job. In *As You Like It,* one man's jealousy of another's gift for friendship precipitates angry actions that hurt three innocent people. A 35-year-old Rhode Island man says about a friend: "He opens his life up like a novel. I never know how singular I am. He has shared his most private problems with at least three people besides me. I mean, is fucking intimate if you fuck everyone?" A 20-year-old college student files the same complaint about her friend: "It annoys the hell out of me when I hear her tell other people the same secrets she tells me. She thinks she can have a dozen heart-to-heart relationships. I think she spreads herself too thin."

Most people feel that exclusivity is a lover's right but a friend's destruction. Do you object to "promiscuous" friends? Or do you think a friend's demand for distinguishing treatment is a symptom of unhealthy possessiveness? Every friendship makes its own rules.

Money

It has often been said that the finest kind of friendship is between people who expect a great deal of each other but never ask it, especially when money is involved. "If you're tired of a friend, lend him money" instructs an old maxim.

"My friend borrowed money from me" showed up as the sixth most frequent reason for strained friendship in the *PT* survey. "I borrowed money from a friend" was reason number 13.

It happens that I have loaned money to two friends, one a brilliant writer who is absurdly underpaid and underpublished, the other a divorced woman who needed it to send her child to summer camp. Because both debts were repaid within a reasonable time, I have no problem with friends and money. But I know others who have been badly burned.

Patrick loaned a friend $100 just because he asked for it. "I thought that's what friends are for." Six years have passed since then. The two men have continued to see each other in the neighborhood and they hang out at the same bar, but the friend has never mentioned the money. "I kept thinking he'd get around to it. I didn't want to embarrass him. Now I'm too embarrassed to ask. It's not the $100 that bugs me—I just wonder how a friend could do this."

To avoid such problems, many people make a rule against borrowing and lending. A similar rule against business transactions between friends would also save a lot of grief, as Cora learned when she sublet office space to a friend. Because she had furnished the office and paid for a cleaning service, she charged the friend a small amount above her cost. Some months later when he learned of the added charge, he blew up and accused her of profiteering. Though the friendship has been repaired, reverberations of his anger still ring in her ears.

Benjamin, a sculptor, also had a friendship soured by business: "When a friend commissioned a piece from me, I charged him a price that barely covered my costs. Selling cast copies would have helped me recoup, but I told him I wouldn't reproduce the sculpture if he had some sentimental feeling about owning the only one. He said I could duplicate the piece as long as I paid him $500 for every copy sold. Since he was investing in me while I was an unknown, he thought he ought to share in my success when I started selling. I couldn't believe a friend would turn my generosity to his advantage. Now, it's an effort just to be civil to him."

Favors

Asking inappropriate or excessive favors is another way to kill a friendship. It may be okay for you to borrow my car every now and then, but a twice-weekly request suggests that you should have chipped in on the purchase price. By the same token, if I refuse your occasional request to borrow the car, you'd have cause to think me selfish. Where favors are concerned, most friends strike a balance between asking too much and giving too little. But some never quite get the hang of it.

In the asking-too-much department, a writer-friend I'll call Zeke asked me to bring him and his new book to the attention of another friend who hosts a major national television show. I refused, asking Zeke to imagine what an outrageous imposition it would be if I bothered my friend on behalf of everyone I know who wants to be on his show. Zeke accused me of wanting to please a friend I consider more "important." "This has nothing to do with how I feel about either of you—this is a question of refusing to do one friend a favor by exploiting another," I said. "You may be willing to exploit me, but I'm not willing to exploit him." Zeke finally gave up, but in an angry voice he said, "You owe me one."

Tracy, a college student, routinely asks one friend to pick up her mail, another to buy her newspaper, still another to "just add my towels to your laundry"—but always seems unavailable to do favors for anyone else. "Tracy's one of those people who was indulged by her family," explains her roommate. "She just assumes other people were put on this earth to make her life easier."

Al, who owns a wine importing firm, says his friends often ask him to donate wines to charitable events. "I don't mind doing it," he insists, "but I do mind friends who disappear between favors."

When their son broke out in chicken pox the night before their planned departure for Europe, one couple asked old friends if they could leave him with them. The friends agreed because their own children had already had chicken pox and the little boy was no trouble. Nevertheless, they did think it was asking too much.

On the "giving too little" side of the equation, there is Dan who came up short when his friend Karen asked a modest favor. One night after an argument with her boyfriend she found herself out on the street with her belongings. It was midnight. Dan's house was the nearest. Karen called him and asked to stay overnight; he said he was really sorry but he had an important project due tomorrow at work and couldn't be disturbed. She said she just needed a couch or a sleeping bag. She'd stay out of his way and leave early in the morning. She wasn't in the mood to talk anyway. Dan said he was *really* sorry but having her there would affect his concentration and this assignment was too important to mess up. Finally, a neighbor who had heard the fight with the boyfriend took Karen in. As for Dan, he's an ex-friend now.

In addition to friends who ask too much and give too little, there
is a small tribe of people, usually women, who *give* too much, thereby
unbalancing friendship's intuitive mutuality of exchange.

Norma was one of these compulsive givers. One day her friend
Kitty complained that she never had time to go to the dry cleaners
after work. Norma immediately offered to do it for her once a week.
Typically, when Norma volunteered an extravagant favor, the friend
took her up on it. But this time Kitty shouted, "For God's sake,
stop letting us walk all over you! My dry cleaning is my problem."

"I guess I didn't believe I was worth anybody's friendship unless
I did things to deserve it," says Norma, who is trying to break herself
of the habit.

Also in the category of "Thanks for the favor, but don't do me
any favors," advice-giving has been identified by several researchers
as one of the frequently misplaced generosities of friendship.[11] Some
advice is not only unhelpful, it can be hurtful. ("I know just how
you feel but you'll get over it in time" is infuriating advice to someone
who's bereaved. Just letting the person talk about the deceased and
sharing your best memories of him or her are far more helpful responses.)[12] Other advice can have the effect of blaming us for our
situation or making us feel incompetent. ("Maybe the company wanted
a more assertive person. Next time, come on a little stronger.")

Sometimes, a friend's "helpful" advice damages our self-esteem.
In that case, we actually feel better when we outrightly reject it.

The freedom to reject advice is a sign of an egalitarian friendship.
It establishes our ability to have a different analysis of a problem and
still respect each other. Friends who gracefully accept the rejection
of their advice show themselves to care more about our ultimate
well-being than about being heeded or receiving credit for solving
our problem. People may feel obliged to take the advice of bosses
or parents for fear of insulting or disobeying them. But in a non-
hierarchical relationship, advice is a gift, not a command—and it can
be returned unused if it doesn't fit.

Dependency

Because dependence has for so long been linked with passive,
powerless women, healthy *interdependence* often gets a bad rap too.
It's important to recognize the difference. We want friends we can
depend upon and, in turn, we also pride ourselves on being the rock

in someone else's storm. But the cloying, draining, energy-sucking friend is not a thing of beauty and a joy forever. The ties that bind can also strangle.

Pearl knows this firsthand. "I have friends who are very vulnerable," she confides. "A dish breaks, they call. Everything is a qvetch and a crisis."

Christopher, an unusually nurturant man, told me he sometimes feels physically dragged down by his friends' demands. "I'm carrying a dozen emotional lives on my back," he says. "I enjoy helping people but not giving aid and comfort every forty-five minutes. I finally had to unplug my phone."

"There can be no friendship where there is not freedom," wrote William Penn. "Friendship loves a free air and will not be fenced up in strait and narrow enclosures."

Dependency is a suffocating form of enclosure. And weakness can be a powerful tool of manipulation in the hands of the friend who is incessantly needy or inconsolable, the one who keeps escalating the crises that require your intervention, and the one whose daily conversation resounds with cries of "I'm falling apart." However faint the voice, such pleas can be as coercive as a shout.

Friends are like violin strings: They can make beautiful music, but if drawn too tight, they snap. Unhappy, overly dependent people may need more help than any friendship can provide. Directing them to professional help—as Laura did when she collapsed under the demands of her photographer friend Rosemary—can be the friendliest act of all. If that fails, a forthright retreat may be the only answer.

On the other side of the ledger, some people never ask anything of a friend because they hate to feel obligated or because they think relying on another person is an admission of incompetence. These relentlessly independent people are usually males, who associate need with weakness and find it unbecoming to "a real man," or nontraditional women, who are so accustomed to acting strong in a man's world that they are afraid to let down their guard even with a friend. Two stockbrokers have this problem: "Mona and I are both so self-sufficient, we're like two walls meeting," says Yvonne. "In our friendship, one of us would have to be hemorrhaging to ask the other for help."

Without speculating on the deficiencies of parental love that might create either an emotional parasite or an obsessive loner, we can simply say that what is at issue here is balance. Remember the previously discussed dialectic through which friendship finds its equilibrium: the delicate harmony between the freedom to be dependent and the freedom to be independent. That equilibrium is the difference between leaning on friends and crushing them.

Illness

On the subject of giving too little, I reserve the heaviest indictment for myself. About seven years ago when a friend's child had cancer, I asked after him frequently and sent a package of children's books to the hospital, but, I am ashamed to say, I never visited him. His parents seem not to have condemned me, and, mercifully, the boy has recovered. But I will always know how inadequate a friend I was to them, as I have been to others I love who have been sick or had sickness in their families.

I have a problem with illness. Armchair analysis suggests it is because my mother died of cancer when I was young and I have never been able to visit sick people or hospitals without stirring up those memories. But it may be something more ignoble: cowardice, laziness, a primitive fear of "germs" or the unknown, a self-serving denial of human frailty and the fragility of life. Whatever the cause, it is humiliating to own up to such behavior, and, like any coward, I do so only after having discovered that others are guilty of it too.

Psychologists call it "the leper syndrome." A 3-year-old with herpes is shunned by his friends whose parents won't let them play with him. Children afflicted with AIDS are totally ostracized: "Please bring me friends," says one little boy to his social worker. Chronically ill diabetic children say their friends stigmatize them because of the disease, and 85 percent of cancer patients are aware of their friends' discomfort with their illness.[13]

"I learned who my friends were when I was in the hospital," said Brian Scott, a high school student. His classmates visited (because the school was close to the hospital, he said) but his neighborhood friends did not. One friend said he hadn't come because Brian's mother had not told him where the hospital was. "That was your responsibility to find out," said Brian coldly.[14]

An experimental project matched hospitalized teenagers with teenage visitors who were strangers to them, not friends who remember how they used to look before they had cystic fibrosis or anorexia nervosa or radiation treatments.[15] With these new friends, adolescents tended to relax rather than to worry about the other person's reaction or approval.

"I sat in front of an immense pile of laundry too tired and depressed to put it in the washer and wondered where my friends were," writes a woman with a desperately sick child. Remembering how her mother's friends cooked and did chores for one another whenever there was a childbirth or illness, she says, "perhaps the worst and most puzzling side effect of this long illness has been the disappearance of our friends. After initial expressions of sympathy, they drew back from us, and I am still trying to understand why."[16] Was it because the family was so emotionally needy, no longer had money to spend, had stopped taking pains with their appearance and weren't fun to be with anymore? Then again, wouldn't the family have been less dour and demoralized had their friends stuck by them?

Manuel Garcia's friends did that and more. Beneath a photograph of the Milwaukee auto mechanic with an interracial group of skinheads gathered around him on his porch, the caption read: "His home and neighborhood is teeming with bald heads, all in the cause of love and concern for the 35-year-old Mr. Garcia in his fight against stomach cancer." In July 1985 when he lost his hair to chemotherapy, about fifty of his friends and relatives shaved their heads so he wouldn't feel like "the only one."[17]

In *No Laughing Matter,* Joseph Heller and his co-author Speed Vogel detail Heller's yearlong struggle with a rare, paralyzing nervous disorder and how the visits, gifts, humor, and care of friends like Dustin Hoffman and Mel Brooks helped him endure and slowly recover. He especially appreciated getting a Sony Walkman, cassettes, Chinese puzzles, a harmonica and a water pistol.

"Illness is a proving ground for friendship," says the sister of a professor whose respiratory problem was diagnosed as AIDS. In his case too, the friends proved out. "Not one disappointed him," his sister remembers. "Even casual acquaintances came through; one brought him a file of up-to-date research on AIDS, another offered to shop for his groceries. His best friend gave him a Book-of-the-Month Club membership as if he were going to live forever."

Sonny Wainright's friends donated blood, kept her life together while she was hospitalized, and dealt with the doctors. Before she died, Sonny boasted of "taking all I can take" from friends and knowing "that I deserve what is being offered"—an enviable sense of entitlement and confidence in the mutuality of her friendships.[18]

Three views from the helper's side of the sickbed leave me further humbled. Dwight's friend Tom had a serious drinking problem that strained their friendship. "It's hard to like a guy when liquor changes his personality," says Dwight. But rather than walk out on his friend in disgust, Dwight joined Al-Anon to learn how to deal with his friend's alcoholism.

Carol Ascher's account of her twenty-year off-again on-again friendship with Viola is the saga of both Viola's struggle with multiple sclerosis and Carol's battle against losing a friend to a debilitating, incurable disease. As Viola battled bravely against failing sight, lameness, thinning hair, paralysis, weight gain, the pain of cortisone treatments, and thoughts of suicide, Carol assumed the difficult labor of offering love without pity. In Carol's words: "Oh, how the limits of friendship now seemed cheaply drawn! What good were distant avowals of affection when Viola needed help eating, dressing. . . ."[19]

Jewel's devotion also stretches the bounds of friendship. "When Kathy discovered the lump, we *both* went for her mammography," Jewel says of her friend of thirty years. "The joke was that the lab called *me* with her results. Although the malignancy was obvious, we went for three more oncologists' opinions. We devised a routine to make it easier on Kathy. The doctor would examine Kathy, then she would leave the room and I'd talk to the doctor, take notes, and later tell her the report in a way she could accept. When she had to have surgery, I interviewed the surgeons for her. After the operation, I went with her for her treatments. I stayed with her when her husband wasn't home. We spent weekends together in the country. But no matter what we did, she got more despondent. Then there was a second mastectomy. Now the cancer seems to have beaten her, psychologically more than physically. In the past, she took Valium and sleeping pills; now she is addicted to heavy drugs and her habit is very serious, but I can't force her into treatment. I'm an enabler. I don't know how to cope with a situation where nothing I do helps."

The power of friendship as treatment and cure has yet to be definitively measured, but there are hints in the wind: Diabetics who had good friends controlled their disease better than those who were unhappy with their friendships. Medical students with good friends had better immune systems than those who were lonely. And women with a friend in the delivery room had fewer complications in childbirth than those without.[20] Friends seem to be like aspirin: We don't really know why they make a sick person feel better but they do.

Seeing Someone in a New Light

I'm sure you've had an experience like this: You're driving behind a slow-moving truck thinking "What a road hog" when the driver steers onto the shoulder to let you pass and you think "What a nice guy." In the rush of life, these abrupt changes of attitude—bad to good or vice versa—merit little notice. But seeing a friend in a new light because of something he or she has said or done can suddenly illuminate the person with a harsh glare or an angel's halo. When the insight is negative, instead of a fault being just a foible, it becomes a fatal flaw.

"We discovered that we have very different views on issues that are important to me" was the third most frequently checked cause of friendship strain in the *PT* survey. It brought to mind the differing politics that destroyed many friendships during the Vietnam War. "In 1964 or '65, I could excuse people being ill-informed or uncritical of U.S. policy in Southeast Asia, but by 1968, government apologists or those who refused to protest the war seemed to me unconscionable," comments a veteran of SDS (Students for a Democratic Society). "I never felt the same about these people, not because I insist everyone agree with me but because I felt their politics revealed them to be immoral."

My interview notes are full of descriptions of similar epiphanies caused by the revelation of a friend's racism, sexism, or insensitivity.

- "When Verna started lambasting the Black bourgeoisie while eating very well at my bourgeois dinner table, I wanted to make her throw up and give back my food," says a Black woman about another Black woman she hasn't seen since.

- "One morning the guy I car-pool with said he thought Lyndon LaRouche had an interesting political agenda," says a 30-year-old white man. "Since I think LaRouche is a madman and a threat to democracy, I'm looking for someone else to drive to work with."

- "A fellow teacher amazed me when she said girls can't master computers so boys should have first crack at the school's machines," recalls a fifth-grade teacher. "Suddenly I realized she didn't share my ideas about equal education and I just didn't want to be her friend."

- "We were out to dinner with my oldest friend and her new husband," recalls Terry. "Twice during the meal, the husband browbeat a young waitress, once for not keeping his water glass full and a second time for spilling a drop of wine on the tablecloth. He was so angry you'd think the poor waitress had dumped a bowl of hot soup on his head. I can't understand how my friend can love a man like that, which makes me wonder if I really know her."

- "Max went crazy when his son got engaged to a Puerto Rican girl," Norman explains. "He said dumb, insulting things about Hispanics. When I challenged him, he shouted 'Mind your own business' and slammed out. Days later, he admitted he was wrong and wanted to make up with me. I said 'Sure' but I can't forget the hate I saw in him."

- "The worst thing is when you suddenly realize that you're bored with an old friend," says Naomi, naming another mind-changing insight. "I made all kinds of efforts to recapture what I used to find interesting in this woman but boring is *boring*. I can't keep my mind on what she's saying. If I fake interest, she'll know, because she knows me, and besides who wants to pretend with a friend. The only solution I can think of is to see each other less often and hope a lot of interesting things happen to her in between visits."

- Not boredom but cruelty showed Hal's friend in a new light. "We were setting up for brunch," Hal begins. "My friend was expecting some important people from his company. We were behind schedule, so he asked me to call my daughter, Annie, in from the yard to help us. I reminded him that Annie has perceptual and motor problems and can't always manage manual tasks. He accused me of 'coddling the child'; he called her inside himself, put a huge bowl of pasta salad in her hands, and sent her to the dining room. Seconds later we heard a crash. He started cursing: 'Christ, there's pasta all over the rug, how could anyone be so clumsy!' He was running around shouting, oblivious to Annie's humiliation. We cleaned up in time for the guests, but for me he can never clean up his image. Under that polished exterior is a man who abuses kids."

Besides seeing someone in a bad light because of their politics, boorishness, racism, sexism, dullness, and cruelty, there is always joint travel. "We took a vacation together" was *PT*'s number 7 troublemaker between friends. Sharing an unfamiliar space and place brings out the worst in people because it distills one's habits to their essence. If you are messy, you are messier living out of a suitcase in a small hotel room. If he is compulsive, it will show up starkly in the way he insists on making all the dinner reservations in advance. Such contrasting personalities may find each other interesting back home where their paths cross at will but not on a camping trip where the messy one can snafu the pair's plans because he forgot the tent poles at the last campground, and the compulsive can kill the spontaneity of the trip by refusing to go one step off the itinerary.

To avoid conflicts, Marylin Bender, a seasoned traveler, suggests friends discuss in advance how each feels about:

- *Luxury*—"Must the hotel furniture pass a white glove inspection or can you accept cockroaches and primitive plumbing?"
- *Sightseeing*—"Do you take in the town in one day . . . or do you prefer to digest a few attractions on each visit?"
- *Scheduling*—"Must you arrive at a depot one hour before departure, or can you only board a plane, train or bus after the doors are closed?"
- *Budgeting*—"Are you the last of the big spenders, an economizer, a worrier?"
- *Grace under pressure*—"How tolerant are you likely to be if your companion should break a hip in the ruins of Agrigento?"[21]

Because this chapter is focused on the tensions and trials of friendship, I have concentrated on those instances when you suddenly see a friend in a negative light. However, not all awakenings are disappointments. As psychologist Steen Halling points out, some are gratifying "phenomena of surprise" that bring you a touching or exhilarating insight into a friend's true self:

- When a friend exposes some previously hidden aspect of his or her inner life—a sweet vulnerability maybe or an unexpected playfulness.

- When you reveal yourself and the other person responds "in a particularly poignant way," say, by reaching across the table to touch your hand.

- When you observe friends being themselves with others and you understand them to be valued people apart from you.

- When extraordinary circumstances bring out qualities you never knew a friend had, for instance, when a seemingly inept person takes charge of your affairs in a crisis.[22]

Positive insights illuminate a friend, Halling says, and "a deepening of the relationship" follows "the experience of 'seeing the other as if for the first time.' "

Betrayal

We have indulged freely in criticism of each other when alone, and hotly contended whenever we have differed, but in our friendship of thirty years there has never been a break of one hour. To the world, we always seem to agree and uniformly reflect each other. Like husband and wife, each has the feeling that we must have no differences in public.

Elizabeth Cady Stanton[23]

From Stanton's description, one can deduce why her friendship with Susan B. Anthony remains a model of emotional and intellectual camaraderie despite dramatic differences between the two women.

Public humiliation has long been recognized as fatal to friendship. Solon wrote: "Counsel your friend in private, but never reprove him in public." Pascal declared: "If everyone knew what one said of the other there would not be four friends in the world." Gossip gets an even more emphatic denunciation in the Talmud (Arakin 15b), where "speaking evil" is as serious an offense under Jewish law as the cardinal sins of idolatry, incest, and murder. The "evil tongue" is said to kill three persons: the one who tells, the one who listens, and the one about whom it is told. "I'm only telling the truth" is no defense. In fact, gossip has such an immense power to hurt that, rather than say something true that may wound a friend, the Talmud requires one "to lie for the sake of peace."

The evil tongue gets more generous notices from writer Patricia Ann Meyer Spacks, who reviews the role of gossip in three centuries of literature in her book *Gossip*.[24] Spacks sees gossip as a tool that allows oppressed and powerless people to bond with others. "The freedom, playfulness and power possible in speculative talk about people become crucial resources for those with relatively little control over their destinies," she wrote. Thus, gossip is logically associated with women, who "have assumed private talk as their special province." I'm taken with the elegance of her argument and the notion of gossip as "a language of feeling." But when I identify with the *targets* of this "speculative talk"—who are not always our oppressors but are often our friends—I lean toward the Talmudic interpretation.

Several researchers have found that people give more weight to negative information about others than to positive words, so the potency of gossip is intensified as its critical content increases.[25] If a friend has ever criticized you in the presence of others, you know that it is as searing as a burn, while gossip that meanders back to you second or third hand hurts with a dull ache, like a rotting tooth. When I accused a friend of being gossipy, he answered, "You're only interested in ideas; I'm interested in people." Being interested in people, I submit, is not the same as clapping your hands after the last party guest leaves and saying, "Oh good, now we can talk about everybody."

When I asked people about the flashpoints of their friendships, so many told me stories of exposure and tale-bearing, duplicity and deceit, that I judged betrayal to be the paramount transgression long before I found it at the top of *PT*'s list.

The betrayers are a universally recognizable crew. There's the "friend" who divulged to everyone in the sixth grade your much-despised middle name, which you had told him in confidence. And the "friend" who revealed things she heard about you in her therapy group. And the "friend" who pumped you for information that he later used to undercut your chances of promotion. And the "friend," who broke the oath of intimacy by telling everyone at the office about your facelift. And the "friend" who tried to seduce your wife behind your back.

Betrayal is the terrorism of friendship. You can't prepare for it because you never know where or when it will strike. You can't worry about it because it would poison your life. But once you are its victim, a trusting corner is sliced off your soul. The wounds of betrayal take longer to heal than other injuries. And why shouldn't they? Betrayal is nothing less than friendship's diametrical opposite.

The wonder is that such wounds heal at all and that such "friends" are forgiven.

But that too is what friends do—they forgive each other. Violators repudiate their ignominious acts, victims exact a pledge of renewed fealty, there are rites of atonement, contrition, and reconciliation.

I suppose everyone deserves a second chance, but after hearing some of those betrayals, I confess I preferred the stories that ended not with amnesty but with endings. (More about friendship termination in the next chapter.)

The Negative Rewards of Friendship

Experiencing conflict in situations such as the ten I've enumerated can strengthen and mature you and test and deepen your friendships.

Or it can make you miserable.

That last possibility has only recently been investigated by social scientists and what they've found is chastening.

Although positive experiences far outnumber negative experiences in friendship, the negative ones overshadow them and leave a much greater impact. Karen Rook, a leading scholar in this field, says it is precisely because the negatives are less frequent and not expected that they register so powerfully.[26] Rook's studies reveal that whereas negatives, such as invasions of privacy or criticism from friends, lower one's morale considerably, positives, such as getting emotional support or sharing leisure activities, do not raise one's feelings of well-being to any comparable degree. Put another way, the supportive aspects of friendship are not powerful enough to offset the problems and conflicts of friendship: "A single heated exchange at an otherwise tranquil wedding may ruin the event; a single pleasant exchange in the midst of a wedding marred with strife has little power to restore tranquility."

Negative behavior is more heavily weighted because positive behavior is taken for granted. Positive behavior is, after all, the cultural norm; people are "supposed to be nice," so when someone is nice, you can't necessarily assume that they care about you. Negative behavior is less ambiguous. If someone insults you or lets you down, it is safe to assume they do *not* care about you.

For another thing, support and conflict elicit different reactions on different dimensions of behavior. When we get support from a friend, it affects our *performance,* but when we experience conflict with a friend, it affects our *emotional state.* Obviously, depression leaves a larger dent in the fenders of the psyche than does a good performance. And when we become depressed in front of a friend, the cycle begins again.

Information such as this about friendship's negative experiences is virtually unknown to lay people. Maybe that's another reason why most of us have been led to expect perfection or are utterly bewildered when our friends make us miserable in the act of trying to help us. Besides the example of the misguided advice-giving friend, there are people who misread our state of mind and try to distract us when we really want to talk or who make us talk when we are tired and want to be distracted; or who provide so much help that they make us feel helpless; or who respond inappropriately to something we've said. (When an unmarried friend announced that she was pregnant, a psychologist "made the assumption that this was bad news and spoke accordingly," only to find out that the friend "was quite happy about it.")[27]

Few of us realize that the helping process is a two-way street. Researchers use the words "reciprocal" and "transactional" to explain how the friend under stress reacts to the help-giver and how the help-giver reacts to that reaction. Some people get frustrated when their advice or assistance is ignored or has no visible effect. Then they, too, become a friend under stress. People can feel so much anxiety about speaking to a friend in the throes of a life crisis, such as an illness or death of a loved one, that they provide inappropriate support as a result of trying to control their own discomfort. They may resort to "automatic or ritualized" gestures or offer platitudes, like "things will get better soon." They don't mean to be hurtful, but having been upset by their friend's upset, they do more harm than good.

Thus, despite the best intentions, a friend who receives support can feel *un*supported and a supportive friend can feel unappreciated. In Antonia Abbey's words: "It is possible to feel both loved and misunderstood simultaneously." Unless there is the right "fit" between you, your situation, and the kind of support your friend offers, the friend may be no help at all and in fact may add to your distress.

According to other researchers, you may not need *more* support but rather a combination of succor and the challenge to get up and go. You may need different kinds of help at different times during the same crisis period. You may need one kind of support from a friend who's a coworker and another kind from a friend who's a relative. A listener may fit the bill in one situation, a cheerer-upper in another. Conflict erupts when your friends persist in giving you the kind of support they want to give rather than the kind you require.

When we seek the company of a friend, we do not prepare ourselves for the bad stuff that comes with the good. Consequently, when the bad stuff happens, it hits us harder. This might account for the common feeling of "wanting more" from our friends or for dismissing adequate friendships as "failures." Because we do not understand and anticipate the negatives, they loom large and cancel out the positives. This leaves some people feeling they have "no real friends," when what they have instead is no real preparation for the flashpoints of friendship.

Chapter 7

Exits and Endings

Many people believe friendship is forever. They say once friends are committed, it's for better or worse and nothing should drive them apart. The writer Lynn Sharon Schwartz, for example, declaims at length about fidelity. "When you care about a person, when you become intimate to a certain degree, you accept that this person is in your life, and for me that's it. . . . this person is a permanent part of me. . . . Maybe I'm just a hanger-on; I don't like to drop people."[1]

Yet drop people we do. Some friendships cannot survive things like boredom, bad debts, jealousy, and betrayal. The flashpoint becomes a fire and we burn out. Love is lost. Or as Gertrude Stein would have it (in her poem of 1931): "Before the flowers of friendship faded friendship faded."

Actually, fading is only one way friendships die. Murray Davis, author of *Intimate Relations,* says they either "pass away" or have a "sudden death."[2] As I think of it, there are three styles of termination: baroque, classical, and romantic.

Baroque endings are marked by rococo plots, agitation, hyperbolic accusations, and florid exit speeches, often delivered with such exclamation points as slammed doors and broken crockery. Baroque endings are bombastic, high-flown, and cannot be missed.

Classical endings are carried out with attention to form. There are discussions. Both parties try to be rational, lucid, and calm. Reconciliation may be attempted. The history of the friendship is replayed, its principal themes repeated over and over in the same key, as in a rondo, the last movement of a sonata. The final chord is emphatic, the break appears clean, and the friends maintain their dignity. However it may hurt, a classical ending attempts good taste.

Romantic endings are characterized by fade-outs. The romantic ending may be no less harsh in feeling for being quixotic in form, or, more precisely, form*less*. The cause of the breakup is either unknown, too mystical to grasp, or too distressing to confront; all is shrouded in euphemism and understatement. "Our friendship faded away" is the typical diagnosis, uttered with a distant look. "I guess I lost interest." "She just stopped calling." Whereas baroque endings are showy and unmistakable, ethereal romantic endings are felt rather than seen. And whereas classical endings follow an almost symmetrical form, romantic endings seem to "just happen"—sometimes only in the mind of one person who never quite communicates to the other that the friendship is over.

We may think we can predict which disengagement strategy would be ours or what infraction would break the back of any given relationship, but in many cases both the why and the how come as a complete surprise. Endings are as unique as the friendships they terminate.

How Some Friendships Ended

Baroque Endings

"Addiction isn't limited to only drugs or alcohol. You can be addicted to people too. With Maria, I got hooked on her life force. For five years, we talked on the phone almost every day. We often worked together in the design business. We spent many weekends and holidays together. Every time I saw her, I had great emotional expectations because she puts out so much warmth. She looks like an opera diva and gathers people to her like a mother hen. But I was always disappointed; I came away feeling wrung out. She wanted me around to admire her. At the same time, she made me feel small. Finally I realized she's full of bullshit. Her warmth is bullshit, her idea of closeness is bullshit. She stops talking with one person when someone more important comes along. She's hopelessly self-centered and only interested in people for what they can give her. I told her all of this in one huge outburst about six months ago and we haven't talked or seen each other since. Even though there's a hole in my life without her, I knew the friendship had to end and that I had to end it."

"For twelve years, William and Penny and Joe and I lived across the backyard from each other, like couples in a 1950s TV series. We thought we had the most fantastic four-way friendship in the state of Louisiana. Penny and I were like twins. People said that we'd go to a costume party as 'Me and My Shadow'—if we knew which one was 'Me.' My husband, Joe, thought Penny was a genius. Penny loved Joe's sense of humor. William and Joe admired each other to the point of adoration. And William and I were like kissin' cousins.

"Into this Garden of Eden came a great job offer for Joe. He couldn't turn it down even though it meant moving to California for a year. We missed our friends every day we were gone and had no intention of staying longer, but when Joe's contract was extended for another year with a big raise, we called William and Penny and asked them to come join us. There were jobs in their fields and we thought it might be an adventure for them. They reacted like lunatics. 'How could any job be more important than our friendship?' Penny cried. She accused us of being phonies, hippies, Hollywood druggies, you name it. On their extension phone, William shouted that we were liars and that we must have known from the start that we were never coming back to Louisiana.

"The friendship ended with that phone call. If they begged me, I'd never take them back. People who could call me a liar after a twelve-year friendship like ours deserve to be cut off forever."

"I never thought it possible for a man to be *just* friends with a woman until Liz came to work at the company about a year ago. She is five years older than I and she had a boyfriend, so it was a real straight-shooter friendship and I liked it like that. Liz has this way of cutting through a lot of crap and seeing everything real clear. Her advice was the smartest I ever got—about the job, problems in the union, or the girls I was seeing. I used to tell her everything. Then, dammit, I got roaring drunk at the Christmas party and made a pass at her. I don't know what got into me. I must have been real crude because she slapped me in the face and went home crying. The day we came back to work I found her right away and apologized. I tried to explain how I sometimes get when I have one too many.

She acted like she didn't hear me. She doesn't even look at me anymore."

Classical Endings

"It took years of psychoanalysis for me to understand why I let this friendship rot away. I have vivid memories of sulking around the apartment and of Miriam trying to make me feel better. During the years we shared an apartment, she was always giving me pep talks or arranging activities to get me out of my funks. When I made self-pitying lists of my faults, she pointed out things I should be proud of. The nicer she was, the more sullen I was. I don't know why she put up with me. Maybe because she never had much family life. Even though she praised me, I saw myself as inferior to her in every way. I wanted her friendship but I couldn't get pleasure out of it. I saw everything that happened to her as happening against me, as if her life existed just to put mine in poor contrast. I was jealous that she loved her work. I was jealous when she got married; still, she asked me to be the maid of honor at her wedding. I was awful when she had her baby. I never showed any interest. We'd see each other for lunch or talk on the phone and I hardly mentioned the child. We talked about me, we dissected our relationship. She reminded me of all the memories we shared, said how much I meant to her, asked if I wanted to join her women's group. I went to a few meetings, but I felt like Cinderella so I quit. Next, she referred a client to me. Then she invited me and my boyfriend to dinner, and we had a great time but I never called to thank her. Finally, she gave up. I mean she's sentimental and she loved me like family but she's not a masochist."

"Wally and I met in 1968 when I was 16 and he was a college sophomore who came to my school to speak about the civil rights movement. We hit it off so well that he asked me to work with him in SNCC [Student Nonviolent Coordinating Committee]. He became my inspiration and best friend. I was amazed that two people who were in such perfect harmony could have met in the same century. He was everything I thought a man should be: a Hall of Fame athlete, a Rhodes scholar, and a swinger with girls. I was a bit of a stud too—until I met the woman who became my wife.

"It was 1973 and she was very involved in the women's movement, which affected our marriage and led me to make a lot of changes in my behavior. I talked to Wally about what I was going through. Because of his feelings about racism, I thought he'd understand sexism too. At least, I expected him to be less macho around me. Instead he got worse. At meetings he made derogatory remarks about the women speakers. When he came over to my house, he ignored my wife and told crude stories of his sexual exploits. In 1974 he married a meek little woman who gave birth to two children in two years. He also kept fooling around on the side. I couldn't understand how such a brilliant guy could be such a Neanderthal about women. Still, he was great in so many other ways, so I figured, nobody's perfect.

"In 1976 I moved 300 miles away. The friendship stagnated, yet we kept up with each other. He met a woman he called the one true love of his life. He and his wife separated. Meanwhile, my marriage was terrific; I had two kids and a job I loved, and I'd become involved in the men's movement. Early in 1984 I was in his city for a conference so I stayed at his house. He had converted to a fundamentalist Christian sect. He'd gone back to his wife and they'd had another child. He didn't cheat on her or ogle women anymore, but his sexism now had religious authority behind it. He gave me a lecture on the concept of 'headship': how males are the head and females the heart, how women should never speak in public or stand up for themselves, and some other stuff he lives by. I said I prefer to live with an equal. I talked about how sex discrimination hurts my daughters. He quoted scripture at me. He was a complete stranger. My best friend was gone and someone had invaded his body. We argued politely and ate together, but those few days were a slow torture. When I left, the friendship was dead."

"This is the most civilized ending you'll ever hear about. Frances and I were as close as two girls can get. We went to the same parochial schools. We spent thousands of hours together playing trading cards, selling lemonade, reading movie magazines, trying on make-up, listening to records, and talking about boys. After high school, I had a scholarship to college; Frances went to nursing school. We got together during my vacations and still were each other's best friends.

"I'm not exactly sure when it began to change. She went to work in the local hospital. After graduation, I went to business school. I noticed that she tuned out whenever I talked about my courses, and when I got this job in banking and moved into the city, she joked about my dress-for-success suits. She was the first to comment that we didn't have much in common anymore. She said she'd always be the type to read the *National Enquirer* and I was reading *Foreign Affairs* and the *Wall Street Journal*.

"The problem came to a head when she married this monosyllabic guy. I hate to think of myself as a snob, but I couldn't see coming out to visit them if the evening consisted of sitting in front of the TV set. I was single, living alone, and had an M.B.A. Frances's life was nothing like mine. Finally, we had to face it: Our lives had gone in such different directions it was silly to force ourselves to stay friends. We kind of hugged each other and that was it—except we still send birthday cards."

Romantic Endings

"I met Jordie on the beach surfing. We found out we both work with cars: I do valet parking and he manages a repair shop. After I broke up with my girlfriend, I asked him if he wanted to move in and share the rent, and we got along real good for six months. We hung out together almost every night after work. We liked the same music. Went to the bars, had pizza, stuff like that. I thought he was a friend. Was I ever surprised when he moved out. He never said nothin' was wrong. I called him a couple of times but he never called back. I guess I liked him better than he liked me. My mom says you're not a bad person if not everyone likes you, but I don't understand why he left. I just don't get it."

"My father taught me to treat a friend as if he may become an enemy and an enemy as if he may become a friend. Following that advice, I tried to be nice to everyone. Friends were my number one priority. But now that I'm in my thirties, I'm dropping them left and right because I've discovered most of the people in my life don't mean as much to me as I thought. The way I drop them is just by not pursuing. Most of them just let it happen. The ones who kept after me are my real friends. Now I have a lot more time for them. And for my daughter and my boyfriend.

"The weird thing is, I've dropped about ten friends this year and I don't even miss them."

* * *

"I offended a friend who was bone of my bone and I still don't know what I did wrong. I didn't even realize she'd cut me off because I went away for a month to set up a branch of my company and when I came home it took me a while to notice she wouldn't get together with me. She kept saying she was busy or sick or her kids had problems, one excuse after another. Finally, I asked what was wrong; she said, 'nothing' and I decided to just let it go.

"We didn't see each other for four years, even though we live in the same town. At first, I missed her terribly. There were a lot of ways she had given me courage and confidence. Losing our friendship meant I had to develop in myself some of the strengths I'd found in her. When we finally met again, I had become the person I admired in her. Actually, I'd outgrown her.

"Our last meeting came about because I'd heard she was going through a brutal divorce and I wanted to offer my help if she needed it. I drove up to her house, sat in the car worrying about what to say, then made myself get out and ring the bell. She didn't reject me but she wasn't her old self either. What annoyed me was her contempt. She acted as if I was incapable of understanding what was wrong. To this day, she still hasn't told me."

"Finally, without telling him, I made my decision to fade from his life. . . . I simply disappeared into the wires of my answering service. . . . I vanished into my private calendar of things-to-be-done that could not include him, even though he called and insisted; I had my 'conferences to attend,' 'clients to see,' 'business trips,' 'reports to write,' 'an engagement with my wife that night,' and so forth. I dropped him and moved on without any social need to offer a real explanation."[3]

These case histories might inspire us to repeat the line attributed to Coco Chanel: "My friends, there *are* no friends." Certainly they bring to mind Christina Rossetti's poem, "A Chilly Night":

My friends had failed one by one
Middle aged, young and old,
Till the ghosts were warmer to me
Than my friends that had grown cold.

But looked at another way, endings can be said to prove not the vapidity of friendship but its striving for perfectability. Although we are suspicious of someone who never keeps a friend, the ability to detach from a nonsustaining relationship is as much a sign of mental health as the ability to form nourishing attachments. A mature person manages to grow both roots and wings.

Maybe we leave so often because we demand so much. Or maybe— as the book *Brief Encounters* contends—time, stability, and permanence are not "the ultimate criteria" of a worthwhile friendship; it could be just as important for us to get the most out of short-term relationships and "to develop rituals and techniques for bringing about closure."[4]

How Friends Call It Quits

When we decide to spread our wings, there is a why and a how. As was evident in the preceding accounts, the reasons *why* friends split apart are singular and complex, but *how* they do it follows a few discernible patterns. Although I like my baroque/classical/romantic construct, communication psychologists seek more precise answers to the question "how do people end their friendships?"

Distancing and disassociating are the key features of friendship termination, says Mark Knapp in *Social Intercourse: From Greeting to Goodbye*.[5] Knapp's stage theory presents the breakdown of a relationship as if it were the film of my chapter "Passage to Intimacy" run backwards: There is a retreat from proximity and self-disclosure; differences become more salient than similarities; there is stagnation, avoidance, and finally the break.

During the "decay stages," Knapp says, people stop trying to make each other feel special. They start feeling awkward in each other's presence. They close the lines of communication. They say things like "I just don't want to talk about that." Or "I know what you're going to say, and you know what I'm going to say, so what's there to talk about?" Or, "I can't stay long." Or, "I'm so busy, I just don't know when I'll be able to see you." Until one day, they deliver the Farewell Address—sometimes directly, sometimes not.

Leslie Baxter, a professor of communications who studied friendship terminations, came up with forty strategies people use to disengage from an unwanted friend, including: "Avoid contact with the person as much as possible; disclose little about my personal activities and interests whenever we talk; pick an argument with the other person as an excuse to disengage; ask a third party to break the disengagement news to the person; inform the person of my feelings in writing only; threaten the person if s/he didn't accept disengagement; try to convince the other person that disengagement was in both our interests; try to prevent us leaving on a 'sour note' with one another; verbally blame the other person for causing the disengagement, even if I thought s/he weren't totally to blame; try to make the other person feel guilty if s/he wanted to keep me in the relationship; try to find reasons for the disengagement other than things about our relationship (e.g., a job offer, graduation, etc.); 'wait it out' until conditions were conducive to a disengagement (e.g., until vacation time); make the relationship more costly for the other person by being bitchy, demanding, etc."[6]

After analyzing the unifying factors in everyone's disengagement methods, Baxter condensed them into four general groups: *"withdrawal and avoidance, intentional manipulation, strategies of positive concern,* and *open confrontation."*

In my model, baroque endings are most characteristic of manipulation and confrontation; classical endings fit strategies of concern and controlled confrontation; and romantic endings follow the route of withdrawal and avoidance.

What determines which method we use to call it quits? Why does one relationship end in a fade-out, another in a fit of rage?

Baxter's research indicates that "mere friends" favor avoidance and manipulation strategies, whereas "close friends" prefer to exit with positive concern or open discussion of their differences. Most adults and grade-school children choose direct confrontation; adolescents prefer avoidance. Androgynous people take the confrontational route, and masculine sex-typed persons elect the avoidance strategies.

Another expert points out that the closer the relationship, the more interwoven the lives of the participants, so that by the time friends break apart, they often are equally involved with the same people and projects. To disentangle themselves, these intimates are more likely to end their relationship decisively and openly, partly to clarify the terms of departure to everyone else involved. Friends who are less intertwined can just withdraw and let the friendship atrophy without regard for innocent bystanders. Close friends are also more prone to choose strategies of concern, which protect each other's feelings, and less apt to use manipulation strategies, which are more devious. These choices are not always made for virtuous motives but because close friends know so much about one another that their "betrayer potential" is threatening. To protect against future reprisals, none of us wants to make an enemy of someone who was privy to so much private information. As a sage once said:

> He who has a thousand friends never has one to spare
> But he who has one enemy will meet him everywhere.

Where friendships end mutually, withdrawal and avoidance are the strategies of choice. Both X and Y can let the friendship dissolve, as it were, into thin air. But when termination is unilateral, X, the one being abandoned, usually puts up a struggle. To get away with a minimum of guilt, Y may try to provoke X to get angry enough to want out too. If Y doesn't care about what X thinks or feels, this hostile manipulative strategy is almost guaranteed to do the trick.

Feeling Our Way

Psychologist Phyllis Katz believes, "Most people really don't expect marriages to last forever but they do expect their friendships will." Katz told me she herself has experienced only one friendship termination. She broke a plate she had borrowed from a friend she'd known since childhood and the friend never stopped bothering her about it. "We couldn't get past her guilt-tripping me so the relationship had to end. I still find it emotionally wrenching to think that an old friend could just disappear from my life."

In the ecology of human relations, endings can be as useful to friendship as a spontaneous forest fire is to the balance of nature; both make space for new seedlings and let in the sun. We can't keep "stockpiling" friends, as one writer put it. So we clean house now and then. At least that is how we want to see it. But is that how endings make us *feel?*

When I ask people about feelings, I begin with the assumption that we're hurt by some endings and relieved by others, depending on whether we are the X or the Y in a termination experience. What I'm really getting at though, is how do we feel about the fact that a once-deep human connection can be so abruptly severed? If we can walk away from someone we once liked so much, does this mean people are disposable, replaceable—like paper plates? Why can't we enjoy our friendships while they last without expecting them to last forever? Is the time spent in an aborted friendship *wasted?* Must we have something to show for every relationship we've ever had? Why do we feel guilty if we did nothing wrong? And, for that matter, must we feel guilty if we *do* end a friendship we found unsatisfying?

Furthermore, what does it mean when a voluntary parting, an ending we know we wanted, registers in our heart as a loss? Why do some long-gone friends keep reappearing in our dreams like ghost dancers in communion with our memories? Why do other separations—from the womb, from the breast, from our parents' house, from loved ones—cast their long shadow on the leave-takings of friendship?

The answers to such questions lie beyond the purview of this book in the kingdoms of psychoanalysis and religion where the comings-in and goings-out of life are sometimes made fathomable. In these pages I feel it is enough to ask the more pragmatic questions that were suggested to me by people with experience in exits and endings, people who consider themselves experts at letting go.

If you are the one ending the friendship, ask yourself:

- Have I been fair? Have I given my friend the benefit of the doubt? (Never dissolve a friendship on hearsay evidence.)
- Am I fed up with what the friend *did* or what the friend *is?* (Isolating a particular infraction and putting the rest of the person in perspective sometimes permits reconsideration.)
- If there is no chance of reconciliation, have I been firm and clear about it so there can be no misunderstanding?
- Even though the parting is my choice, am I prepared to feel pangs of guilt and regret later?

If you are the accused and you want to fight for the friendship, think about these questions:

- Am I able to acknowledge my mistakes or explain my actions without defensiveness or rancor?

- Should I do it by phone, in writing, or in person? On my turf or my friend's? In a public place (where we are less likely to make a scene), in a restaurant (where it is harder for my friend to escape), or in a private setting?

- Do I really want to make up, or do I want to get back together so I can take revenge?

- If I resolve to change, can I keep my promise? Do I really want the friendship if I have to change? Is a clean slate possible or will we be too self-conscious?

- Can my friend and I learn to disagree on some things and still get along or is it just a matter of time until we have another major blowup?

- How many rejections will convince me to let the friendship go?

If a friend's rejection is final, do not flagellate yourself. Assume you did all you could and make a clean break. Forgive the friend for not forgiving you. Retaliation is wasted energy. You even the score best by denying an ex-friend the power to haunt you.

When a Friend Dies

We have been speaking of the death of friendship; now we must talk about the death of a friend. This is the ending that neither person wants and no strategy can ease. Death is friendship's final closure. It devastates us at any age but more so when it strikes in the prime of life, adding existential terror to our loss. The young confront the incredible: If it could happen to my friend, it could happen to me. Those in mid-life wonder, how much time do I have left? The old watch the crowds thin around them. When a friend dies, there is Self and Other in our grief. We mourn the end of the friend's life and the end of our life with the friend. We weep for what we didn't do and for what we can never do again.

A psychiatrist who became involved over a thirteen-year period with four dying friends says it made him question the meaning of his own life and his incessant busyness. Sharing "the dying experience" also aroused in him such anxieties about his own death that his paper on the subject is titled not "With Dying Friends" but "Dying with Friends."[7]

During those years, he felt helpless and responded with classic defense mechanisms: "denial of affect" and "retreat into a detached, emotionally unavailable state." His wife accused him of withdrawing from her. He became preoccupied with trivial tasks because anything was more manageable than dealing with the dying friends. He dreamed he discovered a cure for one friend's terminal lung disease. When going to visit one man, he found that he had unconsciously driven to a hospital miles away from where his friend was a patient. What made him able to spend so many years "dying with friends"? He concludes that the desire to feel himself a hero played an important role in keeping him available to his friends despite the oppressive distress and anxiety.

The historian Jonathan Spence wrote in his biography of Matteo Ricci, the sixteenth-century Jesuit author of *On Friendship:*

> From Seneca, Ricci quoted the thought that he had no regrets for his dead friends, since he had anticipated their loss while they lived and remembered them as still living after they had died.[8]

What an ideal—and what an impossibility, I thought. Then my friend Ene Riisna wrote to me about her closest friend, Dorriet Kavanna, who had just died at the age of 38, and Seneca's notion was confirmed:

> Dorriet and I were like a two-woman club. We had a childhood in common: She was born into a grim family and ran away when she was 15; I was a refugee from Estonia. Both of us sought our place in the world, and never quite found it. We shared our thoughts on this subject in different ways over ten years.
>
> I watched Dorriet recreate herself, invent a bold new identity and then live up to it. She was born Dorothy Kirschner in Cincinnati, Ohio, yet by the time she died she had become Dorriet Kavanna, a great opera singer with an international reputation and on her passport she'd listed her birthplace as Barcelona, Spain.
>
> I once sent her a Rilke quote: "We are born, so to speak,

provisionally, it doesn't matter where. It is only gradually that we compose within ourselves our true place of origin so that we may be born there retrospectively and each day more definitely." After she died I found the quote folded up in her wallet.

She was always interesting to me: brilliant, original, fearless, and full of fun. For dinner, she once ordered all the desserts on the menu and nothing else. When I was miserable over a man, she would sing me to sleep. On my birthday, she wrote to me: "Your present couch has become the symbol of all your hard days, so I am buying you a plush new sofa, one to make love on or fall into when you return home and have lonely feelings. I want to know that if I'm not here, you are in comfort."

Since Dorriet's death, I have no longer been concerned with the meaning of life. I think I *know* what it means and it seems very simple. It is one of the gifts that keeps coming to me from Dorriet. I still feel the feeling of her and it makes me happier at the same time as I am sadder. Were she alive, I would rather spend time with her than anyone. As she is not, I have been very happy with others, because I learned a lot from her about being happy as a way of life.

Deena Metzger entitled her funeral remarks for Barbara Myerhoff "The Story of a Friendship": "I have been lucky; I have had this friendship for twenty-seven years and it has been the finest work of my life. I knew it would be when I first met her and I knew it each day we met, each hour of our meeting whether it was ordinary (and it never was) or extraordinary (and it always was). . . . We had risked everything, everything, in the fight for her life and we lost the fight for life but did not lose the friendship. On the last day, she said to me, 'You did not ask for this,' and I recited the traditional marriage vows: 'For richer, for poorer, in sickness and in health . . .' "[9]

Though friends suffer at losing one another, that doesn't mean we want those we love to die without us, nor do we want to die alone. It's been said that on his deathbed Benedict Arnold, the Revolutionary War traitor, was asked if he needed anything. "Yes," he answered, "a friend."

At the recent funeral of a friend's father I thought about George Herbert's comment: "Life without a friend is death without a witness." One of the speakers at the memorial made reference to the man's remarkable penchant for friendship, yet there were few in attendance at the service or the graveside. At 82, the man had outlived his friends. Sometimes death without a witness is merely a measure of longevity. But those who do live long enough to witness a friend's death want to be allowed to be part of it.

"When Josh was dying, his wife and children monopolized every last minute for themselves; they couldn't share him," says Josh's friend Brian, who felt pushed aside at the end when the family looked to *their* friends for support but kept Josh's friends at a distance. "Someone from the family was always around the hospital bed. I wanted to ask them to leave us alone for a minute, but they seemed to resent that I was there at all. I wasn't able to tie up the loose ends before he died," Brian whispers. "People should realize that friends too need to say good-bye."

Part Two

Connections and Crossings

Chapter 8

Living the Social Life

Now that we've charted the life of friendship from its birth to its death, let's pull back to a wide-angle view of America's search for community. How do we "work at" being social? Where do we meet new friends, and how do we affirm or intensify the friendships we already have?

Obviously, people continue to meet each other in all the old familiar places: at school and work, in bars, on vacation, walking our dogs, and looking after our children. Some of us meet on airplanes, and because we never have to see each other again, we may tell each other the story of our lives. Others meet across a bridge of shared frustration in a doctor's waiting room, the welfare office, standing on line at the bank or the supermarket. And, now as always, we meet and murmur to each other at the scene of an accident, fire, or wherever humanity huddles together staring at its own mortality. Beyond these chance meetings, however, people make many creative and highly conscious efforts to encounter others—efforts that are often touching, always revealing, and somehow unique to our time.

Partying

John, an insurance agent, goes to parties. Not just parties given by people he knows but parties he pays to attend. When he first said this, I thought he was speaking euphemistically about sex orgies or swingers clubs. But he meant parties in the old Coke and pretzels, ask-a-stranger-to-dance sense of the word. These parties are publicized in church and synagogue bulletins, college publications, and alternative newspapers in such neighborhoods as Greenwich Village and Berkeley. Some party-makers advertise in the general press, making a point of describing the caliber of guest they seek to attract. ("Are you a remarkable person?") Party organizers charge a membership or admission fee in return for which they provide a space, some taped music, minimal refreshments, and the chance to meet new people. Some say bring your own booze, others just want your good intentions. John claims he goes to these parties not to find potential clients or sexual partners but to make friends.

Every Tuesday evening Jerry Rubin, the 1960s yippie turned 1980s yuppie and entrepreneur, runs a professional networking party at the Palladium nightclub in New York City. He started giving these parties five years ago in his house but the crowds outgrew the place. Now, more than 5000 upwardly mobile men and women show up; they present a business card and a $6 admission fee and in return get the chance to hear a special guest (such as publisher Malcolm Forbes) and to meet and mingle with each other for purposes of business, romance, or friendship.[1]

Although parties play a concrete role in the development of friendship networks, for most people the party route to making friends would be only slightly more enjoyable than hanging by their hair over Niagara Falls. Even Rudolf Nureyev, the world renowned ballet star, says he has to force himself to attend parties: "I get too comfortable sitting home and you cannot do that or you will begin to lose people. You must go out."[2] Of the hundreds of men and women recently surveyed, 75 percent said "a party with strangers" gave them more anxiety than:

- giving a speech
- being asked personal questions in public
- meeting a date's parents
- spending the first day on a new job
- being the victim of a practical joke
- talking with someone in authority
- having a job interview

- attending a formal dinner party
- going on a blind date[3]

It's not hard to hate big parties: the crush, the smoke, the superficial chatter, darting eyes, sore feet. Moreover, many of us suffer from painful shyness or social phobias stemming from a sense of being scrutinized and judged or a fear of making fools of ourselves. In extreme cases, rather than be subject to anxiety attacks, some people refuse to go to a party even when it is by invitation and they know every guest. Yet here is John and a gaggle of similar go-getters all over the country willingly depositing themselves in a crowd of strangers with a wet glass in one hand and a soggy canapé in the other—just to make friends.

Joining

In the best-seller . . . *And Ladies of the Club,* Helen Hooven Santmyer structures her plot around a nineteenth-century "sociable reading group," which is very much like the one that 34-year-old Amy now belongs to in a small city in Oregon. While reading itself is a solitary and arguably antisocial activity, book discussion groups are distinctly friendly. Amy started out knowing only one other member, the woman who brought her in; now she considers all five members her close friends. What cements the group is a shared love of literature and respect for one another's critical skills, she says. "With most of my female friends, I know everything about their feelings, but these women are special because I know their minds."

Reading clubs, interest groups, professional associations, and other kinds of social organizations have always had both good and bad points. As the Dutch historian Johan Huizinga noted:

> The club is a very ancient institution but . . . besides promoting the precious qualities of friendship and loyalty [clubs] are also hotbeds of sectarianism, intolerance, suspicion, superciliousness and quick to defend any illusion that flatters self-love or group consciousness.[4]

Although Huizinga missed a few of the bad points—cruel initiation rites, coercion, mindless conformity—the good points can be very good indeed. Groups help people define their personal identities. Groups enable the young—and the not so young—to separate in a healthy way from their parents. Even religious and ideological cults can be positive, says psychiatrist and cult expert Saul Levine, if they serve the purpose of helping someone get out of the house and grow up. Groups allow individuals to escape from all sorts of destructive circumstances—family violence, alcoholism, poverty, sexual abuse— and find support among other human beings.[5] And when it comes to agitating for one's rights or breaking through the anonymous exterior of a new town or finding fellow clock collectors or environmentalists, nothing beats joining a group.

Belonging to a group is just that: *belonging*. At its best, it is doing what you like to do with others who like to do it too. In Linda Wolfe's *New York* magazine article "Friendship in the City," comedian Carl Waxman extols the benefits of having a large population as a source for friends of every taste and type. "Even if you are one in a million," he says, "there are seven more of you in New York."[6] A minimum population of 1 million people is what a British sociologist claims is necessary to provide a professional person with twenty interesting, compatible friends. Happily, that ratio becomes as irrelevant as it is ridiculous when people join an affinity group and dive right into a pool of like-minded aficionados. I know of only one group that failed to produce a single friendship: a Friendship Club in Brighton, England, which had no objective other than "making friends."[7] But groups that require cooperation to achieve a larger goal usually result in what has been referred to as "unintentional network building"—in other words, friendship.

Not surprisingly, many people told me they found friends through a church or a synagogue affiliation. Susannah Risley, who works in an artists' colony on the outskirts of a small New England town, confides: "This place is so isolated, and I was so depressed when each round of writers and artists came and went, that I turned to the local church out of desperation even though I grew up in an atheist home. What hooked me was how the minister and the congregants have established a tight community of people who really are committed to helping and loving each other. Just last Sunday, when the minister baptized this baby, a group of small children surrounded the infant and promised to be his friend. I have exchanged that same promise with several people I've met here."

Beyond the well-trod path to religious centers, during the last ten years the number of hobby organizations increased 70 percent, sports associations went up 47 percent, and public interest organizations doubled, according to the *Statistical Abstract of the United States, 1984*. With our combined motives of self-improvement, social activism, and the search for community, we have been joining like mad. Men and women are joining health clubs, country clubs, motorcycle clubs, political clubs, the PTA, dozens of volunteer and charitable organizations, and groups that travel together, cook together, go running together, and play or sing together.

Every other Friday night for the last twenty-five years, Lil Appel has brought together a pride of vocalizers at her home. From ten to fifty of her friends arrive with their banjos, guitars, Autoharps, and a zest for singing folk songs and playing bluegrass music. They range from teenagers to a 90-year-old, from a man who is a lawyer to a woman who drives a taxi. "Occasionally one of the regulars will bring someone special," says Lil, "like a bagpipe player. If I live to be a hundred, I'll never forget the guy in a top hat and tails who sang the songs of Stephen Foster or the clogger who came with her own floor to dance on."

Male friendships are tended in a variety of settings. There are, of course, the Kiwanis, Lions, Rotary, Junior Chamber of Commerce, and oak-paneled university clubs and financial associations. And then there are more quirky men's groups, such as the Lunch Bunch, five older men in Littleton, Colorado, who lunch together each Saturday,[8] and the Wednesday Ten, which is actually a group of twenty-five men from business, finance, the arts, and the media who meet in New York City for dinner once a month. In addition to many thousands of sacrosanct poker games—like the one in which playwright David Mamet plays every week,[9] where thousands of dollars are won and lost and the conversation is likely to wax literary—there is a nationwide network of hundreds of less competitive, more intimate men's support groups, many of them coordinated by the National Organization for Changing Men.[10]

Women too have their traditional organizations and their newly formed professional associations such as the Women's Forum (leaders in business and the arts) and Les Dames d'Escoffier (food professionals), and a wide spectrum of issue-oriented groups, such as the Coalition of Neighborhood Women, the Coalition of Labor Union Women, and the National Women's Political Caucus.

Both sexes belong to groups devoted to civil rights and economic

development, social welfare and education, ethnic unity and charitable goals. And countless grass-roots lobbying and support groups
have been organized by artists, disabled people, homosexuals, single
parents, procrastinators, ex-offenders, drug abusers, people with
phobias, widows, fat people, families of alcoholics, incest survivors,
victims of crime, parents of missing children, and the poor and
elderly. My interviewees tell me that friendships forged in these
groups are a giant step ahead of other relationships because members
already know each other's most absorbing problems.

There are even groups for those who cannot get out to join a
group. For the housebound, there is a telephone club, volunteers
"who would like to call you up if you are lonely. They will just chat
and pay you a friendly visit on the telephone. They will call you
once or twice a week."[11] Local social service source books list "companionship services" and "telephone reassurance" people to "provide
social contact and relieve loneliness and isolation."[12] In an effort to
prevent jail suicides, volunteers at the Adolescent Center at Riker's
Island prison in New York City visit inmates who have not seen a
friend in more than thirty days.[13] And several hospice programs
provide "friends" for the terminally ill who are grateful for companions less distraught than their own friends and family.[14] Such
innovations can be looked at as institutionalized emotions—a sub-
stitution of form (the phone call, the programmed caring) for substance. But from another perspective, group-joining attests to the
vitality of the social self, the impulse to make connections any way
we can, and the great healing power of human contact.

Many people believe that group membership is to friendship what
group sex is to love: an escape from intimacy. Yet groups such as
those mentioned have shown themselves to have a ready capacity to
build shared goals into friendship. I realize that this doesn't always
happen, but the potential is there. I also understand that people in
groups may employ the gestures and language of intimates without
actually engaging one another emotionally. Nevertheless, I maintain—from personal experience and the testimony of others—that
meaningful friendships can and do develop between members who
are working collectively toward a goal. What's more, the cause that
drew them in the first place tends to exert a centripetal pull that keeps
the attraction alive long past the first romance of new friendship.

Friends whose relationship originated in a group situation often
describe themselves in words that suggest they feel "united" but not

"intertwined"; they seem to strike a different sort of equilibrium between freedom and intimacy—not better or worse than other friends, just different. So while I share with Louise Bernikow a fondness for "eye to eye" intimacy,[15] my experience with group-based friendship also supports Saint-Exupéry's assertion that sometimes "love does not consist in gazing at each other but in looking together in the same direction."

Claude Fischer's friendship survey supports my view and adds a fascinating postscript: *The more organizations people belong to, the more group members they call friends and the more friends they have in general.* These active joiners are more likely to go out socially with their friends and to discuss their interests and personal problems with them. Thus, says Fischer, "organizations complement, rather than substitute for, personal relations."

Celebrating

Unlike birth or marriage, the beginnings of friendship usually go unnoticed. No rite or ceremony marks the moment when two free-floating human beings become a caring unit. Few friends can remember the date they met, fewer still the date of their passage to intimacy. Since friendship is essentially a relationship without rules, most people have not known what to expect, what makes a good friendship, or how to formally recognize what their friends mean to them. But today friendship is beginning to be heralded in ways that honor both the friends and the entity they have created. And despite the old chestnut that women know how to celebrate only three things, marriage, pregnancy, and losing weight, it is women even more than men who are especially gifted at celebrating friendship.

Susan Fisher, a senior vice president at Manufacturers and Traders Trust Company, has been called a World Class friend. One time she tracked down three far-flung old friends that her friend Jeanne Golly hadn't seen in years and made them the surprise present at Jeanne's birthday party. Susan keeps tabs on dozens of friends' lives. Once a month she checks through her address book, notes the people she hasn't spoken to in a month, and calls them. She maintains a file called "Accomplishments of My Friends," sends them congratulatory notes, flowers, anniversary presents, and press clippings of special interest. She gives business to her friends, patronizes their shops, gets clients for them, and puts people together who, she thinks, might like or help each other. When asked about this flurry of networking, she just says, "I'm in a position to help my friends, so I do." One year Susan's friend Jeanne threw what she called "A Susan Fisher Party." Every guest was someone who had become Jeanne's friend because of Susan. There were *thirty* of them.

Amy Medine Stein, a camp director, used her own fortieth birthday party as an occasion to celebrate her forty closest friends. She composed and delivered an individualized "appreciation," telling each how much she or he meant to her. "My therapist thought it would be healthier if I'd let *them* praise *me,*" she says. "But I'm a performer: It's my style to get up on the piano in a crowd. Being able to thank my friends was one of the high points of my life."

Joni, a market researcher, is 36 and happily unmarried. Her friends range in age from their late twenties to their early forties, all single, and all perfectly content to be among women, celebrating themselves. Joni gives an annual Valentine's Day tea. She asks her five closest friends to come in 1940s "Ladies Luncheon" outfits. They arrive wearing muffs or cotton gloves and grinning through their veils, as Joni greets them at the door in a Joan Crawford dress and a little piqué apron. "We eat heart-shaped sandwiches and drink tea out of Fiesta Ware cups," she laughs. "Then we indulge in old-fashioned girl talk until it's time to break out the jugs of wine, toast each other with insulting aphorisms, and get smashed." Her toast this year: "Here's to more friends like you—and less need for them."

"In a way, it's a sophisticated pajama party or group therapy without neuroses," says Judy Licht, a television newswoman, about the celebration she organizes with Barbara Walz, a photographer. Their Valentine's Day lunches, which now include as many as fifty women, require a whole restaurant.[16]

Linda Wolfe says, "The dinner party is the crucible of city friendship,"[17] and as Chapter 1 suggests, it is my favorite friendship ritual. But there are more inventive celebrations of friendship: A nurse buys two season tickets to a Philharmonic series, then invites a different friend to join her at each concert; an artist invites friends to an annual Thanksgiving breakfast with entertainment—the Macy's parade rolls past her living room windows; a psychiatrist with a taste for formal manners sends out a card announcing evenings when he is "at home" to receive drop-in friends.

I found a Minnesota couple who started a tradition of monthly beer tastings with their friends. "It's not as ritzy as a wine tasting but we have a great time!" says the husband.

Many single people are consciously joining forces—even having holiday dinners together rather than with relatives for whom they may feel more obligation than affection. The Sullivanian Community, which formally replaces family with friends, does so with such doctrinaire rigor that some people view it as a conspiracy against parents. The Sullivanians maintain group housing and "a fevered socializing"—parties, trips, a theater group, their own nutritional plan, and regimen of psychotherapy. "Sullivanians don't marry, but they raise their children communally and meet all personal needs that might otherwise be met in a family," says a former member of the closed community. "They destroy your sense of where you come from and teach you to make a new self connected only to your friends. It's very seductive if you've come from an unhappy home life."

I know two lesbians who stopped going home for Christmas because their visits were ruined by their parents' hostility toward their partners; now they surround their turkey with friends. And for the past ten years I too have participated in a ritual that usually transpires in the bosom of one's family. It is a feminist seder run by and for women on the third night of Passover. Some have already sat through two traditional seders with relatives; others attend only the women's seder. All of us consider the event a declaration of faith—in Judaism, feminism, and friendship.

More and more "chosen families" are replacing absent or incompatible relatives at holidays and life-cycle festivities once virtually restricted to kin. But while some say that this is another symptom of the new renunciation of family values, anthropologists remind us that there is nothing new about the impulse to elevate close friends to the status of kin. Long before the modern humanistic usage of "brotherhood" and "sisterhood," tribal cultures recognized the closeness of friends with elaborate rites of "blood brotherhood" and obligations that far exceeded those expected of biological brothers. Here in the United States, many ethnic groups create "fictive kin" by calling a friend "Aunt" or "Cousin" or establishing a godparent relationship without the imprimatur of religious ceremony.

Rena Gropper, an anthropologist and expert on Gypsy culture, has personal experience with this phenomenon. The king of a Gypsy tribe that settled in New York City adopted her as his daughter more than thirty years ago.

"Like many cultures where nonkin are never trusted as much as relatives, the Gypsies like to make their friends into family members," Gropper says. "The ideal way to finalize a Gypsy friendship is to arrange a marriage that transforms friends into in-laws. If marriage or adoption isn't feasible, friends will create an economic partnership as a way of getting close. The women will set up a fortune-telling store together, or the men might arrange to work together as asphalters or metal workers. Whether or not close friends become formally related, they call each other sister, brother, or cousin and they use 'Aunt' and 'Uncle' as terms of respect for older people."

In celebrating friends as family, all that the younger generation and middle classes have added to the "fictive kinship" of ethnic groups is the public exaltation of these especially meaningful friends and some new forms of appreciating them.

As you may have noticed, there is one problem with most celebrations of friendship: They're fattening. People love the festivity and primal purr of a good meal with friends but not its effect on their waistlines. Yet, as Alan Alda has said, "Eating is one of the few sensuous things people can do together that doesn't lead to divorce." So what are the alternatives?

When asked to come up with some "food-free" rituals, writer Lindsy Van Gelder found that, besides going to movies and concerts, friends quilt together, play croquet, cut or color each other's hair, take drives in the country, sit together in hot tubs, do needlepoint or yoga, or nurse their babies together.[18] Several people I interviewed described the following noncaloric activities.

In a ritual as regular as bagels and lox, David and his late friend Sam took walks every Sunday morning. For the past two years, David, 50, a judge, and Sam, 72, a writer, kept a date with one another to stroll together for an hour or so. "For him the walk was a constitutional, but for me it was all in the conversation," explains David. "We talked about his writing, my cases, something one of us had read. Sam was a reflective man with a very deep inner life. It meant a lot to me to have had him all to myself every Sunday."

The Fisherman's Clique—three elderly Black men who live in a Florida retirement community—has a habit that observers describe as follows: "In good weather, they set out three chairs, one beside the lake and two under the ficus tree. The first to arrive begins fishing. . . ." When the others arrive, they sit under the tree and talk. "When the fisherman gets tired, another takes his place, and so they rotate for hours. If they catch a fish, they cook and eat it together. But never, never, does more than one man fish at a time."[19]

Christopher, a musician who considers himself a maestro of friendship, organizes events that bring together the ten or twelve people he loves most in the world. "It's a real job to motivate them," he begins, with mock fatigue. "If I didn't get them organized, they'd never even see a movie. I have to start an hour in advance to get everyone to agree on what to see and which show time is best. Once I didn't check with anyone, I just put out my own money for twelve tickets to the musical *Annie* when it was playing in Boston. Every one of my friends came through; they paid me back and were real happy to see the show even though they hadn't planned to." In perhaps his most ambitious social composition, Christopher borrowed a summer house in Maine and got eight of his friends to take their vacation with him up there. "I like to have my friends around me no matter what I'm doing," he explains.

If he can be believed, he also has about *eighty* somewhat less intimate friends around the world with whom he keeps in touch regularly by phone or letter. "If I lose a friend's address, it drives me crazy," he says. "I number all my letters to friends so I can tell you that I've written an average of sixty letters to the average friend over the past ten years. I do a lot of my phoning when I'm copying music; it's a mindless job, so I like to talk while I do it. When I lived in Europe I made $50,000 worth of phone calls to my friends back in the States by using freebie methods everybody knows—toothpicks, slugs, wires. There are yellow, gray, and blue phones in Paris, and you need a different method for each one. And in Austria, one squeeze of a stove spark-starter gets you 100 shillings' worth of time. I was sorry to cheat the phone companies, but I couldn't have kept up with my friends any other way."

Phyllis and Ramona have a friendship ritual that began for the worst of reasons. It marks the anniversary of the night Ramona tried to kill herself. She had been despondent for months; her father had died, and soon afterward, she lost her job and her boyfriend. Taking a razor to her wrists seemed the only logical response. That night, when Phyllis came in to borrow a record, she found Ramona slumped on the floor, her body half out of the bathroom. "Luckily her bathroom is visible from the front door, or I might never have seen her," Phyllis says. "I wouldn't have looked for her either. We had the kind of neighborly relationship where we popped in and out of each other's apartment whether or not anyone was home, but we didn't do that much talking."

"Phyllis goes to college and I work in a factory so I kind of felt she was better than me," Ramona interrupts. "But after November 26th—after she called the ambulance and stayed with me at the hospital all night—everything's changed."

Phyllis nods. "I'm really glad I saved her life. If she was dead we never would have gotten to know each other." Both women break up laughing.

Ramona and Phyllis commemorate the "real beginning" of their friendship by sending each other a friendship card on the 26th of every month. "I try to choose a message that says something I want to say myself," Ramona explains, pointing to a "You are wonderful" card standing between "I can always count on you" and "You are out of this world." "I know she likes my cards because she keeps them out like that on display."

Of the 7 billion greeting cards sold every year, 2 billion are "non-occasion," or friendship, cards, the fastest growing category in the industry. A good percentage of these are purchased by smitten lovers who consider them a socially acceptable way to express romantic interest, but a large percentage of cards speak for "just friends"— such as Ramona and Phyllis—who want to formalize their affection in print. "We fill a need," says a card manufacturer to explain why the market went from "nowhere in 1979 to $300 million" in 1985— "people are a little lazier and a lot busier."[20]

Making Time

"I'm so busy I don't even have time for me," says Sandra, the mother of three children under age 4.

"Friendship is an occupation," insists Carol, a novelist. "I can be a good friend or I can be a writer. I can't do both."

"I'm too busy to spend time on the phone," says Bernard, who runs a lumberyard. "I'd rather see a friend once a year for six hours than talk in five-minute snatches while my mind's on other things."

In a newspaper story headlined "When Life Is Too Busy to Be

Impromptu," Mario Buatta, a decorator, admits he couldn't find a minute to see a friend who was in from London; they had to arrange a meeting for the next time Mario goes to England. Alfred Morris, a writer, had eight invitations for three spaces on his schedule. Meg Newhouse, director of an art gallery, says, "Four of us wanted to get together. All we did was call each other back and forth to set up a drink for three weeks from now." Honoré Ryan asked a friend to come along on her riding lesson because she had no other time to see him. Julie Hoover, a vice president at ABC, says, "I'm so booked, my definition of a friend is someone who doesn't call me."[21]

Busy seems to be the watchword of the eighties. In 1971 Carole King's song "You've Got a Friend" promised "winter, spring, summer or fall; all you've got to do is call—and I'll be there." Nowadays, the line might go, "And I'll be there . . . a week from Tuesday."

One comedian says, "I always have time for a new fuck, but I don't have time for a new friend." Another comedian advises, "It's easy to recognize a workaholic. He's the one with the words 'have sex' written in his datebook one day a week." The jokes get a laugh because so many of us are too busy to do what we want to do or see those friends we want to see. We say "Let's get together soon" or "I'll give you a call" and mean it when we say it—really mean it—but never find time to pick up the phone.

I wouldn't go as far as Barbara Ehrenreich does in decrying the "cult of conspicuous busyness" because that implies people are complaining about time pressure to let the rest of us know what glamorous lives they lead or how much they are in demand.[22] I don't hear that kind of pretension and pleasure among the busy people I know. Rather, they seem to be suffering from "the tyranny of busyness," an affliction of not only upscale professionals devoted to their jobs and physical fitness but also nonyuppie workaholics of every age, working mothers with too many balls to juggle, and people who have to hold down two jobs to make ends meet.

These are folks who barely have time for their meals, no less their friends. I'm not asking whether busy people are "good people" or whether all that busyness makes them happy. What interests me is that they've reached the point where they've *noticed*. Their desire to see friends is strong enough to make them realize that they have no time to do so. People totally caught up in the rat race don't even stop to examine the imbalance in their lives, or they buy a fifty-minute hour and get from a therapist what most of us get from our friends. I'm impressed by the number of busy people who are talking about the problem and feeling so troubled by it that they've given themselves an assignment: *make time for friends*.

"Every few weeks I put an X on my calendar," says Andrea, a top real estate manager. "On that day I make no morning appointments. I spend the time calling friends just to see how they are or to make plans for a future get-together." Andrea is extremely pleased with her new regimen. However, she adds, "When I call I get the feeling that some of my friends are too busy to talk to me."

Gary Fisketjon, executive editor at Atlantic Monthly Press, says the best way to decompress from the single-minded passions of the publishing world is to call friends who have nothing to do with books. "We can talk about their job, about football, *anything* that changes the subject."[23]

An item in *The New York Times* "Metropolitan Diary" builds on the phone-calling phenomenon by identifying a sub-trend of *not* calling or, more precisely, of calling but not speaking to one's friends. "I hardly ever talk on the phone any more," writes the correspondent. "I talk almost exclusively to answering machines. This is definitely a trend with my peers who are busy. My nonbusy peers don't understand it yet." She further explains that friends who are too busy to see one another have been keeping in touch by phone but spending too much time at it. Now they are starting to converse via each other's answering machines on which they leave messages that are warm but brief.[24]

Kenneth, an architect, showed me the quote he keeps pasted in his address book: "I am careless in replying to my friends, because I believe those whom I really love know me without my writing to them—*Beethoven*." Underneath, Kenneth had scrawled, *"Write at least one letter every week."* "Whenever I eat lunch at my desk, I make it a rule to write letters to my pals back home," he says, adding, "I'm getting too old to make new friends."

Many professionals who have families as well as demanding jobs say the only way they can make time for friends is to schedule social lunch dates on workdays. "Lately I've been eating with friends instead of spending two hours over lunch trying to sell some buyer while he drowns in a double martini," says Todd, a package designer with a wife and two children. "I see a different friend about twice a week, which is all I can afford, given the kind of restaurants I favor."

He smiles. "I'd do it every day if more of my friends were in the business and we could eat on each other's expense accounts."

If my interviews are any indication, working-class people may be just as overcommitted as the expense account set. Zelda, a waitress, and Lorraine, a department store gift-wrapper, work full time and have husbands who don't help out much around the house. Consequently, Zelda and Lorraine are as busy as anyone. Although they managed to keep up their daily phone contact, it bothered them that for several weeks they hadn't found time to get together. Finally, Zelda dropped over to Lorraine's one Saturday morning. Lorraine was in the middle of vacuuming. They couldn't talk above the noise, so Zelda went to make herself a cup of coffee in the kitchen. While she waited for the water to boil, she loaded the dishwasher just to give Lorraine a hand.

That gave her the idea of joining forces and doing their housework together on Saturdays. "There's no other time when we can visit," she says. "Our weeks are full of work, our nights we spend with the husband and kids, but we both have to clean house and we both like to do it on Saturday." First they have a roll and coffee and clean Lorraine's house, then after lunch, they tackle Zelda's. "We listen to music and talk while we work and before we know it we're done. It's great because the work goes faster and we have a nice long visit besides."

Americans' conscious efforts to make time for friendship seem bizarre to people from other countries, as I learned from traveling to Sweden, Morocco, Japan, Korea, China, Israel, and the Caribbean. In these societies, being too busy for friends is unthinkable. Our Swedish friends insisted that we stay with them for two weeks. From our vantage point within their home and family, we learned that friendship is to Swedes what television is to Americans: a form of daily recreation. Although their population is stereotyped as cold and reserved, the dozens of Swedes we met through our friends were much more social and actively involved in one another's lives than most Americans I know.

On a recent visit to Israel, Joel was met at the airport by friends, a couple from Baltimore who had settled in Jerusalem. "Both of them took off from work to spend my first day with me," he recalls. "They took me sight-seeing. The woman insisted I use her car while I was there. She gave me the impression that it would otherwise sit in her driveway, but later I discovered that she had taken the bus to and from work so I could have it for those five days. One evening, they invited an archaeologist to dinner because they thought I would enjoy meeting him. The other nights they offered to take me around unless I had other plans.

"Looking back, I realize they put their own lives on ice to make themselves available to me. They must have had things to do, appointments, chores, reading, errands, just as I do here. But they made me feel my visit was the event of their week. I'm ashamed to remember that when they visited the United States all I could carve out of my schedule was one dinner with them."

Although we may suffer by comparison with other cultures, Americans who are struggling against the tyranny of busyness do so with a valor that elevates friendship. They seem to have decided, in Ehrenreich's words: "It would be sad to have come so far—or at least run so hard—only to lose each other."

Reading

Just as making time to talk or write letters or sit across a lunch table are measures of renewed interest in friendship, so is the spate of articles and books on the subject. Besides the *Psychology Today* friendship survey, the last few years have seen major stories in *Vogue, New York, Ms., Mademoiselle, Self, Glamour, Seventeen, Essence,* and *Esquire* to name a few. Calling friendship "the mystique of the 80s," *Self* declared: "We've always valued our friends, but never before have we prized them as we do today."

Scholars are studying friendship in great detail. Janet Barkas's *Friendship: A Selected, Annotated Bibliography* lists 693 entries, including books, dissertations, journal articles, conference papers, audiovisual materials, and organizations.[25]

In imaginative literature, we're accustomed to male friends of the road and friends of the sea, adventurers whose intimacy is born of mutual endurance rather than disclosure, friends whose closeness is aesthetic or heroic but rarely emotional. But friendship has changed considerably since James Fenimore Cooper's Natty Bumppo and Chingachgook, Melville's Ishmael and Queequeg, or Twain's Huck Finn and Jim.

"After the ambulance corps of American writers went off to feel bad about World War I, male friends were—as if by some committee resolution—abolished in our fiction," says critic John Leonard. "Friends have disappeared from the fiction of John Cheever, John Updike, John Gardner, Jerzy Kosinski, Joseph Heller, Norman Mailer, Philip Roth, Walker Percy, you name him."[26] English professor Elizabeth Abel observes that male friendship was "limited" in *The Sun Also Rises* and "fails" entirely in D. H. Lawrence's *Women in Love*, John Steinbeck's *Of Mice and Men*, and Saul Bellow's *Humboldt's Gift*.[27]

But now—as if by another committee resolution—women writers are filling the breach and luxuriating in the deep pools of friendship.

Francine du Plessix Gray's novel *World Without End* follows a man and two women from their charming first encounter as children through their exploration of the Soviet Union as middle-aged seekers of wisdom. An impressionable young girl and an iconoclastic woman in her forties share a life-changing friendship in Gail Godwin's *The Finishing School*. In *The Color Purple*, Alice Walker gives us Celie and Shug, whose love cuts open the heart of friendship and leaves every reader drenched in truth. Gloria Naylor explores the infinite variety of Black women's connections in *The Women of Brewster Place*. Joyce Carol Oates's *Solstice* tells of a teacher and an artist whose obsessional relationship edges toward metaphysical cannibalism. And an absolutely gemlike evocation of relaxed, all-knowing women's friendship gleams from the pages of Grace Paley's short story "Friends." These works and others, such as Faye Weldon's *Female Friends*, Toni Morrison's *Sula*, Elizabeth Benedict's *Slow Dancing*, Marge Piercy's *Small Changes*, and Joan Didion's *Book of Common Prayer*, prove Virginia Woolf's prophecy that when a woman tells the truth about women's friendship "she will light a torch in that vast chamber where nobody has yet been."[28]

Still another genre of writing, the nonfiction inquiry, illuminates friendship with altogether different insights. In 1982 Dale Carnegie's widow, Dorothy, issued a revised edition of his best-selling "bible," *How to Win Friends and Influence People*, which retains its common-sensical advice for aspiring Horatio Algers who can be inspired by bon mots from Henry Ford. For more up-to-date advice, readers can choose from such titles as: *Friendship: How to Give It, How to Get It* by Joel D. Block, *Just Friends: The Role of Friendship in Our Lives* by Lillian B. Rubin, *Children's Friendships* by Zick Rubin, Stuart Miller's *Best Friends* (original title: *Men & Friendship*), *Women &*

Friendship by Joel D. Block and Diane Greenberg, *Worlds of Friendship* by Robert B. Bell, *The Best of Friends, the Worst of Enemies: Women's Hidden Power Over Women* by Eva Margolies, and *Once My Child, Now My Friend* by Elinor Lenz. I submit, however immodestly, that none of these is as comprehensive or diverting as the book you now hold in your hands, but I list these titles as evidence of a spreading friendship fever. (At least two more friendship books are presently being written.) This rash of publications testifies to the fact that so many of us are concerned not just about the Self but about the Self with Others. If Americans want help in enriching their friendships, I take it as a welcome sign that the Me generation is transforming itself into the We generation at last.

Popularizing

For much the same reason, I take pleasure in the popularization of friendship and even in its commercialization. Some say the exploitation of friendliness cheapens friendship. But I like the SMILE T-shirts and "Have a nice day" buttons, the slogans "You have a friend at Chase Manhattan" and "The Friendly Skies of United," and the Pennsylvania license plates boasting "You've Got a Friend in Pennsylvania." These most public of public symbols demonstrate in gross, unmistakable terms that friendship is recognized to be a powerful motivating force and our culture values interpersonal relationships and is in the grip of a common quest for community.

That's why friendship can be used so effectively to sell ideas and products. "Here's to good friends!" chimes Löwenbräu, using images of male camaraderie to warm the heart and direct one's thirst to the friendly beer. Recently, Madison Avenue has also discovered the true dimensions of women's friendship. No more bedraggled housewives comparing detergents and dishpan hands. What sells products today are evocations of women's spirited affection and support for one another: The ads for both Evyan perfume and General Foods International Coffees depict well-dressed intelligent-looking women who seem to be having a great time together; in an inviting beach scene, six women kick off their Bass shoes and dance in a circle on the sand; and the ad that says "Friends are worth Smirnoff" shows three women in work clothes toasting the grand opening of their spiffy new store. [29]

We can't put a price tag on friendship, but with millions of dollars riding on such campaigns, we can put a price tag on friendship's sex appeal—and it is far from cheap. As for the price of an hour's worth of friendship, two conceptual artists in San Francisco advertised that they would pay $9.99 for someone to be their friend, that is, to listen, admire them, and laugh at their jokes.

When I refer to the commercialization and popularization of friendship, I'm also thinking of the carefully nuanced uses of the word "friend" in public life. For instance, Congressman Robert W. Kastenmeier scolds his fellow Wisconsinite: "Senator Kasten should understand that voting in the U.N. is not a proper standard by which we should be judging who our friends are around the globe."[30] In other words, countries who oppose American policy in Central America, the Middle East, or South Africa should still be called our "friends" if we need them and they aren't Communists. Otherwise, the same behavior wins the title "enemy."

Domestically, we've grown accustomed to the two faces of the word "friend." During the resoundingly unfriendly 1984 Democratic presidential primary campaign, Gary Hart's uxorious claims of friendship with Fritz Mondale made insiders wince.[31] And today, you can drop in on any legislative body and hear the phrase "my friend across the aisle" routinely precede a storm of vituperation. Although the charade can be said to devalue the currency of friendship, it seems to me that deference is paid to friendship even as it is dishonored. You've heard of pretenders to a throne but not to a milking stool.

Finally, when I note a positive side to the commercialization of friendliness I am thinking of what one critic refers to as the "loneliness industry," specifically the computer services that profit from our search for community.[32] Forget-Them-Not will "make sure you never again forget a special occasion"; $30 gets you twenty-four reminders a year about friends' birthdays and anniversaries.[33] Friend Finders International, a "lost and found for friends," has a computer registry that lists lost friends and friend-seekers in the hope of effecting a reunion.[34] And dozens of computer bulletin boards and networks allow people to "speak" to each other without the fuss and bother of face-to-face contact. One can condemn these electronic advances as futuristic forms of depersonalization, or one can view them as a bonus of the modern age: technology harnessed in the service of one's social self.

I have one bad story and one good story to illustrate the role of

computers in friendship. The bad story is told by writer Lindsy Van
Gelder, who introduced me to the wonders of "on-line communication" through the modem hooked up to a PC. Thanks to large
chunks of time spent on the CompuServe network, Lindsy has met
a number of interesting people—some she has since met in person,
others have remained unseen on-line friends. Among the most fascinating unseen personalities was a woman named Joan who used
the handle (code name) "Talkin' Lady." Joan was a neuropsychol-
ogist who had been severely disabled and disfigured in a car accident
that left her in constant pain and unable to walk or talk. But she
could type, so receiving the gift of a computer and modem literally
meant the difference between isolation and community. During two
years of "making friends on-line," says Lindsy, Joan revealed "a
sassy, bright, generous personality that blossomed in a medium where
physicality doesn't count. Joan became enormously popular. . . .
Through her many intense friendships and (in some cases) her on-
line romances, she changed the lives of dozens of women." She
founded a women's issue group within CompuServe, sent gifts when
her computer friends were hurt or sick, inspired a 42-year-old woman
to start college and then helped her write her term papers, gave a lot
of support to other disabled people, counseled women who were
suicidal or alcoholic, "listened" to everyone's sexual problems, and
was the kind of confidante people trusted with extraordinarily intimate information.

The sorry upshot of this almost-fairy tale is that Joan was a fake.
"She" was neither a woman nor disabled but was, actually, an im-
poster Lindsy calls Alex, "a prominent New York psychiatrist in his
early fifties who was engaged in a bizarre, all-consuming experiment
to see what it felt like to be female and to experience the intimacy
of female friendship." Alex may have learned exactly that, but he
also left a lot of women feeling used, tricked, and betrayed. "Many
of us on-line like to believe that we're a utopian community of the
future, and Alex's experiment proved to us all that technology is no
shield against deceit. We lost our innocence, if not our faith."[35]

The *good* computer story involves Christopher, the 35-year-old
musician who numbers his letters and phones his friends all over the
world. Christopher is also a serious computer communicator with
the handle "Ludwig von Bytehoven." Over several months, he developed a stimulating on-line relationship with someone who called
himself "Star Scanner." Here is how "Bytehoven" tells it: "On some

boards, everyone accuses everyone else of being a federal agent and gets paranoid that someone might turn them in for pirating disks. I first noticed Star Scanner because he never got involved in the rubble of the board. He and I began leaving electronic mail for each other, inside tips about new software coming out from the best developers, or advice on how to make copies of certain expensive programs that are supposed to self-destruct if you try to pirate them. The more we talked on the board, the more I liked his humor and enthusiasm. He seemed like a really nice guy, so when we put some biographical stuff on the board and discovered that we lived only twenty miles from each other, we decided to get together at a McDonald's midway between us.

"Well, to make a long story short, he turned out to be 12 years old. I mean, he came to McDonald's with his *parents*. They had to drive him there. I could also understand why they wouldn't want him to meet some computer weirdo by himself. Anyway, once I got over the shock, I really enjoyed myself. The kid was just as terrific as I thought when I thought he was an adult.

"Since our meeting, I've been noticing things he says on the board that I never noticed before. Like he uses a lot of Dungeons and Dragons terminology. He refers to his mother as The Finance Master. He's smart as a whip and full of good ideas. I always wonder how many other people have been fooled. Then I wonder why it matters. His age never really makes a difference in the things we talk about on-line. In fact, I usually don't think about it until he posts something like, 'Can people please watch their language on this board. My mom reads these messages.' "

In her provocative book *The Second Self*, Sherry Turkle has the last word on the chameleonlike nature of this new technology: "Computers are not good or bad; they are powerful."[36] It is up to us to use that power wisely in our quest for friendship.

All this activity and generalized interest in making connections speaks to the *how* and *what* of friendship; now it remains for us to ask about the *who* and *why*. Exactly who is making friends with whom, and why do we become friends with some types of people and not others? The next four chapters will suggest some answers.

Chapter 9

≈   ≈

A Sense of Place,
a Touch of Class

When I was a teenager in the fifties I lived in the Borough of Queens, about thirty minutes from Times Square, but I almost never went into "the city." My social life centered around my high school and my block. In this semi-suburb, there was no shopping mall, no street-corner hangout, no neighborhood candy store where kids gathered after supper or homework. If you weren't going to a party or a movie, the only place to be was home—alone or with friends who were similarly at loose ends.

I knew other teenagers lived differently. I knew about street corners and candy stores from reading *The Amboy Dukes* and about small towns from spending part of every summer with my cousin Pris, in Phoenicia, New York, a town whose teenagers seemed to me to come straight out of an *Archie and Veronica* comic book. In Phoenicia, Pris and I could hang out at the Main Street filling station, where the boys pumped gas and the jukebox blared "Come On-a My House" and "Tennessee Waltz," or stroll into the town drugstore, order a chocolate Coke, jaw on a Sugar Daddy, and pretend to read the greeting cards while waiting for "the crowd."

My husband's high school years were spent in rural New Jersey, in the town of Roosevelt, which was founded in the thirties as an experimental labor movement utopia. In Roosevelt, when teenagers weren't taking part in adult social events, they were engaging in friendship in their fashion: by riding around the back country roads in whatever vehicle they could get their hands on—pickup trucks, farm machinery, old cars—with whoever had a license to drive. Riding around took the place of the city street corner and the small town drugstore. Riding around was the social life you gave your kids the minute you moved to rural New Jersey.

Place as Cause and Context

In a white, affluent hillside neighborhood in Oakland, California, 12-year-olds have to be driven to each other's beautiful homes. They average only one or two friends each and say they select friends with whom they have "something in common." Nearby, in a Black, low-income inner-city neighborhood, children of the same age average four or five close friends, move around in groups, and play outside often and spontaneously with a changing variety of other children.[1]

Because each city, town, and neighborhood has a particular pool of potential friends and its own style of socializing, where you live is what you get. We may be attracted to a location because of its schools, its commuting convenience, or its low rents, but when we move in, we get something we may not have bargained for: its social life. This feature, absent from the real estate ads, determines the identity of children's playmates and what they do with their time. (Studies show that youngsters of high school age are attracted to each other because of neighborhood connection first, and then on the basis of ethnic and class similarity, status in school, and mutual interests.)[2] Where we live determines with whom we cross paths often enough to take that next step beyond acquaintanceship into friendship. Where we live also determines adult social styles; for instance, it's hard to adjust to a closed-door community if you're used to a lot of casual visiting.

In the short term, places mold people; that is, when we move in, we generally adjust to what we find. But over the long haul, people mold places. A place takes on a persona from its inhabitants; then it attracts others who see themselves as similar to its predominant population, people who consider social compatibility as compelling a reason to move somewhere as good schools or low rents. This compatibility breeds group identification, which spawns institutions such as singles clubs, ethnic organizations, special interest newspapers, and religious and cultural celebrations, which in turn encourage more place-based friendship. When neighborhood concentration reaches a "critical mass," inbred social networks develop and perpetuate themselves.

For example, eight out of ten American Blacks live in metropolitan areas. Regardless of whether Blacks live where they live because of personal preference or housing bias, studies show that "race is an important determinant of friendship patterns and that black persons are likely to identify close friends from within the black population." About 80 percent of the Blacks living in cities and 60 percent of those in the suburbs say they have no close white friends in their neighborhoods. (However, Black suburbanites were twice as likely as Black city dwellers to be invited into their white neighbors' homes.) Which city one lives in will further determine racial friendship patterns. In Atlanta, 75 percent of Black people restrict their home guests to other Blacks; but the percentage drops to 59 percent in Houston, 44 percent in Cleveland, and 40 percent in Los Angeles.[3]

Sexual orientation also can affect where people choose to live and, hence, their friendship patterns. About fifty cities and counties have laws prohibiting discrimination based on sexual preference, a protection that can affect a community's atmosphere. Some cities without anti-bias laws nonetheless have hospitable social climates because gay people have settled there in sufficient numbers to have established some turf. Thus, many lesbians and homosexual men prefer New York, San Francisco, Los Angeles, Austin, Miami, or Key West, Florida, where they decrease their chances of encountering discrimination and increase the likelihood of finding other gays and the social institutions that support gay life-styles.

In Austin, says one writer, "There are a dozen gay bars, some primarily for lesbians, a gay hot line, a gay psychological referral service and a gay counseling center, two gay churches (and others where gays are openly welcome), numerous lesbian support groups, two branches of NOW and two gay student associations—one for law students."[4] In New York, the National Gay Task Force operates a monthly "welcome wagon" to introduce newcomers to various city neighborhoods, churches, sports teams, musical groups, volunteer organizations, and vocational groups where gays are welcome.[5] These opportunities for socializing offer attractive alternatives to gay bars and bathhouses. You won't find such services in Provo, Utah.

Disabled people are similarly aware of the influence of place on friendship activities. I've been told that many deaf people favor Boston, Washington, D.C., and Rochester, New York, where there are large communities of hearing-impaired persons and a number of cultural and political events that provide sign language interpreters. People with other disabilities will want to live in places that have made housing, public arenas, and transportation accessible to wheelchairs. As we'll see in Chapter 11 physical accessibility affects social accessibility; that is, certain locales make it easier for people to visit and attend parties, movies, and sports events without worrying about structural impediments that exclude disabled people and therefore frustrate spontaneous friendship.

Ethnic minorities, especially new immigrants, often seek to live near others who speak their language and maintain their customs. Singles gravitate toward areas where other singles are concentrated. Families want to live where there are playmates for their children. Whereas people with strong traditional leanings will probably not choose to settle in Soho or Berkeley where a religious fundamentalist may be hard to find, liberals might put those communities at the top of their list.

"People and place are inseparable," writes Louise Erdrich in an essay on the novelist's sense of place. "One must experience the local blights, hear the proverbs, endure the radio commercials. Through the close study of place, its people and character, its crops, products, paranoias, dialects and failures, we come closer to our own reality."[6]

Place is reality *and* context. It is friendship's stage set: the backdrop, cast, and props you find when you get born someplace or arrive there to join a social world that existed before you and may or may not be there when you're gone.

Sixteen years ago, when Arthur Dobrin moved to Westbury, Long Island, six of the houses on his street were owned by Blacks, six by whites. Today the same racial balance exists, but the Blacks are from Haiti and the surrounding neighbors are Egyptian, Chinese, Central American, and Indian. "One hundred years ago," Dobrin says, "those who lived here couldn't have imagined what Westbury was to become, and sixteen years ago, I didn't expect that on a warm day in spring, I would be listening to voices speaking Creole, Mandarin, Spanish, Arabic, and Gujarati. But then," he adds, "when my grandparents moved to Brooklyn, who there expected Yiddish to take over the street?"[7]

Of course, people come and go and places change, but a house, street, or neighborhood need not be unchanging in reality to be forever itself to those to whom it matters. There is a time in every place—a time that can be evoked by a place. Each of us can bring to mind a person from long ago by remembering where we met, talked, threw snowballs, went snorkeling, watched fireworks—by conjuring up images of the space we shared in the universe.

The South Bronx

The writer Grace Paley grew up in the South Bronx in a neighborhood full of women who yelled out the windows to their kids playing on the street below and men who conducted their pinochle games outdoors. "I just loved the streets, and I love them to this day," Paley says. "We played in the streets all the time, and the grown-ups were in the streets all the time, and we had sandwiches in the streets, and someone would throw an apple down from the fourth floor so that you didn't have to come up. I remember all that with a great deal of affection. The streets are something I care about. I'm never averse to sitting down outside . . . with friends."[8]

A half century later the South Bronx is a different place for Darrel Cabey. Darrel comes from a city housing project where about 13,500 people—more than half of them under 21—live in garbage-strewn, overcrowded buildings with no place for kids to gather, no organized activities, and great criminal temptations. "Kids who live here are under a lot of pressure," says Darrel's mother about her son, one of the four teenagers shot by Bernhard Goetz when they asked him for money in the subway. "I tried to talk to him. I told him, 'You have two strikes against you, you're Black and you're poor, so you better get back to studying.' I told him there's more to life than hanging out in the streets."[9]

Teenagers in this neighborhood say friendship is a very loose term. They use it to describe young men who hang out together, play basketball together, or break into video game machines together. James Knight, now 21, reminisces: "When I was 15, 16, there were four or five guys and we'd ride down to the city and jigger with videos. One guy was Roy and I never knew his last name; and Jones, I never knew his first name, and I haven't seen them for two years now. So is that a friend?"

No, but it's what you get when you live in the South Bronx. If, on the other hand, you happen to live in a middle-class suburb, you get something else entirely.

A Connecticut Suburb

Regina, a 36-year-old housewife and mother, has five close friends, all of whom, incredibly, come from farm communities in the Midwest and have husbands who now work for the large insurance companies in the Hartford area.

"In my town, we just walk into each other's houses without calling ahead," Regina begins. "I sort of resented this when my kids were babies and the only time I had to myself was their naptimes. Now I welcome the visits to break the monotony of housework. In bad weather, or when a child is sick and we're stuck in the house, we talk to each other by phone. We know enough not to call at night when our husbands are home, because the men demand their wives' full attention. Also, no one will give up a Saturday to go somewhere with another woman because that's their day with their husbands. But otherwise, these women are really there for me. They listen to my problems, shop for me, take my kids when I can't get a sitter, feed my husband when I'm in the hospital having another baby," Regina laughs. She has five kids.

For many suburban women, friendships function as mutual self-help networks where women service each other's most vital needs, from providing child care to emotional support to transportation for friends who have no car. Rosalie Genovese describes a suburban friendship network in which the women share household equipment and maternity clothes, buy food and garden products in bulk and divide them, organize product parties to sell each other housewares, fabrics, plants, and cosmetics, and plan joint holiday dinners together. One woman works out of her home as a hairdresser for the others; another does clothing alterations for her friends, while they baby-sit for her children. Although the men share tools or rented equipment and have a regular card game, this is basically a women-centered network and, says Genovese, "an important way for women to gain mastery over environments which otherwise narrow their options."[10]

But not everyone flourishes in the suburbs. There are too few things to do or places to go. Unless they have money to spend on restaurants or country clubs, friends can get together only in domestic settings where children and chores are constant distractions. The distances and lack of services can be isolating, especially for women, cutting them off from contacts, culture, and entertainment; consigning them to car pools, and putting them at the disposal of their husbands and children. "We have created suburban social starvation," wrote psychiatrist Robert Seidenberg in *Corporate Wives— Corporate Casualties?*[11] For many women who stay behind when their husbands go to work, the compensations of friendship may not be enough. And for others, there is simply not enough friendship.

An outgoing woman, appropriately named Sunny, moved from the city to the suburbs in search of community. Early on, she gave a party to which all her neighbors came. None have ever reciprocated. She says the only people who ring her doorbell are sales reps, political candidates, and the letter carrier.

Structural factors explain some of the social starvation: where and how easily friends can meet, whether time and transportation allow them to act on their friendly feelings, and whether homes lend themselves to visiting. Believe it or not, socializing can be affected by something as simple as the location of the front door or what residents can see from their kitchen window.

Close Encounters of a Small Town

The little island village where our family spends summer weekends has fewer than 400 households but more structured catalysts for friendship than the average suburb or city. The daily routines that bring people together require rudimentary friendliness—a nod, a smile, a "Good morning"—and residents meet time and again during the course of a day: on the ferry, at the town's only grocery store, at the beach, recreation hall, softball games, day camp events, post office, and lending library. When people happen to run into each other, they often proffer a spur of the moment invitation for drinks or make arrangements for their children to play together. Small towns everywhere have this potential for "encountering." Only the scenery changes with the region.

In the affluent, bucolic town of Wellesley, Massachusetts, the garbage dump, a model of neatness with labeled bins and shelves of giveaway books, has become *the* locale for casual encountering when the townsfolk leave their trash, pick over their neighbors' rejects, and hang around to talk.

In a small midwestern town called Appleton (population: 3160), the most important social center is Lucille's coffee shop. "Every day at ten o'clock, you won't find anybody in their shops or offices," says one local businessman. "Everybody is having coffee there and discussing the affairs of the town."[12] *Everybody* means the shop owners, doctors, lawyers, ministers, newspaper editor, police chief, judge, and school superintendent. The most long-standing members of the group even have coffee mugs with their names on them.

Fifteen years ago, the public place that functioned as a private preserve for the white males of Camden, Alabama, was described by a man who felt at home there: "If you have business with anyone in Camden, you sit under the pecan tree. Sooner or later everyone in town goes by. . . . There's not a bit of gossip that doesn't pass as evidence. Under the pecan tree, men think they're so smart. They talk about foreign affairs like they got a Ph.D. from Harvard. Women aren't allowed and the colored have a bench around the corner."[13]

Which reminds me of a common characteristic of small towns that is often denied by our rosy nostalgia: the potential to inflict pain—the sting of being dealt out of the only game in town, fishbowl visibility, social entropy, a limited society.

"This town is cliqueish and narrow-minded," says a Montana resident. "It's hard to find a good friend . . . one who shares your background, education, goals, pains, experience. . . . For those who move to this town and are not on the inside, it is awesome and lonely and defeating." A woman whose nearest neighbor lives nine miles away adds: "Everybody knows everybody in the community. I hate it. People put you in a box—everybody has a box and everybody knows which one you're supposed to fit into. If you don't fit in, you're headed for gossip and misunderstanding. . . . Lonely women are all over here—miles separate us—men can go to bars and socialize. If you don't drink, you rarely socialize. People are lonely here, but they don't even know why."[14]

Urban Friendship: Rich, Middle, and Poor

By 1985, three out of four Americans lived not in small towns but in urban areas. What you get if you live in Casper, Wyoming, the country's least settled metropolitan area, is 13 people per square mile. In the most populous area, Jersey City, New Jersey, you get 12,000 people living in the same space.[15] But not to worry. Contrary to the belief that urban life weakens social ties, research shows that city people have no fewer friends and are no lonelier than people in smaller places. It's just that it takes a little longer for urbanites to make friends because cities structure our lives differently.

In the city you have to *create* opportunities for casual encountering; they are not built into daily life. People lock their doors. There is no general store, pecan tree or town dump to attract the locals, no lawns to tend while striking up friendly conversation. Urbanites are busy, wary of "interpersonal overload," loathe to make eye contact, not to mention conversation. Although cities have distinctive neighborhoods, overt neighborliness is unusual. As the cliché has it, residents of the same apartment house can be total strangers. But beneath these outward signs of alienation, the dour and suspicious city dweller may actually have more meaningful friendships than the cheerful small town greeter who has a dozen smiling encounters per day. In fact, research shows that urbanites' social networks are more likely to be tailor-made to their individual tastes and that city dwellers have a greater variety of friends.[16]

Each city has a particular friendship climate, a set of customs and a social flavor all its own. In Hollywood, California, for instance, more often than not, there is a hidden agenda behind seemingly social activities. Everyone is selling something, and a party, says Daniel Selznick, "is the chance to see people who don't necessarily answer phone calls."[17] Actors, writers, and directors are cozying up to producers, producers are trying to ingratiate themselves with studio heads, and so on up and down the line. It's hard to trust friendship when everyone is trying to create an image in such a marketplace atmosphere. You don't have to live in Hollywood to feel that Greater Los Angeles is a one-industry town. "Even the psychiatrists and hotel clerks talk about the movie business with their friends," says a book salesman. "It's in the air."

In Washington, D.C., politics are in the air. Whether you're making conversation with a cabdriver or hobnobbing with a four-star general, you have to know everything that transpired that day in the White House, Congress, and the State Department and to have read at least three newspapers. Among Washington's Prominent and Powerful, say the cognoscenti, nothing is "purely social"; every get-together has a motive. Well-placed Washingtonians feel it necessary to drop in on several cocktail parties per night, and once there, they expect to "work the room." Dinner parties are often paralyzed by protocol. People have been known to sneak into the dining room before dinner and switch place cards to get a "good seat" (next to a VIP or diplomat). And don't forget, here's where the phrase "my good friend" means nothing of the kind. Says columnist Meg Greenfield, "members of Congress sometimes call their real friends 'friends' but they always call their enemies 'friends.' "[18] Such tribal customs can be bewildering to the uninitiated, but people from other places who sweep in with each new administration seem to master the rules in no time.

Susan, a songwriter who grew up in a small town in Texas, has lived in New York for the last twenty years, hating every minute of it. "I have to be here if I want to make a living," she says. "But not a day goes by without my longing to be back in Texas where people know how to just *be* together. New York friendships exhaust me. Everyone's an intellectual; everyone has to say or do something brilliant and creative every day. I never feel serene with my New York friends."

In her *New York* magazine article "Friendship in the City" (actually upper-middle-class friendship in the city), Linda Wolfe described New Yorkers who are too busy to see their friends, New Yorkers who feel they have too many friends, New Yorkers who make friends for professional advantage and drop them when their prestige ebbs, New Yorkers who serve cheaper food to lesser friends— but also New Yorkers who work hard at friendship and are rewarded with deep and dependable relationships.

Gerard and Alexandra savor the vitality of friendship in New York where they've lived for the last four years. He grew up in New England; she was born in China, the daughter of missionaries, and since their marriage they've lived in Africa, South America, and an Indiana college town. "In Indiana, we came to know our friends only *too* well," Gerard told me. "It got to be a game—before we went to a party Alexandra and I would guess who would be there, what they'd be wearing, what food would be served, and what subjects would be discussed. So much happened as we predicted that the party itself was an anticlimax. When we moved to New York, we felt we'd finally found home. Here, our friends are wonderfully diverse and we love the intensity of New York conversation and the unpredictability of every get-together. The only problem is we've become typical New Yorkers: We don't have enough time for all these friends we enjoy so much."

"Since I've lived in both places I know that Seattle is a very different city from New York," Jane Adams, a writer, said in an interview. "What's important out here is living a balanced life and making sure we have enough time for friends. People in Seattle may be ambitious but that's not why we're here. If work was so important, we'd live in New York where everyone's caught up in the rat race.

"When I'm in New York having coffee with a friend, I'm aware that her clock is ticking. I know she's thinking, 'Should I sit here listening to Jane's life or should I go home and do the extra work that might get me a raise or promotion?' I've heard New Yorkers say 'Let me look at my datebook' before they can have a Coke together. When I lived in Manhattan, I felt like if I died over the weekend, no one would notice. In Seattle, if I don't answer the phone for thirty-six hours, ten people would show up at my door to see if I'm okay.

"Another thing is that we're more physical here. People *do* things together rather than sit around being entertained. We work together on each other's home repairs, we garden, we do sports. We can be in the outdoors twelve months a year without having to drive four hours to find the countryside. If we decide to go skiing after work on a Friday night, we can be on the mountain half an hour later. I live within a twenty-minute drive of all my friends and I can park in front of their houses. I don't think anything of driving twenty minutes just to have coffee with a friend.

"New Yorkers spend so much energy going to and from work, shopping, finding a parking place, and beating the traffic out of town for the weekend that they don't have much left for friends. Out here, we're able to be more available to each other because everyday life is kinder to us."

For the middle-class city dweller, social structures often substitute for the cohesion of place. The block association, workplace, and the restaurant where the waiter knows one's name become the small town within the metropolis. Although the city affords middle-class single people the greatest variety of social options, urban friends cannot always pay the price to do things together. Because of the high cost of dining and entertainment, educated young people have rediscovered reading, and singles are building their get-togethers around games such as Trivial Pursuit, potluck dinners, and cheap movie rentals (assuming they can afford the initial investment in a VCR).

As for the effect of city life on the friendships of family people, a Cornell University study of Syracuse, New York, is revealing.[19] It finds a solid sense of community in the city's middle-income neighborhoods with their tree-lined streets, parks, and many recreational facilities. Here, people describe each other as "friendly, helpful, skilled in getting along with others and respectful of privacy." They say things like "We really help each other" and "We keep an eye on each other's kids." Virtually everyone sees each community resident, young or old, "as a source of stimulation and support." As a result, such neighborhoods encourage children's friendships and friendly relations, if not deeper connections, among the parents.

The contrast with the poor sections of Syracuse is striking. Here, structural factors not only don't facilitate friendship, they actually impede it. Dilapidated housing, unkempt yards, heavy traffic, and dangerous-looking street people discourage neighboring. Parents consider other children and adults not as potential friends for their children but as potential sources of bad habits, bad language, physical harm, and corruption. "Almost everyone here keeps their kids to themselves," says one mother. "They don't let their children play with other children, or at least they try to prevent it . . . and it makes it hard for the kids to find something to do."[20] There are a few parks, but they are carpeted in broken glass and menaced by teens who drink, use drugs, and harass others. The lack of play space, the sense of being in an uncaring, unsafe, or antagonistic environment, and the fear of crime and lack of mutual trust and support from neighbors lead poor people to withdraw into the family, which creates extreme loneliness and isolation for both parents and children.

This doesn't happen, however, in the Mexican-American community centered around 32nd Street in Chicago even though the neighborhood is officially designated a "slum" by city officials. Indeed, it has its gang violence, crumbling empty buildings, and dismal alleyways. But, wrote the sociologist who studied the area, "other more important aspects of community life make 32nd Street a desirable place to live and bring up a family. The many close ties with friends and relatives and the 'Mexican-ness' of the area are the reasons many residents will not leave the area when they can afford to do so. The extensive personal network of friends and family is important to most residents. It is impossible to walk or drive one block without meeting a relative or friend. . . . People know where their friends spend their time and who the friends of their friends are."[21]

Although contact does not ensure friendship, lack of contact guarantees lack of friendship. In Montreal, the division of the city into French and English sectors and the existence of de facto segregation explain why a person's six closest friends tend to be of the same ethnic origin. Recently, however, "the concentration of entertainment in the downtown area, readily available from any point in the city by comfortable, relatively inexpensive, and readily-accessible metro (subway) and bus service, seems to bring together many teenagers, young adults, older singles and married couples to discotheques, restaurants, movies and businesses where people from different ethnic groups meet or participate in one another's different languages and ethnicities."[22] Montreal seems to be encouraging contact across ethnic and class schisms by building bridges through recreation.

So every place has its advantages and drawbacks for the making and maintenance of friendships. The suburb can be an arid "wasteland" or a warm, sustaining network such as Regina enjoys in Connecticut. The small town can be a cheerful setting for casual encountering or a hothouse of sameness and predictability. And the city can be a place of hostility or belonging for the poor, a world of social pressures or possibilities for the rich and anything in between.

Class Loyalty

The raw emotions of friendship are universal, but the way they are expressed varies not only with place but with age, class, race, gender, religion, ethnicity, disability, sexuality, and marital status. Although this book deals with each factor separately, in life they are usually intertwined; class, race, and gender, for instance, are often inseparable. Social class is an especially complex category of inquiry because in our deeply class-divided and class-prejudiced American society almost everyone identifies as "middle class" and then claims that class doesn't matter. But call it what we may, *most of us spend our free time with others of our own class*. Sociologist Lois Verbrugge puts it this way: "The more similar two adults are in social status, the more likely they will be close friends."[23]

This is a fairly straightforward case of homophily, that familiar birds-of-a-feather friendship pattern we noted earlier. Now the question is, do all the species make friends the same way? How does our social class influence the way each of us makes friends? Who has more friends—the poor, the working class, or the upper class—and who gets the most out of their friendships? And if the classes socialize differently among themselves, how can meaningful friendships form across class boundaries?

Class Differences in Friendship

Working-class people tend to confine their social relations to particular situations, such as the workplace, church, or pub; middle-class friends don't restrict their relationships to the situations in which they originated but let their friendships "flower out" into other contexts.

The average middle-class person uses the home as a place to entertain friends, thus extending, deepening, and personalizing the friendship, while working-class people usually consider the home as "the exclusive preserve of the family." Those rare nonrelatives who *are* invited in are people who cannot otherwise be seen in any structured setting—maybe because they no longer work in the same place or because their favorite pub closed down. And, as anthropologist Micaela di Leonardo notes about working-class Italians, they're never casual about home entertaining. Most middle-aged Italian-American women try to be very genteel in their social lives, says di Leonardo. "They pride themselves on doing everything *just so* when friends visit. But their attempt to adhere to a middle class code of gentility actually makes them appear distinctly working class; the rarely-used front room saved for company, the doilies on the sofas, the display of porcelain statues—these are things the middle class hasn't had for generations."[24]

Middle-class friends tend to plan ahead to meet, thus emphasizing their desire to enjoy each other's company. Working-class friends see their interactions as "the unplanned consequence of being in the same place or taking part in the same activity," says sociologist Graham Allan. ("I met Sam because I went to the union hall" rather than "I went to the union hall to meet Sam.") In the light of these differences, Allan suggests that the term "friend" itself may be class-

bound and that most working-class people would be more comfortable with his definition of the word "mate": A mate is "someone
you see because he happens to be there, but he is not someone you
plan your involvement with for involvement's sake."[25]

A good example of "mateship" may be found at the neighborhood bar, which one research team calls "the public society of intimates."[26] In contrast to middle-class cocktail lounges and singles
bars, where transiency is expected, corner pubs "encourage and develop groups of 'regulars'—people who come into the bar several
times during the week and come to constitute a recurrent group."
Regular patrons kid one another, buy each other rounds, take care
that a regular who has overindulged gets home safely, and confide
in the bartender, who functions as the social director. In such a group,
being able to drink is merely an entry card to barroom sociability,
said psychologist Robert Weiss. "You also have to know how to
participate in barroom interchange and practice the accepted social
forms."

Finally, as sociologist Claude Fischer reminds us, there are *material*
differences between the social classes that affect their friendships.
"Education provides skills and contacts that people use to build networks. Money makes it possible to entertain, to travel, to telephone,
to exchange gifts, and to provide others with aid."[27] Furthermore,
as we've seen, working-class and poor people are often distracted
from social relations by their concern for bad influences on their
children, fear of crime, drug and alcohol abuse, infelicitous living
environments, and a host of basic economic worries.

The Domino Effect

A college education is a common socioeconomic dividing line—
and the first advantage of class; colleges are great places to meet
people. Second, having an education broadens our interests and enhances our self-confidence and social competence. Third, a college
education also allows us to make more money, which gives us greater
mobility and access to more people and resources. Fourth, a college
degree also facilitates our membership in professional and other organizations where we can form still more personal relationships.
These geometrically increasing class privileges account for the positive domino effect of class on friendship.

That sociality among working-class and poor people is superior is a romantic notion; in reality, their lack of mobility and reduced social and financial resources constrain them to relationships with close kin, neighbors, church members, and nearby coworkers. Fischer discovered that educated and affluent people tend to have deeper and larger social networks, and the larger a person's network, the happier the person reported feeling.

Educated people also have more *multi-stranded* relationships. (In a single-stranded relationship, you and I might have a workplace in common. If we also socialize away from work, our relationship is double-stranded: We share both occupational and personal experiences. If we also serve together on the school board, we have a triple-stranded relationship, and so on.) Fischer found that the more multi-stranded a friendship, the stronger and more satisfying the bond.

Continuing the domino effect of class privilege, the educated classes also get the most social support from their friends: more counseling, more companionship, and even more practical help. In contrast, those most at risk because of inadequate support are older people, mothers of young children, minorities (particularly Black women), the undereducated, and the poor. These are the most isolated people in our society, the most hard-pressed, the least likely to have the time and resources to share with others.

Kin, neighbors, and church members are not enough. According to Fischer, the most supportive community is the friendship network that is most common in the middle and upper classes. Confronting his own results, Fischer remarks wryly: "These findings confirm the venerable philosophical verity that 'them that's got, gets.'"

Who Knows Who and Where

Network "density" is a term that describes how many of our friends are also friends of each other. We have a low-density network when our friends are like parallel lines that never meet. A high-density network is one with many crisscrossed relationships; everybody knows everybody. High-density networks are more common in the lower social strata among people who are longtime residents of stable neighborhoods or those who are confined by social or physical impediments to the company of kin and neighbors. This is not to say that kin and neighbors are inadequate friends or even that they are necessarily of the same social class. The point is that when our activities are limited to a few social contexts the radius of friendship choice is narrow.

Of the people who were content with high-density networks and did not long for "more people to talk to or have fun with," most earned under $15,000 a year. For more affluent people, "the denser the network . . . the *worse* they felt."

Why the class difference in subjective reactions? One explanation is that low-income people feel gratified by the familiarity of inbred relationships, while educated people experience these friendships as insular because they're aware of a wider world beyond their interconnected circle. Another reason is that large, geographically dispersed networks pose economic and logistical problems for the poor, while middle-class people have the time and money to pursue wide-ranging friendships and feel cheated if their social circle is small.

The Power Quotient

There is yet another class difference in friendship that bears upon each group's happiness and well-being: the power quotient, not the power *over* but the power *to*—the power to accomplish something on behalf of oneself or one's friends. Entertaining or not entertaining friends at home is a matter of style; but being able to help a friend's child land a plum summer internship is a matter of power. Call it empowerment. In other words, although friendship's *feelings* may be very much the same across class lines, friendship's *instrumentalities* show significant class differences.

About twenty years ago, my husband, Bert, participated in an experiment to determine how many people it took to get from a Starter person to a Target person who was from a different social class and another part of the country. The one requirement was that each connecting link had to be personally acquainted with the next connecting link. The presumption was, the higher the social class of the Starter, the fewer in-between people would be required to leapfrog over millions of Americans to the Target.

In Bert's experiment, the Starter was an attorney in California and the Target was the manager of Sutter's Bakery in Greenwich Village, New York. The first thing the California man did was to consult his law school alumni directory to find a former classmate of his who might be living in Greenwich Village—that was my husband. Since the two knew each other personally, the Starter could call Bert directly and ask if he knew the manager of the bakeshop. Although we shopped at Sutter's, Bert did not know the manager personally, but he knew that our landlady had been the man's friend since childhood. Bert went upstairs and asked *her* to call the manager. Voilà! Only two connecting people between Starter and Target.

If I remember correctly, the study found that more links were required in the chain of people leading to the Target when the Starter was low on the social scale, except when such Starters turned for help to their doctor, employer, or minister, which moved the process up into the more privileged classes where it then zoomed to its Target.

The consequences of this experiment should be obvious. To be able to reach the person who can help you, to get someone on the phone—even "a friend of a friend"—to cut through red tape, to "take advantage" of friendship in the best sense as an available network of helpers, is to possess human resources that have no price. (Successful people who claim they made it all by themselves are not taking into account the invisible resource of their powerful, supportive friends.)

Despite the reported emotional satisfactions of high-density "everybody knows everybody" networks, it is clear that lower-class people are afforded minimal opportunities to benefit from such outreach and influence. The "who you know" game played out in the following success story illustrates how education and class yield powerful friendship connections that pay off throughout life.

When Heidi and Rocco Landesman wanted to produce a musical based on *Huckleberry Finn,* they called on their friend William Hauptman, a former classmate of theirs at the Yale Drama School and a published playwright, to write the stage version of Mark Twain's book. Next, the Landesmans and Hauptman went to Robert Brustein, their former Yale professor, who is now director of the American Repertory Theatre in Cambridge, Massachusetts, and he agreed to present the first stage adaptation. Still another Yale connection was classmate Michael David, who agreed to coproduce and who got *his* friend Des McAnuff to direct and try out the show at the La Jolla Playhouse in California, where he happens to be the artistic director. Together, this team of ex-Yalies took the show to Broadway where, under the title *Big River,* it won seven Tony Awards.[28] The play's underlying theme? The triumph of friendship.

How Class-conscious Are We?

Despite such impressive examples of the educated and affluent using "who you know" power, the average person is largely unaware of class influences on friendship. Instead, the myth of a classless society continues to animate Americans' collective self-image—maybe because an acceptance of class would imply an acceptance of the economic inequalities that cause it. To most of those I interviewed, class was taboo. Only when pushed did some people acknowledge that education, occupation, and income might play a role in determining how and with whom they socialize. Even then, people prefaced their remarks with apologetic disclaimers: "I know it sounds snobbish . . . ," "I don't mean this as a put-down . . . ," "It's probably just me, but . . ."

A financial analyst comments, "My friends are all well-traveled, well-read, serious about art and music, and comfortable with intellectual discourse. Some might say I'm class-conscious but all I look for is intellectual congruity. That's not as snobbish as it sounds," she adds quickly. "I don't care what color people are, what they do, or how much money they make as long as they have the brain-power."

"I'm *friendly* with my secretary but she'd die laughing if I said we were *friends*," reports a corporation president. Embarrassed by how rigidly he draws the status lines, he nonetheless recognizes the interplay between power and class. He admits that his "real friends" tend to be highly placed professional people "who speak the same language I do."

At first I blamed the culture of calibration for what I took to be upper-class snobbery. But that's an oversimplification. Lois Verbrugge has found that those with the most education and occupational prestige prefer higher status friends but because few people are above them they end up with almost all friends of their own class. Verbrugge says people on the lowest socioeconomic edge want friends who are their social inferiors (to make them look good in comparison), but because it's hard to find a class lower than the bottom, they too end up with same-status friends. And in my interviews, I found lower-status people as uninterested in those "above" them as upper-class people were in those "beneath" them.

"We've had big-time intellectuals over to the house—professors with Ph.D.'s and Nobel prizes—and after they left I felt drained," confesses a full-time mother, a high school graduate who lives with her husband, a software designer, in a modest suburb of Boston. "My husband meets Harvard and MIT people through his job, so it's important for him to exchange information with them, but underneath he admits it's a strain for him too. He's never happier than when he's poking around under a car hood with the other guys on the block. Me, I want to be able to talk about rug shampoo and kids' tantrums with my friends. I don't want to have to be *on*."

Others felt more disdain than social strain. "I cannot be friends with people who accept money from their parents or have trust funds," says a band musician who identifies with the working class. "I work hard for every buck. I scrounge for play dates. I teach talentless students. I hassle to get the rent paid. I'm not going to pal around with some dependent 30-year-old whose parents buy him a Steinway and a Mercedes in the same year."

A Kansas City man told the authors of *Social Standing in America*, "I'm a carpenter and I wouldn't fit in with doctors and lawyers or in country club society. We have different interests and want to do different things. We don't always understand each other. . . . I hate to say there are classes but it's just that people are more comfortable with people of like backgrounds."[29]

Sociologist Herbert Gans maintains that the preference for friends of one's own class is a matter of economics rather than psychology. "Income similarity is valued by the less affluent, not as an end in itself, but because people who must watch every penny cannot long be comfortable with more affluent neighbors, particularly when children come home demanding toys or clothes they have seen next door."[30]

A machinist echoes that view: "Our friends make about the same money we do so I know I'm not gonna suddenly see one of 'em bust out with a whole new wardrobe or an air conditioner in every room. We're all pretty satisfied, not like those rich folks on the TV. I wouldn't be their friend if you paid me. They got fancy clothes and big houses but none of 'em is happy."

Because class snobbishness is expressed in all strata doesn't make it any more palatable. But it does suggest that class bias may be only part prejudice; the rest may be attributable to homophily. Since similarity is a by-product of common experience and common experience is rooted in one's educational and financial circumstances, the whole social dynamic has a circular inevitability.

Varieties of Social Eating

"I'm not impressed with upper-class socializing," says a waiter who works the banquets in an elegant hotel ballroom. "When you have to wear a penguin suit every night like I do, a tuxedo is no big deal. I feel sorry for those society types; they get all dressed up to have a dinner of five string beans, a mushroom, and a steak the size of a sink plug. Where I come from, a good time is when you wear drip-dry clothes and eat until you're full."

In an interview, sociologist Gaye Tuchman said food figures into friendship in different ways in different classes: "Upper-middle-class and upper-class people practice gourmet sociability; they build their friendships around food. For the working class, food goes with family. They tend to have a meal with their family of origin at least once a month if geography permits."

The dinner party, a mainstay of middle- and upper-class social relations, is not a strictly social event. We might seat one of our business "contacts" beside a lifelong friend who needs venture capital and a subtle appeal made between the soup and the salad may be the precursor of a deal cemented days later on the telephone. Friends who can do favors for other friends are introduced to each other with attendant raves as are potential donors, dates, collaborators, clients, buyers, or sellers. None of this happens around the working-class supper table, which is basically a place to have supper.

Says a working-class wife, "I've never given a dinner party. I don't know that I've ever been to one. You know, every now and then—it isn't often, because it costs too much and besides it's too much trouble—I just have people down for dinner, but it's not what you'd call a dinner party."[31]

When I interviewed sociologist David Riesman he said he has found that the dinner party, for all its up-scale formalities and apparent social manipulations, is actually more intrinsically democratic than the lower-class "potluck supper," which appears more naturalistic. At the potluck, where people choose their own seating, they tend to stay with those they already know, whereas the hosts of a dinner party seat their friends beside *new* acquaintances and rarely put wives and husbands together. At the potluck, conversation is random and unguided; at the dinner party, the hosts may orchestrate the conversation so that many subjects are covered and every guest has a chance to be heard. Without determining which is "better," we can agree that the potluck supper and the dinner party yield very different social experiences. The potluck may be more relaxed than the dinner party, which requires a certain "performance sociability," but the dinner party may be more stimulating than the potluck at which no one is called upon to "be interesting." The dinner party usually opens the possibility of new friendships and new information; the typical potluck offers a good supply of familiar faces and easy talk about easy subjects.

Upward and Downward Mobility

Although the United States is not a classless society, it *is* a society in which class is not immutable. Over a lifetime, our social status can change several times, and our friendships with it. Thus, once having decoded the friendship style of one socioeconomic class, we may have to do it all over again. Education produces the first upgrading from the class of our family of origin. Career or financial success accounts for another jump. Winning the lottery can be quite a boost, and marrying "up" or "down" may alter class in either direction.

"I have a friend who inherited major wealth and never let it corrupt her," said Tuchman. "But when she married a middle-class man, she went from riche to nouveau riche overnight. Suddenly her lampshades had to match her drapes—and we stopped being friends."

Divorce too affects class. "I felt myself losing status when my husband left me," comments Stephanie, a graphic artist and the mother of two. "Single women with children are automatically de-classed. Ex-wives of successful men even more so. Look at me. I'm the same person with the same job I had when I was married, but now that I'm alone, some friends have disowned me."

For Martha, the mayor of a small city, political fame was the status-changer. "Winning public office gave my husband and me the *illusion* of classing up," she explains. "It increased our standing on the social ladder, but mayors aren't paid much and my husband is a civil service employee, so we can't afford to keep up with the wealthy contributors who want to be our friends. At the same time, less affluent people hold back because *they* can't reciprocate, or maybe they're intimidated. New friends feel we should invite them to our house because if they invite us it looks like they're currying favor. Old friends get insulted because official business prevents me from socializing the way I used to. The upshot is, we have fewer friends now than we had when I was an ordinary citizen."

When an old friend rises out of her or his class, are old friendships doomed? No, but there are problems. Male college freshmen whose neighborhood friends didn't attend college exhibited more fear of success than freshmen whose high school friends *had* gone on to college.[32] The college men were anxious about moving beyond the social class of their peers for fear they would find themselves in the position of having increased status at the expense of friendship.

Gene, who started with one restaurant and in eight years became a multimillionaire in the franchising business, has several old friends who had to make major adjustments in their relationship with him. "Since his sudden wealth, he eats in four-star places where I don't even try to reach for the bill," says one man. "I might be able to split the dinner check, but I can't cover a $200 bottle of wine, and Gene orders *two* of them. No matter how gracious he is about paying, not being able to reciprocate gives me a bad feeling. So we've developed a little charade: He takes me out to four-star dinners; I spring for lunch at a health food place near my office."

Another of Gene's friends has more serious objections to the multimillionaire's new life-style: "I think he and his wife are imprisoned by their wealth. They require a degree of luxury that limits my relationship with them. In the old days, I'd invite them out to my converted barn in the country and we'd hike, pick berries, browse through the flea markets, cook up a batch of pasta, and sit around all evening in our jeans, just yakking. *Now* that kind of weekend wouldn't be enough for them. They've become jaded. They need a $5 million house in the Hamptons with an art collection, a screening room, and a gourmet cook. The only way we've stayed friends is for me to accept the imbalance. I let Gene be the perennial host. We do things his way in his world on his money."

Another friend, an investment banker and no piker himself, blames his own competitiveness for the difficulty he had in coming to terms with Gene's success. "When Gene began to make it big, I was real happy for him. We've been pals for twenty years and I've always wished him well. But I have to admit there was pain in the pleasure because he was outdoing me so dramatically. First he bought a couple of sports cars, then a yacht, a private jet, houses in London and on the island of Ibiza. Finally he got out so far ahead that I couldn't even dream of catching up. At that point I stopped competing. Now I just relax and enjoy his success with him. He's such a generous guy—it's impossible to resent him."

For his part, Gene exhibits no awareness that the class differential matters to his friends. His face is unclouded by doubt as he says, "My wealth is unimportant. My three closest friends are all extremely successful at what they do. Each of them has stature. They have interesting lives, they're involved in the world, they travel. We go back a long way together. I'm sure they don't care who has more money."

Gloom at the Top

While class discrepancies may create discomfort for people with higher status friends, what the high status person worries about is: "How do I tell an authentic friend from an opportunist?"

People from celebrity families often feel isolated, have few friends, and are suspicious of people's motives. They "aren't expressing paranoia," says one researcher, "their suspicions really do reflect their experiences."[33] Dozens of acquaintances want them for celebrity-by-association. Or the prominent person tells a friend something intimate only to see the item appear in the gossip columns.

I heard such a story from an heiress I'll call Penelope. As a result of her recognizable fourteen-carat surname, she was constantly sought after by people who seemed to want to be her friend but before long asked her to contribute to some business or charitable project. She felt like a sitting duck. To escape the barrage, she started to use her husband's name in her social life and did all her philanthropic giving anonymously. Over time, her Rich Kid identity faded. "In the last few years," she says, "I got my real estate license under my married name, made some friends through business, made other friends through my kids' schools where few people know who I am. Now if someone is interested in me, I try to believe it's genuine."

An actor enjoying first-class stardom protects himself against false friends by hiding behind an army of agents, lawyers, and secretaries. When he meets new people, he says he can tell a lot about them from the first conversation. "If they only talk about me, my movies, or my co-stars, they're usually sycophants and celebrity-hunters. When they can talk interestingly about themselves—who they are and what they think—it feels more like the start of a sincere friendship."

Obviously, some basic rules are reversed among the upper classes. Most of us were taught to be proud of our identity; the heiress makes friends by masking hers. We were taught to show interest in others; the actor likes people who talk about themselves. Most of us believe you have to start by trusting people. Grace, the president of a small college, starts with distrust to protect herself against disappointment. "To be a close friend of mine you'd have to be someone who couldn't possibly be trying to use me," she says. "That lets out just about everybody I know: students, parents, faculty, alumni, my trustees, my former coworkers who now work for me, the townspeople who often want a favor or have an ax to grind. They all have reason to want to be my friend, so I can't be sure they really *are* my friend. If I lost my job, I'd lose my power too; then I'd see who my real friends are. But why put anyone to the test; it's easier to have a lot of casual friends and not to assume too much."

Making Friends Across Class Lines

All other class problems seem to pale beside the ambivalence and guilt surrounding the issue of cross-class friendship.

Luke and Harry met while serving together in World War II. They each married and had two children, but there the demographic similarity ends. Luke is a manufacturing magnate and Harry runs a driving school. Nevertheless, they have kept their ties through the years. "He's like family," Luke says of Harry. "I'm godfather to his daughter. We talk now and then. We'll go to a ball game together. But I can't invite him to my parties. I had him over once and he suffered terribly in the company of my other guests. The desire to be friends with someone of a different class is not the same as doing it. My friendship with Harry requires extra sensitivity. I always have to think ahead to avoid his embarrassment."

Many people regret the class homogeneity of their friends and wish they had social relations outside their own class.

A lawyer told me, "My friends are my socioeconomic clones. I don't know anybody who works for the post office, the sanitation service, or the subways. My friends in government are elected or appointed officials not civil service workers. I know teachers but not janitors, journalists but not printing trades people, union leaders but not assembly-line workers, lawyers and judges but not legal secretaries and court stenographers. I feel I'm missing a large part of the world."

Esther Newton, an anthropologist and a lesbian, wrote: "I came out in 1959 in working class bars. . . . My lover comes from a working class family. . . . Living in New York City, I know there are many Latin, Black, Asian, Native American lesbians—I see them on the streets, in bars, at women's bookstores." Yet, "as a white college professor who knows mostly other white intellectuals, my social world is more class and race segregated than I would like."[34] Newton says research in the gay community shows that, for their lovers, lesbians choose women of like status, while gay men choose lovers of unlike status. But for their *friends,* both gay men and lesbians choose people from their own status group.

Millie, a corporate speechwriter says, "A few working-class people live in my neighborhood and I see them at tenants' rights meetings but they're not my *friends.* I have some highly educated women friends who are poor because so many single mothers and underemployed women are poor, but they're not really lower class. I look at them and think there but for the grace of God go I.

"The money difference between us is a constant unspoken problem," Millie continues. "I'm afraid of overestimating what they can afford. I don't think twice about spending five bucks for a movie but many of them do. When we travel around the city, I pay for the taxi. I tell them, 'I would have taken one anyway.'

"I've gone to meetings at homes where everyone sat on boxes, folding chairs, and the bare floor. When it was my turn to host a meeting, I made up some excuse about having a sick mother at home. My living room is full of upholstered furniture and Oriental rugs. I could not bear the idea that my friends would be hurt by the comparison."

Millie described another friend who lives in a much more opulent apartment and often hosts meetings for disadvantaged groups. "When I asked her if she thought these other friends might be uncomfortable in her plush surroundings, my friend answered, 'I'm not going to patronize these people or fake poverty. Downward mobility is the worst kind of radical chic. I used to be poor, now I can afford a nice home. I'm fighting for everyone to be able to live like this.'

"I thought her answer was terrific," says Millie, "until I attended a meeting at her house and saw the poor people sitting around staring at the elegant furnishings with a mixture of awe and longing. The logical answer fits my politics but the emotional truth doesn't."

James and Doug are a homosexual couple who live in Texas. James is a wealthy developer; Doug was a refrigerator repairman and is now a $200-an-hour hairstylist. Their problem is finding gay friends in their own socioeconomic class. "We're always wishing for other gay couples who might travel with us and go out with us on the town," says James. "It sounds weird, but we're too rich for our own good." Most of their friendships are cross-class by default. They go to bars and parties with their less affluent gay friends, but often they feel uncomfortable. "I think some people resent us, like we're slumming," says Doug. When the two men want company in expensive places or on their round-the-world jaunts, they team up with their straight friends who can afford it. "We can't get the sexual life-style and the economic life-style together in one friendship."

Nobody I interviewed had found a way to avoid the discomfort of discrepant possessions and privileges. Middle- and upper-class people squirmed when I asked if they had any friends of unlike status. They named their baby-sitters, secretaries, domestic workers, the supers of their buildings, but further probing made it plain that these were pleasant employer-employee relations, not friendships.

When I asked working-class people if they had cross-class friends, the reaction ranged from impatience to amusement. "I'm no social climber," said a telephone operator. And her husband, a house painter, added, "What would we do if we had a friend in one of them three-piece suits? Give him chili? Take him dirt-bike riding or bowling?" He laughed at the idea.

For upper-class people, like-status friends confirm their elite identity and help them further differentiate themselves from "lesser" stock. But why do members of lower classes also resist cross-class friendship? The answer might be the attraction of equality.

Friendship and Equality

Friendship is seldom lasting but between equals.

Samuel Johnson

For centuries, thinkers have recognized that friendship cannot flourish without equality. Francis Bacon understood what a problem that presents to kings. Kings are supposed to have no equals, only subjects. Thus, to gain friends, says Bacon, monarchs must "raise some persons to be, as it were, companions and almost equals to themselves."[35] While a monarch can elevate someone by royal fiat, the rest of us have neither the power nor the resources to move people from one socioeconomic class to another as much as we might want to ensure across-the-board equality for ourselves and our friends.

Anne, a psychotherapist and single mother, complains: "I have wonderful colleagues who are feminists and who have children as I do, but they live so far away it's impossible to share daily life with them. My neighbors close by are single women who work in stores or factories. They're kind and caring, but I can't think of them as close friends because they're not feminists or mothers or intellectual equals."

No matter how fond they may be of one another, people of disparate status are rarely close friends, be they unequal neighbors, boss and worker, client and expert, student and mentor, or rich and poor. True friendship requires equality.

Equality presumes that neither partner has more "fate control" over the other. Equality eliminates power imbalances. Equality is what distinguishes love from adoration, sharing from supplication, caring from condescension, and entitlement from gratitude.

In its best light, class loyalty is the homage friendship pays to equality. Think of friends as "class-mates" rather than "classifiers" to understand what I mean. As long as our culture ranks human beings, and as long as we subscribe to the *felt* differences embedded in class distinctions, then choosing friends with occupations, incomes, and education similar to our own may appear to be the quickest route to a certain kind of equality in friendship. There would be nothing wrong with this if the shortcut didn't close off the longer route—if we were also willing both to open ourselves to some people who have different class profiles than our own and to work a little harder to find out where our similarities lie.

Crossing class lines does not mean learning to like people you have nothing in common with. It means looking beyond tired old socioeconomic clues to discover equality in another dimension.

As one man put it, "My friend and I came from different worlds but we found out we have the same heart. And now all the rest doesn't seem to matter."

Chapter 10

≈ ——————— ≈

Our Own Kind

Friendship within Racial and Ethnic Groups

Brother. Landsman. Compadre. Paesan.

Words that distinguish "us" from "them." (Their masculine form excludes women from full "us-ness" but that's another subject.) In any language, the words that convey shared origins also suggest shared secrets and ties as binding as an oath. And along with the assumed loyalty and instinctual understanding is the presumption that a stranger who is one of our own kind is potentially a friend.

Ties That Bind

After a full review of the childhood friendship research, Professor M. L. Clark states: "The most consistent finding concerning the influence of race on friendship selection is that both black and white children of all ages prefer friends that are of the same race."[1] Sociologist Wayne Usui found the same thing among the elderly: 97 percent of Blacks and 99 percent of whites said their three closest friends are people of their own race.[2]

Not only do we prefer our own kind, we *know* our own kind and their habits, or think we do, as these sweeping generalizations suggest:

- "Even in the middle of WASP heaven, Italians hit it off to-gether in a special way. I can feel it when another Italian who works at my company sees me, and says, 'Aah, *campare* Mar-ianna!' and we wink."

- "Friends are absolutely essential to Hispanics because of the conditions under which most Mexican-Americans and Puerto Ricans live."

- "The French are more formal than Americans. We drink a lot of wine and break a lot of bread together before we call a person a friend."

- "Asians don't let another person get too close because of the fear of losing face. If you care about family honor, you do not talk about family problems with your friends."

- "I hate the stereotype of the Irish drinker but I have to admit that if there was no such thing as beer and booze, I'm not sure what would happen to Irish friendship."

- "Jews are very comfortable sharing neuroses. We make friends through complaining and exchanging self-deprecating humor. Those are our contact gestures."

- "Black people have a kind of shorthand. We know the mean-ing of our meanings. We like 'gettin' down' together, which means going back to our roots and being comfortable enough to be yourself. With Black friends, you don't have to watch your ass or your language."

In one sense, ethnic and racial homogeneity in friendship is a sign of healthy group identity and pride. In another sense, of course, it also speaks of rejecting or being rejected by others. Claude Fischer discovered "more culturally encapsulated networks" among Blacks, Jews, Asians, Mexican-Americans, and the foreign-born than among comparable Anglos.[3] Surely it is no accident that the groups that most tend to stay among themselves are also those most stigmatized by the white Christian majority. The issue of cross-race and cross-ethnic friendship will be covered in the next chapter. Here, we are going to examine friendships formed *within* racial and ethnic groups and how intragroup friendships help people maintain their identity and boundaries.

Although we all look for the same basic support from our friends (see Chapter 4), there *are* differences stemming from culture, race, and ethnic experience that affect the way particular groups make and maintain their friendships. I see two relevant kinds of differences: *questions of fact*—the objective economic and social realities of one's life—*and questions of style*—the special ways that members of one's racial or ethnic group signal interest in one another and pleasure in their friendship.

Some questions of fact are more crucial to one's friendship identity than others. For instance, it matters if your Jewish friend is the child of Holocaust survivors, your Black friend is descended from slaves, or your Japanese-American friend was born in one of the detention camps in which the United States quarantined its Japanese citizens during World War II.

Questions of style would include an ethnic group's distinctive greetings and leave-takings, the food and atmosphere at their mealtimes and parties, the meaning of a nod or a stare, the amount of eye contact and touching that is considered comfortable between friends, and how verbal and nonverbal communication differs from one culture to another.

"People take their folk gestures seriously," says one communications scholar.[4] Different ethnic groups "organize their senses differently," says Edward T. Hall, an ethnologist and an expert on communication styles. What one culture considers intimate, another culture might consider appropriate in public behavior.[5] These transactions, learned in earliest childhood, become social instincts that distinguish the insider from the outsider. If friendship is to develop across racial and ethnic lines, outsiders have to learn to recognize and respect these cultural codes if not to use them themselves.

Cultural Do's and Don'ts

Interpersonal Spacing. Most Americans conduct business at a distance of four to twelve feet from one another, but when friends talk face to face, they stand about an arm's length apart (one and a half to two feet away). If they find themselves closer than this, they will gradually separate or show signs of discomfort. If a Jew from Southeastern Europe attempts conversation a foot away from a white Anglo, who tends to prefer much wider interpersonal spacing, "a high degree of irritation results."[6] The same would be true for Scandinavians speaking to Arabs who "consistently breathe on people when they talk," says Hall. "To the Arab, smells are pleasing and a way of being involved with each other. To smell one's friend is not only nice but desirable, for to deny him your breath is to act ashamed."[7]

Touching.　Indonesians, as compared with Australians, and Latins, as opposed to Anglos, stand closer and do more touching and more smiling.[8] Mediterraneans, Near Easterners, Far Easterners, and Americans all exhibit different patterns of touching and touch avoidance. Middle Easterners and French people touch each other in public much more than do Americans.[9]

Eye Contact.　The French "really look at you," says Hall. "Arabs look each other in the eye when talking with an intensity that makes most Americans highly uncomfortable." Americans are taught not to stare, but "proper English listening behavior includes immobilization of the eyes." Americans nod their heads and grunt to indicate understanding and agreement; the English blink their eyes.[10]

Verbal Communication.　When standing at arm's length, most Americans talk louder to their friends than do Southeast Asians, the Japanese, or upper-class British folk, but not as loud as Spaniards, Arabs, South Asians, Indians, or Russians. The Japanese habit of "indirection"—talking around and around a point—is maddening to most Americans, but our habit of getting straight to the point is maddening to them. To the average Arab, too, speaking directly to the point can seem rude, and particular inflections and voice emphasis can convey very different meanings in our two cultures. (Those who are unconscious of these subtleties may find themselves unwittingly insulting their friends.) Arab greetings tend to be elaborate and drawn out. Among Bedouins, casual salutations are not always returned because a greeting is considered a serious guarantee that the person greeted will be protected by the greeter's kin and tribe.[11]

Nonverbal Communication.　To Chicanos, staring at someone or failing to shake hands may be interpreted not just as bad manners but as violations of personal honor and "attempts to demean an individual."[12] Arabs refuse food three times before accepting it, but Americans would consider it overbearing to pressure someone who had twice refused to eat.[13] Among themselves, the French understand ten French-style gestures that communicate amazement, disbelief, and power, among other emotions.[14] Well-bred European women pay their respects to friendship by attending at-home luncheons dressed in suits, silk dresses, jewelry, and high-heeled shoes; their American counterparts wear slacks, sweaters, and flats.[15] Germans close doors unless there's a reason for them to be open; Americans keep them open unless there's a reason to close them (such as sex, dressing, private meetings). When Americans want to be alone, they go into a room and shut the door. When the Arabs or British want solitude they don't seek closed space, they just stop talking.

Hall tells of an Englishman who complained of his American roommate: "Whenever I want to be alone, my roommate starts talking to me. Pretty soon, he's asking what's the matter and wants to know if I'm angry." For the Englishman, breaking in on his silence is an invasion of privacy; for the American, sitting in the same room and refusing to talk to someone is rejection.[16]

Openness and Accessibility. Latins are more likely to be open and friendly than are Anglos.[17] Brazilians expect somewhat more support and intimacy from friendship than do Australians.[18] Blacks or Hasidic Jews will often exchange nods or brief greetings when they see one of their own in a public place. Mutual accessibility is assumed when strangers recognize each other as members of the same disadvantaged or special group.

Personal Compliments. The Japanese give each other far fewer compliments than do Americans, and each culture finds the other's complimenting style somewhat troubling.[19] Japanese compliments tend to be indirect and tentative: "Your short hair is nice but I like it long too"—as if too much praise of the new hairdo would suggest that the old hairdo has been disliked all along. American compliments are direct and often overstated: "Fantastic! You look great! I love your haircut." Most Japanese hear such raves as empty flattery. Scholars attribute the difference in complimenting to each nation's social ideal: The United States extols individual excellence, whereas Japan promotes group effort and harmony.

Values. In contrast to most Americans, says Hall, "Europeans allow more time for virtually everything involving important human relationships." Among themselves, the French share an unspoken value system, which includes twelve commonly held assumptions about individualism, intellectualism, the art of living, realism, "le bon sens," and friendship.[20] People from Thailand "may not seem serious to Western eyes" because of their Buddhist "detachment from life and acceptance of fate. Americans value activity and doing; Thais value interpersonal relations."[21] Turks "emphasize companionship, sharing and loyalty in their friendships, are less competitive, and more involved in the friend's psychological and personal development . . . report more similarity, less jealousy and less overt quarreling with their best friends than Americans do. The Americans report that freedom for each friend to be himself/herself is basic to an enduring relationship, while Turks cite openness and honesty."[22]

A Sampling of Friendship Cultures

This smorgasbord of behaviors and attitudes reflects just a smattering of what might be called "the culture of friendship." To bring these cultures to life, we turn to a few representative groups. The term "Perspectives" is used to introduce each discussion to emphasize that the views expressed are individual rather than conclusive statements about friendship in each community.

Black Perspectives

Despite some intragroup difficulties, which we'll get to shortly, Blacks show a strong pattern of commitment to friendship and often to kin friends in particular. As the research indicates, Black children form friendships more rapidly, have more stable friendships, and make twice as many best friend choices as do white children. Evaluating these findings, M. L. Clark and M. Ayers speculate that intragroup friendships may be more important in the Black social support system than in the white system because, along with the stresses of adolescence, Black students must contend with racial prejudice.[23] White racism does not *cause* Black friendship, but the burden of racism seems to make friendship particularly precious, sustaining, and necessary to Black people.

As noted earlier, Blacks are among the groups whose social networks are predominantly made up of their own kind. In addition, R. P. Coleman and L. Rainwater found that nearly 100 percent of the Blacks they questioned said they and their five closest friends were of the same religion.[24] As is the case with every group, the general preference Blacks show for other Blacks is based on many factors.

"I like my friends to be cool, together people, and mostly that's the brothers," says Roy, a 22-year-old security guard who reports that all his friends are Black. "I like my friends to look sharp but not be show-offs. They got to know how to talk smooth and not let anyone push them around. They got to know how to rap and style. They got to make some money and be willing to spend it but also be decent and help out they mama when she be needing money for the rent or food."

Helping out is a way of life in The Flats, a poor Black community studied by anthropologist Carol Stack. In this community, funds from low-paying jobs and welfare don't cover the necessities of life, thus friends have to bridge the gaps. As Magnolia explains, "If you have a friend, you should learn to trust them and share everything that you have. When I have a friend and I need something, I don't ask, they just automatically tell me that they going to give it to me. I don't have to ask. And that's the way friends should be, for how long it lasts. But sometimes when you help a person they end up making a fool out of you. If a friend ain't giving me anything in return for what I'm giving her, shit, she can't get nothing else. . . . You can't care for no one that don't give a damn for you."

Stack explains how Black friendship meshes with fictive kinship: "Individuals in The Flats continually evaluate their friendships by gossip and conversation. They talk about whether others are 'acting right' or 'doing right by them. . . .' When friends more than adequately share the exchange of goods and services, they are called kinsmen. . . . For example, if two women of the same age are helping one another, they call their friend 'just a sister,' or say that they are 'going for sisters.' . . . When a friendship ends because individuals 'let one another down,' this concludes both their expectations of one another and their kin relationship."[25]

Bernice Powell, a widow in her thirties, is a well-educated, highly paid consultant with prominent and powerful friends all over the world. She maintains a brownstone in a gracious middle-class pocket of Harlem. "I have lived a very different life than the people I grew up with," she confessed in a recent conversation. "I've seen places, done things and known people wildly removed from my neighbors' lives. It's painful to admit I've outgrown those Black people, but I have to accept that we really aren't friends as I now define friends.

"My friends are women and men who are making something of themselves but who have never forgotten they're Black," she explains. "They and I are as at home in an all-white boardroom as in a Black church. We can talk Ivy League English or rap with the best of the brothers. We still make chitlins and sweet potato pie but we serve it on fine china. We may be beyond our neighbors in terms of money and mainstream sophistication, but we aren't ashamed of where we came from and we never turn our backs on Black folks." What this means is that Powell and her friends make good salaries and put a lot of money and time back into the Black community. They serve as Big Sisters or Big Brothers to Black youngsters. They work on voter registration and welfare reform, lobby for economic equity, protest apartheid, help run programs for teenage mothers, dropouts, and drug users. Powell says, "Sharing those activities and having one foot in the ghetto and one foot in The Man's world can make people very close friends."

Bernice Powell's friendships remind me of the middle-class Black clubwomen of the late nineteenth and the early twentieth century who are described in Paula Giddings' celebrated book *When and Where I Enter: The Impact of Black Women on Race and Sex in America*. In taking on "a race-conscious mission" to educate and empower their people, these women developed friendships that were special "because they were working together in the trenches, founding Black schools, working for suffrage, withstanding all kinds of abuse, but also sharing in the fruits of their labor when a child or woman moved forward."[26]

Claudette, a psychologist, talked about how having a multi-leveled vision affects her friendships. "Middle-class Blacks have to be tri-cultural: We have to be sensitive to the white world, the Black world, and the class issues in both worlds. Take my schizophrenic reaction to being confronted by a wino or some other antisocial, threatening-looking Black man in the street. I have three simultaneous responses: One, I'm ashamed because I see him as white people see him—as a living stereotype; two, I'm angry at white society, which is in many ways responsible for his condition; and three, I'm angry at the man because I think you should work hard and do better even if the odds are against you. When I'm with a Black friend, I can express any of those three responses and my friend will understand that the one I show isn't my only one. A white person would misinterpret and oversimplify my reaction and thereby distort it."

Black friends can rely on the bonds of common experience, Claudette says. "For instance, if I bring a girlfriend to one of my family's big gatherings, she might meet a relative of mine who's a doctor and another one who's a welfare mother or an ex-convict. If my friend is Black, chances are she comes from the same kind of mixed-up background or that she would understand at least that there's tremendous variety in American Black families because Black progress has been so erratic in the last two generations. But a white friend would probably find it very bizarre and I'd feel embarrassed."

In her experience, Claudette adds, Blacks of all classes express friendship differently than do most whites. "We have a long tradition of socializing at home rather than going out with friends, partly because we were poor—there was no Black bourgeoisie until World War II—and partly because segregation didn't allow us access to many places."

I ask if she sees a particular Black social style.

"Our relationships are more physical," she replies. "We drape our arms around each other or trade friendly slaps. We communicate with our eyes or with the pitch of our voices. We have a large vocabulary of facial expressions and body language that can escalate emotionally from a tilt of the head to a hard stare that says 'you gotta be kidding,' to looks that 'kill,' to physical confrontation."

That anger has a different meaning in Black relationships was mentioned by many people. "Loud verbal contests are a recurrent part of those social occasions during which the men regard themselves as 'having a good time,'" Ulf Hannerz wrote of men in the urban ghetto. "The arguments at times result in violence [but]. . . . Fleeting contests like these leave no trace in the continued relationships between peers which seem elastically enough defined to allow such momentary shows of aggression."[27]

Both the volatility and the elasticity appear in a university setting as readily as in the ghetto. "We express anger in dramatic, explosive terms and know it will blow over and be forgotten," says a Black academic. "But it drives white administrators up the wall. They exaggerate the threat of Black anger because they don't understand that you just have to wait it out. Sometimes, we even put out a more extreme position than we feel, just for emphasis. When a Black gets mad at you, you hear it right away. Whites are just the opposite. As they're sharpening their knives, they smile and say 'let's have lunch.' Next thing you know, you have a hole in your gut."

Claudette agrees that loud confrontational anger doesn't destroy friendship among Blacks. "For whites, it's frightening, for us it's cultural adaptation. Don't forget, a white person can call the police and assume they'll be on his or her side; a Black person can't. When you don't have the resources of law or other institutions at your disposal to express your feelings or save face or get help, intimidation becomes your best defense. I think that's why Blacks tolerate more expressions of hostility in friendship."

A practice that institutionalizes friendly hostility at an early age is "doing the dozens"—also called "signifying," "sounding," or "joning"—a kind of initiation rite among young Blacks (boys more than girls). "The dozens" is an exchange of claiming and debunking that youngsters use to make contact, check out one another's vulnerability, and test their wit and verbal acuity. Its goal is one-upmanship; its by-product is laughter.

"You mama, she so skinny, if she swallow a bee, she look six months' pregnant."
"Well, you mama, she so fat, when she sit around the house, honey, she sit *around* the house."

Gabe, an elected official, says Black men move on to adult forms of verbal parrying and insult repartee. They usually learn to steer clear of mother-defamation, but at heart they're still doing the dozens, no matter how educated or successful they are. Away from white people, Gabe and his friends relax by "talkin' Black," he says, referring to an oral culture refined in various kinds of joking, gibing, slang, and the adoption of exaggerated accents. "Even college professors do it. It's a signal we're among friends and we know who we are no matter where we're at in the white world."

Claudette believes these "articulation rituals" are important because Black men do not have as many ways to measure their manhood as do white men. "They can't really compete in terms of wages or possessions or economic power, so they compete on outverbalizing whites," she says. "The image of the smooth-talking Black man fits E. Franklin Frazier's observation that Black men tend to develop more distinctive personalities than white men. Think of Muhammad

Ali or Jesse Jackson as opposed to the much blander Ingemar Johansson or Walter Mondale. Black men use talk to impress friends, seduce women, and outmaneuver whites."

"The skill of talking well is widely appreciated among ghetto men," noted Hannerz; "although it is hardly itself a sign of masculinity, it can be very helpful in realizing one's wishes. 'Rapping,' persuasive speech, can be used to manipulate others to one's own advantage. . . . A man with good stories well told and with a quick repartee in arguments is certain to be appreciated for his entertainment value."[28]

Bill Tatum, publisher and chairman of the *Amsterdam News,* also emphasizes the power of talk. "With Black friends I can use a shorthand language to describe a wider range of conditions or emotions. I can say something is 'boss' or 'Baby, that's righteous,' and a Black will understand me. We have a long history of coded communication. It was a mark of solidarity and a means of survival. When the slaves sang 'Go tell it on the mountain,' they weren't only singing about God or Jesus, they were passing messages; they were planning insurrection.

"To us, tone and circumstance mean more than words alone. For instance, take the word 'motherfucker.' When I'm walking down the street with a white woman and some white guy grumbles 'You motherfucker,' I hear it a lot differently than when a Black friend slaps my palm and says 'Hey, you old mu'fucka!' The same is true of the word 'nigger.' It's an insult from a white and in some tones from a Black. But it can also be a term of affection between Black friends. We have a saying, 'you my nigger if you don't git no bigger; and even if you git any bigger, you still my bigger nigger.' That means I'll take you any way you come."

Tatum has strong, thoughtful views on friendship and a great many affiliations of all descriptions. Of his four closest friends, two are Black (both women) and two are white (a woman and a man). "It troubles me that I number no Black men among my dearest friends," he admits. "I have enormous problems getting close to Black men. Many have a chip on their shoulder and so much rage inside. When Black males get together, the first issue between them is always, 'Let's talk about what Whitey done to me lately?' While I am well aware of what Whitey has done, I won't let it take over my life. Besides, there are some white people I truly love."

Others who have spoken honestly about the problems besetting

Black friendship have cited conflicts that seemingly center on one's place of origin but actually have more to do with differing regional economic histories and sociopolitical responses to racism.

Frank, a southern-reared New York City Black, says, "Poll the Black leadership in any city and I'll bet 90 percent were born in the South. Southerners are fighters. We knew we had to work for our freedom; northern Blacks thought they already were free. New England Blacks are the most uptight and assimilated. Racism is the same everywhere but Blacks aren't."

Holding opposite regional generalizations is a Black civil rights worker who was born in Detroit and now lives in Georgia. He says he finds southern Blacks too weak and accommodating: "There's been a brain drain down here because the best Blacks went North to better themselves. In the two years I've been down here, I haven't made any friends that match my relationships up North."

Another schism that affects intra-Black friendship was described to me by several Caribbean-born Blacks who feel estranged from American-born Blacks, whether from the North or South. Cecilia, who came from Jamaica, teaches high school math and runs a tutoring service on the side. "Caribbeans are different. In our countries, Blacks are the majority," she explains. "Self-rule has given us self-esteem, leadership models, and a tradition of business ownership."

"I stay with my own kind," says Nigel, a co-owner of an office supplies store. "I can't be bothered with people who are always bitching about the white man keeping them down while they are just sitting on their butts. Trinidadians have no use for folks who think the world owes them a living."

Griselda, a 42-year-old Brooklyn housekeeper, was born in Barbados. Although she has both Caribbean and American-born friends, she thinks common values make the island people closer. "We talk about life, kids, what a penny used to buy, the way the world is changing with drugs and computers and all. We do with what we have and don't worry none about what we don't have."

Griselda's best friend is another Barbadian, Gwen, whose husband died fifteen years ago, leaving her with seven children to rear alone. "Watching Gwen has helped me raise my daughter," says Griselda, describing an extended family relationship familiar to single mothers everywhere. "I bring Gwen my problems and she puts me on the right track, like she always told me how you have to keep the lines of communication open with your kids or you lose them. I've followed her advice and sure enough my daughter and I get along real well. She's a good student and she don't take drugs."

A number of Blacks of Caribbean origin say they offer instant friendship to new arrivals, helping them get settled, find work, and deal with immigration. Griselda, who is now a U.S. citizen, told me about another friend who was an illegal immigrant from an island in the Lesser Antilles. "She and I are not very close, but when the government caught up with her, I signed a paper saying I'll be financially responsible for her until her green card comes through. I help her out because she has a new baby to feed and her nephew needs books for school. Everyone needs help to get a start."

Latin Perspectives

"Before we can think about Latino *friendship*, we have to ask what is *Latino?*" cautions David Hayes Bautista, a specialist in health policy at the University of California at Berkeley. "Is it language? Which language? We speak Spanish, French, Portuguese, or Indian dialects, depending on where we come from. Is it race? Then are we Black, Asian, or Indian? Our class divisions are sharp and strict. There are tremendous differences by rural and urban origin, by regional or national identity, and by nativity. Mexicans think Cubans behave weirdly; Puerto Ricans think Brazilians are odd; Argentinians see themselves as a piece of Europe, they see Mexicans as a bunch of Indians whooping it up, and Brazil as a Black ghetto. The Hispanos in northern New Mexico, whose ancestors arrived in 1590, regard themselves as having nothing in common with either the more recently arrived Mexican-Americans from the Los Angeles barrio or Mexicans from Mexico. So what do we mean by Latino cultural identity?

"My colleagues and I have argued this question into the ground and we still have no answer, yet when we are outside our culture we know we have crossed a boundary."

I ask Bautista for an example relevant to friendship.

"A party," he answers. "At an Anglo party, you have a group of adults who eat hors d'oeuvres, drink, talk for a while, and go home. At a Latino party, the table is groaning with food, there is animated conversation, someone plays a guitar, you sing and dance. Whole families are there, grandparents, babies, kids running around, and there's a great emphasis on relationships.

"To us, friendship is a big deal. When someone comes over to your house, you don't just put an extra cup of water in the soup. Latinos practice more social interaction. They don't get together with their friends every six months; instead, they have lunch or dinner together once or twice a week. The *abrazo* (embrace) is commonplace among male friends once they feel any degree of familiarity. Argentinians go even further: The men kiss each other on the mouth. We often joke about how if you try to give Anglo men a hug or a kiss, they stiffen and back away. Among Latinos, it is legitimate for a man to cry; he shouldn't be a crybaby, but anyone who doesn't demonstrate emotion is considered a weird bird. Of course, it's not okay to express weakness, that wouldn't be *macho*."

I have a long telephone conversation with Maxine Baca Zinn, a Chicana who teaches at the University of Michigan and writes on sex roles, race, and ethnic relations. "Between Hispanics from New York, New Mexico, and San Francisco, there are greater similarities than differences," she says. "Our ethnicity is broad enough—in the way we experience the world and how it treats us—so that long-term friendships can develop between Chicanos and other Latinos. The only problem might be class differences; for instance, a working-class Chicana would have no hesitation about inviting me in for a meal; she'd set out her best dishes for me. But a middle-class Chicana might have some feeling of apology about her situation because I am an academic and the Hispanic middle class is still very tenuous and self-conscious.

"Our friendships reflect the we/they feelings that most of us have in the United States. Chicanos are a racial ethnic group, a people of color who have been colonized. We need ethnic friendship for cultural regeneration, for like-self affirmation of our roots, sometimes even for survival. Our *compadrazgo* system provides for godparents and co-parents, who have more social than religious significance. They are friends who will take care of you and your children in times of need when the rest of your family can't. I am a scholar and a modern woman, but in a crisis, what matters to me is being Mexican and having compadres."

Hilton Nuñez, a building superintendent and co-owner of a grocery store, was born in the Dominican Republic, came here in 1969 at the age of 17, and is now in the process of becoming a citizen. His family comes first, he tells me, referring to his wife, also a Dominican, and three children, ages 10, 7, and 5. After them, come his friends at the Los Bravos Bowling Club, which operates bowling and softball teams and offers games and socializing at its clubhouse. About 300 people belong for a $50 membership fee and $15 a month dues.

"Many Friday nights we go bowling at about 9 p.m. and then end up at the clubhouse for Bingo, Ping-Pong, or pool," he says. "We do everything in family groups. When my wife and I have people to our apartment, they come with their children. The men talk to the men, the women talk to the women, and the kids play among themselves. The men are crazy to talk about baseball because about forty-five major league players are from my country. And we talk about women when our wives are not listening. The women talk about kids and men, but also about their problems. The only problems I would tell another man are money problems. I can always get financial help from my friends."

"I just came back from a weekend at a campsite in the Catskill Mountains that attracts Hispanic working-class people with a middle-class vacation style," says Aida Alvarez, vice president of Public Affairs for the New York City Health and Hospitals Corporation. "I went to be in the great outdoors but I must have been thinking in an Anglo mode. I forgot what happens when you get that many Latino families in one place. They dragged me from trailer to trailer, saying, 'Have a soda, have a beer, sit down, spend a while.' Latinos are seriously offended when their invitations are refused, so I spent my outdoorsy weekend inside visiting."

Alvarez, who came to the United States from Puerto Rico at the age of 1, recently returned to her hometown of Aguadilla for the first time in fifteen years.

"What struck me is how much I am a part of that world even though I have been a professional for years." By "that world" she means a generalized Puerto Rican society in which women friends walk hand in hand and children are greatly valued.

"The kids are everywhere—they sit on laps, they eat with you, they just blend in and you don't think 'Hey, this is a 9-year-old speaking so why should I listen.' People actually pay attention to what children say.

"Family is my cultural base. I talk to my parents every day. When

I gave a housewarming for my apartment, I invited my mother and sister, and all my New York City TV and reporter friends were surprised. An Anglo single woman doesn't usually have her family to her parties. But I don't think I could have *just* friends."

Class, color, and nationality are woven into Angie Smith's reminiscences about her friendships. For her first eighteen years, she was a child of privilege in an upper-class Puerto Rican family. Then she came to the United States for college and stayed on. Now married to an American and the mother of four children, she is also an interior designer who shuttles between New York and Tokyo.

"At home I was very different from my cousins and friends. I wasn't your typical Spanish girl; I was outspoken and interested in a career and the big issues of life. My girlfriends were superficial. They talked about clothes and giggled about boys and sex.

"Our parents didn't allow us to go to the beach. All of us were light-skinned and there's a premium on light skin among Puerto Ricans. They didn't want us to get a tan, so we never learned to swim. Imagine, we grew up on an island and we never learned to swim.

"Everyone had their national prejudices too. After the Castro revolution, a lot of Cubans came to Puerto Rico but there was very little mixing. Puerto Ricans resented them because the ones who came were extremely arrogant and wealthy. 'Did Cuba have any poor people?' we wondered."

For a charming view of friendship among poor Cubans, look to Fresh Pond, a housing complex for the elderly in North Miami. "More spontaneous socializing occurs among the Cubans than among the Blacks or Anglos," say two observers of the scene. "A direct personal network links all the Cubans, in all the buildings, to one another. They call to friends from the windows; drop over to chat; spend hours on the phone. The two self-appointed Cuban gardeners greet everyone who passes. As part of this conversational flow, what we call the Morning Mop-Shaking Ritual has developed. Around 10:30 a.m. a Cuban woman appears on her porch to shake her mop. Soon another woman, also shaking a mop, appears on a nearby porch and they start chatting. Suddenly, a number of others appear on their respective porches, all shaking mops and calling to one another. This ritual lasts about fifteen minutes."

The Cuban Domino Game, a more organized social ritual, is the only activity that "has operated continuously since Fresh Pond was opened. Monday and Friday nights, five to ten Cuban men play a serious but friendly game of dominoes for small stakes. The lively game requires four vociferous fans to every three players."[29]

"I grew up in a large working-class Mexican-American family where people made very quick judgments about others," says Patricia Zavella, an anthropologist. "After one meeting, for instance, you might be characterized as a 'slime dog.' My old friends are quick to object if I use academic jargon or big words. With my Chicano friends who are professionals I can relax in terms of class compatibility but their Latino sexism still gets on my nerves."

Zavella describes other features of Chicano friendships. "When we greet each other after an absence, we spend more time in a hug than Anglos do; I always notice that my Anglo friends detach from a hug a split second sooner than feels right to me." She says Chicano men tend to have fewer friends than do the women; nor do they speak about their friendships with any depth of emotion, whereas the women make a point of emphasizing how much they rely on their friends. Hispanics who meet for the first time go through a ritual of self-disclosure, asking each other where they are from and what they do. "The answers immediately evoke a reaction," she says. "Mexicans look down at Chicanos as *pochos;* they think we don't speak the language well and don't really know our Mexican heritage. Working-class Mexican-Americans look down at Mexican immigrants because they don't know American ways. Educated Mexican-Americans look *up* to Mexicans because they come from the homeland and the cradle of our culture. Chicanos from Texas identify as Mexicans because they interact with those from south of the border, whereas people from southern California identify more as Mexican-American. New Mexicans, regardless of class, possess an inner sense of worth because they've been on this continent since before the Europeans. Add to this the differences in Spanish accents and in regional dress and you can see why many Hispanics are not likely to meet each other in the first place, much less become friends."

Carole Hill, who studied ethnicity in Atlanta, found sharp class and nationality divisions among the mixed Latin American population, the city's largest ethnic group other than Blacks. The more affluent Latins organized themselves into the Spanish-American council, a cultural-professional association. The less affluent founded the Hispanic Society, basically a social service agency. The affluent identify with white society, seek roles in the white power structure, and don't want Latin identity to be associated with the poor. In the lower socioeconomic levels where survival issues take precedence, people have tried to use ethnic identity to unite across class and origins so all Latins can prosper. Whether they can form friendships that subordinate class to culture Hill says is an open question.[30]

Asian Perspectives

Judith Klein, a clinical psychologist who specializes in ethnotherapy, has many Asian-American clients who are dealing with the effects of their racial and cultural heritage on their emotional lives. "Coming from very strong shame cultures, the men feel relieved to get things off their chests in therapy because they do not confide in one another," she says. "Most of them are highly achievement-oriented, trying to make it in U.S. society and to overcome memories of fathers who were houseboys and menials. Whatever energy they have left after work goes to dealing with their families. They have little time or inclination for friendship. The women have *action* friendships; they help each other, they do for each other, but they're not big talkers either."

"It all depends on which generation you're referring to," says Sasha Hohri, a foundation field director and a *Sansei* (third-generation Japanese-American). "The *Issei* [first generation] stay with each other because of the language barrier and their unfamiliarity with American culture. Both Issei and Nisei [second generation] consider most Americans really rude and self-promoting, so they're not that eager to mix.[31]

"Probably the thing that most influences friendship for the Nisei is the Japanese-American concentration camp experience," she continues. "They feel they have to stick together, not necessarily out of choice but out of an inability to trust others. They do not feel safe here. Americans admire Japanese technology and business techniques and we're proud of that, but we're also afraid of the anti-Asian violence that has erupted around the issue of Japanese imports. Such incidents convince Japanese-Americans of the need for keeping tight within our own group."

Hohri says that when Japanese socialize, which is not very often, their gatherings are more subdued than most American get-togethers, and certain traditional rules of courtesy apply no matter what the class of the participants.

"I don't like all the constraints on our behavior, but if the Japanese-American community means anything to you, you have to learn the art of self-deprecation," she explains. "You always have to think about other people, not just in the sense of trying to please but in the sense of telling yourself over and over what my parents told me a million times: 'You are not the center of the universe.' That is supposed to be our guiding principle."

When I mention the research about how rarely Japanese compliment one another, Hohri exclaims: "Oh, yes. If a friend says something nice about you, you're supposed to say, 'No, no, that's not true.' You're not to draw attention to yourself; it's too disruptive. Japanese society is highly structured and stratified, everyone has a role to play. No one is supposed to stand out."

Bartender Charlie Chin emphasizes what a problem it is to describe Chinese relationships in terms of American ideas of friendship. "The big difference is how much blood and geography counts to us. One of the first things we know is that we are part of a group related to other groups. For the Chinese to feel comfortable, they want to know where you stand and where they stand. The word 'friend' is much too simple for these relations.

"Our first responsibility is to our family, then our extended family (which can be enormous), then our village relations, then occupational brotherhoods. Also, if two people have the same last name there is automatic warmth and obligations between you. I can ask a member of my clan for anything; they know I will bend over backwards for them. Because Americans consider themselves not as members of a group but as individuals, they see only our obligations, not the pleasures of belonging.

"We have different ideas of intimacy. The Chinese style of being polite is considered stuck-up or standoffish by Americans, but we think it presumptuous to do otherwise. For instance, a friend of mine was insulted when other friends joked about his love relationships and called him a 'ladies' man.' He thought it degrading. He discussed his feelings with one friend who he knew would tell everyone else. That way, he made his objections known without a confrontation."

Elizabeth Tejada, a bookkeeper and business manager, came from the Philippines in 1973 at age 18. When I ask her what ethnic issues are relevant to Filipino friendship, she speaks of competitiveness between people from different regions, of language barriers, and of the tensions between modern and traditional ways: "If you want to spend Christmas with your friends, Anglo or otherwise, or you hang out a lot with them, the older generation says, 'Aha, now you're an American,' and they mean it as an insult."

Tejada also says Filipinos do not accept the idea of men and women being friends. "Besides her husband, a woman can be friends only with a male relative or the husband of a woman friend," she explains. "With anyone else, it's assumed to be an affair. My mother has given up scolding me for my friendships with men. 'I just don't know where I went wrong with you,' she says."

Communication among Filipinos can be difficult because the older generation speaks Spanish, the national language is Tagalog, of which there are many dialects, and English is the main language taught in the schools.

"My friends and I speak 'Taglish,' " laughs Tejada. "Rarely does anyone say a complete sentence that is either all English or all Tagalog. About three-quarters of my friends are Filipinos of my generation who share the same speaking style and the same politics. I was a member of the Coalition Against the Marcos Dictatorship and I'm active in the American women's movement. I protest Filipino regionalism because internal divisions make it harder to organize for social change. When I attend a gathering of my parents' traditional friends, I always try to change some of their backward thinking. I always mix friendship and politics."

Jewish Perspectives

Jews have been variously defined as a religion, a race, and an ethnic group. As a Jew myself, I have always felt most comfortable with the term "a people," which stuffs an admixture of theological, historical, experiential, and ethnic identity into one kreplach. However, the interactions of class, regionalism, national origin, language, and degree of religious practice make it as hard to talk about "Jews" as a single entity as it is to generalize about Latins.

Jewish friendship patterns vary, depending on whether your first language is English, Yiddish, Hebrew, or some other tongue. It depends on whether you live in a Lower East Side housing project, an affluent suburb like Shaker Heights, or a small town in Tennessee. (The tendency to be conscious of their Jewish identity is more likely to occur among small-town Jews than among urban Jews, and small-town Jews are more involved with one another.) It also depends on

whether you're an *Our Crowd* German-Jewish aristocrat with four
or more generations of American-born children, or descended from
the great wave of East European immigration, or a more recent
newcomer from one of the Arab countries, the Soviet Union, Israel,
or Ethiopia. And it depends on whether you define "Jewish" to mean
religiously Orthodox, Conservative, Reform, or Reconstructionist
and whether you include your historiopolitical identity—that is,
whether you are motivated by post-Holocaust consciousness and
concern for Israel's survival or simply call yourself "an American."

Despite this morass of variables, there are some generalizations
to be made about Jews and friendship. Actually, it's more like the
old joke: Where there are two Jews there are at least three generalizations, and some are even statistically grounded.

Steven M. Cohen, a sociologist who polls Jewish attitudes and
behavior, found that most Jews have many more Jewish friends than
Jewish coworkers and neighbors. In other words, the more intimate
the relationship, the more Jewish the network. Looked at another
way, Jews, like other ethnic groups, exhibit homophily in friendship,
but, unlike other ethnic groups, they do not necessarily choose to
live and work among their own kind. This may be a measure of the
particular Jewish schizophrenia of being economically assimilated but
psychosocially ghettoized or it may just prove that there are not
enough Jews to go around.

"I see three interaction styles among Jews," Cohen said in an
interview. "The first belongs to my father's generation of relatively
uneducated petit bourgeoisie. When the men are with their friends,
they talk about their businesses and how successful they are; the
women tell each other their feelings and experiences, compare information about vacations, restaurants, or clothing; and both women
and men trot out the achievements of their children.

"The second style belongs to the educated younger people: the
Wall Street genius, the head of cardiology at some prestigious hospital, the brilliant libel lawyer. Their friendships are based on doing
things and having things, not on playing with ideas, but I am eth-
nocentric enough to believe that they are still more socially conscious
than the average gentile yuppie.

"The third group, the intellectuals, do with subtlety what my
father's generation does flagrantly. They let you know what they've
got, only it's a grant or a new book, not a store or factory, and they
seem blasé about it.

"At the end of any evening with friends, my wife will tell me how I managed to drop forty-two names of articles, books, and people. To me, it's not impression management, it's inadvertent. I tell her, 'I'm not proving I'm smart; I *am* smart and these are the subjects that interest me. *This* is how I socialize.' "

Ethnotherapist Judith Klein told me Jewish men practice a version of "the dozens," which is based on intellectual one-upmanship: "They'll trade references to a recent article in *The New Republic* or *Mother Jones* or make fun of some important political figure. The question they seem to have to settle between themselves is 'How much can we commit to irony together?' "

Steven Cohen says that his three closest friends are all intellectual and Jewish-identified but in different ways: "Harry, who is the most stereotypical in terms of Jewish mannerisms and political radicalism, gives me the most emotional nurturance, but I can't count on him to follow through for me, say with the Motor Vehicles Bureau. He's disorganized but wonderful to talk with. We talk on the phone. We meet for late-night walks to talk. We arrange our teaching schedules so we can be together.

"Arlene is an enlightened Modern Orthodox woman with a very religious background. Though I can't plug in to her kind of spirituality, we have shared many Jewish-located experiences and talked endlessly about Jewish public affairs and organizational issues.

"Sam was born in a displaced persons camp, went to Columbia University, is very leftist, very politically sophisticated. We talk about progressive Jewish causes, our families and careers; we borrow each other's house and car.

"With all my friends, what I like to do best is talk."

Not every Jew is as consciously and deeply embedded in the Jewish community as are Cohen and his friends, but for those who are, relationships can be made and broken over a person's positions on the key issues of the day: Israeli politics, affirmative action, Palestinian self-determination, and the ordination of women rabbis, to name a few. And if conflicting opinions can be divisive, differing degrees of religious observance can make friendship impossible. Jews who don't "keep kosher" cannot easily invite a kosher friend for a meal at home. And those who observe the dietary laws and the laws of the Sabbath and holidays cannot join friends at a public restaurant or double-date on a Friday night or go for a drive on Saturday. Thus, an orthodox and a reform Jew might be completely stymied in their friendship by the fact that they lead such different lives.

Just as in-group friendship is a symbol of ethnic affirmation, *avoidance* of one's own kind is a sign of self-hatred, says Klein. "Although people may not connect the two facts, those who have trouble with their own Jewishness generally do not have a lot of Jewish friends."

My interviews yielded many Jews who said they were not conscious of the role their Jewishness played in their social lives, but I found none who had no Jewish friends whatsoever. Sociologist Rela Geffen Monson found more than half the Jewish college students she questioned said "all or most" of their close friends were Jews, while only 3 percent said they had no close Jewish friends at all.[32] The students who were most likely to have all or mostly Jewish friends were those who had attended Hebrew school or Jewish youth groups and who were reared by parents who observed Jewish law and were involved in the Jewish community.

Judith Klein, who described typical Jewish contact gestures as "sharing neuroses . . . complaining and exchanging self-deprecating humor" and spoke of Jewish men's verbal competitiveness, says this about Jewish women: "Personal revelations that members of another ethnic group would only share with old and intimate friends, Jewish women will exchange in the act of *getting* to know one another. Traditional Jewish women are very comfortable talking about themselves as nurturers or participants in relationships. Intellectual Jewish women might talk in terms of opinions and ideas, but they also can get impacted taking care of the emotional stuff. In general, Jewish women could do with a lot more attention to the outer world."

Judging from Marv's experiences, Jewish men can get just as buried in "emotional stuff." When he lived in New York City in the early seventies, Marv belonged to a consciousness-raising group of seven Jewish men who met weekly for three years to deal with every aspect of being male. "There were no taboos. The group's level of involvement was so deep that we sometimes got stuck in the groove of emotional pain. When one of the men came out as a homosexual, the rest of us spent seven or eight months supporting him and helping him deal with telling his wife.

"About eight years ago I moved out West and joined a men's group in which I was the only Jew. The difference was remarkable. In the non-Jewish group, suffering wasn't accepted. These were very

physical, very pleasure-oriented men. They could admit sexual inadequacy sooner than fear or anxiety. There was a lot of denial of
emotional pain in the interest of getting on with life. So there was
no catharsis. They also didn't put much of a premium on monogamy.
As a husband and father in that group, I felt my ethnic difference
keenly. My non-Jewish friends out here seem much less self-sacri-
ficing. They expect independence and autonomy from their kids.
The men in the New York Jewish group had been more involved
with their wives and children and more concerned about giving them
material things."

Marsha, a homemaker and mother of four, has no non-Jewish
friends. "I don't cross paths with them," she explains. "We live in
a Jewish suburb, my children go to Yeshiva, and my husband works
in the garment business, which is mostly Jewish. We go to our
synagogue every Friday night and Saturday morning. My husband
has his Sunday morning bagel breakfasts at the Jewish Center and I
belong to Hadassah and Sisterhood. Once in a while I get together
with some other ladies to play cards or Scrabble, or we go to the
lectures sponsored by the synagogue, but not very often.

"My husband and I both come from big families. We visit each
other's houses about once a month. It's nothing to have sixteen people
sitting down to a five-course meal, two or three generations with
babies in playpens and grandparents and great-grandparents. With
my four kids and all these relatives, I don't have much time left for
friends."

Bea, a union organizer, is a veteran of every social movement of
the last twenty years—civil rights, anti-war, feminism, gay rights,
and now the nuclear freeze—but she has never been involved in
Jewish causes and is not affiliated with a synagogue. Nevertheless,
she says she feels "very Jewish," and most of her friends are Jews.

"I can't put my finger on what attracts me to other Jews, but I
know it when I see it," she laughs. "Maybe it's the cultural and
political thing; once I'm at home with that, it's much easier for the
emotional intimacy to follow. I guess what appeals to me most is
Jewish humor. And the way we talk fast and get excited about issues.
Jews interrupt each other without getting insulted. We enjoy a good
argument. I also like the idea that when I talk about the Rosenbergs
or the Hollywood Ten, my Jewish friends know what I'm talking
about and agree with my politics. And when I say I'm making grie-

bens [crisp rendered chicken fat] or haroses [chopped apples, nuts, and wine—a ritual dish for Passover], they salivate along with me. Lots of Americans have eaten knishes or chopped liver, but only a Jew knows from griebens and haroses."

Other Ethnic Perspectives

As I spoke with other minority group members, I was struck by the many different interpretations of the connection between ethnic identity and friendship. Some people saw their ethnic heritage as the *cause* of their way of practicing friendship. Others viewed their friends as the link to their ethnicity. And still others described their concept of friendship as inseparable from their ethnic identity.

Pat Walsh and Anne Keegan share a fierce and spirited Irish identity in the context of their friendship. "Christmas is my religious Holy Day but St. Patrick is my ethnic holiday," says Anne. "Every March 17, Pat and I wear our green and watch the parade from the steps of St. Patrick's Cathedral. We watch every minute of it until the end when the old men from the Counties Galway, Dublin, Cork, and Limerick march by. Then it's back to my house for corned beef and cabbage, Irish soda bread, Irish music on the phonograph, and Irish coffee."

That reminds me. What about the stereotype of beer, booze, and Irish friendship, I ask.

"Oh, the Irish like to drink a few with friends," Anne replies. "But I don't think we're much different from, say, the Italians; they'll have wine with their soup and tortellini, and we'll have beer with our meat and potatoes."

There's a smile in her voice when Toni Lopopolo talks about the idiosyncratic Italian friendship network of her father, a California businessman-rancher who owns vineyards and an olive oil factory. "He had no family in this country but he did have his *paisans* from Bisceglie who settled in the Fresno area. They always got together for festivals, weddings, and holidays and I remember it being *wonderful*. My father's friends would dance with us little girls and there were acres of food. On the feast day after Easter, the whole group came to our ranch.

"During the Second World War, when we lived in L.A., my father started to buy horses and enter horse shows where famous actors sponsored prizes for the benefit of U.S. War Bonds. My father's horses kept winning these prizes, so he got to know a number of the Italian-American movie stars. He was befriended by Leo Carrillo, who played Pancho in *Cisco Kid,* and Lou Costello from Abbott and Costello. Then he met Robert Alda and his family and we all hit it off really well. We used to go to Italian films with them."

For Italians, says anthropologist Micaela di Leonardo, "work and ethnic identity exist in relation to one another and clients and friends are one and the same."[33]

Rudy Martin, a member of the Tewa, one of the Pueblo tribes in New Mexico, told me, "Friend is such a limited word for people who are like my spiritual brothers and sisters. We are all very respectful of each other's spaces and possessions. Good behavior is expected between people. That's why there is no word for 'thank you' in any Indian language."

Ethnicity and friendship are fused when Martin and his friends go once a month to a sweat lodge, the Indian version of a sauna. "We build a wigwam, a hogan made of branches and leaves. We fast, abstain from drinking, have a vision quest, build a fire, heat stones, and make steam. After we sweat and purify our bodies, we jump into a stream. Then we smoke the pipe of sweet grass and sage as a symbolic gesture of health and community and have a feast."

Is it easy to make friends with people from other tribes? I ask, mindful of the cliché of Indians at war with one another. "Relations between nations have never been better," he answers. "We're amiable people. We've always felt things can be worked out around the fire."

Jacqueline Showell, a member of the Shinnecock tribe, is less sanguine. "Sometimes I think the Mohawks don't want to be friends," she says. "They're very uppity. And a lot of Midwest Indians don't like East Coast Indians. My great-grandmother taught me to love everyone. I had a friend, a Chippewa from Michigan, who came here to work straight off the reservation. She wasn't used to the city, so I took her around. I baby-sat for her son. She and I had a lot in common as women. I invited her to my nation's powwow on Labor Day. We did earth dances, rain dances, bird dances. We ate samp [bean or corn soup], fry bread, and lots of seafood and rice. We smoked the peace pipe and felt together in spirit. Material things don't matter to Indians, but when she went back to the reservation I gave her my moccasins and she gave me her sacred silver earrings."

Pluralistic Friendship

The United States is home to more than 100 nationalities. About 188 million of us identify as white, 27 million as Black, 15 million as Hispanic, and 7 million as "other races." Almost a third of all Americans are of mixed ancestry. Fourteen million of us are foreign-born.[34]

Even these bare demographic facts suggest that humanity is a smorgasbord, not a stew. Rather than boil down this marvelous diversity in a "melting pot," rather than subsume our various friendships in the bland togetherness of a UNICEF card or a soft-drink commercial, I'd like to see us aspire to a "pluralistic friendship" ideal that celebrates *genuine* differences arising out of life experience and culture but rejects *socially constructed* differences resulting from stereotypes or discrimination. In rethinking what ethnicity means to friendship, consider these points:

- Ethnicity is both cognitive and economic, emotional *and* material, a self-defined label *and* an imposed status.
- Ethnicity always interacts with the historical, economic, political and social reality of a person's life.
- "Class equals culture" is a misleading precept. As we've seen, class sometimes overrides culture. Also, people who appear middle class have not necessarily lost their ethnicity.
- The texture of ethnic friendship often rests on the labor of women. Women are expected to create the festive meals and parties, the holiday celebrations, the warmth, food and closeness—the "symbolically-laden environment" that allows friendship to flourish. Some traditions can be oppressive. Yet the current wave of conservative "rhetorical nostalgia" romanticizes all tradition in the interest of preserving the sex role division of labor and the patriarchal family. It should not be mistaken for authentic cultural ethnicity and it should not justify preserving culture on the backs of women.[35]

Ethnicity is friendship-enhancing when it is not oppressive to anyone.

Ethnicity is friendship-enhancing when it does not make another group into an "Other" group.

Ethnicity is friendship-enhancing when we make it an "and," not a "but." The difference is palpable: "She's my friend *and* she's Jewish" allows me the pride of difference that a "but" would destroy.

Group identity spawns both pride *and* prejudice. What makes a group special also makes it different. For some people, "different" must mean "better" or it is experienced as "worse." But people who do not need ethnic supremacy to feel ethnic pride find comfort and cultural regeneration among their "own kind" and also are able to make friends across racial and ethnic boundaries.

It is to those relationships that we turn next.

Chapter 11

The Same and Different

Crossing Boundaries of Color, Culture, Sexual Preference, Disability, and Age

On August 21, 1985, as they had done several times before, twenty-one men from a work unit at a factory in Mount Vernon, New York, each chipped in a dollar, signed a handwritten contract agreeing to "share the money equaly [sic] & fairly to each other," and bought a ticket in the New York State Lottery. The next day, their ticket was picked as one of three winners of the largest jackpot in history: $41 million.

The story of the Mount Vernon 21 captivated millions not just because of the size of the pot of gold but because of the rainbow of people who won it. Black, white, yellow, and brown had scribbled their names on that contract—Mariano Martinez, Chit Wah Tse, Jaroslaw Siwy, and Peter Lee—all immigrants from countries ranging from Paraguay to Poland, from Trinidad to Thailand.

"We're like a big family here," said Peter Lee. "We thought by pooling our efforts we would increase our luck—and we were right."[1]

The men's good fortune is a metaphor for the possibility that friendships across ethnic and racial boundaries may be the winning ticket for everyone. This is not to say that crossing boundaries is a snap. It isn't. There are checkpoints along the way where psychic border guards put up a fuss and credentials must be reviewed. We look at a prospective friend and ask, "Do they want something from me?" Is this someone who sees personal advantage in having a friend of another race at his school, in her company, at this moment in history? Is it Brotherhood Week? Does this person understand that "crossing friendships" require more care and feeding than in-group friendship, that it takes extra work?

Explaining

Most of the extra work can be summed up in one word: *explaining*. Whatever the boundary being crossed—race, ethnicity, or any other social category—both partners in a crossing friendship usually find they have to do a lot of explaining—to themselves, to each other, and to their respective communities.

Explaining to Yourself

One way or another, you ask yourself, "What is the meaning of my being friends with someone not like me?"

In his classic study, *The Nature of Prejudice,* Gordon Allport distinguishes between the in-group, which is the group to which you factually belong, and the reference group, which is the group to which you relate or aspire.[2] Allport gives the example of Blacks who so wish to partake of white skin privilege that they seek only white friends, disdain their own group, and become self-hating. One could as easily cite Jews who assume a WASP identity or "Anglicized Chicanos" who gain education and facility in English and then sever their ties of kinship and friendship with other Mexican-Americans.[3]

When you have a friend from another racial or ethnic group, you ask yourself whether you are sincerely fond of this person or might be using him or her as an entrée into a group that is your unconscious reference group. The explaining you do to yourself helps you understand your own motivations. It helps you ascertain whether the friend complements or denies your identity, and whether your crossing friendships are in reasonable balance with your in-group relationships.

Explaining to Each Other

Ongoing mutual clarification is one of the healthiest characteristics of crossing friendships. The Black friend explains why your saying "going ape" offends him, and the Jewish friend reminds you she can't eat your famous barbecued pork. Both of you try to be honest about your cultural sore points and to forgive the other person's initial ignorance or insensitivities. You give one another the benefit of the doubt. Step by step, you discover which aspects of the other person's "in-groupness" you can share and where you must accept exclusion with grace.

David Osborne, a white, describes his close and treasured friendship with an American Indian from Montana: "Steve was tall and athletic—the classic image of the noble full-blooded Indian chief. We were in the same dorm in my freshman year at Stanford at a time when there were only one or two other Native Americans in the whole university. He had no choice but to live in a white world. Our friendship began when our English professor gave an assignment to write about race. Steve and I got together to talk about it. We explored stuff people don't usually discuss openly. After that, we started spending a lot of time together. We played intramural sports. We were amazingly honest with each other, but we were also comfortable being silent.

"When I drove him home for spring vacation, we stopped off at a battlefield that had seen a major war between Chief Joseph's tribe and the U.S. Cavalry. Suddenly it hit me that, had we lived then, Steve and I would have been fighting on opposite sides, and we talked about the past. Another time, an owl flew onto our windowsill and Steve was very frightened. He told me the owl was a symbol of bad luck to Indians. I took it very seriously. We were so in touch, so in sync, that I felt the plausibility of his superstitions. I was open to his mysticism."

Mutual respect, acceptance, tolerance for the faux pas and the occasional closed door, open discussion and patient mutual education, all this gives crossing friendships—when they work at all—a special kind of depth.

Explaining to Your Community of Origin

Accountability to one's own group can present the most difficult challenge to the maintenance of crossing friendships. In 1950 the authors of The Lonely Crowd said that interracial contact runs risks not only from whites but from Blacks who may "interpret friendliness as Uncle Tomism."[4] The intervening years have not eliminated such group censure.

In her article "Friendship in Black and White," Bebe Moore

Campbell wrote: "For whites, the phrase 'nigger lover' and for Blacks, the accusation of 'trying to be white' are the pressure the group applies to discourage social interaction."[5] Even without overt attacks, people's worry about group reaction inspires self-censorship. Henry, a Black man with a fair complexion, told me he dropped a white friendship that became a touchy subject during the Black Power years. "We'd just come out of a period when many light-skinned Negroes tried to pass for white and I wasn't about to be mistaken for one of them," he explains. "My racial identity mattered more to me than any white friend."

Black-white friendships are " 'conducted underground,' " says Campbell, quoting a Black social worker, who chooses to limit her intimacy with whites rather than fight the system. " 'I'd feel comfortable at my white friend's parties because everybody there would be a liberal, but I'd never invite her to mine because I have some friends who just don't like white people and I didn't want anybody to be embarrassed.' "

If a white friend of mine said she hated Blacks, I would not just keep my Black friends away from her, I would find it impossible to maintain the friendship. However, the converse is not comparable. Most Blacks have at some point been wounded by racism, while whites have not been victimized from the other direction. Understanding the experiences *behind* the reaction allows decent Black people to remain friends with anti-white Blacks. That these Blacks may have reason to hate certain whites does not excuse their hating all whites, but it does explain it.

For instance, several Blacks admitted feeling a diffuse anger toward white women because so many white women have had affairs with Black men; some even think that white women use their friendship with Black women as a way to meet Black men. "Every one of our men who's taken away by a white woman is felt as a serious loss," says Harriet Michel, president of the New York Urban League. Since poverty, prison, and drug addiction have created a demographic deficit of marriageable Black men and because homosexuality further depletes the pool, Michel says it's understandable that Black women become suspicious of each other's white friends.

Ethnic communities also may disapprove of outsiders. Patricia Zavella recalls the tension she felt when her best friend, an Italian-American, first showed enthusiasm for their friendship. "I was afraid to get close to her because to have a white friend is frowned upon in the Mexican-American community. But now that more and more Chicanos are becoming professionals and learning how friendships develop around mutual interests, the criticism is subsiding."

Historically, of course, the biggest enemies of boundary-crossing friendships have not been Blacks or ethnic minorities but majority whites. Because whites gain the most from social inequality, they have the most to lose from crossing friendships, which, by their existence, deny the relevance of ethnic and racial hierarchies. More important, the empowered whites can put muscle behind their disapproval by restricting access to clubs, schools, and businesses.

If you sense that your community of origin condemns one of your crossing friendships, the amount of explaining or justifying you do will depend on how conformist you are and and whether you feel entitled to a happiness of your own making.

Rejecters and Rejectees

Some people use the extra work of "explaining" as an excuse not to bother with crossing friendships at all. But for all those who stick to their own kind because it is "easier," there are many more who do so because they reject or are rejected by others. Usually, it is the dominant white group that does the rejecting, but sometimes it works the other way, and minority groups choose their own kind in preference to mixing with outsiders. Or the pattern can be more complex.

Asian students seem to have three social networks: co-nationals, "whose function is to affirm and express the culture of origin"; American classmates, who help them with their academic studies; and multinational friends, "whose main function is recreational."[6] Their friendships reflect their transitional consciousness: They have chosen a like-self group for comfort, an American group for learning the ropes of this culture, and a mixed group with whom to practice the universal pursuit of fun.

Overall, Chinese-American students have roughly a third of each kind of friendship. Interestingly, however, the students with the strongest ethnic identity tend to have more Caucasian than Chinese friends (maybe they operate from a stronger psychological base and can "afford" to expand their social circles into the white majority community). Also, the Chinese were as intimate with their white friends as they were with their Chinese friends.[7] Most likely, the two groups have become comfortable with each other because as students they share one set of values.

Much of the rejection of outsiders by immigrants has to do with having sets of values that differ from the values of the majority population and feeling estranged as a result. Rejecting others because *you* feel alien is one thing; rejecting them because you think *they* are alien is something else. This second and more common attitude is based on racial or ethnic stereotyping: the projection of negative traits onto a whole category of "Others."

To prove that they are different, that is, better than the Others, some people distance themselves from the stigmatized group, never giving themselves the opportunity to discover whether a particular member of the group may in fact be likeable or have similar interests. Of course, if they *were* to discover they were compatible with one of the Others, they could no longer believe themselves superior to the whole group. Friendship—a relationship of equals—is out of the question because affinity would prove mutual inferiority.

The dynamics of stereotyping are the subject for another book. What I'm asking here is *how can we repudiate stereotypes and at the same time honor authentic racial and ethnic distinctions* such as those discussed in the previous chapter? According to the *PT* friendship survey, not even four out of ten Americans have a close friend of a different race and fewer than half have a close friend from a different ethnic group. I'm interested in how more of us can learn to cross boundaries and find friends without losing ourselves.

Testing Your Assumptions

As we saw in Chapter 5, "The Passage to Intimacy"—and as many ethnic studies confirm—most friendship is based on a similarity of values and beliefs, not of status or personal background.[8]

Think for a moment of friends of yours: How much of your closeness is attributable to your common biographical origins as opposed to your shared values? Have you ever known someone of exactly the same racial, religious, and ethnic background with beliefs so antithetical to yours that the two of you may as well have come from different planets? If you have friends who are of another race or ethnic origin, did the two of you become friends despite your differences or because of them? Were you interesting to each other for being different or were you so similar you didn't notice?

If you don't have any crossing friendships, think about whether you have enough opportunities to interact in positive ways with people of different racial or ethnic groups. Friendship needs proximity, but under favorable conditions. Under *unfavorable* conditions, such as job competition or in a tense, polarized neighborhood, frequent contact can actually increase prejudice and resistance. Have you been in pleasant circumstances with people who are different from yourself? That is the more accurate test of your receptivity to crossing friendships.

What happens to your ruminations when you try to tease out the influence of class? Does being at the same socioeconomic level "smooth out" the racial or ethnic differences between you and your friends? If you have no friend to whom to apply this question, imagine that you are an educated affluent Latin. Do you think you would have more in common with another Latin person who is an uneducated member of the working class or with an educated affluent Anglo? And if class, race, and ethnicity aren't marble cake enough, what happens when religion is added to the mix? Would an Italian-Catholic engineering student more likely be friends with *any* Catholic with an eighth-grade education or with a Jew from her engineering class? And would that modern second-generation Jew have more in common with her modern second-generation Italian classmate or with a Jewish immigrant who is Orthodox?

Class vs. Race vs. Ethnicity

Although it's easy to understand how class differs from culture, experts cannot agree on which factor is more controlling in friendship formation. It's a hard call but I see class, race, ethnicity, and religion as *interactive* influences with class outweighing race in some situations (and gender outweighing them all).

Specifically, Blacks and whites seem to get along well in residential communities where they are "similar in socioeconomic level and in the visible cultural aspects of class." South African academics developed better racial-ethnic attitudes and more intergroup friendship when whites and "coloureds" of equal status had regular professional contact.[9] And if American whites have occupational and residential contact with Blacks of equal or higher status, they become "more friendly, less fearful and less stereotyped in their views" than whites in segregated situations.[10]

Class also overrules ethnicity, says a researcher who studied friendship in a mixed community in Newfoundland. "Ethnicity is more a question of personal predilection and choice, while class serves as a constraint. And while class divisions are a result of structural barriers, ethnicity is not."[11] I take issue with that analysis on two grounds: first, because being a *racial* ethnic, say, a dark-skinned Indian or Latin, is not a matter of "personal predilection and choice," and second, because race and ethnicity are often intertwined and because racism erects structural barriers that are at least as impermeable as class barriers.

During a high school trip to the Soviet Union, Matt Spector became friends with a Puerto Rican boy, a talented break-dancer. "We were in a neutral environment with nothing around to define our differences, no big house versus small house, no private versus public school. In Russia we were just two Americans."

In this country, as historian Bonnie Thornton Dill points out, racial structures have taken on "a life of their own and cannot now be considered merely reflections of class structure."[12] If racial bias can still undercut the benefits of education for Blacks, the "complex connection" between race and class must be accounted for. While accounting for it, I cannot ignore the evidence that class commonalities can surmount other differences and make friendship possible.

Double Consciousness

"Possible" doesn't mean easy. To maintain crossing friendships that do not compromise their respective identities, two friends must honor both their similarities and differences. This balancing act requires a double consciousness that is expressed succinctly in these lines attributed to poet Pat Parker:

> For the white person who wants to know
> how to be my friend
> The first thing you do is to forget I'm Black.
> Second, you must never forget that I'm Black.

This position is seconded by a Black woman who told Campbell: "If you don't see color, then you don't see the essence of me." The message: Be color-blind *and* color-conscious. Remember we are both human beings. The same. But also remember that I am different and special in my way. The same and different. That double consciousness is the hallmark of crossing friendships.

The Same but Never Quite the Same

"I go coon hunting with Tobe Spencer," said former police officer L. C. Albritton about his Black friend in Camden, Alabama. "We're good friends. We stay in town during the day for all the hullabaloo and at night we go home and load up the truck with three dogs and go way down into the swamps. We let the dogs go and sit on a log, take out our knives and a big chew of tobacco . . . and just let the rest of the world go by."

Looking at a picture of himself and Spencer taken in 1966, Albritton mused: "It's funny that a police officer like me is standing up there smiling and talking to a nigger because we were having marches and trouble at that time. . . . Old Tobe Spencer—ain't nothing wrong with that nigger. He's always neat and clean as a pin. He'll help you too. Call him at midnight and he'll come running just like that."[13]

Two friends with the same leisure-time pleasures, two men at ease together in the lonely night of the swamps. Yet race makes a difference. Not only does the white man use the derogatory "nigger," but he differentiates his friend Tobe from the rest of "them" who, presumably, are not neat and clean and helpful. *The same but never quite the same.*

Leonard Fein, the editor of *Moment,* a magazine of progressive Jewish opinion, gave me "the controlling vignette" of his cross-ethnic friendships: "An Irish-Catholic couple was among our dearest friends, but on that morning in 1967 when we first heard that Israel was being bombed, my wife said, 'Who can we huddle with tonight to get through this ordeal,' and we picked three Jewish couples. Our Irish friends were deeply offended. 'Don't you think we would have felt for you?' they asked. 'Yes,' we said, 'but it wasn't sympathy we wanted, it was people with whom, if necessary, we could have mourned the death of Israel—and that could only be other Jews.'

"The following week, when the war was over, my wife and I went to Israel. The people who came to live in our house and take

care of our children were our Irish friends. They had understood
they were our closest friends yet they could never be exactly like
us."

The eternal difference of the Jews, said Fein, is symbolized by
Shylock's speech in *The Merchant of Venice:*

"I will buy with you, sell with you,
Talk with you, walk with you and so following;
But I will not eat with you, drink with you,
Nor pray with you."

"Can we buy, sell, walk and talk with someone but not eat, drink
or pray with them, and still expect a full-fledged friendship to develop?" Fein asks. "Whether it's because of Jews' relationship to
kosher food, the synagogue, or Israel, by being different in overt
and crucial ways, by holding ourselves apart in certain contexts,
perhaps we can never totally bond with non-Jews."

For Raoul, a phenomenally successful advertising man, crossing
friendships have been just about the only game in town. He remi-
nisced with me about growing up in a Puerto Rican family in a
Manhattan neighborhood populated mostly by Irish, Italians, and
Jews:

"In the fifties I hung out with all kinds of guys. I sang on street
corners—do-wopping in the night—played kick the can, and belonged to six different basketball clubs, from the Police Athletic
League to the YMCA. My high school had 6000 kids in it—street
kids who hung out in gangs like The Beacons, The Fanwoods, The
Guinea Dukes, The Irish Lords, and The Diablos from Spanish Harlem and Jewish kids who never hung out because they were home
studying. The gang members were bullies and punks who protected
their own two-block area. They wore leather jackets and some of
them carried zip guns and knives. I managed to be acceptable to all
of them just because I was good at sports. I was the best athlete in
the school and president of the class. So I was protected by the gangs
and admired by the Jewish kids and I had a lot of friends."

Raoul's athletic prowess won him a scholarship to a large midwestern university where he was the first Puerto Rican to be en-
countered by some people. "They wanted me to sing the whole
sound track of *West Side Story*. They asked to see my switchblade.
And I was as amazed by the midwesterners as they were by me. My

first hayride was a real shock. Same with hearing people saying 'Good morning' to each other. Every one of my friends—my roommate, teammates, and fraternity brothers, Blacks from Chicago and Detroit and whites from the farms—they were all gentle and nice. And gigantic and strong. Boy, if one of them had moved into my neighborhood back home, he'd have owned the block.

"After graduation, a college friend went to work in a New York City ad agency that played in a Central Park league and needed a softball pitcher. He had me brought in for an interview. Even though I knew nothing about advertising, I was a helluva pitcher, and the owner of the agency took sports seriously. So he hired me. I always say I had the only athletic scholarship in the history of advertising. I pitched for the agency, I played basketball with the owner, and I learned the business. So I found my friends and my career through sports. Even though I may have been a Spic to most everyone, sports opened all the doors."

The same but never quite the same.

Sal, who has an Italian father and a Jewish mother, grew up in a Black neighborhood in Pittsburgh. "All my friends were Black until junior high school when my family moved south," he says. "It was a real culture shock. There were no Blacks in my new school and the whites were real WASPy and cliquish. They didn't accept me because to gain entry into that social set you had to have the WASP symbols, primarily the right clothes. First of all, I couldn't afford what they wore. And second, I didn't want to look like them. I was reading *Time* magazine and copying the Beatles who, in those days, the southern kids ridiculed as 'hippie.' Most of them knew I was Italian from my last name. Had they known I was also Jewish it would have been worse for me. One of my nonfriends did find out and he nicknamed me WEJ for Jew spelled backwards.

"In the summer I went away to a Y camp that attracted lots of Blacks from the cities. For me it was like coming home. They didn't look like me but they were more like me than all the southern whites put together."

The same but never quite the same.

"At the beginning, because of difficulties of adaptation, we immigrants protect ourselves by getting together with people from the same culture who speak the same language," says Luis Marcos, a psychiatrist, who came to the United States from Seville, Spain. "Next, when we feel more comfortable, we reach out to people who do the same work we do, mostly those who help us or those we help in some way. Then we have a basis for friendship. My mentor, the director of psychiatry at Bellevue, is a native-born American and a Jew. He helped me in my area of research and now he's one of my best friends. I also began to teach and to make friends with my medical students as they grew and advanced."

That Marcos and his friends have the health profession in common has not prevented misunderstandings. "When we first went out for meals together, my impulse was to pay for both of us," he says of another doctor, a Black woman who taught him not to leave his own behavior unexamined. "It wasn't that I thought she couldn't afford to pay; we were equally able to pick up the check. It was just that the cultural habit of paying for a woman was ingrained in my personality. But she misconstrued it. She felt I was trying to take care of her and put her down as a Black, a professional, and a woman. In order for our friendship to survive, she had to explain how she experiences things that I don't even think about."

Moving in One Another's World

Ethnotherapist Judith Klein revels in her crossing friendships. "My interest in people who are different from me may be explained by the fact that I'm a twin. Many people look to be mirrored in friendship; I've had mirroring through my sister, so I can use friendship for other things. One thing I use it for is to extend my own life. People who aren't exactly like me enhance my knowledge and experience. They let me be a vicarious voyager in their world."

As much as friends try to explain one another's world, certain differences remain particular barriers to intimacy.

Luis Marcos mentions the language barrier. "No matter how well I speak, I can never overcome my accent," he says. "And some people mistake the way I talk for lack of comprehension. They are afraid I won't understand an American joke, or if I choose to use aggressive words, they don't think I mean it, they blame my 'language problem.' "

While many Americans assume people with an accent are ignorant, many ethnics assume, just as incorrectly, that someone *without* an accent is smart. Some Americans have a habit of blaming the other person for doing or saying whatever is not understandable to Americans. Ethnics also have been known to blame their own culture—to use their "foreignness" as an excuse for behavior for which an American would have to take personal responsibility. "I can't help it if we Latins are hot-tempered" is a way of generalizing one's culpability.

Of course, the strongest barrier to friendship is outright resistance. After two years of off-and-on living in Tokyo, Angie Smith came to terms with the fact that "the Japanese do not socialize the way we do." She found, as many have, that in Japan friendship is considered an obligation more than a pleasure and is almost always associated with business.[14]

"Three times I invited two couples for dinner—the men were my husband's business associates—and three times the men came and the women didn't," Smith recalls. "They sent charming little notes with flowers, but they would not have been comfortable in our house for an evening of social conversation. Yet these same Japanese women would go out to lunch with me and tell me more intimate things than they tell each other. While we were in Japan, I just had to get used to sex-divided socializing and not having any couple friendships."

When people's differences are grounded in racism rather than alien styles of socializing, it can be especially painful to move in the other person's world.

"I felt myself a slave and the idea of speaking to white people weighed me down," wrote Frederick Douglass a century ago.[15] Today, most Blacks refuse to be weighed down by whites. They do not "need" white friends. Some doubt that true friendship is possible between the races until institutional racism is destroyed. Feminists of every shade have debated the question "Is Sisterhood Possible?" Despite the issues that affect *all* women, such as sexual violence, many Black women resist working together for social change or organizing with white women because they believe most whites don't care enough about welfare reform, housing, teen pregnancies, or school dropouts—issues that are of primary concern to Blacks.

Bell Hooks, a writer and a professor of Afro-American studies, wrote: "All too frequently in the women's movement it was assumed one could be free of sexist thinking by simply adopting the appropriate feminist rhetoric; it was further assumed that identifying oneself as oppressed freed one from being an oppressor. To a very great extent, such thinking prevented white feminists from understanding and overcoming their own sexist-racist attitudes toward black women. They could pay lip service to the idea of sisterhood and solidarity between women but at the same time dismiss black women."[16]

Phyllis Marynick Palmer, a historian, says white women are confounded by Black women's strong family role and work experience, which challenge the white stereotype of female incapacity. White women also criticize Black women for making solidarity with their brothers a priority rather than confronting Black men's sexism. In turn, Black women get angry at white women who ignore "their own history of racism and the benefits that white women have gained at the expense of black women."[17] With all this, how could sisterhood be possible? How can friendship be possible?

"I would argue for the abandonment of the concept of sisterhood as a global construct based on unexamined assumptions about our similarities," answers Dill, "and I would substitute a more pluralistic approach that recognizes and accepts the objective differences between women."

Again the word "pluralistic" is associated with friendship. An emphasis on double consciousness, not a denial of differences. The importance of feeling both the same and different, of acknowledging "the essence of me," of understanding that friends need not *transcend* race or ethnicity but can embrace differences and be enriched by them. The people who have managed to incorporate these precepts say that they are pretty reliable guidelines for good crossing friendships. But sometimes it's harder than it looks. Sometimes, the "vicarious voyage" into another world can be a bad trip.

The Hazards of Crossing

"Anglo wannabes" are a particular peeve of David Hayes Bautista. "These are Anglos who wanna be so at home with us that they try too hard to go native. For instance, Mexicans have a certain way that we yell along with the music of a mariachi band. When someone brought along an Anglo friend and he yelled 'Yahoo, Yahoo' all night, every Chicano in the place squirmed."

Maxine Baca Zinn gives the reverse perspective: of a Chicano in an Anglo environment. "Once, when I was to speak at the University of California, a Chicana friend who was there told me that the minute I walked into that white academic world my spine straightened up. I carried myself differently. I talked differently around them and I didn't even know it." Was Zinn just nervous about giving her speech or did she tighten up in anticipation of the tensions Chicanos feel in non-Hispanic settings? She's not certain.

When Charlie Chin, a bartender, started work in a new place, a white coworker quipped, "One thing you have to watch out for, Charlie, are all the Chinks around here." I winced when Chin said this, but he told me, "I just smiled at the guy. I'm used to those jokes. That's the way whites break the ice with Asians. That's the American idea of being friendly."

Anthropologist Rena Gropper remembers the problems that destroyed her friendship with a Hindu couple. "The husband was a physicist, the wife a high school teacher. They presented themselves as a modern couple but I noticed that she had no say in the household and that he expected her to serve him the minute they both came home from work. She told me she wanted to get pregnant, to try for a daughter, but he had refused, saying two sons were enough for him. I could tease him because I'm an American, but he also knew I was *her* ally. Then, she broke her hip. I wanted to come over and do the housework for her but the husband wouldn't permit it. I'm not sure if it was because he thought I would pollute his house or if he was too proud to let me see his dirty dishes. Anyway, I could not keep making excuses for the way he behaved and for her tolerating it." The friendship dissolved over these differences.

David Osborne talks about losing his dear Indian friend when Stanford began actively recruiting Native Americans. "By our junior year there were a hundred American Indian students on campus and Steve was becoming part of that separate world. He slowly moved away from me, away from our talks about books and philosophy. For a while I tried getting to know some of his friends but their anti-intellectualism made me uncomfortable. They enjoyed drinking, watching *Star Trek,* and talking about getting laid. Once when Steve was drunk, he called me his 'white middle-class friend.' Another time, when he came back to school after Christmas, he said, 'People are drinking themselves to death on my reservation. You can't imagine it. It's a totally different world from this country club.'

"At the beginning of our senior year, we ran into each other and I invited him for dinner. He didn't show up. Two weeks later he came over unannounced with a Native American girl. We had trouble finding things to say. He seemed confused about his identity. Everyone expected him to go to law school and become a champion of

Indian rights. But he seemed to be rebelling against succeeding in the white world. After graduation, we lost touch completely."

For another pair of friends, having different sensitivities did not destroy the relationship but did create a temporary misunderstanding. Yvonne, a Black woman, was offended when her white friend, Fran, came to visit, took off her shoes, and put her feet up on the couch. "I felt it showed her disregard for me and I blamed it on race," says Yvonne. "Black people believe the way you behave in someone's home indicates the respect you have for that person. Also, furniture means a lot to us because we buy it with such hard-won wages." Weeks later, Yvonne saw one of Fran's white friends do the same thing while sitting on Fran's couch. Yvonne realized that the behavior had nothing to do with lack of respect for Blacks. "For all I know millions of whites all over America put their feet up when they relax—I'd just never seen that part of their world before."

What Bill Tatum discovered about a couple of his white friends was not so easy to explain away. When the couple asked Tatum to take some food to Helen, their Black housekeeper who was sick, he asked her name and address. They knew her only as "Helen" but were able to get her address from their 6-year-old who had spent a week at her apartment when they had been on vacation.

"I arrived to find a filthy, urine-smelling building, with addicts hanging out on the front stoop. Rags were stuffed in the broken windows in Helen's apartment. She was wearing a bag of asafetida around her neck, a concoction made by southern Blacks to ward off bad luck and colds. She was old, sick, and feverish. She said she'd never been sick before and her employers—my friends—had provided her with no health insurance. Obviously, they'd never imagined where or how this poor woman might live—or else they wouldn't have left their little girl with her. They treated their Black housekeeper with none of the respect and concern they showed me, their Black *friend* and a member of their economic class."

Until that experience, if anyone had ever accused the couple of racism, Tatum says he'd have gone to the mat defending them. Now he has to square what he's seen with his old love for them and he is finding it very, very difficult.

He makes another point about moving in the world of white friends. "Some whites make me feel completely comfortable because they say exactly what they think even if it contradicts whatever I've said. But other whites never disagree with me on anything. They act as if Blacks can't defend their positions, or they're afraid it would look like a put-down to challenge what I say even though they would challenge a white person's opinion in a minute."

While Tatum resents whites' misguided protectiveness, he also finds fault with "many Blacks who are climbing socially and are too damned careful of what *they* say. They won't advance an opinion until they have a sense of what the white friend is thinking." Not only is that not good conversation, he says, "that's not good friendship."

Horizontal Hostility

Despite finding many happy crossing friendships, I was surprised by the number of times members of minority groups spoke ill of other minority groups. Blacks said they had white ethnic friends but that it was hard to be friends with Hispanics. Asians told me it's easier for them to relate to whites than to Blacks. Gentiles said they have individual Jewish friends but problems with Jews in general. English girls of interracial parentage chose white friends over Black friends. A Medical Corps captain said that in his sixty-bed treatment center Blacks and whites sometimes become friends but never Blacks and Filipinos. An Irish-American high school girl was afraid to invite her Black friend home because her uncle "doesn't know any Black people and doesn't want to. He's hard-core Irish. I mean, he doesn't even like Italians."[18]

Micaela di Leonardo reported that scapegoating inside of the Italian-American community takes the form of *campanilismo,* solidarity based on region of origin. Northern Italians ridicule Sicilians and southern Italians and try to distance themselves from the southern stereotype. These regional differences are largely unrecognized in the outside world where "an Italian is an Italian" or, worse yet, a "dago" or a "wop." Although many Italian-Americans have felt the sting of bigotry, they themselves sometimes express negative feelings toward Blacks, Chicanos, and Asians, depending on which group impinges on their work or residential area. Cetta Longhinotti and her office colleagues allowed their biases to deprive them of a lovely tradition. In the days when the whole staff was made up of Italian-Americans, the women gave each other birthday presents. After a Black and an Asian were hired, the Italians couldn't celebrate each other and leave the minority women out but they wouldn't include them in either. So the gift-giving ritual died.[19]

In California, Claude Fischer found all kinds of ethnic biases among all kinds of ethnics. Charlie Chin admits that he and other Asian-American activists are constantly working to dispel Chinese prejudice against Blacks. And in the housing complex mentioned in the previous chapter, where that charming mop-shaking ritual and the domino game take place, researchers found that both Cubans and Blacks prefer to interact with Anglos rather than with each other.

Horizontal hostility is nothing new. (The phrase belongs to radical lawyer Flo Kennedy.) In 1950 Gordon Allport found that people of all ethnic groups considered English and Canadians most desirable for social relationships and Hindus, Turks, and Blacks least acceptable. Allport was "forced to conclude" that most minority groups conform to the majority's attitudes, including its prejudices. Regrettably, much the same bigotry is still with us. In recent decades, the growth of ethnic and racial pride may have helped minorities to repudiate negative stereotypes of their own group but it has not inspired them to do the same about other groups.

What accounts for the persistence of this friendship bias? Why are minorities more likely to have crossing friendships with the white majority than with other racial or ethnic minorities? Is there so much to be gained from acceptance by a majority person? Have minorities so deeply absorbed the majority's negative views of ethnic groups that they cannot make up their own minds about each other?

Although psychological and cultural factors undeniably contribute to horizontal hostility, there is another equally powerful divisive force: *Friendship follows economics*. Minority groups that are made to feel they are direct competitors for a finite number of jobs or "handouts" are not likely to feel particularly friendly to one another. In Atlanta, for example, unskilled Cubans, Vietnamese, and Blacks compete for jobs, federal money, social services, city resources, and respect for their cultural heritages.[20] In Montreal, the same situation exists for different ethnic competitors, and the economic rivalry is far from conducive to friendship.[21]

Despite the lip service paid to "brotherhood," only naive idealists could believe that the ruling majority has anything to gain by intergroup unity. Divide and conquer remains the policy that best protects the economic interests of the "haves." A widespread proliferation of crossing friendships among "have-nots" would carry significant and subversive political ramifications. It could signal the start of a revolution.

The Problem with "Them" Is "Us"

If you're a young, heterosexual, nondisabled person and you do not have one friend who is either gay, old, or disabled, there might be something wrong with *you*. If you're gay, old, or disabled and all your friends are just like you, it may not be because you prefer it that way.

Gay people, the elderly, and disabled people get the same pleasure from companionship and intimacy and have the same problems with friendship as does anyone else. They merit a separate discussion in this book for the same reason that class, race, and ethnicity required special discussion: because on top of the usual friendship concerns, they experience additional barriers.

In essence, the barriers exist because we don't *know* each other. Many people—some of whom are homophobic (have a fear of homosexuality)—reach adulthood without ever to their knowledge meeting a homosexual or a lesbian. Many have neither known someone who is blind or deaf or who uses a wheelchair nor spent time with an old person other than their grandparents. That there are such things as Gay Pride marches, disability rights organizations, and the Gray Panthers does not mean that these groups have achieved equal treatment under the law or full humanity in the eyes of the world. To a large degree, our society still wants to keep them out of sight—the gays for "flaunting their alternative life-styles," the disabled for not "getting better," and the old for reminding us of our eventual fate.

As a result of our hang-ups, these populations may be even more segregated than racial or ethnic minorities. When these groups are segregated, "we" don't have to think about "them." Out of sight, out of mind, out of friendship. People told me they had no gay, elderly, or disabled friends because "we live in two different worlds" or because "they" are so different—meaning threatening, unsettling, or strange. Closer analysis reveals, however, that we *keep* them different by making this world so hard for them to live in and by defining human norms so narrowly. It is our world—the homophobic, youth-worshipping, disability-fearing world—that is threatening, unsettling, and strange to them. In other words, their biggest problem is us.

To make friends, we have to cross our self-made boundaries and grant to other people the right to be both distinctive and equal.

Gay-Straight Friendship

Forming relationships across gay-straight boundaries can be as challenging as crossing racial and ethnic lines because it too requires the extra work of "explaining":

- Explaining to yourself why, if you're gay, you need this straight friend ("Am I unconsciously trying to keep my heterosexual credentials in order?"), or why, if you're straight, you need this gay friend ("Am I a latent homosexual?")

- Explaining to each other what your lives are like—telling the straight friend what's behind the words "heavy leather" or explaining to the gay friend just why he *cannot* bring his transvestite lover to a Bar Mitzvah

- Explaining to your respective communities why you have such a close relationship with one of "them"

Gay-straight friendship is a challenge not only because the heterosexual world stigmatizes gays but because homosexual society is a culture unto itself. Straights who relate comfortably with their gay friends say they get along so well because they respect the distinctive qualities of gay culture—almost as if it were an ethnic group. Interestingly enough, a Toronto sociologist has determined that gay men have the same institutions, "sense of peoplehood," and friendship networks as an ethnic community; all that gays lack is the emphasis on family.[22] And in places where lesbians congregate, such as San Francisco, there are women's bars, music, bookstores, publications, folklore, and dress styles—an elaborate self-contained culture.[23]

Since gay men and lesbians have to function in a straight world during most of their lives, it's not too much to ask a straight friend to occasionally accommodate to an environment defined by homosexuals. But even when both friends accommodate, gay-straight relations can be strained by disagreements over provocative issues.

GAY-STRAIGHT DEBATE

The Gay's View	The Straight's View
On Homophobia	

You're not relaxed with me. You think gayness rubs off or friendship might lead to sex. You act like every gay person wants to seduce you. You fear others will think you're gay. You are repulsed by gay sex though you try to hide it. You bear some responsibility for the discrimination against gays and if you're my friend, you'll fight it with me.	I am the product of a traditional upbringing. I cannot help being afraid or ignorant of homosexuality. My religion taught me that homosexuality is a sin. I'm trying to overcome these biases and still be honest with you about my feelings. I support gay rights, but I cannot be responsible for everyone else's homophobia.

On AIDS

Ever since the AIDS epidemic, you have not touched me or drunk from a glass in my house. I resent your paranoia. I shouldn't have to watch my gay friends die and at the same time feel that my straight friends are treating me like a leper. If I did get AIDS, I'm afraid you would blame the victim and abandon me. Can I trust a friend like that?	I *am* afraid. I don't know how contagious the AIDS virus is or how it's transmitted. From what I read, no one does. All I know is that AIDS is fatal, homosexuals are the primary victims, and you are a homosexual. I'm caught between my affection for you and my terror of the disease. I don't know what's right and you're in no position to tell me.

On Lesbian Politics

Lesbianism is not just sexual, it's political. Every woman	I support lesbian rights and even lesbian separatism if

should call herself a lesbian, become woman-identified, and reject everything masculinist. Women who love men and live in the nuclear family contribute to the entrenchment of patriarchal power and the oppression of women. Authentic female friendship can only exist in lesbian communities. If you don't accept "lesbian" as a positive identity, it will be used to condemn all women who are not dependent on men.

lesbians choose it. I believe lesbian mothers must be permitted to keep their children. I oppose all discrimination and defamation of lesbians. I believe that lesbian feminists and straight women can work together and be friends, *but* I resent lesbian coercion and political strong-arming. I also resent your more-radical-than-thou attitude toward heterosexuals. Like you, what I do with my body is my business.

On Acceptance

You want me to act straight whenever having a gay friend might embarrass you. I'm not going to tone down my speech or dress to please your friends or family. I do not enjoy being treated as a second-class couple when my lover and I go out with you and your spouse. If you can kiss and hold hands, we should be able to show affection in public. If straights ask each other how they met or how long they have been married, they should ask us how we met and how long we've been together.

You refuse to understand how difficult it is to explain gay life-styles to a child or an 80-year-old. You make me feel like a square in comparison with your flashy gay friends. You treat married people like Mr. and Mrs. Tepid, as if the only true passion is gay passion. Your friends make me feel unwanted on gay turf and at political events when I'm there to support gay rights. You put down all straights before you know them. It's hard to be your friend if I can't introduce you to other people without your feeling hostile or judging their every word.

*   *   *

Despite so much potential for conflict, 29 percent of *PT*'s respondents have a homosexual friend, although only 5 percent identify themselves as homosexual. When gays and straights sustain close friendships, they do so in roughly this order of frequency:

- straight women and gay men
- straight women and lesbians
- straight men and gay men
- lesbians and gay men
- lesbians and straight men

Although basically friendship is friendship—and the most striking distinctions relate to gender not sexuality—there are some interesting points to be made about the influence of sexual orientation on those five configurations of friendship.

Straight Women and Gay Men. "Brad's not my friend *because* he's gay or *even though* he's gay; he's my friend who *happens* to be gay," says a straight woman about a relationship that others in her life haven't accepted and don't understand. "My mother couldn't believe Brad is a homosexual because he's he-man sexy, not faggy, and he's very successful. She wanted me to date him and try to, y'know, change him. My best girlfriend thought our relationship was sick because, *yuck,* he sleeps with men. My husband was jealous until he made himself think of Brad as one of my girlfriends. But I don't think of him that way. And I don't think about what he does in bed or who he does it with. To me he's a funny, fun-loving guy and a great friend."

"Everyone thinks all gay men are hairdressers, ballet dancers, and interior decorators because those professions allow men to openly express who they are," says Michael, a tax lawyer. "I'm not about to wear my Fire Island caftan to the office. And even though I tend to like flamboyant speech and campy humor, I know better than to relax my guard with straight men. I would lose masculinity points and lawyerlike authority. The real me would scare their socks off. But with my women friends, I can be totally myself. They enjoy my style. I enjoy their honesty and warmth. They don't judge me, they like me."

The Kinsey Institute found that two-thirds of gay men have some female friends.[24] John Malone, author of *Straight Women/Gay Men: A Special Relationship*, reports that "the number of gay men with some straight women friends is in the millions."[25] Malone, who reviewed all the existing research on these relationships, believes such partners are drawn together by "a similar process of redefinition"— gay men are redefining masculinity, straight women are redefining womanhood. They are also united by their common adversaries: conservatives and people who are sexist and homophobic.

Enemies of gay rights are often similarly vehement against women's rights. They find homosexuality and feminism equally threatening, and they see any relaxation of sex-role stereotypes as an attack on "nature" and The Family. More often than not, those who call homosexual relations sinful also oppose abortion; in both cases their objection is to *nonreproductive sex*—sex for pleasure—which millions of women and gay men now dare to consider their right.

Even when common issues are not consciously acknowledged and neither partner is militant on behalf of gay rights or women's causes, many such friends say they feel a mutuality of status. In our culture, the straight woman is still second class for being female and the homosexual is "like a woman" because he too allows himself to be sexually used by men.

Simone, a Black woman, sees gay/straight friendship as an equalizer in a sexist society. "When my friend George announced he had to talk to me about a serious problem, I knew he was either going to tell me that he was marrying a white woman or that he was gay. Those are the two things that make Black men vulnerable in the Black community and vulnerability makes men a woman's equal. Black men will reject us for another color or sex, then tell us about it, 'cause we're friends. Sure enough, George was gay."

Although both straight women and gay men are sexually attracted to men, rivalry for the same lover is rare. Instead, they commiserate about their respective male partners without the competition that besets same-sex confidants or the sexual tension that complicates cross-sex friendship between straights. Many gay men say women are good sounding boards (straight men say the same) and more accepting of gay sex than straight men are. Likewise, Malone found, women discuss their sex lives and feelings more openly with gay male friends because most straight men "assume that a woman who talks about sex is looking for sex" and because gay men don't get aroused by women's frankness. As one homosexual told the authors of *The New Couple: Women and Gay Men*, "Being gay and having experienced what creeps men are, I can relate to a lot of things women feel."[26]

True friends trade intimacies; confederates, you'll recall, satisfy one another's more limited needs: The gay man needs a female companion for "cover," and the straight woman wants a social escort with no sexual hassles. Whether they're true friends or confederates, a woman who spends time with a homosexual man is called a "fag hag" or "fruit fly," labels of disdain for a woman who doesn't choose to upgrade herself with a "real man." Any male-female relationship that is nonsexual is a mystery to orthodox thinkers. If a woman and a man don't want each other's body, what could they possibly want?

Psychoanalytic explanations range from "he wants mothering" to "she's afraid of sex." This may describe neurotic unions but not every friendship between straight women and gay men.

"Gay men give me more than most men but less than most women," says Sherry, a college senior, in summing up her many gay friends. "They let their anima out. I love their dramatic pace. They love me when I'm being outrageous—when I'd be too much for most straight men to handle. But even if they didn't approve, I wouldn't feel that I was being unloved by A Man. Gay men are my no-risk friends. The ones who flirt confirm my attractiveness. The ones who don't make me feel neuter. With so much emphasis on sex in my age group, it's a relief to be asexual for a change."

Straight Women and Lesbians.   Sherry has had several negative experiences with lesbians: "Judging by the number of gay men in my life, you'd think I'd have at least one gay woman friend. But I've felt terrible hostility from the lesbians on campus. They're so politically correct. They're intolerant of any woman who doesn't go on record hating men. One lesbian accused me of selling out just because I wear make-up. When I took a course on Gertrude Stein, the lesbians in the class made me feel I didn't belong. They just assume that every straight is homophobic."

Actually, there is less homophobia among women than among men. First, little girls are largely spared the indoctrination that equates affection with sexual orientation, propaganda that squelches boys' expressiveness. Second, masculinity is more prized than femininity and is more rigorously standardized and guarded. Thus, the fear of being thought "unmanly" coerces men into harsher anti-gay attitudes and allows the expletive "sissy" to wound far more deeply than "tomboy." (Tomboy may even carry implicit admiration for a girl.) Third, there is less female homophobia because the women's movement has emphasized common female needs and raised the consciousness of straight women about lesbian reality.

Nevertheless, when a lesbian "comes out," her straight friends may not know how to handle it. "Although I considered myself sophisticated and had known gay women in the past, having a close friend suddenly disclose the fact that she was homosexual was vaguely terrifying," says Pam Black. "She didn't look or act any different and yet I had to stifle the urge to stare at her as if she were now a complete stranger. How would she and I now interact? Should I treat her the way I would treat a man? Did she now view me as a potential sex partner?"[27]

To avoid having to absorb such reactions, some lesbians retreat altogether from their straight friends: "It would've been too hard to look Roz in the eyes after all these years of pretense," says Lynne, who stopped calling Roz as soon as she came out. On her side, Roz feels betrayed. "Wasn't I important enough for her to at least test me? Why couldn't she give me a chance?"

If they do give it a chance, both friends may experience a relationship that is greater than the sum of its parts. "I enjoy my lesbian friends more because they know more about themselves as women," says Babette, a psychologist. "My straight friends are too busy relating to men."

Lesbian feminists tend to feel closer to *all* women than to any men, including their gay brothers. "Straight and gay women may have different agendas but we end up in the same boat with men at the helm," says Jo, a lesbian whose best friend, Carla, is married to an abusive man who has forbidden her to see Jo. (Jealousy is not the usual male response to these friendships. Many men so underrate female sexuality that they cannot conceive of a lesbian being a sexual predator or a viable alternative to themselves.) Nevertheless, Carla and Jo continue to meet secretly. "She gives me something more important than sex," says Carla. "She gives me self-respect."

Feminists Esther Newton and Shirley Walton have known each other for twenty-seven years, ever since their freshman year in college. In 1970 when Newton became active in Gay Liberation and

Walton was married and pregnant, they asked themselves, "Do we still have anything in common?" The answer was a book called *Womenfriends,* alternating pages from their joint journals.[28] "Lovers come and go," says Newton, "but this friendship is forever."

Straight Men and Gay Men. "My longest lasting, firmest friends happen to be straight men," says Nick, who came out five years ago after living duplicitously in a twenty-year marriage. "In general, I find gay men superficial, self-absorbed, and narcissistic. I'm 54 years old. I need friends with real maturity. The man I turn to most is my business partner of the last seventeen years. Even though he never knew I was gay, he's been my escape from the tensions of gay life. I trust him more than anyone else in the world. When I was ready to come out, I told him before I told my wife. It was a helluva shock for him but now, with the lie out of the way, we're even closer."

Several gay men were reminded of how hard it was to be one of the boys when they were teenagers. "Some kid would be telling me about his crush on a girl while I had a crush on *him,*" laughs Rob, whose best friend today is his college roommate. "The minute we met I knew my roommate was straight as an arrow. I'd resolved not to hide my homosexuality like I did in high school, so I told him right off the bat. He was very uncomfortable at first, but I said he could ask me anything about it and then if he wanted to request a room change, I'd understand. Our talks probably helped us get to know each other sooner and better than most roommates. He decided he could hack it. That was three years ago."

Since most gay men have painful memories of being taunted or rebuffed by boys and men friends who discovered "the truth," it's no surprise that many still find straight friendships too trying. "I can't be myself with straight people, even when they know I'm gay," one man told psychologist Lillian Rubin. "I mean being gay influences my whole life—how I look at politics, at sex, just about everything. Let's say I'm walking down the street with some men from the office and they see a pretty girl. That's all they talk about; you know, all the things men say. But if I see some cute guy who turns me on, can I say the same things about him? You bet your sweets I can't. But I *have* to listen to their shit if I'm with them because they're the 'normal' ones, and I'd be just another goddamned faggot if I opened up and said what I was thinking."

Lesbians and Gay Men. On paper, they cross the same gender boundaries as do straight women and men, but in reality their friendships are quite different. Straight men and women have the potential for sexual union but not many ideological grounds for common cause. Lesbians and gay men, on the other hand, have virtually no sexual tension but many grounds for solidarity on gay issues. Why then do lesbians have more gay than straight male friends whereas gay men have many more straight women than lesbian friends?

A few speculations: Lesbians may be more open to friendship with homosexuals because they need the political support of the relatively stronger male wing of the gay rights movement. (Of course, this impetus is diminished if they also are competing for the same media attention or social service dollars.) For another thing, many lesbians consciously distinguish between straight men who oppress women and gays who have little involvement with women. Gay men may distinguish between straight women and lesbians on more superficial grounds of personal style and "stridency." Also, gay men can get supplementary affirmation of their attractiveness from straight women. Most lesbians neither offer that bonus nor seek it from men of any sexual persuasion.

"They don't need men for nothin'," sneered a gay man who neither has nor wants a lesbian as a friend. "They're angry at men and I'm a man. Besides, they're no fun; they take themselves too seriously. I'd rather be marooned on a desert island with two heterosexual lovebirds than one lesbian."

Arlene, a lesbian, accounts for her many gay male friends this way: "Even though lesbians are into intimacy, and gay men generally are sexually promiscuous, we're both emotionally expressive, so it's easier to be friends with a gay guy than a straight guy."

Some lesbians even think it is easier to be friends with a gay man than with another lesbian. In *The New Couple,* a lesbian named Jane says she prefers male homosexuals' hangouts because she finds lesbian bars "notoriously godawful. They're just dykes, the old syndrome. They look terrible. I just don't like them. But I have always had a number of gay male friends."[29]

Christine Burton, a columnist for the largest gay and lesbian newspaper in New England, told me she regrets that women such as Jane need men to validate themselves. "These lesbians suffer from internalized homophobia. They feel less valuable, so they see other lesbians as less valuable and unworthy as friends." Burton herself deals with gay men professionally but says, "I don't fraternize with them. They were brought up like other men, to put women down."

Among the crossing friends who express unqualified enthusiasm for each other and often go out together is a handsome gay man and a lesbian of extraordinary beauty. "She's the lure," he jokes. "When straight men fall for her, I come in for the kill." The two friends play at heterosexual flirtation but are really soulmates who tell each other everything. "He's all I want in a man," she smiles, "only I don't want a man."

In *The New Couple*, a gay doctor says of his secretary, who is a lesbian, "I have an emotional attachment to Susan, not physical, not love, but Susan is very important to me." Another gay man has this praise for his best friend, a lesbian: "Candy was the first woman who taught me that I could be comfortable around women. . . . Before that I had divided people into females, those insipid little things, and males. . . . Candy was the first person, man or woman, I could talk to about being gay, what it meant to both of us. She could also discuss being female. That relationship turned my whole world around."[30]

Lesbians and Straight Men.   Straight men who need admiring women to verify their sexual appeal and lesbians who see straight men as impediments to both gay and women's liberation are about as compatible as oil and water, and indeed these friendship pairs are hard to find. Straight men typically snickered at the very idea of their having a lesbian friend, and most lesbians could not imagine trusting their inner lives to "one of the oppressors."

But then, I met a few people like Donna and her straight friend, Jay, who is like a brother to her. They were childhood neighbors who played marbles, stickball, and Monopoly together. Now in their thirties, they jog, play tennis, and share a ski house. "Jay and I don't give a damn about labels," she says in tones that suggest this is the last word on gay-straight friendship. "We just care about each other."

Disabled and Nondisabled Friendship

About 36 million Americans have a disabling limitation in their hearing, seeing, speaking, walking, moving, or thinking. Few nondisabled people are as sensitive to the experiences of this population as are those with close friends who are disabled.

"Last week," recalls Barbara Sprung, "I went to have a drink at a midtown hotel with a friend who uses a wheelchair. Obviously it's not important to this hotel to have disabled patrons because we had to wait for the so-called accessible elevator for thirty minutes. Anyone who waits with the disabled is amazed at how long the disabled have to wait for everything."

"In graduate school, one of my friends was a young man with cerebral palsy," says Rena Gropper. "Because he articulated slowly and with great difficulty, everyone thought he was dumb and always interrupted him, but if you let him finish, you heard how bright and original his thinking was."

Terry Keegan, an interpreter for the deaf, has become friends with many deaf people and roomed for two years with a coworker who is deaf. "If they don't understand what we're saying it's not because they're stupid but because we aren't speaking front face or we can't sign." Keegan believes all hearing people should learn 100 basic words in Ameslan, American Sign Language. "Historically, this wonderful language has been suppressed. Deaf people were forced to use speech, lipreading, and hearing aids so they would not look handicapped and would 'fit in' with the rest of us. Their hands were slapped when they tried to sign. This deprived them of a superior communication method. Deafness is not a pathology, it's a difference. When we deny deaf people their deafness, we deny them their identity."

Many nondisabled people have become sensitized to idioms that sound like racial epithets to the disabled, such as "the blind leading the blind" or "that's a lame excuse." Some find "handicapped" demeaning because it derives from "cap in hand." A man who wears leg braces says the issue is accuracy. "*I'm* not handicapped, people's attitudes about me handicap me." Merle Froschl, a nondisabled member of the Women and Disability Awareness Project, points out that the opposite of "disabled" is "*not* disabled"; thus, "nondisabled" is the most neutral term. Disabled people are infuriated by being contrasted with "normal" people—it implies that the disabled are "abnormal" and everyone else is perfect. And the term "able-bodied" inspires the question, Able to do what: Run a marathon? See without glasses? Isn't it all relative?

"Differently abled" and "physically challenged" had a brief vogue, but, says Harilyn Rousso, those terms "made me feel I really had something to hide." Rousso, a psychotherapist who has cerebral palsy, emphasizes, "Friends who care the most sometimes think they're doing you a favor by using euphemisms or saying 'I never think of you as disabled.' The reason they don't want to acknowledge my disability is that they think it's so negative. Meanwhile, I'm trying to recognize it as a valid part of me. I'm more complex than my disability and I don't want my friends to be obsessed by it. But it's clearly there, like my eye color, and I want my friends to appreciate and accept me with it."

The point is not that there is a "right way" to talk to people who are disabled but that friendship carries with it the obligation to *know thy friends,* their sore points and their preferences. That includes knowing what words hurt their feelings as well as when and how to help them do what they cannot do for themselves.

"Each disabled person sends out messages about what they need," says Froschl. "One friend who is blind makes me feel comfortable about taking her arm crossing the street, another dislikes physical contact and wants to negotiate by cane. I've learned not to automatically do things for disabled people since they often experience help as patronizing."

"I need someone to pour cream in my coffee, but in this culture, it's not acceptable to ask for help," says Rousso, adding that women's ordinary problems with dependency are intensified by disability. "I have to feel very comfortable with my friends before I can explain my needs openly and trust that their reaction will not humiliate both of us. For some people it raises too many anxieties."

Anxieties that surround the unknown are dissipated by familiarity. Maybe that explains why so many disabled-nondisabled friendships are composed of classmates or coworkers who spend a lot of time together.

"There are those who can deal with disability and those who can't," says Phil Draper, a quadriplegic whose spinal cord was injured in a car accident. "If they can't—if they get quiet or talk nervously or avoid our eyes—the work of the relationship falls entirely on us. We need friends who won't treat us as weirdo asexual second-class children or expect us to be 'Supercrips'—miracle cripples who work like crazy to make themselves whole again. Ninety-nine percent of us aren't going to be whole no matter what we do. We want to be accepted the way we are."

To accept friends like Phil Draper, the nondisabled have to confront their unconscious fears of vulnerability and death. In one study,

80 percent of nondisabled people said they would be comfortable having someone in a wheelchair as their friend. But "being in a wheelchair" came immediately after "blind" and "deaf-mute" as the affliction they themselves would least want to have.[31] If we fear being what our friend *is*, that feeling is somewhere in the friendship.

Nondisabled people also have to disavow the cult of perfectability. Disabled people are not going to "get better" because they are not "sick"; they are generally healthy people who are not allowed to function fully in this society—as friends or as anything else.

"Friendship is based on people's ability to communicate," says Judy Heumann, the first postpolio person to get a teacher's license in New York City and now a leader of the disability rights movement. "But barriers such as inaccessible homes make it hard for disabled people to just drop in. Spontaneity is something disabled people enjoy infrequently and the nondisabled take for granted.

"While more public places have ramps and bathrooms that accommodate wheelchairs, many parties still occur in inaccessible spaces. If I have to be carried upstairs or if I can't have a drink because I know I won't be able to use the bathroom later, I'll probably decide not to go at all. One way I measure my friends is by whether they have put in the effort and money to make their houses wheelchair-accessible. It shows their sensitivity to me as a person.

"Good friends are conscious of the fact that a movie theater or concert hall has to be accessible before I can join them; they share my anger and frustration if it's not. They understand why I'm not crazy about big parties where all the nondisabled are standing up and I'm at ass-level. It makes me able to function more as an equal within the group if people sit down to talk to me. I can't pretend I'm part of things if I can't hear anyone. I don't want to *not* be invited to large parties—I just want people to be sensitive to my needs.

"I always need help cooking, cleaning, driving, going to the bathroom, getting dressed. I pay an attendant to do most of those things for me but sometimes I have to ask a friend for help, which presents a lot of opportunities for rejection. Often, the friends who come through best are other disabled people whose disabilities complement mine. I can help a blind woman with her reading, child care, and traveling around town; she can do the physical things I need. And we don't have to appreciate each other's help, we can just accept it."

Ariel, a psychotherapist and doctoral candidate who is blind, says,

"In general, I don't pick my friends, they pick me. I've met people I'd like to get to know but they don't stick around long enough to be known. My blindness so startles them that it obscures everything else I am. The only category they can fit blindness into is terror. When I was 10 I remember lamenting to my family that I was having trouble making friends. My father, who was very outgoing and gregarious, said I would always have to go more than halfway to break down people's barriers. To this day, I usually take the initiative and ask someone to a movie or a restaurant because so many sighted people assume the blind can't eat in public or enjoy a movie."

Despite such strains, Ariel has some remarkable friendships, two of which date back to college in the sixties. With poignant candor, her friends Maureen and Eloise define an intimacy that transcends all barriers.

"Ariel and I are incredibly alike in hundreds of ways," Maureen says. "We even sound alike. The most important things between us have nothing to do with the fact that she's blind, but that doesn't mean I'm unaware that she can't see. It took me years to find a middle ground between infantilizing her and not giving her enough help. Whenever we went out into the world together I'd do all the dealing because people assume that if you can't see you can't talk or hear either. I learned how to let *her* take over. When a cabdriver asked, 'Where does she want to go?' I said, 'I no speak English.' Nowadays people tell me I 'think blind' because I check out the hedges, the stairs, the cracks in the sidewalk to see how I would find a friend's house if I had a cane. I 'see' the world from Ariel's perspective."

"Because I'm a Quaker," Eloise explains, "when I first met Ariel, I thought it was my moral duty to overcome my fear of someone so different. Then I found her disability didn't get in the way of our love of good conversation or good music. Her difficulty is not that she doesn't see—which I can't do anything about and which she can't imagine doing anyway—but that other people won't let her participate in life. I *can* do something about that. Pity is a waste of time. It is also antithetical to friendship. You cannot feel equal to someone when you're thinking 'Oh, how awful my life would be if I was like that.' I'll admit there's some nuisance connected to her disability. But I've come to see her limitations as part of a continuum of human difficulties. Everyone has disabilities and all friendship involves mutual assistance.

"What do I get from Ariel in return for the extra 'burden'? I get a great adviser, a wonderful companion, and, to be absolutely honest, I get pleasure from being there for her when so many people aren't."

Cross-Age Friendship

I am now 46, my husband is 51. Among our good friends are two couples who are old enough to be our parents. One woman, a poet, can be counted on for the latest word on political protests and promising writers. She and I once spent a month together at a writers' colony. The other woman—as energetic and as well-read as anyone I know—is also involved in progressive causes. Although the men of both couples have each had a life-threatening illness, the one with a heart condition is a brilliant civil liberties lawyer and the one who had a stroke is a prizewinning novelist with stunning imaginative powers. The lawyer taught our son to play chess when he was 5. The novelist has encouraged our daughters to write stories ever since they could read. The men have been fine surrogate grandfathers.

When I described these couples to someone my own age, he said, "Ah, it's easy to be friends with *interesting* old people, but what about the dull ones?" The answer is, I am not friends with dull young or middle-aged people so why should I want to be friends with dull old people? And why does he immediately think in terms of old people *not* being interesting? Perhaps the crux of the problem with cross-generational friendship is this *double* double standard. First, to think we "ought" to be friends with the elderly—as a class—denies old people the dignity of individuality and devalues their friendship through condescension. But second, to assume that those who are young or in mid-life will necessarily be more interesting and attractive than those over 65 maintains a double standard of expectation that cheats younger people of friends like ours.

Ageism hurts all ages. And it begins early: Studies show that 3-year-olds already see old people as sick, tired, and ugly and don't want to associate with them.[32] Older people also have their biases about youthful behavior. Some 70-year-olds think children are undependable, unappreciative, ask too many questions, and must be told what to do. They believe teenagers are callow, impatient, and unseasoned.[33]

The authors of *Grandparents/Grandchildren* write, "We shouldn't blame adolescents for not being adults. To become adults, the young need to be around adults."[34] But age segregation keeps us apart. Without benefit of mutual acquaintance, stereotypes mount, brick by brick, until there is a wall high enough to conceal the real human beings on either side.

Another big problem is miscommunication. Conversations between young and old often founder because "sensory, physical, or cognitive differences" cause "distortion, message failure, and social discomfort."[35] That's a fancy way of saying they can't understand each other. And anyone who has ever talked with a young person whose span of concentration is the length of a TV commercial or with an old person whose mind wanders to the blizzard of '48 when asked how to dress for today's weather will understand how each generation's communication style can be a problem for the other.

But stereotypes and miscommunication do not entirely account for the gulf between young and old. Homophily—the attraction to the similar self—is the missing link. Those who are going through the same thing at the same time find it comforting to have friends who mirror their problems and meet their needs, and, usually, people of similar chronological age are going through parallel experiences with wage-earning, setting up house, child-rearing, and other life-cycle events.

Age-mates also tend to have in common the same angle of vision on history and culture. Two 65-year-olds watching a film about the Depression or World War II can exchange memories and emotional responses that are unavailable to a 30-year-old who did not live through those cataclysms. And while a person of 18 and one of 75 might both love Vivaldi, their simultaneous appreciation for Bruce Springsteen is unlikely.

Claude Fischer's studies reveal that more than half of all friend-partners are fewer than five years apart. But the span is reduced to two years if their relationship dates back to their youth when age gradations matter the most and the places where youngsters meet—school, camp, military service, and entry-level jobs—are more age-segregated. Contrary to popular wisdom, elderly people, like the rest of us, prefer friends of their own age. The more old people there are in a given community, the more likely it is that each one will have a preponderance of same-age friends. And, believe it or not, a majority of old people say they think it's more important for them to have age-mates than family as their intimates.

Given this overwhelming preference for homophily at every age, why am I on the bandwagon for cross-generational friendship? Because when it's good, it's very, very good—both for friends of different ages who are undergoing similar experiences at the same time and for friends of different ages who are enjoying their differences.

- A 38-year-old woman meets 22-year-olds in her contracts class at law school.

- A couple in their early forties enrolled in a natural childbirth course make friends with parents-to-be who are twenty years younger.

- Three fathers commiserate about the high cost of college; two are in their forties, the third is a 60-year-old educating his second family.

Age-crossing friendships become less unusual as Americans follow more idiosyncratic schedules for marrying, having children, and making career decisions.

But there are other reasons for feeling that age is immaterial to friendship. Marie Wilson, a 45-year-old foundation executive who has five children of high school age or older, told me, "My friends are in their early thirties, and they have kids under 8. But these women are where I am in my head. We became close working together on organizing self-help for the poor. Most women my age are more involved in suburban life or planning their own career moves."

Sharing important interests can be as strong a basis for friendship as is experiencing the same life-cycle events. However, without either of those links, the age difference can sit between the young and the old like a stranger. I'm not asking that we deny that difference but that we free ourselves from what Victoria Secunda calls "the tyranny of age assumptions"[36] and that we entertain the possibility of enriching ourselves through our differences.

Thea, a 30-year-old graduate of Vassar, works as a waitress when she's not writing her first novel. Dawn, an 18-year-old single mother, *always* works as a waitress because that's how she supports herself and her child. The two women met on the job. "Dawn's as smart as anyone I went to school with," says Thea. "She's just had all the bad breaks. After her mother died, she moved in with her boyfriend, had a baby at 16, and dropped out of school. We talk about how she'll get her high school equivalency degree or how I'll overcome my writer's block. She's a great listener, a great manager of emotions. I'm the educated adult but I need her to get me through the day."

An age spread may foretell differences in experience but it does not in itself preclude equality. This is true even when the age gap is a yawning half century or more. Sometimes, the very young and the very old are equalized by shared feelings of powerlessness: Kids are answerable to their parents and old people are answerable to their children, that is, both are answerable to the generation in the middle. When their mutual powerlessness is transformed into mutual empowerment, young and old can become natural allies and empathetic friends.

Many such relationships already exist. Some communities have arranged for children to visit with elderly friends, read to them, play checkers with them, and listen to their stories because "both enjoy repetition; children ask to hear the same story; older people love to tell it."[37] Foster grandparents and "grand-friends" are serving as resource persons in early childhood classrooms and as surrogate parents to troubled teens. An elderly Florida man ran an ad saying he was available for "adoption," and a single mother took him up on it because her children had no grandparents.[38] The Adopt-a-Grandparent program in New Haven brought together 20-year-old Susan Crone and 85-year-old Boris Shukman. "I never had a real friendship with an older person," says Crone. "I really get a lot out of it."[39]

Middle-aged adults say their young friends heighten their awareness of ordinary life and make them feel more connected to the future. Susan Jacoby, who is childless, realized at age 37 that she wanted and needed "closer contact with children of all ages—as a caretaker, teacher, adult confidante, and friend. . . . One of the greatest pleasures of my middle years has been the discovery that this newly emerging emotional need of mine is not only a boon to my friends (who need someone to give them temporary breaks from their parental responsibilities) but an important source of support for their children who need to see models of adult lives different from, as well as similar to, those of their parents."[40]

Cross-generational friendships are proliferating as a result of not only individual efforts but also several homogenizing social currents. A 50 percent divorce rate means that young people and second-timers are forming new families at the same time. Television and computers unite all ages in a common culture. Educational differences that used to accentuate the generation gap are disappearing as more Americans finish high school and go on to college. Unexpected ideological groupings have made strange bedfellows: On the left, the old out-radicalize the young, while on the right, a growing contingent of young conservatives are a sight for sore eyes. At work, three generations labor shoulder to shoulder as more seniors postpone retirement; at play, those who retire pursue the same travels and hobbies that engage the young before they "settle down."

As we cross all these lines and meet at many points along the life cycle, people of diverse ages, like people of every class and condition, are discovering that we who are in so many ways "the same and different" can also be friends.

Part Three

Forging New Meanings

Chapter 12

≋   ≋

Friends at Work

In the fifty years since Dale Carnegie first published *How to Win Friends and Influence People,*[1] the book has carved its own niche in the pantheon of best-sellers. The reason for its huge and enduring appeal is its premise: how to achieve business success through friendship. Today, however, people want something more; they want to know how to find friendship through business. Today, many people devote almost as much energy to making friends as to making money. And today, for many of us, at work is where our friends are.

Commenting on a Detroit study in which up to a third of those questioned named work colleagues among their closest friends, sociologist Lois Verbrugge said coworkers (along with kin and neighbors) tend to establish ties that are "more secure and holistic" because, in addition to feelings of friendship, they (1) are easily accessible, (2) share common interests and experiences, and (3) are able to give each other practical help and emotional support.[2] Of course, there can be liabilities associated with work friendship and we'll get to them in a moment; but let's begin with the credit side of the ledger.

Adding Up the Assets

First of all, coworkers have proximity. If company policy, coffee breaks, and the layout of office partitions allow frequent interaction, coworkers don't have to go out of their way to meet people. Face-to-face contact doesn't guarantee intimacy but it does facilitate friendship. Second, unlike most acquaintances, coworkers start with at least one major life experience in common: their job. They needn't flounder around in small talk or try to visualize what one another does all day; they have a basic understanding of each other's daily pressures and concerns. Third, they share an environment, both its comforts and hazards, and in this environment day after day they accumulate shared memories large and small. Fourth, they travel the same orbit with the same constellation of people who talk the same funny language—whether it's "What's the CPM?" (cost per thousand) or "What are his transitional objects?" (a teddy bear or baby blanket) or "What happened when she went up?" (forgot her lines).

I admit to a thoroughgoing enjoyment of shoptalk. Maybe this is because my "shop" is the book and magazine world where the personalities are often larger than life and the talk-of-the-trade is particularly lively. But I've stood in countless elevators in the fashion district, where my office is, listening to animated conversation about "crazy Moe who thinks this is the Year of the Belt" and which dress house is cutting velvet and who overbought on buttons. And whether or not I understand ladies' garments, the fish business, or risk arbitrage, I'm sure the insiders in those fields find their shoptalk just as lively and their personalities just as interesting.

A Personal Case History

Some of my most satisfying friendships have come about because of my work: I first met one of the dear friends I described in Chapter 4 when we were both starting out in the book publishing business, and the woman who was my secretary for much of the 1960s is still a good friend today. The surprising fact is that during nearly thirty years and ten different publishing or writing jobs even my casual colleagues have felt like friends. When people have a meaningful activity in common they are more than mere passersby in each other's lives.

I've also discovered that coworkers who are not very close can still constitute an extended family and that longevity can approximate closeness. My husband has been with his law firm since before our children were born and the personnel has changed very little through the nearly thirty years. As a result, the kids have come to consider their father's colleagues as "lawyers-in-law." His partners and associates and their spouses and children are as familiar as our cousins, if not more so.

Throughout my working life, my extended family has included peers, mentors, and apprentices. Although I rarely socialized with my bosses, from time to time I have called them for advice and they've helped me with patience and enthusiasm; and wherever we meet, I feel genuine affection between us. After I left book publishing to become a writer and magazine editor, my daily contact with most of these old colleagues ceased. I would not say they're my friends today, but I would say I "feel friendship" for them.

During fifteen years at *Ms.* magazine, I have developed a few close friends with whom I fully expect to grow old and gray, rocking side by side on the reviewing stand of the twenty-first century. They are my friends who happen to be coworkers. But there also have been coworkers who happened to be friends—women who were in my life just for then. There was a young layout artist who baby-sat for my children, several coworkers who were my research assistants for this and other books, a colleague who has given me computer lessons, the company accountant who offers tax advice, and several of the magazine's publicists who have helped promote my books. At the same time there have been a number of interns whom I've helped get fellowships or permanent jobs, four colleagues whose book contracts I've negotiated or revised, one I helped with a loan, and two others for whom I found a woman rabbi—one for a marriage, one for a funeral. Is this feminism or is this friendship? For me, it's both.

This personal digression is meant to prove one simple point: *A job is a place where coworkers can become friends.* They don't have to, but they can. Somewhere in your company, office, factory, store, or work unit, there is almost always someone worth adding to your circle if you choose to, someone who can be both your coworker and your friend.

Work Can Make Friendship Easier

Meaningful work friendships show up in all classes and occupational groups and some people think they are the best kind. Wendy Weil, my literary agent, is a good example of a professional who feels that it is perfectly logical that the people closest to her have been her colleagues. "A profession is like a college dormitory," she says. "You're thrown together, day after day, so you get to know people you wouldn't necessarily have gravitated toward. You're in the same situation. You know the same people. You build up a history together, then you're friends." Weil's historic close friends are Judy, who started out with her in the Doubleday training program twenty-five years ago; Martha, formerly her assistant; and Jonathan, formerly a publisher, now an agent. She also counts a few of her clients as real friends—"not just people who like me as a listener."

What do you talk about? I ask, wondering if relationships that start at work might remain work-oriented.

"What *don't* we talk about," she answers. "Our adventures, marriages, aging parents, illnesses, all our ongoing dramas. We're friends like any other friends."

That makes sense to me. What doesn't make sense is some people's insistence that there are immutable differences between workfriends and other friends. Like the word "kin," I read "coworker" as a status, not an emotional connection. And like the word "family," I read "workplace" as a context within which one can be anything from estranged to adored. Once again, the main point: You can have coworkers who just happen to be friends or friends who just happen to be coworkers. *You* determine which role is primary. The job situation merely provides the opportunity and the setting.

Russell Baker, the humor columnist, understands the unsung social benefits of the workplace. "People lucky enough to have an office to go to can partake of a wide array of gossip; form alliances against members of the social unity they dislike; plot schemes of vengeance, adultery and well-poisoning, and revel in the companionship of an interesting variety of personalities who help alleviate the tedium of work."[3]

Although, as usual, his tongue is firmly in his cheek, Baker is right to worry about whether the home computer will eventually eliminate the need for people to go to the office. The workplace has become the extended family, village well, and small town, all rolled into one. For many people, socializing at work is the most effortless socializing of their complex lives.

Megan Ryan, an administrative assistant, says, "I'm married and the mother of a young child, I rehearse and perform in a chorus, and

I'm a full-time worker. I don't have time to sit in the playground with other mothers or make dinner parties for my husband's associates. The only time I have for friendship is while I'm working. Luckily, my best friend is the woman I sit next to at the office. We're really comfortable talking about anything together. We schmooze like women used to do across the back fence."

No one says a job should be a laugh riot. And I'm not recommending that people squander work time in endless schmoozing. But it is my impression that employees who are happy together are also more productive. For the worker who has no other outlet for stress, having a friend on the spot—someone to whom you let off steam or turn to for advice—can save a company many dollars in absenteeism or medical expenses. A little on-site friendship goes a long way toward morale-building.

They certainly subscribe to that view in the military, which Roger Little calls "a unique occupational culture,"[4] where bonding, or esprit de corps, is "deliberately fostered as an objective of training." Since military personnel live away from kin and civilian society, use the same base facilities (commissary, school, chapel, barracks), share an identity and a uniform, and do everything in a group context, it is both easy and necessary for them to make friends.

When a married officer or an enlisted person is away on assignment, his or her family depends on the base friendship network for emotional sustenance and social activity. "Each family becomes an extended family for the others," says Dr. Theodore Williams, a retired Medical Corps captain who is now in private psychiatric practice. "Though we've all been on the move, once a friendship is established, we can call each other at any time and pick up where we left off."

Since service people are transferred so often, they tend to develop an aptitude for making friends quickly but not deeply. "You don't share all of yourself if you know you're leaving," says Dr. Richard Ridenour, the Navy's chief adviser in psychiatry. "Nevertheless, some friendships are quite intense. If we're stationed at the Fargo, North Dakota, Air Force Base, feeling that the outside world doesn't understand us, and spending more time together than most people spend with anyone ever, we might end up with a very close friendship. Or if two Navy doctors are away for twelve months on a carrier off Beirut and there's an explosion and they have eighty injured bodies to deal with, those two guys are going to get to *know* each other. They might even become lifelong friends. That just doesn't happen in a nine-to-five job."

For all its friendship benefits, the military is notoriously class-bound. "We're no more elitist than most people, we're just more up-front about it," protests Ridenour. "Instead of class, we call it rate and rank. Socializing beneath one's rank is called fraternization and it's forbidden; it may even be cause for court-martial. If you're an executive officer, fraternization with a subordinate smacks of favoritism. It erodes your ability to discipline your troops. And if there is a marked age difference between the two fraternizers, whether they are the same or opposite sex, it also smacks of sexual involvement." Ridenour feels cross-status friendships are "unhealthy" in civilian life too. "I'd worry about a physician who hung out with street people or whose main group of friends worked in the local factory," he says. "I'd worry about his identity."

Friends Can Make Bad Jobs Better

For people who get no particular pleasure from their jobs, co-worker friendship can be an important compensation.

In her studies of Chicano cannery workers in San Francisco, Patricia Zavella pays special attention to why women's on-site friendships are so important to them.[5] She describes how the production workers stand at a conveyor belt sorting produce and placing it in various chutes. The work is noisy, smelly, nauseating, and repetitive. The workers must wear earphones and are prohibited from talking with coworkers. Nevertheless, the women do talk during the half-hour lunch period and two 12-minute breaks, and they show great skill at forming relationships that reduce the monotony and help them get the job done. Whether they are kin, fictive kin, or friends, veteran workers train the novices, teaching them unauthorized short-cuts that help piece-rate workers earn more. They cooperate with one another on the production line. They sing, joke, talk about the supervisors, share information, and minimize their disputes so that no one gets into trouble.

"Friendships initiated on the job function to 'humanize' the work-place," Zavella says, "and the camaraderie women develop in this process becomes an important positive feature of the job . . . [and] a focal point of their private lives." Off-season, the women cultivate their friendships outside the factories. They visit one another, go shopping, or have lunch or drinks. Some introduce their husbands into the fun. The couples have parties and barbecues and take weekend trips and vacations together. Work-related factory friendship networks also provide the same sort of practical help that is often available at offices: baby-sitters, advice, assistance, and, in more than one workplace, comrades in a women's caucus organized to press for improved working conditions and one woman supports another when she resists an overbearing husband.

Occupations Have Personalities Too

Certain occupations encourage workers to be more involved with one another because of such features as:

- *isolation* (an oil rig)
- *unusual working periods* (the night shift, an archaeological dig, or a long tour of duty at sea)
- *shared social stigma* (sanitation workers)
- *shared danger* (firefighters or coal miners)
- *common ethnic background* (Chicana cannery workers; American Indian ironworkers; Irish cops)
- *team organization* (IBM or professional sports)
- *recruitment through personal ties* (legacy jobs in TV camera work or the building trades)

In addition, certain occupations create a more distinct group identity than others and are thus more likely to foster camaraderie between coworkers. For example, dancers, typographers, politicians, journalists, athletes, and steelworkers usually have more of a social world than file clerks, telephone operators, sales people, insurance adjusters, and stenographers.

Finally, full-time workers tend to be more involved with each other than part-timers are. Full-timers have less free time for their friends away from work—good reason for them to put more energy into their work friendships. "The fewer choices people have for making social ties, the likelier they are to rely on the workplace," says Claude Fischer, who found that homemakers are the workers who are most likely to restrict their friendships to other homemakers.[6] While they have more flexibility than factory coworkers, homemakers have no alternative location in which to develop relationships or seek more varied friends.

Blurring the Lines: Work Friends vs. "Real" Friends

In my best of all possible worlds, the homemaker would have more social options but other workers would have more of what the homemaker has: a permeable membrane between the worlds of work, family, and friends. I welcome any sign of a breakdown between categories, be they racial or gender categories or the rigid dividing lines between the personal and professional aspects of our lives. Blurring these arbitrary lines helps us understand that, in reality, everything we do and feel is connected: If we're having friendship problems, it affects our work, and if we're having child care problems, it affects our friendships, and if we're feeling good in one arena, it spills over into the others.

The friendship networks of the cannery workers strengthened women to the point where they could stand up for their rights in the workplace and also be more assertive with their husbands. Sometimes the spillover flows in the other direction and family matters strengthen workplace relations. This was the case with women factory workers in apparel and electronics plants who formed friendly relationships across barriers of language, culture, and age by "bringing the family to work."[7] With that phrase, Louise Lamphere summarizes many activities: workers sharing news of their family events, illnesses, and vacations; showing each other photographs of their holiday ceremonies and, through the pictures, explaining their ethnic customs; and celebrating each other's birthdays, engagements, marriages, anniversaries, childbirths, and retirements. (Women in "opposing" ethnic camps got together to contribute money for gifts, cooperatively wrap baby presents, and make potlucks, showers, and surprise parties for each other.)

Some observers believe these friendly practices foster complacency by taking the edge off unacceptable working conditions. Others see work friendships as the prelude to resistance because repeated interaction across ethnic and age boundaries builds solidarity for future job actions or union organizing efforts. One thing is certain: Warm family-oriented celebrations at the workplace cut through ethnic tension and job competition and even blur the distinctions between labor and management. The class struggle may not be well-served when supervisors participate in workers' friendship circles or when management makes it easier for these celebrations to take place at work (the unions call it co-optation). But friendship is the victor as workers rise above divisive interest groupings to celebrate what they have in common as human beings: family pride, a love of love, and the excitement of personal milestones.

It is one thing to humanize the workplace with more personal touches and quite another thing to allow impersonal workplace habits to spill over into one's friendships. Marilyn Machlowitz, a psychologist and author of studies on workaholics and "whiz kids" (young business successes), is concerned because so many fast-trackers treat their friends the way they treat business acquaintances. "Promising 'I'll call you in the morning to confirm our lunch date' and then canceling if something more important comes along is acceptable behavior in business but not among friends," she told me. "And when you offer, 'let's have a drink and get to know each other,' and the other person wonders what you want from them, it's a sign that friendship has become a more suspect motive than getting ahead."

She added another example: "Since I went to mostly male schools and I now work in a mostly male profession, I was hungry for women's friendship, so I decided to invite eight women colleagues to monthly Dutch-treat dinners at the Yale Club. I invited those particular women because I like them and I wanted to get to know them better. At the end of the dinner, when three of them asked if they could each bring a friend to the next gathering, and the rest started exchanging business cards, I knew my idea had been misunderstood."

She felt these actions depersonalized her intentions and made the dinner a networking event rather than an act of friendship. I see her guests' request to invite others and their exchange of cards as expressions of enthusiasm for the unique experience of having dinner at the Yale Club with a group of professional peers who were *all* women. I too would want to share such dinners with other friends. And I'd collect business cards to be sure I could reach the women I'd met that night to further develop these new friendships on my own. Furthermore, if all eight of them subsequently did business with one another, I'd rejoice that women have come so far from the days when the only thing we had to give each other was recipes.

I applaud most developments that interweave humanity's private and public selves—for instance, when businesses establish child care centers or sponsor social events for coworkers and their families. As Freud maintained, we are happy when we are satisfied both in love and in work. Inside each of us, love and work are mingled waters. When they are dammed into separate sectors, the pressure builds and something bursts. I don't want to see personal relations get more businesslike but I do want to see business relations get more personal. For our health and the health of our friendships, mixing business and pleasure sounds like just what the doctor ordered.

The Debits: Why Work Friendships Don't Always Work

Obviously, the workplace is no bed of roses and not every coworker becomes a pal, a mentor, a friend, or a member of your extended family. Sometimes friendship is stopped at the starting gate. Other times, things go wrong on the track. If the potential for positive relationships is not easily realized, the problem may be traced to one of these stumbling blocks:

- The friendship was situation-bound.
- One friend suffered a power failure.
- Discrimination destroyed mutual access.
- Competition destroyed mutual trust.

Think about your own coworkers—the friends you've lost or never made—and see whether one of these problems explains your experience.

Situation-Bound Friendship

The two of you are intensely close while you are working together, but at the end of the day or the conference or the project, your friend cuts off completely. Gone. Kaput.

This phenomenon is well known to anyone who has ever worked

in an election campaign. The whole campaign apparatus rises out of the mists like Brigadoon. Everyone works together at fever pitch with an intensity usually associated with medical emergencies. People eat every meal together, pull all-nighters, sleep at each other's homes, deliver huge hunks of emotional information to one another—all in a concentrated period of time. The passion for the candidate and the issues, the time pressure, and the sense of mission combine to create a fervent intimacy that makes coworkers feel they've been friends since childhood. "Then, the day after the election, most of them vanish," says Rhoda. "Off to the next job or the next candidate. And when I see them around, they act like we were casual acquaintances and never friends at all."

Rhoda's experience is typical of "situation-bound" friendship: a closeness that depends on a given context. The context can be an airplane seat, a neighborhood bar, a stalled subway car, or a work situation such as a research project, a convention of anesthesiologists, or a troupe of actors who become deeply enmeshed during the run of a play but go their separate ways when the show closes. For some people the situation is the *start* of something great, but for others the situation is the beginning, middle, and end, and the intimacy associated with it registers only as long as the situation exists.

Not everything about this phenomenon is bad. If we know that certain situations are conducive to friendship, we might purposely create them specifically to bring about social interaction. This is just what happened when a unifying work project was offered to elderly people: They got caught up in a "web of sociability" around the cooperative task.[8]

Sociologist Herbert Wong makes another positive point: You can have a *periodic* but significant friendship with the same person when you meet for a week twice a year at a sales conference. The duration or frequency of a relationship does not necessarily "affect its quality in terms of self-disclosure, sharing, trust or emotional security."[9]

Situational friendship is not necessarily less meaningful, but people who have a history of such friendships often assume it is a signal that they may be "afraid of intimacy." They worry that they may be the type who attracts superficial people, when, in fact, the pattern may not be due to personality or temperament at all but may be a result of factors beyond their control, such as the demands of their work schedule, the nature of their work, the atmosphere in their workplace, or the life-style associated with their particular occupation.

In other cases, situation-bound friendship is simply a matter of out of sight, out of mind. For instance, Lloyd and Dennis met when they were claim clerks at the same insurance company. They had been friends for almost two years when Lloyd left the company for a higher-paying job. Before a month was out, they were finding reasons for not getting together after work for their traditional shot and beer.

"Once we couldn't complain about the overtime, or our bosses, or talk about people we both knew, there was nothing much to say," Lloyd explained. "Dennis wasn't all that interested in hearing about my new job, and after a while, I was tired of gossiping about the old gang. To be honest, I think we got bored with each other."

Nothing odd about that fade-out. Without a shared situation, the two men discovered they had little else in common. In the case of Herb and Mary Ellen, two colleagues at a large law firm, the situation that bound the two of them was geographical convenience. When inconvenience was introduced, their friendship wasn't strong enough to overcome it even though they still had a lot in common. "I'd gotten into the habit of dropping in on Mary Ellen because her office was on the route to the men's room," Herb explains. "Those conversations really added up, since I went to the bathroom at least twice a day." He grins. "Many times, when I popped in, if we discovered that neither of us had a business lunch, we'd run out for a bite together. But last fall, the firm moved Mary Ellen's department to the thirty-fourth floor. That killed the spontaneity. Now it's a hassle to get on the intercom or take the elevator for a five-minute conversation. We keep saying we will, but we don't."

At all levels and in all occupations, friendships often fail because of a physical break in the links between coworkers—someone leaves, moves, works a different shift, is transferred. In general, this can't be helped, although employers can stimulate friendship by expanding the opportunities for coworker interaction beyond the work situation—hosting company picnics, outings, holiday celebrations, and team sports. (Incidentally, the companies most likely to offer sports activities are those that employ the most educated people.[10] Once again, as with so many friendship advantages, "them that's got, gets.")

Power Failures

Situation-bound friendships can atrophy from lack of contact at all job levels. But power failures—friendships that fade when the power fades—are unique to the upper echelon. Such was the experience of Morrie Goldfischer. Relieved of his duties after twenty-five years as a publishing executive, he began to free-lance but found himself deserted by his friends in the business. "It seems that leaving the mainstream of publishing life confers instant pariah-hood," he complains. "Your name mysteriously disappears from all Rolodexes and you become, if not an untouchable, an unreachable." He quotes Samuel Butler: " 'Friendship is like money, easier made than kept.' "[11]

In trying to figure out why Goldfischer's perceptions of publishing people were so different from mine, I thought at first that he might have been bitter about being laid off or that he had misjudged the isolation inherent in self-employment. But, more likely, the difference lies in our expectations. While I expected most of my daily "contacts" to disengage from my life once I left the business, he considered these associates his *friends* for life. He had not understood that, unless both partners work to make them otherwise, the "friendships" of business are almost invariably exchange relationships. They are based on mutual back scratching, and when we are not in a position to return a scratch—when we leave a job and no longer have the influence or power to do anyone any good—we are easily forgotten.

Given standard business practices, this fact is neither hard to understand nor unforgivable. It only becomes a problem when people believe they are being loved for themselves, instead of their position. As the Spanish proverb has it, "He is my friend who grinds at my mill." Without one friend's wheat and the other's mill, two colleagues lose the underlying reason for their interaction. Without the wheat and the mill, there is only each other.

In Washington, D.C., people understand that colleague friendships "represent mutual convenience verging on mutual opportunism," says Meg Greenfield.[12] Politicians seem well aware of the roles played by the wheat and the mill in their relations. But corporate executives and academics often resist seeing that they too may be relating to their colleagues position-to-position rather than person-to-person.

Gardner, a college professor, observes: "One's place in the academic hierarchy is so important that there's almost no possibility of an honest, selfless friendship taking root in this setting. Ambition eats up whatever intimacy might develop between scholars. We spend so much time on superficial colleagueship and so little on real intimacy. We read and cite each other's work and recommend each other for tenure—or not—but we don't share our feelings or talk about our worries or mistakes. We're out to impress, not to help." Gardner's self-awareness is atypical. Most academics are taken by surprise when they change universities and their ex-colleagues become instant ex-friends. "Our camaraderie is based on loyalty to the institution, not to each other," he says.

So here are the disappointments lying in wait for coworkers who are friends (as opposed to friends who are coworkers): They can turn out to be foul-weather friends like Lloyd and Dennis, who were close only when they had physical proximity and common complaints. Or, they can turn out to be fair-weather friends, like Morrie's or Gardner's former colleagues, who are close only when they are able to trade favors. Fair or foul, both are quintessential exchange relations and both can disappoint you if you think otherwise.

Coworkers who happen to be friends need to understand the limitations of such friendships. For instance, they may feel solidarity in the face of poor working conditions, but those same working conditions also subvert their friendship: They are more closely supervised or their socializing is crammed into short periods. And because some of that closeness stems from shared discontents, it may wither if they lose their common enemy or if one member of the pair becomes successful—exactly what happened when a woman at the San Francisco cannery was promoted to a supervisory job and her former coworkers made petty, jealous remarks about her.

While foul-weather friendship can't survive success, fair-weather colleagues *require* it. Powerful people are good at applauding one another's strengths and enjoying one another's influence, but they may not stand firm with someone who falters or leaves the scene of the action. In relationships both fair and foul, the parties function as coworkers first, so when that identity changes, the friendship changes. This does not happen with friends who just happen to be coworkers—they remain close no matter what happens to their careers.

Eight years ago Jennifer and Diedre became buddies when they worked together on a project that Diedre supervised. Then Diedre married the president of the corporation and lost her job because of the company rule against nepotism. Ironically, her husband was fired shortly thereafter. Since then, Jennifer has risen in the company, though not high enough to hire Diedre who has never found another job. "It's been really hard on her," says Jennifer, "but at least she knows I love her whether she's got a fancy title or not."

Discriminating Friends

It stands to reason that new job opportunities for women and minority men should have increased the incidence of cross-sex and cross-race friendships, but as you may have noticed around your own shop, it hasn't happened. Research done by Rosabeth Moss Kanter tells us why: White males perpetuate closed friendship circles and restrict key corporate information and strategies to members of those circles.[13]

A 1985 human resources report states: "Women executives suffer from isolation in the workplace to a far greater degree than do their male counterparts."[14] Since women at the top of the corporate hierarchy are excluded from male friendship circles, the report says, "an increasing number of the country's corporations are creating small peer groups to seek out and identify the human needs that executives have for companionship and understanding."

In academia, compared with their male counterparts, female professors have fewer male collegial friendships even though there are more males in virtually every academic discipline (enough for every woman to have a few as friends) and more males in power positions in most departments. It is not paranoid to suggest, as the researcher does, "that isolation from these informal collegial contacts leaves women at a professional disadvantage."[15]

Why haven't cross-sex and cross-race friendships developed on the job? Part of the answer is, as earlier chapters make clear, that people feel more comfortable with friends who are like themselves. In the workplace, say sociologists James Lincoln and Jon Miller, people choose friends of their own sex and race because of "the need to eliminate uncertainty from organizational arrangements."[16] Theoretically, then, the attraction of white males to their white male coworkers is no different from other kinds of homophily, whether it be the attraction of kids from the same neighborhood or Hispanics from the same social class.

But there *are* important differences. In the first place, most friendship homophily is motivated by the search for equality—for the
soulmate in an impersonal world. But in work situations, white male
homophily is motivated by the desire to protect the white male's
dominance of corporate power. You might say that the major "uncertainty" these men want "to eliminate from organizational arrangements" is the uncertainty that comes with having to compete
with new categories of workers. Given the already high level of
competition endemic to male relationships, the added presence of
female and nonwhite male competitors understandably makes white
men get a little hot under the collar—white collar or blue—and cool
to the idea of befriending newcomers.

In the second place, excluding people from workplace networks
has serious economic consequences for the excluded. Civil rights
laws supposedly temper the worst expressions of racism and sexism
on the job, but it is almost impossible to prove discrimination in
friendship. Employers demand functional cooperation between
workers, regardless of sex or race, in the company interest. And
many men exhibit superficially friendly behavior toward women or
minority men simply because of good breeding. But what counts
toward career advancement is what happens beyond the encounters
that are pragmatic and polite, for the attachments that affect who
gets the extras are informal, nonorganizational, and voluntary. As
Lincoln and Miller put it: "Friendship networks in organizations are
not merely sets of linked friends. They are systems for making decisions, mobilizing resources, concealing or transmitting information." When women and minority men are excluded from these vital
systems, it costs them as surely as if they were being left out of the
company health plan. For example:

- Somehow, everyone in the accounting department decided to
  reapportion office space on the day Luis, a Puerto Rican, was
  out sick.

- On the golf course Sunday, three company vice presidents (all
  male) came up with a marketing plan that impressed the president on Monday morning. Another vice president, Sue, could
  not share the credit—she's never been invited to play golf
  with the men.

- When Jonah, a Black, entered the bathroom, the conversation between two of his white coworkers came to a dead stop. Later that week, the two white men and three of their friends quit their jobs and found work at another plant. Not long afterward, Jonah learned that his factory would be closing and that he would be out of work along with several hundred others. In hindsight, he realizes that the two men had had advance word of the shutdown. They managed to get relocated before hundreds of laid-off workers—including Jonah—could flood an already depressed labor market.

Competing Interests

In the big economic picture, capitalism, not socialism, generally is considered the breeding ground for competition and worker alienation. What does that mean to coworker friendship?

When people feel alienated from their work, friendships suffer, but when workers feel their work is meaningful and not dog-eat-dog, coworker friendships increase. In other words, the happier we are at work, the more involved we are in everything associated with our jobs, including workplace friends. In two socialist countries in Eastern Europe, salaries are more equal and professionals practice more cooperative approaches to business projects. As a result, "a close friendship group develops."[17]

In America, not too many people think much about capitalism's ethic of competition or its effect on work relationships. When asked about it, most deny there is a connection. Ninety percent of *PT*'s respondents said friendships do not suffer because one friend becomes more successful than the other. However, when asked what accounted for the cooling or termination of their friendships, two of the most common replies were "one of us became markedly more successful at work" and "one of us became much richer."

Most competition between friends is indirect. Coworkers don't go at each other with hammer and tongs; they are stealthy, they make their moves circuitously; when they gain an advantage, they affect surprise. They attack by omission as well as commission— that is, they innocently "forget" to do something to help a friend. Take the experience of unemployed engineers in Boston. When their former colleagues did not actively help them find new jobs, the out-of-work engineers felt deserted. They were oblivious to the rampant competition inherent in any period of widespread layoffs in any field—especially engineering. When jobs are plentiful, colleagues serve as each other's referral sources and two out of three find work through friends. But when jobs are scarce, the networking proportion drops to one in three or four.[18]

I asked dozens of working people about competition and friendship. Some said it was impossible to have a truly trusting relationship with a colleague, precisely because of the nature of most jobs. "In this plant, we aren't judged against some standards posted on the wall, we're judged against each other," says a piece worker. "If I work fast, I earn more, but it makes everybody mad because it shows that they could work faster too. How can I be friends with someone who stands in the way of my making money or resents me for wanting a promotion?"

"If a coworker gets to know you too well, he has ammunition to use against you," insists a chemical company accountant who steers clear of his coworkers for fear of an inevitable conflict between loyalty and self-interest. "Besides, you might have to take sides in a power struggle, and a friendship could hamper your decision. Suppose I have a buddy who's on the bosses' shit list; say the guy's a whistle-blower on some company violation or something. What should I do, turn him in and get a gold star or defend him and watch my career go down the drain? I don't want to have to face that choice, so I keep to myself." The option of valuing a friend enough to sacrifice one's single-minded ambition in favor of a higher principle struck this man as "utopian and naive."

Others say that it's rare for any two employees to be in direct competition and that coworkers are more likely to be in a position to help one another. "I have two close friends who've been here a long time," attests a museum staff member. "They tell me what's going on behind the scenes, where the job openings are, how my boss likes things done, and how my work is evaluated. It's like having six ears not just two."

Still others say they enjoy their work friendships *because* of the competition. "If it doesn't get out of control, it can give you an adrenaline rush and keep your work fresh," insists a graphics designer. "My pal at the next worktable admits he tries to come up with designs that are more original than mine and I do the same with him. It doesn't hurt our friendship to know this."

A "young turk" software inventor has a practical reason for preferring work friends: "When my outside friends get jealous of my
success, they're not in any position to compete with me so they just
become snotty or play 'who has more status symbols.' With people
at work, the competition is for tangible rewards like a raise, a share
of the profits, a vice presidency, or a company car. I prefer my work
friends to my other relationships because their competitiveness is
very honest and up-front."

Other opinions focus on *who* is more competitive. "Men are
usually worse than women, because they've had to be," says a food
services manager. "Most women don't get carried away with the
scramble to the top. But I once had a woman friend who did scramble
and she screwed me royally."

Some women have reason to be street fighters. Many feel they
have to prove themselves to be not simply good at what they do but
"as good as a man" (*which* man is never mentioned). Under this
pressure, they may be excused for out-toughing the competition but
they aren't going to win any popularity polls. Women also need a
sixth sense to know when a friendship with a male coworker might
arouse suspicion of sexual hanky-panky and thus give a competitive
colleague something to use against them. Furthermore, women are
often put in the position of competing solely with other women,
especially in medicine, law, architecture, the construction trades, and
wherever females are still underrepresented. Each woman is made
to feel that she has to be a credit to her sex but also that her sex is
her only competition. It's as though there are two lines of promotion,
male and female, and women are supposed to fight it out among
themselves to win the few top "women's positions." Such a climate
is hardly conducive to workplace friendships, yet research shows that
most women doctors still believe that "friendships with other women
are the key to achieving the strong sense of community they desire."[19]

On the question of whether successful or unsuccessful people are
more competitive, one top retailer says, "successful people make
better friends because they don't suffer from the inferiority feelings
that make people competitive. At a certain level of achievement
people rise above their competitive instincts and just do their best.
They're like the old railroad and banking moguls. They may have
been ruthless in the beginning, but once they made their millions
they became magnanimous philanthropists and loyal friends even to
their former enemies."

A foreman in a plastics plant thinks of competitiveness as a character trait—either you have it or you don't. "Once a competitor always a competitor," he says. "If you like to beat your friends at cards, sports, or arguments, you'll like to beat them at work. I don't have a rule about whether to make friends with people at my job, but I do make it a rule not to trust anyone who has a cold-blooded will to win."

Some of the fiercest competition occurs in a workplace called college. Two seniors I spoke with say they never register for a course if their third roommate intends to register as well—unless they are prepared to put up with his craziness. He rushes out to buy all the books on the syllabus, announces how far ahead he is in his assignments, and sneaks looks at his roommates' class notes, but he never wants to discuss the course with them, refuses to study with them for exams, and brags shamelessly if he gets a better grade than they do. "He's a terrific guy, as long as you stay out of his races," says one roommate. "The only way we'll ever remain friends when we get out of school is if we're in totally different occupations."

A sophomore woman insists, "Compared to high school, this competition is nothing. None of my friends pull me down; if anything, it's a matter of my measuring up to them. We never want the other one to do badly—we just want to do as well."

Although not always aware of it, some people have bypassed competition at work or school by steering clear of their peers and making friends with their underlings. In principle, such relationships are healthy, barrier-crossing friendships but, in fact, they can be touchy situations. They give "superiors" security and status but are rarely intimate because a leader cannot afford to show weakness and an underling cannot afford to criticize the person who has all the power. The equality that is natural to friendship contradicts the authority structure that is natural to business. In other words, you can't be a confiding pal one day and a demanding boss the next.

But you can establish a mentor relationship, and many do. Mentoring seems to appeal to people who don't need work friends because their intimacy needs are satisfied in their marriage or outside friendships. (Alice Rossi speculates that wives play the role of "intimacy mentors" to their husbands, while men play career mentors to each other.) A mentor relationship also satisfies people who are threatened by closeness; to avoid intimacy, they avoid equality and opt for power and distance.

Whatever the motivation, I hope there are always mentors around and young people to learn from them. I had splendid experiences with mentoring from both directions. I've also known people who are better mentors than parents and I've known people who are more available to their workplace subordinates than to their friends. This is sad for their children and friends but I don't think it means all mentoring is a zero-sum game. And I don't see anything wrong with people expressing their parenting impulses on the job. (Again, a nice blurring of the lines.) Not everyone has to be a biological parent; adopting an apprentice can be better than rearing a child if you're not suited to it. And, for that matter, having children of your own shouldn't stop you from wanting to help and empower the young people you work with.

Mentoring is a sweet antidote to competition but its effects are only temporary. While mentor-apprentice pairs are unequal for the moment, if the mentor is effective, the relationship is eventually transformed into a friendship of equals. In fact, your apprentices may grow up to be your toughest competition—because *you* trained them.

Competition mentioned in connection with friendship is usually a scare word because of its association with dog-eat-dog careerists. But when we stop dividing things into strict categories, we see that competition is an across-the-board fact of life. It is not an isolated workplace problem. It affects not only coworkers but neighbors who compete with their showcase lawns or classy cars and wives and husbands whose conversational contests can ruin a party or sour a marriage. And when married people compete for earnings or status, when they bad-mouth and belittle each other, hide their assets, or manipulate their finances, they make rival coworkers look like loving altruists.

Although you may encounter one of the four stumbling blocks that thwart friendship in the workplace—a friendship that is situation-bound or victimized by power politics, discrimination, or excessive competition—that doesn't make the workplace a bad place for friendship. Conversely, friends that you meet at school or church are not automatically more intimate, self-disclosing, loyal, unbiased, or noncompetitive than the people you meet at work. It's a mistake to confuse the *context* with the *content* of friendship: Your roommate can be the most competitive person on earth and the friend you met at church can be a selfish pig.

Remember, the workplace is only a place. What happens to

friendship on the job depends on dozens of variables, from the location of the water cooler to the smoking habits of the person at the next desk. The only generalization you can safely make about co-worker friendships is that they are basically no different from other friendships; they are just as complicated, just as quirky, and potentially just as satisfying.

Chapter 13

≈   ≈

Men's Togetherness

Why am I rounding the homestretch of this book by devoting the next three chapters to friendship and the sexes? After discussing the thousands of variables among friends, how can I resort to the crude divisions of male/female—especially when, of all human relations, friendship is supposed to be the most *human* and the least sexual?

Because I am not talking about friendship and eroticism but about which sex is friends with which sex and how their friendships differ. It would be naive to ignore the nose-on-your-face truth about social relations in America: That although we are a relentlessly *heterosexual* society, our nonromantic interactions are overwhelmingly *"homosocial."* Jean Lipman-Blumen coined that term to describe men's and women's preference for the company of the same sex.[1] She views this as part of a sex-linked system of power that has political, economic, and social consequences. She argues that men seek one another's company both because of their desire for a like-self soulmate and because, as those in control of society's resources, they are able to offer those resources to each other. Thus, the cycle continues: Men's homosocial friendships reinforce the all-male club, the old boy network, sex segregation in the workplace, and other institutions of patriarchy, which, in turn, enforce traditional sex roles and perpetuate male supremacy.

I subscribe to this theory not just because I believe homosocial friendship keeps women out of power but because it keeps men in chains of their own. The largest gender gap in American life exists not in electoral politics but in social relations, where men emerge as the disadvantaged group. In short, male friendship is in trouble.

Male Bonding Revisited

Can this be true? For centuries, friendship between men was the paradigm of human comradeship, mutual trust, loyalty, compatibility, and selfless love. From the biblical story of Jonathan and David, the Babylonian epic of Gilgamesh and Enkidu, the Greek concepts of platonic love and *Philia,* the Christian distinction between Eros and Agape, to more modern philosophic rankings which place brotherly love above romance and sexual desire, the friendship of men has been described as transcending anything women might feel for each other.

Hundreds if not thousands of writers and social scientists from Homer to Freud have shared the view that women are incapable of deep, enduring friendship for various reasons, ranging from their supposed solipsism and superficiality to their competition for husbands and their inferior psychosexual development. These sentiments of Montaigne, from his essay "Of Friendship," are typical: "The ordinary capacity of women is inadequate for the communion and fellowship which is the muse of the sacred bond of friendship, nor does their soul feel firm enough to endure the strain of so tight and durable a knot."

In our own time, the adventure novel and buddy movie (such as *Butch Cassidy and the Sundance Kid, The Deerhunter, The Sunshine Boys,* and *The Sting*) have personified male comradeship in the popular culture and made women's affiliations seem silly or boring in comparison. In 1969 anthropologist Lionel Tiger gave fellowship a "scientific" shot in the arm with his theory that men are better friends because "male bonding" was biologically necessary for human survival during the sweep of evolution.[2]

Then, in the 1970s and 1980s, the whole picture changed. Systematic reality checks not only failed to prove Tiger's thesis but cast doubt on the entire mystique of male camaraderie. "The male bonding described by Tiger may indicate sociability, but it does not necessarily indicate intimacy," said sex-role expert Joseph Pleck.[3] One team of researchers discovered that men in groups exhibit not male bonding but "male hostility vis-à-vis other males."[4] Elizabeth Aries of Amherst College found "competition and aggression" in all-male groups.[5] Sociologist Robert Bell described men as being "stuck within themselves."[6] And the latest Kinsey Institute study reported that homosexual men have "more good, close friends" than heterosexual men do.[7]

A few indictments were issued with sad reluctance. After interviewing 1000 Americans and Europeans in his three-year search for "true friendship among adult men," psychologist Stuart Miller found "most men clearly admitting that they had no real male friends and most of the rest pretending or thinking they did when they did not."[8] Daniel Levinson's life-span study of adult male development states: "In our interviews, friendship was largely noticeable by its absence. As a tentative generalization, we would say that close friendship with a man or a woman is rarely experienced by American men."[9] And in 1985, after a decade-long study of 5000 men and women, Michael McGill wrote:

> To say that men have no intimate friends seems on the surface too harsh, and it raises quick objections from most men. But the data indicate that it is not far from the truth. Even the most intimate of friendships (of which there are very few) rarely approach the depth of disclosure a woman commonly has with many other women. . . . Men do not value friendship. Their relationships with other men are superficial, even shallow.[10]

The Four "Incompletes" of Male Friendship

Time and again, researchers have come up with the same results: Men have *more* friends than women but women's friendships are richer, deeper, and more meaningful. Let's put it this way: If friendship were a course of study, men would get "incompletes" in four significant subjects.

Men Do Not Give Each Other Affection

"He just sat there," says a 28-year-old man, about his closest friend. "I was crying about how my dad had hardly touched me or showed me any love and now he was dead and it was too late, and here was my best friend sitting there watching me sob, not touching me and not giving me any love—just like my old man."

Whenever men discourse on the male condition, one of them inevitably mentions father deprivation. He recalls hating that he had to graduate to paternal roughhousing and man-to-man handshakes while his sister continued to receive Dad's hugs; hating that he was denied embraces and words of paternal affection and was given, instead, a playful jab on the chin as a sign of his father's love, if indeed his father was there at all.

To deal with this legacy, a 45-year-old Rhode Island man joined one of the men's support groups that proliferated in the wake of women's consciousness-raising groups. "At first all we talked about was how angry we are at our fathers. Everyone had a father who didn't give a shit or who never had anything good to say about him. One guy felt so remote from his father that he labeled his conception as 'all egg.' Another guy told how his father came home from work every night, ate supper, and then went to bed, never speaking a word to him. Now the father's in a nursing home and he can't talk at all. By the end of his story, the guy was bawling like a baby."

When I tell this to other men, many nod somberly, like witnesses at a criminal trial, and say that they too were exiled from Daddy's lap. In a sense, grown sons *are* testifying to a crime: the theft of father-love, spirited away by homophobia and buried by countless reminders to his little boy to "act like a man" and "don't come running to Daddy." As a result, the intimacy quotient of the average father-son relationship leaves much to be desired. Just consider the fact that four out of five college women named their mothers among their close friends, while *none* of the young men mentioned their dads.[11] But beneath the overt complaints about nondemonstrative fathers I hear a broader cry of distress that men are too embarrassed to state outright. "We are starved for male affection" is what they're saying. "And maybe, if our fathers had been affectionate with us, we could be affectionate with each other."

Actually, the root cause of the problem is not fathers but narrow notions of manhood to which fathers, like all men, have been forced to succumb. A "Real Man" learns that *affection is sexual and emotional* and is acceptable, therefore, only in encounters with women.

Yet, many men now admit that they want to be able to say to another man what they feel about him and to hear each other say it and to physically express their feelings for a man without having to be in a foxhole or football game to make it "kosher." They want permission to use another body language besides the athletic, the violent, and the erotic.

When Joseph LaBonte, 20, was serving a six-month prison sentence, a sad, frightened 18-year-old was assigned to his cell and the two became fast friends. "He always brightened my day whenever I was with him," Joseph told his mother when he asked her to take his friend into their family when his prison term was over. Shortly afterward, the warden separated the two young men on suspicion of homosexuality, although Joseph insisted their relationship was "brotherly" and that they had never had sex. Says Joseph, "I felt like crying because I couldn't see how a man with so little understanding of the needs of a prisoner could get the job he has."[12]

At one point in Stuart Miller's search for friendship, he rigorously dissects his "rosy good feeling" for a particular man, trying to determine whether it is a signal of homosexual desire. "Do I want to fuck him?" he asks himself in alarm, then answers: "No. . . . My true problem, rather, is what to do with my *tenderness* toward him." Miller can do nothing, given the limited lexicon of masculine emotional expression. "I sit in my chair and feel what I feel. But I do not caress that tired head. And he probably could use it."[13]

Men want to be able to show tenderness without calling their sexuality into question in their own minds or anyone else's. "The desire to touch is a natural outgrowth of friendship," says 32-year-old Jed, "but I touch men friends at my peril. They just can't handle it. They make a joke about how we're all turning gay, but you can see they're freaking out. It's easier to be friends with women because they accept touching as part of feeling good about a person. Men aren't like that."

In much of Europe, Africa, Latin America, and the Middle East, men *are* like that. They openly embrace each other and stroll the streets arm in arm. I saw men holding hands in every city of the People's Republic of China. In airport lounges and sidewalk cafés all over the world, one can watch men friends (and fathers and grown sons) greet one another with hugs and kisses. But in America, sex-role rigidity and homophobic paranoia censor the body language natural to the discourse of friends.

"My friend Rob and I have been accused of homosexuality just because we spend a lot of time together," says Nik Weinstein, a high school senior. "Can you imagine what they'd say if we ever hugged?"

"My friends and I hug when we haven't seen each other for three months in the summer," protested my son, David, at age 17. "Well, actually it's more like an affectionate tackle."

"Affection is in such short supply in a man's life that whatever I do really registers," says Andrew, a high-ranking elected official. "I'm a toucher. I handle people, hold their hands in mine, grip their shoulders, put my arm around them, give them bear hugs even. I like to believe men enjoy the unfamiliar feeling of nonthreatening male body contact, but maybe I get away with it because they like being touched by someone in power."

For a politician, warmth is part of the strategy to win public support. But Andrew makes it clear that his inordinate physical expressiveness is related to his body's energy cycles and his own need for affection: "Sometimes, when I feel drained or my motor overheats, I wish I had a friend who'd say, 'Gee, you look tired, let me run a bath for you'; someone who'd stroke my hair and rub my back. But no man is going to give me that. Only my wife and kids rejuvenate me with that kind of caring."

At present, while our generation is in transition between old and new forms of masculinity, one man's idea of affection can be another man's homophobic nightmare. For instance, psychologist Joseph Pleck posits a "new brotherhood" that ranges from men who accept a man-to-man hug as "just one way of expressing warm feelings for someone" to men who can see themselves "sharing sexually with another man if it felt right in a particular relationship." But Herbert Gold, the novelist, describes being taken aback simply by another man's questions:

> We were enjoying a meeting of the minds about the deep matter of friendship, and I thought we understood each other. Then he asked, "Do you kiss your friend?"
> "What?"
> "On the lips?" he asked.
> I began to laugh, and he looked hurt. I was laughing be-

cause I had thought we understood each other and we didn't; he was hurt because he had in mind a model for friendship based on the credo of his former wife's women's group, and evidently I didn't have that in mind.[14]

Spoken affection between men is almost as hard to come by as the physical kind. A national survey found that 58 percent of all males had not told their best friend that they liked him. "If the disclosure of liking one another is so difficult, it is little wonder that hugging, holding hands, caressing and kissing, which are allowed between close friends in some cultures, are not often observed in our culture," says sex-role researcher Robert A. Lewis.[15]

John Updike describes his novel *The Centaur* as his favorite, partly because "it's a portrait of my father; and I loved my father, and really could only say it in that book—I don't think I ever said it to him."[16] As for saying it to friends, Steve Tesich, a playwright and screenwriter (*Breaking Away*), says, "I can tell women I love them. Not only can I tell them, I am compulsive about it. I can hardly wait to tell them. But I can't tell the men. I just can't. And they can't tell me. Emotions are never nailed down."[17]

Some men die not knowing how much they mattered to their friends, and others outlive their friends knowing they withheld the information. "I tend not to admit that I love someone if he is male, until after he can't hear me," wrote critic John Leonard. "This is a cold witness."[18]

So many of the men I interviewed confessed the same reticence.

What would have been so hard about telling your friends how you feel? I ask.

"Hard?" they repeat, surprised at being accused of shirking a challenge. "It didn't come up," they answer. "We weren't like that." "We didn't need it."

Affection Substitutes. What sometimes takes the place of forthright verbal or physical affection are coded messages that men pride themselves on deciphering. Andrew Neuwirth, a high school student, says, "I've been forced to be more open with my female friends. With the guys, I can articulate a lot less and they understand." Although studies find that women engage in more nonverbal communication than do men, the male code-breakers insist that they exchange unspoken words with a pal, then read between the lines.[19] "Let the women play show-and-tell; we men just *know* when we're good buddies" they say, claiming to get their insights from a glance or a grin. If one partner happens to miss the message or to read it wrong, of course he is spared humiliation. Since nothing was said, nothing need be retracted; since no affection was shown, none was rebuffed. Intimacy imagined is intimacy controlled: The closeness may be illusory but it's also risk-free.

Another substitute for forthright affection is the hail fellowship of self-proclaimed "outcasts together." Such men describe themselves as mutual mavericks or hint at becoming friends by default because each guy is more than most other people can handle. "It's him and me against the world" they declare, hiding the bulges of dependence and sentimentality beneath a curmudgeon's disguise, the favored stance of several pairs Paul Feinberg interviewed for the book *Friends:*

> "Our personalities are so goddam churlish most folks won't put up with the degree of bullshit that we both hand out, so each of us had to find somebody to be tolerant of the other," says Larry King, the author and playwright about his friend Warren Edsel Burnett.

> "Nobody likes him but me," laughs bank president Taylor Burke, referring to his friend, Captain Billy Tyndell. "I'm the only person in town who will talk to him. Everybody has to have one friend, the burdens we take on, and mine is being a friend to Captain Billy."

> "I don't want to be his friend; I'm just stuck with him," snarls Jesse Huey about his fellow octogenarian. "But he's a gentleman. One of nature's noblemen."[20]

Nothing corny. No gushing testimonials. The love-hate quality in these grudging admissions of affection stamps each friendship with the imprimatur of manliness. But we glimpse a crack in the tough exterior—one man's eyes water a little as he speaks, the other's face creases like a crumpled letter, written but never sent—and we know these two will cry more bitterly afterward if they do not manage to say "I love you" before one of them dies.

Men Do Not Talk to Other Men
about Intimate Things

According to *The McGill Report on Male Intimacy*, "One man in ten has a friend with whom he discusses work, money, marriage; only one in more than *twenty* has a friendship where he discloses his feelings about himself or his sexual feelings."[21]

"Men like to talk, but not necessarily with their close friends," says journalist Maurice Carroll. "That is why God invented bartenders."[22] It also may be why God invented women.

Tony and Bill work as camera operators at the same TV station and eat lunch together every day. "We bitch and moan about whatever happens on the set and trust each other not to carry tales," says Bill, "but I can't say we're totally honest about personal stuff. When his oldest kid had a major drinking problem and dropped out of college, Tony didn't tell me, I found out months later from my wife who heard it from Tony's wife."

Men talk to wives and other women when they talk at all. When denied a female ear but in need of talk, they resort to bartenders or support groups.

After separating from his wife of twenty-two years, Ted Lewis, an insurance executive, formed a support group for divorced men because he was unable to talk about his feelings with any of his friends: "If you sought out male companionship for anything else but business or sport you were treated with suspicion."[23] Even without an emotional subject on the agenda, the very idea of purposeless conversation makes many men anxious.

> I once called a friend to suggest that we have dinner together.
> "Okay," he said. "What's up?"
> I felt uncomfortable telling him that I just wanted to talk, that there was no other reason for the invitation.[24]

Donald Bell, author of *Being a Man: The Paradox of Masculinity*, also joined a couple of men's groups in search of honest talk. But after exhausting the "big issues," the groups dissolved as the men found more compelling things to do: "Sustaining intimate contact and dealing on a close and personal basis proved to be too difficult for us."[25]

What do friends talk about? Most women communicate with their best friends on three levels: *topical* (politics, work, events), *relational* (the friendship itself), and *personal* (one's thoughts and feelings). Most men, however, generally restrict their exchanges to the topical.[26] Furthermore, many men *perceive* their conversations as intimate when they are actually topical. "We are pretty open with each other, I guess," said one fellow about his best friend. "Mostly we talk about sex, horses, guns, and the army."

"I'm very open with Robert," boasts another man about his closest confidant. "I'll tell him anything. If I think his girlfriend looks like a rabbit, I'll tell him." These proudly "open" guys remind me of a man I interviewed who pronounced a friendship intimate on the grounds that "we know each other's salaries."

While half the women in one survey say they talk by phone to their closest friend ten minutes or more either daily or weekly, only 19 percent of the men say they have that much contact. Both sexes seem to get together with their friends equally often; the women do it in twosomes, the men in groups.[27]

In mixed-sex groups, men engage in more one-to-one conversation, taking their cue from the women, but when men are in all-male groups, they often address their remarks to the full assemblage.[28] Are they testing their power and influence by demanding to be seen and heard by all? Is talking to a whole group a way of evading the close personal contact that makes so many men uncomfortable? Or is it that addressing the whole gathering at once lets a man establish his credentials more efficiently—which men may feel more pressured to do in an all-male group?

What They Talk About. Of all the patterns charted by systematic friendship research, the most consistent finding is that males and females talk about very different things in very different ways. *The average man's idea of an intimate exchange is the average woman's idea of casual conversation.* The two sexes often approach the same subject from completely different directions. When a party broke into sex-segregated clusters and both groups were discussing the *Achille Lauro* hijacking, the men debated which country should prosecute the terrorists who killed Leon Klinghoffer, while the women tried to analyze what kind of a person could shoot an old man in a wheelchair.

In childhood, girls talk to their girlfriends about school, wishes, and needs, while boys talk about sports, motors, and locations.[29]

From late adolescence on, Elizabeth Aries says, "males, unlike females, avoid a high degree of intimacy with members of their own
sex and acknowledge warmth and friendship in the form of joking
and laughter."[30] Women talk about themselves, their feelings, doubts,
fears, love relationships, families, homes, and problems; men talk
about competition and aggression, and things they have seen or
heard. They discuss work, sports, politics, social issues, money,
business, cars, weather, and traffic. When sociologists studied gossip—"conversation about any third person"—they found that, contrary to stereotype, men's gossip is just as catty and derogatory as
is women's. The only difference is that men's gossip is most likely
to be about sports figures.[31] "Males engage in dramatizing and
storytelling, jumping from one anecdote to another, and achieving a camaraderie and closeness through the sharing of stories and
laughter. Females discuss one topic for a half hour or more, revealing more feelings and gaining closeness through more intimate self-
revelation."[32]

Basically, what women talk about most is *relationships*. The only
topic about which men talk frequently and in great depth is *sports*.[33]
A few days after I told this to my husband, Bert, he had lunch with
five middle-aged men. Somehow their conversation proceeded from
a review of the Giants-Redskins game, in which Joe Thiesmann's leg
was broken, to a heartwarming discussion of the 1950 Phillies. The
men went around the table naming the infield players, contributing
a fact or two about each, then doing the same for the outfield,
pitching staff, and catchers, proud of their ability to recall one old
name after another and to reconstruct the games of yesteryear. At
the end of the meal, Bert pointed out that, typical of men, they had
done nothing but discuss sports; in two hours no one had said a
single intimate thing. One of the men protested that they *were* intimate because they all had very warm feelings for the 1950 Phillies
and the discussion was very nostalgic. Bert said nostalgia wasn't the
same as intimacy and besides, you can't be intimate on the subject
of a baseball team. "We could have the same discussion with a group
of strangers and the feelings would have been identical," he insisted.
To this, the other man answered, "What are we supposed to do, tell
each other I love you?"

Are those the only alternatives for men: sports talk or I love you?

"For younger, unmarried men, sex is almost as popular a topic
as sports," says the *McGill Report*. "Curiously, the two topics are

discussed in much the same way, with anecdotes of past and present conquests and analyses of the players, but rarely a personal revelation."

Sex talk is very often sexist (and heterosexist). Misogyny, homophobia, and the denigration of women are used as the currency of exchange in much of male conversation. Straight men distance themselves from both femininity and homosexuality by advertising the number of women they've "had" and how emotionally uninvolved they were. Their conversation is about "scoring," not love.

This was certainly true of the friends portrayed in David Rabe's drama *Hurlyburly*. Even allowing for the Hollywood drug culture setting and the characters' show biz arrogance, the sex talk between these men objectified females in ways that made some women in the audiences boo and hiss. In the movie *Diner,* the young men who hang out together make sexual bets and divide the female world into girls for sex and girls for marriage. The author of the men's column in *Glamour* magazine, who is known simply as Jake, admits to his readers: "The problem with this male camaraderie is that it insists I act like someone I'm not. Even though I'm no sexist, you'd surely believe I was if you heard Steve and me rating women from one to ten as they pass on the street. . . . After a date, we always greet each other with the same single question: 'Any luck?' "[34]

A woman who overheard a group of young men talking in her college dining hall says, "It blew my mind. They were checking out all the females like we were at a cattle auction. Then one of them said 'Let's go get us some freshmen.' I felt weird, hearing how these guys look at women and seeing us as they see us."

One of Stuart Miller's subjects told him: "I learned years ago that the most important step with a man is to get beyond the level of friendship where you think you're intimate because you talk about women. You've got to get beyond talking about women. You've got to talk about yourself, about the other guy; above all, you've got to be willing to talk about the relationship."

Judging by most reports, that reasonable prescription is just so much pie in the sky. In *Essence* magazine, Martin Simmons describes what a Black man can and can't talk about with his friends: "Just let him go bopping down to the corner talking about how gentle or tender he is. Or let him try to tell the guys over a beer that he doesn't control his woman, that he doesn't sock it to her because he can't or doesn't want to. He'd be laughed out of the bar, and branded a punk, a chump, a fool—maybe even a faggot. In front of the boys, he'd better have made it with every woman he has ever said he wanted. He'd better be rough, tough, don't take no stuff."[35]

The Black men who were regulars at an urban barbershop "repeatedly revealed their sexual exploits with women and/or took decidedly misogynist positions on sex-role issues"—and the men with the most contempt for women were found to be the most admired. Although there was some talk about world affairs, most of their conversations focused on women's genitals, "screwing," rape, how women "ask for it," criticism of working mothers, gays, how women "can't do men's work like men," and other subjects relating to sex and sex roles—subjects through which men "negotiate" their masculinity.[36] Much the same was true of the men at the Oasis Tavern, a blue-collar haven for white working-class men;[37] and though the words may be better spoken, similar topics are covered in the all-male secret societies of the Ivy League.[38]

Whatever the ostensible subject of men's talk—sex, sports, politics—it is really about proving one's manhood and ending up on top. For instance, William Howarth, a veterinarian, and Bill Gunesch, a wholesale florist, who met twenty-five years ago at the Rotary Club, spend their time competing to grow the earliest squash, competing to raise the most money for the Colorado Interfaith Task Force Walk, and quizzing each other on facts about Colorado.[39] "Winning isn't everything, it's the only thing," said the legendary football coach Vince Lombardi, summarizing masculine ideology in a slogan that speaks to the goals of governments, armies, athletic teams, and individual men alike. When physical competition is inappropriate, men's conversations substitute as the Olympic qualifying event that separates the winners from the losers. As we've seen, these competitive rituals may take the form of intellectual one-upmanship among educated males, doing "the dozens" in the Black adolescent subculture, or negotiating masculinity in the barbershop.

Man talk is, in one man's words, "an ongoing pissing contest." Regardless of style, the goal of competitive conversation is the same: to test one's own strengths against the other guy's weaknesses to determine *who's the best?* Men trade gibes to prove who's the wittiest. They trade information to prove who knows the most. They trade war stories or sex sagas to prove who is the most heroic or the biggest stud.

The one thing most men do not trade with their buddies is the *truth* about themselves.

What They Don't Talk About. Telling the truth would mean admitting some loss (nobody is a winner all the time) and no man can afford to reveal his losses to a competitor. He can tell a woman pieces of this truth because no matter how much he diminishes himself in the telling, society allows all men to feel superior to all women. A female confidante may comfort him or boost his ego but she can't provide ultimate reassurance of his manhood. The "second sex" does not have the stature to grade its "betters." Only another man can help a man figure out who he is and where he stands in the world. Without such a friend "to walk with, relate to, bounce thoughts off," wrote Martin Simmons, "you can easily lose sight of the real meaning of power and manhood."

By late adolescence, male emotions are well-defended. "A guy has to be a *very* close friend before I'll ask his advice," says Steve Lemme, 18. "When you ask for advice, you're showing your weakness." Our culture teaches boys that power is manhood. To maintain control, a man has to put up a front, often using humor as both a weapon and a shield. Humor more than any other tactic serves men "as a guise for intimacy and as a guard against it," says the *McGill Report,* but you have to play by the rules. "For example, it is acceptable for a friend to call his slightly overweight buddy a 'lard ass.' A woman would never make such a reference to a friend. Male rules dictate that such an insult should be taken with a laugh and returned in kind. Those men who take offense at such gibes or cannot make a retort soon find themselves excluded from friendship groups, as do those who go beyond a man's public self to a more intimate private or personal attack."

If that slightly overweight friend is hurting, he takes it "like a man"; he suffers in silence. He doesn't tell his friends when he feels insulted. A Real Man also doesn't tell them when he is confused or frightened, doubts his ability, is obsessed about losing his hair, talent, or stamina, has problems with his wife and children, or worries about sex, health, money, failure, aging, and death. In a crisis, he has no one for solace or counsel. Without his sense of humor, he is alone.

"To talk to other men about cowardice is unthinkable," wrote John Leonard. "When I am devastated—on the breaking up, for example, of a marriage—I call a male friend, who is appalled and silent. He doesn't know what to think; he listens and nods; his forgiveness is a blank check, but he doesn't want to leak any of his own pain for fear of seeming less than manly. And then of course, when he cracks up, I behave in the same way. We want to be friends without talking about it."[40]

Or men *avoid* their friends so they don't have to talk about it—whatever "it" is. Journalist Tom Powers tells of a man who ran in the opposite direction when he saw an old friend. He wanted "to get the hell out of there before he was trapped into talking over old times" and coming face to face with what he once wanted to be. Failure—or falling short of one's dream of success—puts an impossible burden on friendship. "At the very moment when a man is confronted with the limits of the self, and most needs to consider himself a part of a human community rather than a humbled Napoleon, he finds that he is nevertheless cutting himself off from old friends," wrote Powers. "I don't ask certain friends what they are working on now because I know how much they will suffer if they tell me, and certain friends don't ask such questions of me. So we speak, when we speak at all, of neutral things and take a long time to be at ease with each other and let years go by without meeting just as if we had five lifetimes in which to be friends and could afford to squander this one."[41]

But if close friends cannot talk about "it," how does their relationship satisfy the most basic criterion of intimacy? It doesn't. While those who *do* overcome their reluctance to talk openly tend to become much closer, better friends—and having truly close friendships has been linked with greater levels of health and happiness—most men do not exchange intimacies until some tragedy, some existential epiphany, helps them see that they really have nothing to lose.

Arny Lipin has Lou Gehrig's disease, a muscular degeneration. Arnie Carr has Hodgkin's disease, a form of cancer. The two men found their way out of competitive male rituals the hard way, by "letting go of the same things—of ego and ambition," says Carr. "The more he lost his physical powers and his body fell away, the more his heart seemed to open." And Lipin admits: "I lived most of my life without allowing people to get close to me. When I became ill, many things started changing for me besides what was going on in my body. I was no longer competing with anyone. . . . Most of my friendships before had been based exclusively on doing things. . . . I never let any of them in because deep down I was afraid that what they might discover about me was unworthy. . . . There's nothing unspoken now. Arnie and I show ourselves to be scared. We embrace each other and give open affection to each other. There are no judgments or expectations."[42]

Confronting sickness and death, some men continue to play the eternal winner; they mask their fears the way a shaman masks his mortality behind a facade of ancestral invincibility. For other men, a life-threatening episode helps them see the flimsiness of their masquerade. Like Arnie and Arny, they find the trappings of manhood empty and invalid. (Yes, invalids often discover what is invalid.) In weakness, they discover the enormous power of male intimacy, a resource that is *always there*—an endowment fund whose principal is untouched while one lives on the interest. Pity that a man must be incapacitated—"invalid-ated"—before he permits himself to draw upon that capital sum and invest it wisely in a few good friends.

Men Do Not Nurture Each Other

Male friends are good at friendship when there is a bike to be borrowed, a house to be painted, or something to get, do, buy, make, find, or fight for. As valuable as this form of help may be, it is very different from the kind we call *nurture*.

Four men volunteered information about male nurturing or the lack thereof:

"Phil was the only man who really cared about me at a time when I was more anxious and depressed than I'd ever been in my life. My wife had left me a week before. My business was losing a fortune. I just couldn't see any light at the end of the tunnel. Late one night, I had a real panic attack—chills, trembling, paranoia, the works. I called Phil who came right over. He let me talk awhile, then insisted on sleeping over even though all I have is a loveseat in my living room. The next day, after he left, I couldn't bring myself to go to work and that night again I was afraid to be alone. I called another friend and asked him to keep me company. He said he would but after a couple of hours when he hadn't arrived, I called him. I heard someone pick up the phone, listen to my voice, then hang up. I felt like killing myself. I thought I had no friends, I couldn't work, eat, or sleep; I swear I considered jumping out the window. Then, the doorbell rang. It was Phil. He said he was going to stay another night to make sure I'd be okay. He crammed himself into that little couch and told me to wake him if I needed anything. I've never forgotten it."

"Quincy and I had been involved with women other than our wives and we both got found out at about the same time. His love affair was more serious than mine, but my wife's reaction was more extreme than his. I wasn't sure if my marriage would survive. I was terribly upset and ashamed. I unloaded all my misery on Quincy. He unloaded only about 25 percent of *his*. He's never been in touch with his own pain but he was amazingly insightful and good at healing mine. I've felt safe with him ever since. If you go through big trouble with a friend it brings you closer than togetherness in tranquil times, and if a man's responses to your troubles are acceptable, it builds trust."

"When I got fired from my job, I was in such a state of shock I can't even remember how I got home from work. My best friend, Charlie, and I had tickets for a hockey play-off game that night but there was no way I was going anywhere. I was sure Charlie would give up his ticket too and come help me cry in my beer. But he never even offered. He gave my ticket to another guy and off they went to the game. Since then he's been very awkward around me. I'm out of work for the first time in twelve years and the guy never even asks me how I feel."

"When I meet people I like, I pursue them. I turn off all the burglar alarms. I talk rhapsodically to and about them. I kind of take hostages. Most of my friends are women or fellow recovering alcoholics. I've never had anyone call just to see how I am, other than a lover or another recovering alcoholic. I envy the way women take care of each other. If I can't make a spiritual connection with my men friends, I'd rather spend my time on my boat alone with my cat."

A nurturant person is one who "gives help or counsel to people who are having difficulty" and "manifests a genuine interest in the problems of others." Given this definition, a large sample of men rated their women friends highest in nurturance but gave their male friends the lowest ratings.[43]

Some men can be helping and caring to women—maybe it's part
of the chivalrous ideal—but most men will not nurture *other men*.
By sexism's perverse logic, they see giving comfort and asking for
it as equally emasculating. This hurts men coming and going. A Real
Man can neither disclose his own needs nor respond to a friend's
unhappiness because he imagines *both* behaviors would undermine
his manhood. Supposedly, women can accept a man's care-giving
under the rubric of masculine strength, but other men perceive nurturant behavior as inherently feminine. After all, it is what the average
male has come to expect from his mother, wife, or lover, not his
father, brother, or pals. Until warmth and empathy are culturally
neutralized (or defeminized or humanized), men will continue to feel
that it is more important to conform to the rugged, self-reliant,
macho image than to establish satisfying and authentic give-and-take
relations with their friends.

Another reason men resist comforting their male friends is simply
that they are too accustomed to competing with them. However
good-natured men's bantering style, it does tend to lock them into
a nongiving groove. For some, the resistance to nurture is coldly
self-aggrandizing: By leaving his friend unassisted, he can, for the
moment, enjoy knowing, without a referee, which one is the wimp
and which the winner. For other men, the resistance to nurture is
cowardly. They think weakness is contagious. Getting too close to
a friend who is emotionally needy reminds them of their own hairline
vulnerability and their own essential powerlessness to "fix" everything.

Whatever the diagnosis, the sorry result of nonnurturant friendship is this: *Men do not relieve each other's loneliness.* Psychologists have
determined that loneliness is due not to physical isolation but to the
absence of "meaningful interaction." Both sexes need the same things
to make a friendship meaningful: "disclosure, intimacy, pleasantness,
and satisfaction"—but these are qualities that women are far more
adept at providing. In fact, male-male interactions have been found
to be less meaningful even when the participants were best friends.
The plain truth is, the *best* of male friendship isn't good enough, and
the more time a man spends with *women,* the less lonely he is.[44]

What is it about the emotional style our culture breeds in women
that makes interaction with them feel more fulfilling? We will explore
that question more extensively in the next two chapters, but for the

moment let's just call it a *willingness to disclose* and a *will to care,* two qualities that most women actively cultivate and most men actively suppress in their pursuit of manly stolidity. The males who exhibit these qualities—the ones who can give help, ask for it, and accept it; the men who have freed themselves from the rigid demands of the male sex-role in favor of a more flexible, androgynous way of engaging with other people—are the ones who have meaningful friendships with other men.[45]

This finding points up one of the most crucial themes of this book: *Traditional sex roles have a negative effect on friendship.* We know a lot about how sex-role socialization stunts child development, women's potential, men's emotions, and everyone's sexuality and love relations. But the damage done to and within *friendship* has been relatively unacknowledged. A woman can ask her best friend to be her roommate, cry on her best friend's shoulder, tell her best friend her most secret secret. A Real Man can't—not without raising eyebrows and rumors of homosexuality. As masculinity-posturing bankrupts men's relations with humanity and exacts ever more soul-shrinking sacrifices, the question for every man to consider is whether the rewards of manhood are worth the price. If that question can be avoided by most men most of the time, it is because, in place of nurturing, men friends have two things that make them *feel* close: They have fun and they have loyalty. With these compensations (and with women friends in the wings for emergency succor), men seem to make it through the emotional desert.

The Cult of Fun and Loyalty. Although I've enjoyed some of my biggest laughs with women, and I'd be the last to say women have no sense of humor or joie de vivre, in most cases, "having fun" is not the reason we women get together. For men, however, friendship and fun are synonymous. Like humor, fun compensates for shortfalls in intimacy at the same time that it substitutes for intimacy. Yet because fun is also so visible, it is often the criterion by which male friendships are judged "best."

In his book *The Best of Friends,* David Michaelis profiles seven pairs of men friends—among them John F. Kennedy and LeMoyne Billings and Dan Aykroyd and John Belushi.[46] Each of these accounts is fully-fleshed and unique, but all seven stories seem remarkably similar in tone and structure because, for the most part, they are profiles of fun. Each friendship is made up of anecdotes—recollections of banter and activities—that tie man to man with a rope of "remember whens . . ."

For young Kennedy and Billings at Choate School, fun was founding an illegal club of close friends who shared "the exclusive privilege of listening to Kennedy's Victrola between Chapel and dinner"—and nearly getting expelled for it. Fun was taking a convertible coupe for a forbidden drive off campus, being pursued by the school proctors, ending their wild car chase in a barn—and getting away with it. Then there were years of tennis, sailing, and softball at Hyannis Port, risqué songs, dares, bets, funny telegrams, double-dating, two months together in Europe, adulthood, the presidency, and still more practical jokes and weekends of backgammon and golf—a deep friendship. "Oh, man," Billings mused looking backward, "we just had the best fun. The best fun—ever."

Fun is the third presence in a rowboat with two guys fishing at dawn. Fun is hitching across country, telling shaggy dog stories around a bonfire, tossing a ball around, and storing up anecdotes. I understand all that, sometimes even envy it. The thing I find so odd about most men's fun is how so little goes such a long way. "Bob and I have the greatest times together," one man tells me; then I learn that he and Bob haven't seen each other for a year. "There's nothing like going to a party with Mort," says Stanley. When I ask how often he and Mort have been at the same parties, he says, "Oh, two or three times."

To most men, nurture is "touchy-feely," having fun is "real"; you can chew on it during the next social famine or talk about it in front of others. When a man tells me one of those Boy-did-we-have fun! anecdotes, I see him turning over the evanescent experiences of friendship as if they were concrete possessions he could hold in his hands, like photographs or souvenirs, icons of the great old times. Fun is the *thing* that saves men from having to deal with feelings. Fun is what men have in order to avoid coming home to an empty house.

Loyalty is the other prize in the Cracker Jack box of male friendship. Men who make do without affection and nurture get a splashy payoff: They promise to save each other's lives. Male loyalty feeds on heroism, on oaths, initiations, and codes of conduct, on the romance of blood brotherhood, on legends of rescue, danger, and sacrifice, on myth and melodrama.

In *Friends and Lovers,* anthropologist Robert Brain describes a bonding ceremony among the Azande of Africa:

> The two blood friends cut each other's chest and arms and smear their blood on pieces of wood which are exchanged, swallowed, and then "talked to" within the stomach. Two peanuts from the same pod are used to symbolize the equality between friends, and the enumeration of obligations and sanctions underlines the reciprocal nature of the relationship. Loyalty to a friend is placed above that to a chief.[47]

In Western societies, Brain says, certain men are more likely than others to unite through formal pacts "and achieve their solidarity through culturally developed rituals." Prisoners sometimes form such friendships in alliance against authority and confinement. Fishermen, coal miners, cops, seamen, and soldiers are among several categories of men whose mutual loyalty springs from their "feeling of identity and equality" and their vital interdependence "in situations involving a high element of risk or danger." Often, occupational brotherhoods have secret incantations, superstitions, taboos, nicknames, and mascots with which they acknowledge their shared destiny. Men's clubs, lodges, and fraternities establish similar "magical sanctions against the failure of the bonds of friendship."

There is a torturous double message at work here: a prohibition against male intimacy but *for* masculine loyalty; a social imperative to keep men attached to women—to keep men heterosexual—by offering women's nurture, while also keeping men attached to other men—mutual guardians of male institutions and power—yet condemning "too much" affection; a prescription for enough friendship to ensure male solidarity but not so much that it depletes male energies that must go to country, corporation, and the nuclear family. The double message makes men's social attachments so intrinsically tenuous that they need magic or oaths of loyalty to encode their togetherness. Street gangs establish trust through reciprocal exchanges of favors, money, and information. High school and college fraternities seal brotherly solidarity through initiation rites, pledging, secret handshakes, and hazing. And every so often, when there's a scandal, we glimpse the dark side of fraternal fervor: violence and the brothers' collective mistreatment of women, and I don't mean "panty raids."

Friendship, Violence, and Death. The Association of American Colleges (AAC) reports fifty cases of documented campus rape between 1983 and 1985, nearly all of them involving fraternities.[48] "If fraternities constituted a state of the union, it would be a very small one, with about half the population of Vermont," says Andrew Merton, a professor at the University of New Hampshire. "If, in a state that size, fifty confirmed gang rapes took place within two or three years, impartial observers might begin to wonder about the place."[49] Yet the rapes are prosecuted quietly if at all, and the rapists rarely have to worry about witnesses testifying against them. The brotherhood protects them.

Suggesting why most rape happens in fraternities, the AAC report says: "A man in a gang rape situation may be acting out not only hostility toward women, but expressing strong emotions he feels for other men. Often one man is the 'leader'; the others willingly follow him. 'Men rape for other men.' "

Sixteen-year-old John Isaacson was a victim of another perversion of fraternal "friendship." He arrived in a hospital emergency room with "enormous purple welts all over him" and underwent surgery for abdominal bleeding resulting from blows received in a high school fraternity initiation ceremony. At first, he refused to divulge who assaulted him. "I didn't want to tell on anyone," he said. "They were supposed to be my friends." Chuck Stenzel didn't live to prove his loyalty. He was killed by alcohol poisoning and exposure to freezing weather while locked in the trunk of a car during his fraternity initiation at Alfred University. Nationwide, twenty-nine hazing deaths were recorded between 1978 and 1985.[50]

While loyalty to the death sometimes means dying for nothing, what men seem to both esteem and take for granted is the intersection of friendship with death and violence. Philosopher David Hume wrote: "The difficulty is not so great to die for a friend as to find a friend worth dying for." Patroclus took Achilles' place in battle, sacrificing his life for his friend. That Damon and Pythias were willing to die for each other so impressed the tyrant who had threatened to execute one of them that he freed them both and asked for their friendship.

Some have interpreted David's eulogy of Jonathan—"Thy love for me was wonderful, surpassing the love of women"—as evidence that the two men had a sexual attachment. But most commentators understand this statement to laud the transcendence of male friendship over the carnal love of a woman. What interests me is how this Bible story has come to symbolize only *male* devotion when it *also* tells how Michal (David's wife and Jonathan's sister) saved David's life. Why hasn't the tale come to epitomize the loyalty of wives? I think the answer lies in the fact that male friendships are so rare they must be protected and mythologized, whereas women's altruism is so commonplace, it can be assumed. Man's devotion to man—or rather to the values of Man—is too important to allow the Jonathan and David story to be diluted by other themes. Man's loyalty to man "proves" the supremacy of male fellowship above men's ties to women and props up the "defend to the death" ideology of men in war. As D. H. Lawrence wrote: "Woman is inadequate for the last merging. So the next step is the merging of man-for-man love. And this is on the brink of death."[51]

Being "on the brink of death" gives men their only acceptable excuse to love one another. War takes the onus off man-to-man affection and emotion. War gives men ample opportunity for apocalyptic tests of friendship and enactment of the rescue fantasies of boyhood. Even if falling on a grenade to save a buddy or pulling a pal out of a burning tank are not commonplace experiences, the *possibility* of self-sacrifice heightens the intensity of male comradeship in combat.

War codifies loyalty, gives it basic training, makes it a survival tactic. War polishes male friendship as if it were a rifle to be kept in working order. Men who don't quite know how to act around other men in civilian life have it all set out for them in wartime. In a disturbing essay titled "Why Men Love War," William Broyles, Jr., wrote: "War replaces the difficult gray areas of daily life with an eerie, serene clarity. In war, you usually know who is your enemy and who is your friend, and are given means of dealing with both. . . . A comrade in war is a man you can trust with anything because you trust him with your life."[52]

For all that, it doesn't last. Roger Little, an expert on friendship in the military, wrote: "However intensive the buddy relationship was in combat, it quickly dissolved when the necessity of mutual survival was over. Even when buddies were in the reserve bivouac rather than 'on the line' in direct contact with the enemy, they became more contentious and less mutually supportive. When they left the unit they always promised to write to their buddies about life in 'the world' (the United States), or to visit one another when both had returned, but they rarely did. Departure from the battlefield terminated the relationship."[53]

War is a "situation-specific" maker of friends. Remove the external enemy and men resume business as usual. Competition replaces comradeship, masculine independence replaces military *inter*dependence, and sentimentality replaces intimacy. After a war, wrote Broyles, "veterans' reunions are invariably filled with boozy awkwardness, forced camaraderie ending in sadness and tears: you are together again, these are the men who were your brothers, but it's not the same, can never be the same."

Back home, without the impetus of a deadly game, without the rules and the risks, these men who once would have died for each other now let their friendships die.

Ordinary Loyalty. Without a war, men prove their devotion in ways that fit the masculine imperatives of this era.

At his twenty-fifth college reunion, Mike publicly tongue-lashed his 18-year-old son, Kevin, for his bad manners. Kevin struck back by asking Mike's best friend, Frank, "How come you never get on your son's case the way my dad gets on mine?"

"Maybe my son doesn't need it," answered Frank.

Kevin looked stung. "Sorry, kid," Frank laughed, tousling the boy's hair. "But after twenty years of friendship, you didn't think I'd turn on your dad, did you?"

Among Mexican-Americans, *cuatismo* (from the word for twin brothers) describes a male partnership so strong that in extreme cases a man will go to jail for his friend.

Sugar Ray Leonard, the boxer, and his friend Joe Broady, a security guard, met when they were sparring partners in neighborhood backyards. "He was there before I had anything," says Leonard. "Joe will always be there."

How does Joe see it?

"One of us made it, one of us didn't," he says.[54] Despite his disappointment, Joe Broady has become that special breed of friend, the loyal retainer, the guy who knew you when, the pal who keeps his pride intact and thereby invalidates status differences with the force of his friendship. Loyalty of this sort earns one a seat at court, not quite as an underling but at the right hand of the champion. Richard Nixon had his Bebe Rebozo, New York City Mayor Ed Koch has his Daniel Wolff, and Sugar Ray Leonard has his Joe Broady.

"I'll give you an example of how much I think of him," says Alexander Reynolds, a hotel doorman, about his pal, a hotel porter. "I told my wife a few weeks ago that if I should die unexpectedly she is to go first to James Boyd if she is in any difficulties. He will know what to do, and he will do it. That is a friend."[55]

Bacon and Shakespeare would agree with Reynolds. "If a man have a true friend," wrote Bacon, "he may rest almost secure that the care of those things will continue after him." And Shakespeare has the dying Hamlet beseech his friend, Horatio, "To tell my story."

In patriarchal societies, each man is concerned to have things "continue after him"—his name, his property, his accomplishments. The loyal friend facilitates this goal. Furthermore, sex-role norms demand that if a man cannot take responsibility for "his dependents," he looks to another man to do it. David and Jonathan pledged to care for one another's children after death. Latins have the institution of the *padrino*, or godfather. American men do not share fathering in the sense of baby-sitting for each other's children, but they may share the "manly" financial or decision-making responsibilities associated with the father role. Several men I interviewed mentioned having give their best male friend power of attorney or named him executor of their wills or guardian of their children in the event of both parents' deaths. A few who had not made such formal arrangements nonetheless said they expected the friend to "keep an eye on things if anything happens to me."

That is all well and good. Loyalty, like fun, belongs in every relationship. But it is absurd to measure friendship by an applause meter marked "Laughs" or to substitute apocalyptic tests of devotion for ongoing intimacy. As criteria of true friendship, fun is too small and loyalty is too big. Most men are missing out on the great middle— the comfort zone where speaking openly and giving comfort are the *everyday* activities of friends, not their special events.

Men Do Not Have Holistic Friendships

"I had a friend I jogged with for two years," says Marty. "He was my neighbor, a shy guy who little by little revealed himself to be brilliant. We'd run and talk three times a week. At first I did all the talking. But when he opened up, wow, what a mind. It was like having a session with Plato or Aristotle. I began saving up huge cosmic questions for our runs because he always had such incredible responses. I looked forward to every minute with him, but somehow we never went on from there to socialize together. Then, last June, he moved about thirty miles away and I never saw him again."

Men see their friends "not as total human beings but as persons filling particular roles," says sociologist Robert Bell.[56] In Marty's case, his neighbor was someone to run with. Period. The average American man has a friend for each purpose and a purpose for each friend, but virtually every man applies the word "friend" to anyone he does things with on a regular basis: his work colleagues, the men he commutes with, hangs out with, gets drunk with, or watches TV with, the pals who go to the same meetings or ball games or health club. Friendship expert Paul Wright found that "men were better friends and considered one another more interesting and stimulating if they agreed . . . on specific day-to-day activities."[57]

In addition to men's activity-orientation, according to the *McGill Report,* "the most common male friendship pattern is for a man to have many 'friends,' each of whom knows something of the man's public self and therefore a little about him, but not one of whom knows more than a small piece of the whole." In other words, men's friendships are not holistic; they are atomized. John may regard Jim as a "good friend" with respect to generosity but not with respect to intellect, sportsmanship, or politics. In contrast, a woman tends to regard her good friends as good "across the board," says Wright. "The difference may be summed up metaphorically by saying that for men, there are friends and there are friends; while for women, a friend is a friend."

Psychoanalysts explain male friendship behavior through early family scenarios: The boy's developmental "task" is to achieve separation and individuation from the mother (object and source of the infant's love) and to make identification with the father (who is often shadowy, authoritarian, or absent). To ensure that he accomplishes this difficult task and emerges from the Oedipal crisis as a "normal" heterosexual, a boy must not only detach from the caring mother but disavow everything female and try to focus on what is attractive and rewarding about being male. Men's avoidance of intimacy in friendship is one legacy of the male child's repudiation of his mother and the loving behaviors with which she is associated.

The sociological explanation of the same phenomenon highlights the cultural and environmental forces that shape individuals, tracing men's friendship style to early play activities and team sports, which are presumed responsive to the physiology of growing boys but actually *program* them to define their maleness by what they *do*. (Girls just have to *be* female.) If what males *do* is to have any reality, it must be witnessed and approved by the relevant peer group. A man cannot have his athletic prowess validated by a girl or even by a boy who's a bookworm; he needs his jock friends to confirm that he's a jock. Male friendships are specialized for the various aspects of masculinity-training.

Rather than argue the causes of traditional masculine behavior, it is enough to become aware of the debilitating and coercive *effects* of sex-role conformity in friendship. Because men are expected to police each other's masculinity on society's behalf, they cannot become too open or attached to other men; this would create a conflict of interests. They must learn to resist the closeness that would make them vulnerable in themselves or unable to demand high standards of maleness in others. They must protect their flanks by compartmentalizing their lives.

For women, "a friend is a friend," not a catalyst to gender identity. Although, as we'll see in the next chapter, women suffer sex-role excesses of another sort, most feel comfortable enough *as* women to allow themselves to open up to a friend. And because they become emotionally intertwined, women tend to work through their feelings and mend their bonds when a problem develops. Men, on the other hand, expect less. They learn to enjoy their friends but not *depend* on them. Since they do not invest heavily in any one person, they can tolerate strains without feeling compelled to confront them. One might argue that men overlook a friend's shortcomings because they are more interested in preserving the friendship. But at what price? Pretense? Annoyance? Repressed anger? At some point the swallowed complaints and papered-over tensions amount to a *fake* friendship not a tolerant one.

Some argue further that, when added together, men's specialized friendships can prove just as satisfying as the more holistic friendships of women. That additive approach to human relations—intimacy by accretion, if you will—covers the territory but misses the depths. It gives a man many pals but rarely a soulmate. It cheats him of the intoxicating experience of knowing another person fully and completely and of *being* known himself—all because of "manhood," a mythic abstraction that reigns like a jealous god.

Chapter 14

≈ ——————————— ≈

Women's Intimacy

By now, after years of being misperceived, maligned, or ignored, female friendship is the acknowledged "state of the art."

- "The truth is that friendship is to me every bit as sacred and eternal as marriage"—Katherine Mansfield, writer.

- "Women love their best friend of the same sex about as much as they love their opposite sex lover; men do not"—Robert Sternburg, Yale University, psychologist.

- "Friendship between women can take different forms. It can run like a river, quietly and sustainingly through life: it can be an intermittent, sometime thing; or it can explode like a meteor, altering the atmosphere so that nothing ever feels or looks the same again"—Molly Haskell, critic.

- "I don't think any woman in power really has a happy life unless she's got a large number of women friends . . . because you sometimes must go and sit down and let down your hair with someone you can trust totally"—Prime Minister Margaret Thatcher.

- "I think women know how to be friends. That's what saves our lives"—Alice Adams, novelist.

Let's not belabor what research confirms: That women honor friendship and love their friends; that two women can be as open, honest, warm, and helpful to each other as the best of blood or love relations; that most women are far more empathic and emotionally intimate with their casual friends than men are with their closest friends. So what's the problem?

- Friendship is something women do best so being good at friendship is not highly valued.

- Being *too* affiliative is as bad for women as being not-affiliative-enough is for men.

- Some women are so good at friendship that they let it divert them from Life.

Picking up on the last chapter's metaphoric college course on friendship, if Man gets four "incompletes," Woman overprepares, tutors her classmates, earns an "A," then discovers it's a noncredit course. Plus, she was so busy helping her friends that she missed a chance to run for office and a Tina Turner concert. And nobody thanked her besides.

That's the problem.

While male friendship is so rare it must be mythologized, good female friends are so abundant that they're often taken for granted. Even the most gregarious, giving woman is seen as just "doin' what comes naturally"—like taking care of children. And, like taking care of children, taking care of friends is only noticed when a woman won't do it, or doesn't do it well, or nearly kills herself trying to do it better. Friendship is what women are "supposed" to be good at even if we're not good at anything else. Our friends are the "precious possessions" that make up for our having little status, property, money, or control over our own lives. Most men expect us to be good at friendship (ours *and* theirs) because they usually benefit from it, and when they don't benefit from it they downgrade it, which we'll get to later.

Why Women Befriend

As with male friendship patterns, you can take your pick of theories to explain women's affiliative skill.

Biological determinism sees it as an instinct associated with childbearing.

Current psychoanalytic thinking asserts that it originates in the mother-daughter bond of the pre-Oedipal period: Because the girl child never gives up her primary identification with the mother, she supposedly never forms distinct ego boundaries and thus goes through life seeking fusion and defining her "self" as a "self-in-relationship" with an "other."[1]

The social learning theorists uncover the source of women's affiliative skills in the female sex-role catechism taught to little girls with their alphabet. From earliest childhood, the girl learns that it is her job to take care of relationships. Year after year—with her dolls, siblings, baby-sitting charges, boyfriends—she learns to notice other people's needs, to empathize with their feelings and want to help them. While males are rewarded for developing independence, females are rewarded for getting along with others.

They learn their lessons well. Child psychologist Jean Piaget found that in childhood games boys are more concerned with the rules, while girls are more concerned with the relationships among the players, even if the game suffers in the process.[2] Girls and boys develop in opposite directions; she feels strongest when she is leaning or being leaned on; he feels strongest when he stands alone. Writes Harvard psychologist Carol Gilligan: "Since masculinity is defined through separation while feminity is defined through attachment, male gender identity is threatened by intimacy while female gender identity is threatened by separation."[3] Women are good at friendship because girls are trained to get pleasure from giving pleasure and gaining external approval.

"Women not only define themselves in a context of human relationship but also judge themselves in terms of their ability to care," writes Gilligan, whose book *In a Different Voice* recognizes and legitimates "female-style" moral development and its emphasis on caring. While reading her provocative arguments, however, I keep hearing echoes of an old joke: "If you're so smart, why aren't you rich?" For indeed, women might ask, "If we're so good at intimacy, why aren't we happy?"

Too Much of a Good Thing

Female friendship is warm and satisfying, yes; but it can also be deceptively pleasing. Like sugar or sweet cream, too much of a good thing is dangerous. Little girls who are overtrained in the art of affiliation grow up to become *relationship-junkies,* women who need to be needed before they can feel worthwhile and alive. They require other people to validate what they do and how they feel. They form symbiotic attachments of mutual dependence or, worse yet, parasitic fusions, allowing themselves to become obliterated, their unique properties expropriated by friends who feed off their energy and invade their lives.

They get hooked on relationships because without a mirror they are not sure who they are.

"For many women the threat of disruption of an affiliation is perceived not just as a loss of a relationship but as something closer to a total loss of self," says Jean Baker Miller, psychoanalyst and author of *Toward a New Psychology of Women.* However, she points out, blaming women for this behavior is like blaming the victim. Women are reared to relate, connect, attach; they cannot then be "punished for making affiliations central in their lives."[4]

But they *are* punished. Research on stress-related diseases suggests "that the importance that women place on relationships may have health costs." This is as true of relationships with friends as with lovers and families. "Because they care so much more about others than men do, women tend to experience the troubles of those close to them as their own."[5]

"As far back as the records go, we see that women have been the archetypical givers," wrote Elinor Lenz, an educator, and Barbara Myerhoff, an anthropologist. "Being needed became woman's justification, her profession and in many cases her bondage. . . . Why are women often unable to keep themselves from empathy and identification even when it is not in their best interest to do so?"[6]

I am no more interested in arguing about *why* women get hooked on friendship than I was in settling once and for all why men do not. What concerns me are the *effects* of these phenomena. Rather than just congratulate women for getting honors in intimacy, let's figure out what it may cost them and who profits from it.

Obviously, the honors are premature if women's talent for intimacy is intended first and foremost to serve the hidden agenda of sex-role conformity and patriarchal economics.

What's Really Happening?

"Girls are encouraged to be specialists in human relations, to develop few but highly emotional relationships—and thus prepare to become mothers and wives who will invest much in a very limited set of others," wrote Beth Hess in analyzing friendship's relevance to sex roles. "Boys are expected to have extensive networks of buddies; to share all kinds of team experiences, typically goal-directed; to be gregarious—precisely the type who should do well in the American occupational structure." Thus, "friendship patterns adopted by boys and girls are highly functional to the adult roles they will assume, and highly preservative of societies."[7]

Not only do women who are relationship junkies play into this master plan, and not only do these women lose the self in others, but *we* also lose *them*. Society loses their work, ideas, and involvement in the universe of public concerns. Burrowing deeper into the contained, manageable details of a few private lives, they turn away from the world as if it was not their responsibility, ignoring the fact that what happens between nations, rulers, classes, genders, and races are *relationships* as well and could greatly benefit from their attention.

While some friendships are catalysts for women's personal growth and collective action, others have the effect of an emotional addiction, a tranquilizer for the discontents of women's lives. And whereas catalytic friends rock the boat, tranquilizing friendships that distract women from their own oppression—and from the grit and struggle of the public sphere—assure smooth sailing for the status quo. No wonder women's friendship has been called so many names.

Whenever it is viewed as a safe, diversionary preoccupation for the fair sex, friendship is romanticized as a luxury of the privileged or a great natural gift, like playing the piano (the goal being to keep women in the music room.) When it is called something on the order of a "lesbian-feminist Marxist-Leninist cabal," you can bet women's solidarity is felt as a threat. And when it is described as "gossip, giggling and girl talk" or "catty, bitchy, narcissistic and competitive," it is perceived to be in its preferred condition: trivial, harmless, and working like a charm.

These shifting characterizations tell us more about sexism's strategies than about women's actual behavior. The cultural ideal of female friendship, like the male's, matches up with the needs of the sex-role system. Since our culture assigns all nonsexual intimate relationships to women, being "feminine" means being "good at friendship." A Real Woman should busy herself by exhibiting warmth, affection, and understanding; by creating a climate of friendliness and tracking its barometric pressure; by doing the labor of friendship: visiting, calling, giving gifts, writing thank-you notes, making coffee, soothing the depressed, comforting the enraged who might otherwise make trouble, and paying attention to how people *feel*, not to who has the power that affects how we feel. Being "good at friendship" means being a "nice girl" who takes from her own life huge chunks of her time and her thinking and her doing and gives them to other people.

In the preceding chapter I asked whether it was worth it to men to give up true friends for that abstraction known as "manhood." Here, I am asking if it is worth it to women to gain friends through behavior that is often eagerly, self-sacrificially feminine.

I am asking if being so good at friendship is always so good for women. This is much the same question many women have posed about motherhood and other roles and institutions that support traditional patterns of dominance and inequality. Although some women are gifted mothers, we've learned that too much mothering not only damages children but stunts women's lives; now our goal is to distribute child-rearing more equitably and sensibly to *both* parents (and to others in the child's life). By the same token, although some women are talented at being friends, too much "befriending" of the sort associated with the stereotypical female social role not only incurs health costs and fosters dependency on relationships but displaces women's impact on society. Our next goal should be to distribute both the labors and pleasures of friendship more equitably and sensibly to *both* sexes.

As D. W. Winnicott offered the concept of the "good enough" mother,[8] we need to create a model for a "good enough" friend who gives enough to establish intimacy but does not set herself impossible standards of altruism and devotion to others. There is nothing admirable about always being "there" for one's friends if it makes a woman increasingly absent from herself.

For many women, the talent for friendship is a mixed blessing because it has yet to reach homeostasis, the point where *what the organism does well also does good for the organism*. To achieve this equilibrium, we have to do what men have to do—but in the other direction. We have to move away from polarized roles toward a synthesis of the independent self and the self-in-relationship. To understand how this synthesis might develop, let's look at three current forms of women's friendship, each of which functions as a coping mechanism to mediate between the self and the world. Simply put:

> *Feminine friendship* works to help women function in a man's world.
>
> *Female friendship* operates when women create a world of their own.
>
> *Feminist friendship* works to help women function in the world as it is while making it better.

Although the three forms overlap and intersect in historical time and in the life span of each woman—and many of us have experienced all three within a single relationship—I separate them here to create an organizing framework that takes into account both the personal and the political ramifications of friendship, a relationship that only *appears* to be private.

Feminine Friendship

Feminine friendship, or what I think of as "old-style sisterhood," is an alliance of the weak, but an alliance nonetheless. A woman who (consciously or unconsciously) views her dependence on men as a "fact of life" looks to her women friends to help her function despite her economic and physical powerlessness. Feminine friends share an acceptance of the traditional verity that "It's a man's world" and woman's place in it is both ordained and protected. Friends strengthen her in carrying out (or enduring) her roles as girlfriend, wife, mother, or low-status worker. A great part of the time she spends with friends is taken up with mutual assistance in perfecting the behavior expected of the feminine woman: the beautification of herself and her surroundings and the care of men and children.

To be sure, just as we have been great givers and nurturers, women have been catty, bitchy, narcissistic, and competitive. Weakness breeds adversaries as well as allies. "All friendship between women has a uterine air about it, the air of a slow, bloody, cruel, incomplete exchange, of an original situation being repeated all over again."[9] According to the psychoanalytically inclined writers of that pronouncement, the "original situation" is mother birthing daughter, an inferior like herself, another woman who wants father's love. We might argue instead that the "original situation" is worldwide male supremacy. In either case, the repetitive situation is the lifelong ritual of comparison, one woman with another to see who is the less inferior of the two.

Competition among Women

Research shows that women's competitiveness is no worse than men's—it's just different. But facts are irrelevant if women have internalized the propaganda that "females are not to be trusted" and "women are their own worst enemies." I think of male competition as a jungle where wild plants struggle for the most light and air and of female competition as a hothouse full of cultivated orchids vying to be the prize blossom. Unlike men, however, women engage in this behavior not to prove their gender identity or to gain the respect of other women but to gain the approval of men. Both sexes play to the sex that has the power. Moreover, men's competitiveness is generally portrayed as healthy ambition and men are applauded for their striving or their competitive spirit; in women, such spirit is seen as a nasty character trait. In fact, both forms of competition are the logical outcomes of sex-role training, and the praise that matters comes from those in charge. Whenever men determine that there is room for only one woman, naturally, each of us wants to be the one: the prettiest, the smartest, the one who "thinks like a man," the agreeable one who wins the attention and love of the guys who pass out the goodies. We started competing with other little girls to be the best little girl and some of us have never stopped.

Men compete for manhood; women compete for men. As long as *they* are at the center of *our* vision, men have nothing to fear from female unity. When women are head to head they are not shoulder to shoulder.

A study of single career women found only two friendships in twenty-seven that ended because of rivalry over men.[10] But in a poor Mexican-American community, gangs of young women fight over men.[11] Among whites and Blacks, says Bell Hooks, competition "has always been centered in the arena of sexual politics with white and black women competing against one another for male favor."[12] Wherever traditional *ideas* about womanhood persist, Simone de Beauvoir's words still hold true:

> For most grown-up girls . . . to get a husband—or at least a steady sweetheart—becomes a more important business. This concern is often destructive of feminine friendships. The "best friend" loses her place of honor. The young girl sees rivals rather than allies in her companions. . . . Women feel their solidarity more spontaneously than men; but within this solidarity the transcendence of each does not go out toward the others, for they all face together toward the masculine world, whose values they wish to monopolize each for herself.[13]

Even high achieving college women still vie for men. "I can be in the middle of a story and if a guy walks into the room, my friends all orient themselves toward him," says Joan, a 20-year-old Ivy Leaguer. "You can feel the energy shift."

Among educated or intellectual women, professional competition can be as steamy as romantic rivalry. Louise Bernikow says Virginia Woolf was haunted by "the specter of jealousy, another writer, a younger woman."[14] Both Woolf and the younger Katherine Mansfield shared the "passion for writing," similar gender politics, literary attitudes, and debilitating illness. Each was the only serious woman artist the other knew. Each greatly respected the other's work. But for Woolf, Mansfield's was "the only writing I have ever been jealous of"—as if there were no male writers to envy, as if each generation could admit only one great woman writer to its literary pantheon, as if Woolf might be evicted and Mansfield given her place by the men who decide such things.

Bernikow writes of her own female graduate school classmates of the 1960s: "We stayed away from each other. We tried, in the privacy of our student apartments, to be smarter on the subject of

John Donne or The Victorian Novel than anyone else, but especially
smarter than other women—because there was room for only some
of us, because the jobs that might be waiting were limited and only
a few women would get them, because the struggle to be taken
seriously by our male professors was relentless."

To my dismay, canker sores of feminine jealousy fester even in
avowedly feminist circles. As Bell Hooks says, "the women's movement has become simply another arena in which white and black
women compete to be the chosen female group." Valerie Miner's
"Rumors from the Cauldron" attributes the problem of competition
among feminist writers partly to women's ambivalence about success
and their tendency to confuse *feelings* of competitiveness with the
process of competition and partly to a practical cause: the publishing
marketplace "is a men's emporium. . . . Money is tight and there
are still unofficial quotas on women. . . . Because those in power
are often invisible or inaccessible, we often direct our fury and bit-
terness at sister writers. Some women get ruthless, undermining the
work of others to serve their own careers. After someone wins an
award, her next book may be reviewed with special harshness."[15]

Although I've rarely known women to be as catty, bitchy, and
untrustworthy as some testimony or propaganda suggests, I see competition between women as a very real blot on the portrait of feminine
friendships, as disfiguring in its own way as male competition is to
men's friendships.

"You want to hear about *competitive,* listen to what I do the minute
I arrive at a party," one woman told me in conspiratorial tones. "I
run an elimination tournament in my head. I check out all the women:
'My outfit isn't as sophisticated as Denise's black silk dress,' I tell
myself. 'Grace over there looks dowdy, but she's acting pretty spunky
because of her job promotion. I see Martha has a new boyfriend, so
she's feeling impressed with herself, too. Jo's showing off her new
haircut and she looks great, dammit. Well, at least I'm thinner than
most of them, thank God.' " As crazy as this interior monologue
sounds, my friend says it's the only way she can prepare herself to
function in a group where there are other women and at least one
man she likes. "I've got to feel I'm the best in something before I
can carry on," she admits.

As social worker Margaret Adams has noted, competing for men
establishes a hierarchy of social ties among single women who view
each other as "filler" companions until the real thing comes along.[16]

Cindy, a 24-year-old cashier, accepts second place without question. "It's only natural that guys come first," she says.

Years ago, my roommate and I said the same thing. When we first came to New York after college, we agreed immediately on a modus operandi: No matter what we'd planned to do together, all bets were off if a man asked either of us for a date. Who but a pal could understand the lure of romance? In hindsight, I'm not sure it always *was* romance. I see internalized inferiority instructing us that Saturday night with *any* man was better than just being with "us girls." I've since discovered countless women who made the same deal, resolving not to get in the way of each other's social life, not seeing that *we* were the social life that outlasted all the men.

The Question of Fun

In describing a Saturday night dinner with Gloria, Joan, and Roberta, Kay says: "It was great fun and the conversation was fascinating. We talked about phobias, asking for a raise, Margaret Mead, John Irving, gynecologists, computers, and sex. Gloria and I had the *best* time. She's married and I'm not, but we both agreed it was especially relaxing to be away from the company of men. Joan and Roberta who are single didn't find it so relaxing. Joan said she needs the odor of alertness that's in the air when men are around, and Roberta admitted she was a little nervous about being seen on a Saturday night 'with three dames.' "

Perhaps this is one reason why many women friends seem to have less "fun" than men: because women view each other as substitute companions, not the main event. Or is it just a question of one's definition of fun?

My daughter Robin wrote a piece for her college newspaper about watching young men on the softball field, football field, carousing around the campus on tap night for the all-male singing groups, disappearing into the all-male secret societies; the many times she has envied boys their camaraderie: "I can only feel its power from the outside, its aura of exclusivity, secrecy, even superiority," she wrote. "This potency is not so apparent in men individually; it emanates when they are together."[17]

American culture equates fun with activity, but women's idea of fun may be different from the sports, mischief, and adventure that animate men. Men's fun is an escape from intimacy. Women seem to have the best time together when they are exploring intimacy to the hilt. The women who are "celebrating themselves" (in Chapter 8) choose to do it at lunches and dinners, for the most part—events that facilitate conversation. Since women talk more and *do* less together and since they form pairs more often than groups, it may only *appear* they are less joyful because their fun is less jocular and less noticeable.

Still another possibility: Maybe women need to feel more entitled to the use of public spaces before they can have the sort of fun men have in public. As it stands now, where can women go to be together? Certain places and certain hours are off-limits. There is still the question of "reputation" and the charge of "what's a nice girl like you. . . ." There is still a safety consideration. The bars, streets, gyms, and playing fields are male turf. Women cannot just "hang out"—their mere presence is interpreted as an invitation to be picked up. The actress Lily Tomlin tells the story of a man who approached a woman while she was having a drink with three other women. "Hey, baby, what are you doing here alone?" he asked her.

One more "maybe" might explain women's lesser—or less overt—readiness to have big bursts of fun with their friends. They are protecting their femininity. Surely that explains why there are proportionately so few female comedians. Being raucous or rowdy, bawdy or insulting, prankish or loud is the ultimate in unladylike behavior. For women, fun comes at the risk of "defeminizing." Maybe, in the process of learning to be ladylike, women unlearn spontaneity and allow themselves to become too domesticated to give in to anything indecorous, wild, or corrupting.

"I think about it sometimes," says a 28-year-old working-class woman. "It would be fun to go with my girlfriends sometimes— you know, not to do anything wrong, but to have some fun. But then I worry what would happen if I did. I might get to like it. Then I get afraid, and I think I don't know if I want to taste that life. You know, sometimes when you taste something like that, then you start requiring it. My life is really my husband, my children, and my home. I wouldn't want to risk taking any chances of losing them."[18]

With its contradictions of intimacy and distrust, Feminine friendship very often develops as a *by-product* of women being together, not a goal in itself. Two women meet each other or combine forces because both are engaged in activities oriented toward men. The hours they spend talking about make-up, fashion, the boss, diets,

health, beauty, love, sex, and child-rearing; the time they spend
in helping each other dress, cook, strategize, rearrange furniture, in
doing each other's hair or soothing each other's humiliations, in
discussing how to get rice not to stick to the pan and babies to sleep
through the night—all those woman-hours filled with laughter, advice, weeping, and secrets have at their center men's desires and
expectations: how to make woman, house, and child pleasing to *him?*
It just so happens that in the process of doing things with men in
mind, women share their lives. In the process of acting out their
roles in the same eternal play—of being girlfriends, office servants,
wives, and mothers together—women become friends.

Bitches or buddies. Competitors or companions. The two faces
of Feminine friendship. This old-style sisterhood is an old story. But
now, rather than overlook it as trivial and private, or dismiss it for
being "male-identified" and weak, historians are helping us to understand Feminine friendship as one of the sustaining legacies of
female adaptation and survival.

Found Friends

"Black and white women of the Big House needed each other,"
writes Eugene D. Genovese, a historian specializing in antebellum
southern society, who found a relationship of mutual dependency
between slaves and their mistresses despite the obvious power imbalance between them. "Mistresses with drunken, dissolute,
spendthrift, or brutal husbands poured out their troubles to their
maids, who poured out their own troubles to their mistresses and
to each other. If a woman, white or black, woke up at night terrified
by a dream of impending death, she would run to her maid or her
mistress for comfort. The black and white women of the Big House
reached the peak of intimacy in their involvement in each other's
love lives."[19]

Slave women were intermediaries and purveyors of secrets between mistresses and their beaux, and did not hesitate to offer their
opinions about each prospect, reports Genovese. Mistresses likewise
meddled in the romantic and marital affairs of their servants. It may
not conform to our idea of egalitarian friendship, but it was surely
a more human connection than Black and white *men* were able to
experience at the time.

By analyzing the letters and diaries of privileged white women

of the nineteenth century, Carroll Smith-Rosenberg has discovered
a vast spectrum of women's intimacy in "a world in which men
made but a shadowy appearance." Intense, loving, even sensual feminine friendships were deeply important to Victorian women and
were considered "both socially acceptable and fully compatible with
heterosexual marriage." Mary (Molly) Hallock Foote, for example,
wrote to her beloved friend Helena Gilder: "I wanted so to put my
arms round my girl of all the girls in the world and tell her . . . I
love her as wives do love their husbands, as *friends* who have taken
each other for life."[20]

Older women trained younger women in "domestic skills" and
in how to participate in "the visiting and social activities necessary
to finding a husband." Friends helped ease a woman's courtship,
marriage, frequent pregnancies and childbirths, the rearing of children, the trauma of illness and death. These upper-class ladies spent
their lives on a narrow path between hearth, church, and social visiting. The persona of their Feminine friendship is surprisingly rich
and satisfying for being so claustrophobic, and "young women's
relations with each other were close, often frolicsome, and surprisingly long lasting and devoted."

Married or not, women wrote adoring letters to and about their
friends, were lavish in their praise and physical affection, and "assumed an emotional centrality in each other's lives," says Smith-
Rosenberg. "They valued each other."

Historian Carl Degler found a letter that the same Molly wrote
to Helena after both women were married and Molly was pregnant:
"Yours is the warm close clasping woman's hand leading me step
by step through the sacred mysteries of wifehood and motherhood.
Yes, my darling—even if that last awful mystery must blind my
shuddering eyes—I could bear it better because I know that you have
borne it and lived and kept your sweet faith whole." Years later,
when Molly's husband had succumbed to alcoholism and could not
support his family, Helena provided so much emotional succor that
Molly was ashamed to be a burden: "Now forgive me, and I will
hush. I imagine that you kiss me, with a few quiet tears."[21]

Were these friendships *romantic* or is their effusive intensity an
expression of florid nineteenth-century hyperbole? Were romantic
friendships tolerated because they did not threaten the security of the
family but actually sustained women in their family roles? Can we
judge the affections of women of another era by the standards of

today? Is it reasonable to speculate about erotic activity among upper-class Victorians who themselves would undoubtedly be appalled at the suggestion? Then again, were their loving relationships so different from the fevered adolescent girlfriendships of today? Among adults in the 1980s there are reports of "women who define themselves as heterosexual but find themselves in love with another woman." What should we call two women who have "an emotional passion with no physical counterpart"?[22] Nonsexual lesbians? Romantic friends?

Feminist scholars have long debated these questions. Some, like Lillian Faderman and Adrienne Rich, see the historicity of women's passionate feminine attachments as important validation of the universality of lesbian love.[23] [24] Others argue that friendship is a vast continuum and that we misrepresent women of the past by eroticizing their relationships in hindsight to fit current sexual polarities.

In the absence of definitive answers, I find history's Feminine friendships more interesting for the functions they served in women's lives than for "how far" they went. Today, the line between friendship and sex blurs easily for some and remains sharp for others. Victoria Vetere, a social psychologist, reports that eight out of ten lesbians say they were friends before they became lovers. As with unattached men and women, I have a problem not with two women friends becoming lovers but with the fiction that they can still be "just friends" after they have sex. As one lesbian told Vetere, "The quickest way to lose a friend is to become [her] lover."[25]

Lesbians aside, Feminine friendships that were a haven from inequality and alienation have become less frequent as women's and men's spheres have become less separate. Yet, whenever society decrees a right and wrong way to be a woman, whenever men demand traditional services in the family, Feminine friendships still fulfill those age-old purposes: to help prepare women for marriage and absorb the aftershocks of marital discord.

The perfect example is Nela Rubinstein and Fela Krance, who met as schoolgirls in Poland just after World War I. Fela married a man who became an industrialist; Nela's husband was the great Artur Rubinstein. Fela and Nela stayed in touch through the decades; Fela reared a family in Wisconsin, and Nela and her children lived out of a trunk during Artur's international tours. After Fela's husband died in 1972, the Rubinsteins invited her to live with them in Paris. Every winter, Fela spent two months in their house.

One year, while Artur was writing his memoirs with a co-author,

Annabelle Whitestone, Nela and Fela collaborated on Nela's own book of reminiscences and recipes gathered during her life with Artur. "We traveled so much, and he loved good food," Nela explains.

"Nela is a marvelous trooper; with headaches, miscarriages, four children, she was always at Artur's side," Fela says, validating her friend's wifely existence as she has clearly done hundreds of times. "Nela is a very devoted mother, but she shared Artur's life completely—100 percent."

"I actually sacrificed the children for him—always," Nela agrees. "There were years he played 135 concerts. . . . He was the darling of the whole world. . . . I gave him moral and intellectual support. I was a real partner. I created a family. That completed him in a way, and it came out in his playing. He was really at his most marvelous when he played. Otherwise, he had lots of faults."

In 1982, at age 94, after nearly fifty years of marriage, Artur left Nela to live with his young co-author, Annabelle Whitestone, in whose company he died two years later.

"Too depressing," murmurs Nela.

Instantly, Fela chimes in with a story about the time the two girls captured a blue heron together at her uncle's country estate the summer when they were 12 years old.

Nela says: "We are friends, you know, since, since . . ."

"Oh, come on—for sixty years. Over. Let's be frank."

"Sixty-three years," declares Nela.

"There was hardly a year in our lives when we didn't see each other," says Fela.

"It is a wonderful thing," says Nela. "I think friendship is better than husbands and everything put together."[26]

Friendly Relations

As I have said before, separating friendship from kin relations draws a distinction without a difference, one that glosses over a very large area of Feminine friendship. However, while millions of people count relatives among their close friends, it is *women* who perform what anthropologist di Leonardo calls "the work of kinship"—phoning, keeping in touch by mail, sending gifts and cards, arranging visits, organizing holiday gatherings and celebrations, and doing the mental work of planning these activities.[27] All this takes time and skill that is virtually invisible because women are thought to have the "moral responsibility for family life." The work of kinship doesn't count as labor expended in the creation of friendship and yet it is that and more.

Carol Stack describes how such friendly relations buttress poor Black households by providing services and commodities that would otherwise cost money, such as child care, help with the laundry, gifts of clothes or furniture, things that very close friends do for one another, related or not.[28]

Among certain ethnic groups and lower-middle-class families, women are central to "the web of kinship linking together sets of households," notes anthropologist Sylvia Yanagisako. In the Japanese-American community in Seattle, for instance, a majority of the women have jobs outside the home, yet mother, daughters, sisters, aunts, and cousins may telephone daily, baby-sit, or shop for one another and visit regularly. What the women are actually doing, says Yanagisako, is protecting the masculinity of men who have to "maintain a clear stance of independence from each other to validate the integrity of the nuclear family."[29] The idea of a self-sufficient nuclear family is crucial to Japanese cultural ideology and male self-esteem, yet the men's modest wages do not allow them to be independent. Therefore, each family's needs must be met through interfamily assistance and an exchange of services. The women's friendships do the job of creating a support network between households, while the men can save face by maintaining the appearance of independence from one another.

However warm a woman's feelings for her kin, it is misleading to represent these relationships solely as an expression of female emotionality. They also serve to cover up the failed ethos of male autonomy, the fact that men avoid kin work and yet benefit from it, the economic inadequacies of the nuclear family, and the lack of social options for women.

In this latter regard, I cannot help but think of the Orthodox Jewish women of the Hasidic sect. Differentiated by hundreds of sex-specific tasks and taboos, they are even more alienated from men than were the proper Victorians. Religion, culture, and strict sex-segregation keep Orthodox women tightly interlocked within their family and community, and like any confined group, their friendships grow out of their shared status and responsibilities.

Lis Harris, the author of *Holy Days,* who spent months in a Hasidic community in Brooklyn, observed "what appeared to be a

remarkably energetic, mutually supportive community of women—
an almost Amazonian society, too busy to pause to reflect upon its
distance from the world of men." She describes the private circumscribed domain of women: the separate schools, the shopping street,
the home, and the synagogue, where women are crammed upstairs
in an airless black-screened balcony in which—since they cannot see
or hear the service conducted by the men below—they are as likely
to talk as to pray. Only in the mikvah, the ritual bath where women
go to purify themselves for their husbands, is there no socializing,
"none of the affectionate banter so prevalent in feminine Hasidic
society."[30]

However warm and affectionate, Feminine friendship is most
marked by its prevalence in societies where women are segregated
and confined, either by the psychological and economic confinement
of domesticity, the cultural or religious confinement of the ethnic
enclave, or the literal confinement of a prison.

Friendship Behind Bars

Regardless of the counterconventional behavior that may have
put them in prison, most female inmates believe in conventional sex
roles. According to a report by Rose Giallombardo in 1966 (still the
most extensive study on women's social relationships in prison),
female inmates commonly believe other women are untrustworthy.
They have a full lexicon to describe everyone's clearly defined role
in the social structure. There are "squares," "jive bitches," "rap
buddies," "homeys" (from the same hometown), and a homosexual
cluster that includes the "femme" or "mommy" and the "stud broad"
or "daddy."[31]

My brother-in-law Mark, who is a professor of criminal justice
at the University of Colorado, says, "Women's relationships tend
to imitate romantic or family roles. They play wife, husband, lover,
or mother to each other. Men establish utilitarian relationships, using
threats and intimidation to assure themselves a supply of cigarettes
or sex. For both genders, real friendship is rare in prison."

"We make friends but it's complicated," says a prison inmate
who agreed to give me some firsthand information. "Sometimes a
woman becomes a lesbian out of loneliness when she stops hearing
from her spouse or man. . . . But most of the women have the
wrong conception of lesbianism. They try too hard in role-play-

ing. . . . Some women prefer aggressive women rather than feminine women simply because they want to be with a man."

The same inmate says her conversations with friends outside prison
are "meaningless and so very empty," but she and her friends in
prison "spend time together eating, dancing, acting, singing, working, spending yard time, talking, and loving each other."

"We play cards and chess and talk about our family, freedom,
ourselves," adds another prisoner.

"Also we take out our frustrations on each other and then when
we catch ourselves we are sorry and get even closer," continues the
first. "We hold each other's hand when there is no light in the tunnel
on our sentence appeals. When someone goes home, you're sad because you wish it was you . . . but you also are so happy for the
person who is returning to her family."

An inmate who is doing twenty-five years to life admits that
when a friend gets out it's "really, really rough if you were very
close. Here is a moment to celebrate but you have lost a close friend
and friends matter so much here. . . . People of different races, classes,
and sexual orientations all live *very* closely together here—probably
more mixed than they'd be outside prison—and friendships definitely
cut across all these differences." But, this woman adds, her prison
friendships have "a kind of different quality" with transfers, paroles,
and releases changing the population, like travelers "passing into
someone's life for a moment." As for the lesbian relationships, she
says: "It's pretty rare that they are associated with a feminist consciousness, one of appreciating each other as women. Having no
choice, women take women even though on the street they would
pick a man. . . . There's actually a lot of contempt for women as
women here, and these feelings affect lesbian relationships as well as
other friendships."

Says a fourth inmate: "When friends become lovers and the affair
ends, the friendship ends."

In prison or out, a friendship that is rooted in powerlessness—a
Feminine friendship—is a tender trap. It facilitates women's willingness to make do in a situation that is fundamentally unpleasant
or unfair. It turns women toward or against each other for the benefit
of someone other than either of them. It helps some women feel
"happy." It helps others survive. Feminine friendship is what women
give each other when they accept, or cannot help, the way they are
defined by others.

Female Friendship

Even in periods when women have been domesticated and un-equal, another form of friendship has evolved, one that repudiates traditional sex *roles* but makes a virtue out of what have traditionally been considered distinctly female *traits:* women's sensibility, nurtur-ing, and supposed moral superiority.

If Feminine friendships can be said to develop while women are in the act of serving men, Female friendships develop while women are in the act of saving humanity. Female friendships typically have sprung up in the past among social reformers, settlement house women, churchwomen, organizers of civic and professional women's clubs, women who fought for equal education, for temperance, abolition, and women's suffrage. As Carl Degler notes in *At Odds,* these group relations "took the place of the older, more intimate but still rather confined relations between individual women."

In today's world, while the cult of domesticity has declined and sex roles have relaxed somewhat, Female friendships emerge among women who share a belief in women's special qualities as pacifists, healers, and visionaries in the peace, civil rights, and women's move-ments. Their devotion to their cause fuels the fires of friendship, and each friend in turn buttresses the other in her chosen mission.

The key word here is "chosen." Although many of these women function in a separate sphere, unlike the others we have been dis-cussing, these come together away from men because they choose to, not because someone else demands it. And they feel better not lesser as a result. Often, they are unmarried. Always, they are ori-ented away from the man-pleasing, male-run world, and toward a world of their own in which they escape both domestication and discrimination by establishing women's institutions or espousing fe-male culture. They refuse the imposed separatism of the weak but embrace a separatism of the special.

Historian Blanche Weisen Cook gives us four eminent women of the past whose lives embody this second style of friendship: Lillian Wald, founder of the Henry Street Settlement House, Jane Addams who started Hull House in Chicago, Crystal Eastman, a lawyer and investigative journalist, and Emma Goldman, the legendary anarchist remembered lately as a character in the films *Ragtime* and *Reds.* Of these, Cook says only Goldman "relied predominantly on men for emotional sustenance and political support. . . . Yet throughout her life, Goldman wrote, she 'longed for a friend of my own sex, a kindred spirit with whom I could share the innermost thoughts and feelings I could not express to men. . . . Instead of friendship from women I had met with much antagonism, petty envy and jealousy because men liked me.' "[32]

Goldman's attitude matches the Feminine construct described in the foregoing section. In contrast, Crystal Eastman represents the Feminist attitude we will get to next. "Eastman's comrades were the 'new women' of Greenwich Village. Radical feminists and socialists, they considered men splendid lovers and friends, but they believed that women needed the more egalitarian support of other women," wrote Cook. "Unlike Emma Goldman, who lived almost exclusively among men, Crystal Eastman always had a feminist support group of considerable importance to her life. She was supported by women with whom she had deep and lasting relations: many of the ardent suffragists of the Congressional Union, her friends from Vassar who worked with her in the Woman's Peace Party of New York and who were part of her communal family in Greenwich Village."

As I see it, the other two women represent the Female friendship category. "Jane Addams and Lillian Wald were involved almost exclusively with women who remained throughout their lives a nurturing source of love and support. Henry Street and Hull House were staffed by their closest friends who, night and day, made possible their unrelenting schedules," wrote Cook. These women gave all their time and money to the poor, put nurses and free lunch programs into the public schools, made social activists out of rich society women, campaigned against war and for the women's vote, and worked, traveled, and lived together.

It is beside the point whether or not these women were heterosexual, lesbian, or asexual (as some historians would have us believe). What matters is that they moved in a homosocial universe; they were woman-related and proud of it. Women who attended the newly established women's colleges and co-ed universities were overjoyed to find other women like themselves, females who took themselves seriously and in many cases planned a career outside of marriage if not instead of it. Some relationships between educated women, like those of the Victorian ladies, also suggest a depth of feeling that today's emotional seismographs would find suspicious.

Historian Nancy Sahli describes the eventual repression of a widespread practice called "smashing," in which women undergraduates exchanged bouquets, love notes, and other accoutrements of courtship: "As long as women loved each other as they did for much of the nineteenth century, without threatening the system itself, their relationships either were simply ignored by men or were regarded as an acceptable part of the female sphere. Feminists, college graduates and other independent women, however, were a real threat to the established order."[33]

Another historian, Leila J. Rupp, identifies several long-lasting friendships between autonomous, educated women of the twentieth century who "lived in a world of politically active women friends."[34] Among these were Mary Woolley, president of Mount Holyoke College, and Jeannette Marks, who taught English there; Lena Madesin Phillips, founder of the Federations of Business and Professional Women's Clubs, and actress Marjory Lacey-Baker; and biographer Alma Lutz and librarian Marguerite Smith, who were colleagues in the National Woman's Party—pairs who were part of "friendship networks made up of woman-committed women."

In 1916 sociologist Jessie Taft noted: "Everywhere we find the unmarried woman turning to other women, building up with them a real home, finding in them the sympathy and understanding, the bond of similar standards and values, as well as the same aesthetic and intellectual interests, that are often difficult of realization in a husband, especially in America."

"I wish poets and novelists would celebrate more often the friendships of women, for these are a marked and, generally speaking, wholesome phenomenon in the modern world," wrote Vida Scudder in 1937. Scudder was an English professor at Wellesley for forty years and a co-founder of two settlement houses; her friend for forty years, Florence Converse, was a writer, an editor at the *Atlantic Monthly,* and a worker at Denison House. They were deeply embedded in a "women's subculture which flourished under conditions of the breakdown of the traditional spheres for women and women's familial networks," according to scholar Nan Maglin. They promoted the higher education of women and acknowledged the importance of women's friendships. "These friendships and their extension into communities became, in a sense, a replacement for the traditional nuclear family which many of these women chose not to join. . . . [But] their homosocial world [was] not so radically different from the world of the eighteenth- and nineteenth-century women who married and yet lived in a total female world. These latter-day women just carried the 'irrelevancy' of men to its logical conclusion."[35]

Separate Is Not Equal

The evidence leads us to a subtle but critical distinction: Although Female friendships made *women* women's priority and supported political activism that paved the way for our own feminist enlightenment, these women fall short of the feminist ideal because they did not use their own experience to overtly challenge traditional assumptions about women's role or sexuality; they simply tried to alleviate suffering and live another way themselves. In our own era, the same can be said about some of the friendships formed by women in all-female communes, collectives, convents, or the "women's culture" movement where the accent is on spiritualism. These women, too, alleviate suffering and live another way without necessarily challenging the status quo.

Obviously, a convent, though a woman's world, is not a female institution; it is run by the Church, and churches are male owned and operated. Just the same, as historian Eileen Power points out, in earlier times, nunneries provided women the only respectable career other than marriage, and they still afford "opportunities for education, organization and responsibility, not easy for women to find elsewhere."[36] Furthermore, a convent is not just a religious unit but a homosocial one in which strong female friendships flourish despite strict regimentation and omnipresent homophobia.

One former nun remembers: "We were lectured on the dangers of 'particular friendships.' No one used the word Lesbian. The prohibition of close friendship between two women was based on the ideology of community life: if you restricted your time and attention too much to one person, it limited your availability to the community as a whole."[37]

Another ex-nun says: "The most difficult thing I had to learn during those days was how to live uncritically in such extremely close contact with so many women, many of whom I probably would not have associated with in the outside world." By the end of her novitiate she "keenly felt" that she was "part of a very special group of mostly bright women who were dedicated to working for others."[38]

However admirable this shared moral passion, Female friendship in a female world is not the goal most women are seeking. The price for that kind of friendship is the surrender of honest and equal relations with men and, even more alarmingly, the absence of feminists from mainstream activity.

I am in favor of all-women groups and institutions as a base for feminist theory-making, organizing, and resistance, but not if these are our *only* structures and not if all other institutions and structures are allowed "off the hook" while feminists are busy among themselves. Separatism is an option, and sometimes a strategy, but not a goal. Self-elected separation from the mainstream culture has been, at times, a strengthening experience for women as it has been for Blacks, but over the long haul separate has never been equal.

Feminist theorist Estelle Freedman recognizes women's collective debt to lesbian feminists who, "by affirming the primacy of women's relationships with each other and by providing an alternative feminist culture, forced many nonlesbians to reevaluate their relationships with men, male institutions and male values. In the process, all feminists have put to rest the myth of female dependence on men and rediscovered the significance of woman bonding." At the same time, Freedman warns, we must "use female institutions to combat inequality, not to entrench it."[39]

The larger society will never be influenced by the rearranged priorities of female culture if their "utopia" is closed. When they live in their own world and feed off their own institutions, women have minimal impact on conventional power arrangements; they may as well be cloistered like the nuns. From such friendship, says one critic, "We learn about the world in us, but far less about us in the world."[40] For Female friendship to both feel good and do good for women in the world, it needs to be experienced both privately *and* publicly.

Feminist Friendship

Feminist friendship is not doctrine but practice.

When the relationship of two friends is defined and shaped by the struggles and victories of feminism, when it is a friendship of utter wholeness—of both nurture *and* empowerment—it is a Feminist friendship regardless of whether the friends are active in the women's movement.

Housewives can have it. Molecular biologists can have it. Young or old, single or married, lesbian or straight women can have it. Cagney and Lacey have a Feminist friendship in the TV series of the same name. So do the characters portrayed by Meryl Streep and Cher in the film *Silkwood;* Lillian Hellman and her friend Julia; the pairs of women in the French films *One Sings, the Other Doesn't* and *Entre Nous;* Celie and Shug in *The Color Purple;* and before all of us were born, Elizabeth Cady Stanton and Susan B. Anthony practically invented it:

> So closely interwoven have been our lives, our purposes and experiences that, separated, we have a feeling of incompleteness—united, such a strength of self-assertion that no ordinary obstacles, differences or dangers ever appear to us insurmountable. [41]

Stanton's words illustrate why I see the progress of women's friendships not as a linear hierarchy going from Feminine to Female to Feminist but as a synthesis of all our historic patterns. When Stanton says she and Anthony are incomplete without each other, she speaks not as a relationship junkie, who is nobody without somebody, but as a powerful individual who is even stronger, more effective, *more* complete when united with a dear friend who is herself so strong.

Since the mid-1970s, as American women have gained economic clout and self-esteem, conservatives increasingly claim that they are losing the female art of selfless love; that women are becoming "like men," intimacy-takers not intimacy-givers. But the truth is they are developing what psychologist Janet Surrey calls "relationship-authenticity." [42] Many women have cured themselves of their addictive attachments. They don't aspire to a totally "separate self" who cannot interact and coexist but to a self who "gains vitality and enhancement in relationship and is not reduced or threatened by connections." They see women's talent at self-disclosure as a form of risk-taking that enhances personal identity "without sacrificing feelings of relatedness." [43] They are better equipped to put power behind their love. Power *to,* not power *over.* Power to choose friendship rather than retreat into it. Power to help one's friends, not just to huddle with them.

But there is one stipulation: The new kind of helping must not require self-sacrifice. If women stop sacrificing for men only to do it for other women, they have made no progress: Women should not be "asked to be feminine in the name of female bonding," writes Mary Daly, who believes friendship based on sisterhood "has at its core the affirmation of freedom."[44]

Liberating and comforting, galvanizing and subversive, sisterhood transforms women's friendship because it combines Feminine loving-kindness and Female solidarity with a Feminist consciousness. And it *feels* different.

"It was not that they first found these friendships in movement activities, but rather that the movement supported them in *conceptualizing the value of friendships*," wrote psychologists Ann Seiden and Pauline Bart about the friendships among the feminist activists they studied. "Previously, female friendships had often had a 'pastime' quality, being regarded as outside the arena of major action, something you do until the 'relationship' comes."[45]

Another healthy portrait of Feminist friendship emerges from the work of sociologist Robert Bell, who says that Nonconventional women (who are more apt to subscribe to feminist values) have more "very close friends" than do Conventional women: "Friends are important to them but they do not dominate their lives." Nor do they "usually see their friends in terms of what these friends can do for them." Also, these women are more in demand. "It appears that the aliveness and vibrancy of Nonconventional women are attractive to other women and they are drawn toward them."[46]

A third positive report comes from a group of middle- and working-class women whose lives have been dramatically changed by feminism. Many of these women say their new friendships are unlike any they've ever experienced. "I feel a real sisterhood," says one of those being studied. "I'm very aware of women and not as something to compete with, which is something really nice. It's like we need to be together if we're going to make it, if it's ever going to be any different."[47]

The researchers who worked with this group report: "These new female friendships have a political dimension, they become sources of resistance to the conditions of daily life. . . . For these women, feminism did not mean a celebration of self at the expense of others, but the recognition that control of one's own life was to be found in overcoming the relations of domination which structure all women's lives."

The complaint about the women's movement having spawned hoards of selfish prunes is a transparent defense against what feminism really does spawn: confident individuals who form friendships that unite the self and the other in pride, vitality, and strength. Feminist friendship is an empowering interactive force with enough megawatts to energize each woman who plugs into it. You feel it when you notice yourself assuming the best of a woman, not anticipating hostility or suppressing envy. You feel it when you are interested in what a friend thinks—not just about you and your activities but about *everything*. You feel it when your friends alter your perspective on life, help you sort out your problems, enlarge your goals and help you move toward achieving them, help you see yourself not as one isolated woman treated this way or that but as a vital member of half the human race.

Seven brief case histories hint at the diversity of these ties.

The Odd Couple

Sarah, who is divorced from Ben, the father of her three children, described "the oddest, nicest friendship ever":

"Ben had studiously kept me from meeting Meg, his new wife. I didn't know if he was embarrassed about her or scared of me. He had also been very insensitive to several problems our children were having since the divorce. Last spring it all came to a head when he wouldn't agree to come see our son in his school play. I was so frustrated on behalf of the child, who already felt unloved, that I called Ben's house when I knew he was out and I told Meg the problem.

"She was wonderfully understanding, which inspired me to tell her some of the children's other crises that had been precipitated by their father. She admitted to me that she wants a child, but after watching Ben with the ones he already has, she's decided to postpone getting pregnant. I could see she has a real feeling for kids. When Ben came home, she managed to talk him into attending my son's play.

"Since I had unloaded all these problems on her and she'd shown such interest, I wrote her a follow-up letter about each child's situation. I said I was sorry to bug her, but the kids' problems would end up on her doorstep anyway.

"She suggested we have lunch. We met at some out of the way restaurant and we got along swimmingly. 'Ben has married a replica of you,' she told me and she was right. We're both the unvarnished farm girl type, we have the same value system, she works in a shelter for the abused and I have a job in cancer care. She told me how uncomfortable she is with Ben's aristocratic family. They sit around and quiz each other on the subway systems of major European cities or lines from Proust.

" 'They're too complex,' she said.

" 'No,' I told her. 'They're simple. Simple cruelty is the way that family treats everyone who isn't them. Complex is you sitting across the table from your husband's ex-wife.'

"We've gotten very close since then. When I went to visit my youngest child in camp, Meg came to my house to baby-sit for the other two kids. She has given me more support in a few months than I got from Ben in all the years we were married."

Wife and ex-wife linked by one man. Not competing for him but pulling together as women, for their own needs and for the sake of three children. There are no rules for such a friendship; it is too new, too different. Yet it reminds me of "the bawdy lore of Southern women," an ancient tradition of women warning women of "what they can expect in private out of the men and institutions they are taught to praise in public."[48] The unity of women: as new as lunch with an ex-wife; as old as the hills.

A Sisterhood of Writers

Louise Bernikow describes the vitality of her Feminist friendships with other women writers: "There is a shared sense of risk about our individual lives, as though we were in fact women on the edge of time. . . . We know, whether we live with men or not, that there is no arm to lean on—the figures of the national economy tell us so. So we all worry about money and we do it together."

Louise and her friends read each other's manuscripts and give each other gifts that "become metaphors, describe transactions, are in themselves the language of relations. . . . At Christmas this year, Nancy gave me a scarf that her sister made and I gave her various body lotions. Leeny made a drawing. I baked bread. Rosemary sent running socks, Vicki a photograph of myself with Honor. There was a poem from one of us to another, a pair of hair combs, a soft purse. . . .

"What are these things but a laying on of hands? . . . The glorious gift from Honor sits on my mantel—a leatherbound copy of my last book, marbled paper front and back, deep red covers. In this language, we offer each other double kinds of support—the body and the mind, the woman and the work, each part as valuable as the other."[49]

From Coworkers to Family

Pam Surratt and Joyce Jennings defy the odds. Other women with such divergent life-styles might break apart. This friendship grows deeper through their differences. Ten years ago when Joyce was beginning her career as a social worker and Pam was her supervisor, they ignored the usual hierarchical constraints and became friends. They shared a condo and skiied together. Joyce was promoted. Pam got married. Still the friendship grew. When Pam became a full-time mother and struggled with her new life, Joyce helped. When Joyce moved along in her career and struggled with *her* choices, Pam helped. Joyce keeps Pam in touch with the social work world. Pam asked Joyce to assist at the birth of her second child. Joyce loves to help care for the kids. A room is reserved for her in the Surratt household. She's family. And that "makes my life well-rounded," she says.[50]

Teamwork and Companionship

Jane Smith and Jean Yancey began their collaboration with a lemonade stand in the third grade. At 14, they staged the country's first department store teen fashion show, a huge success. During World War II, they founded a shopper service for servicemen. Jane went on to become a buyer for a boutique and a fashion show commentator; Jean became a business consultant and public speaker. Although their husbands and children never meshed, Jane and Jean stayed connected. Together they traveled without their families all over the globe in the years when women didn't do "that sort of thing." Occasionally, one has stepped in when the other couldn't fulfill a business engagement. They are not just buffers, they're each other's boosters.

"I've always been able to pick up the phone and say, 'Something great has happened. I had this audience and they gave me a standing ovation,' " Jean says. "And her response has always been, 'That's great, go for it.' "

"We've taken different paths but we still come back together," adds Jane. "We laugh a lot. There's no jealousy. We also have a lot of respect for each other's opinions . . . a feeling of roots, a feeling of closeness, and . . . companionship, tremendous companionship."[51]

Friendship with a "Star"

"She's such a famous actress that even in sunglasses she's besieged by autograph hounds," says Michelle, a public relations woman, of her friend whose name is a household word. "But what I love about her has nothing to do with her fame. The fame is just this big weight she has to drag around with her in public places. What makes her so wonderful is the way she is a friend. She's *hamishe,* like one of my Jewish aunts. She cares about what I eat because I'm overweight, so she's always recommending diets and buying me health foods when she barely knows the whereabouts of her own refrigerator. If I'm going to some foreign city, she arms me with a detailed list of what I *must* do and see, the galleries, museums, out of the way shops, her friends who I *must* look up. She encouraged me to let my hair go gray; since I don't have to stay glamorous forever like she does, she insists I shouldn't get enslaved by hair dyes.

"Despite her money and celebrity there are things she relies on me for; like when we gave a joint party at her house, she got as nervous as a kid, dusted all her *tchatkes* five times and asked my advice every two seconds. She's not great at stuff like that but I know how to organize events and people with my left pinky.

"Since we're at such different economic levels, I can never match the elaborate gifts she gives me or thank her enough for paying my way so that she can have my company on vacations I couldn't otherwise afford. But I know she loves me a lot and appreciates my strengths, so it all evens out in the end."

Empathetic Women

"Early in life, I became very female-identified," says Julie. "I adored my mother. I got along fantastically with my girlfriends. I went to a girls' high school and a woman's college. I always get excited when something good happens to a woman in the news; Gerry Ferraro, Sally Ride, even when a little girl gets to play on the boys' football team, I feel the victory like it was my own. I grew up believing it's okay if you can't *help,* but it's unforgivable if you can't *feel.* My women friends can feel whatever I'm feeling. Even though my husband is one of my best friends, he can't satisfy my need for empathetic women. He once asked me what I get from my women friends that I can't get from him. The answer is, the sister I never had, the daughter I might have, the other *me.*"

A Feminist Strike Force

Diane has a coterie of friends—not all soulmates but all help-meets—who help her be what she is: the highest level woman official in her state. "I think of these twelve women as my feminist strike force; they baby-sit, cook, cut the grass, stay with a sick child, make me laugh. I'd never have been able to raise five children and be in politics if they hadn't volunteered to share in the family duties."

Every three months Diane and her "strike force" go away for a two-day retreat. "It's pragmatic feminism," she says. "We have an agenda. We discuss how I can be more effective in office, how I can be a better asset to the cause, and what they can do about it. We brainstorm. We spread paper all over the walls and list mistakes, strategies, strengths, and weaknesses. They're the people I count on and respect most. They recharge my cells."

I've seen some of these women in action at Diane's house, where the door is always open—women are ferrying children in their cars, one is unpacking groceries, one is running around with a clipboard full of to-do's for a party, another is handing Diane her coat and a copy of her speech. Somehow it all works to free her to be a responsible public servant and then come home and be a relaxed mother. "My husband can't do any of this; he has a big job himself. So, in the professionalizing of my staff, my number one priority has been to set up a network to care for the kids. Male politicians have their wives do this behind the scenes stuff for them. Women politicians usually have to pay for this kind of help. My friends do it for me because they're my friends. They were my friends before I got this job and they'll be my friends after."

Each of these women enjoys the homeostasis I mentioned earlier. They find equilibrium in friendship by bringing into balance the dualities that patriarchal thinking polarizes: self and community, autonomy and cooperation, differentiation and fusion, individuality and collectivity, power and love. Rather than dichotomized opposites, these are ingredients to be combined in different measures at different times, never static, never final.

These women and their friends are allies in the world as it is and mutual visionaries of a world that has yet to be. They do for each other what society expects women to do only for men. But they do not lose themselves in the process.

Chapter 15

❦   ❦

Can Women and Men Be Friends?

Name one.

Name one famous friendship between a woman and a man—one admired, esteemed, inspiring, nonromantic, nonsexual friendship between a man and a woman in history or literature.

It's not easy. In every culture, friendship between the sexes has been either inconceivable or forbidden. Inconceivable because women were universally considered men's inferiors; forbidden because each woman was chattel belonging to either her father or husband. Why would she be interested in any other man unless she intended to compromise her virginity or her virtue; why else would he be interested in her when all women were carnal creatures, meant for decoration, fornication, reproduction, and domestic service?

Cross-sex relationships that contradicted these norms usually involved "deviates," Bohemians, artists, people of "lower rank," or offbeat unions that can be otherwise explained.

There was Jesus and Mary Magdalene, but she was a follower more than a friend. And Barak, the biblical warrior, who said to Deborah, the prophet and judge, "If thou wilt go with me, then I will go: but if thou wilt not go with me, then I will not go." Although this echoes Ruth's declaration of fealty to Naomi, Barak was on assignment from Deborah to defend the Jews from the Canaanites. Theirs was a work relationship, not a friendship.

Aspasia was "a woman of considerable intellectual stature who

conversed with Socrates and taught rhetoric. . . . Her friendship with
Socrates caused her to be remembered and written about by his
followers."[1] Plato says that Socrates claimed he could deliver a fine
eulogy thanks to Aspasia, "for she who is my instructor is by no
means weak in the art of rhetoric; on the contrary she has turned
out many fine orators and amongst them one who surpassed all the
other Greeks, Pericles."[2] (Aspasia is thought to be the real author of
Pericles' oration.) "Socrates himself would sometimes go to visit
her, and some of his acquaintance with him; and those who fre-
quented her company would carry their wives with them to listen
to her. . . . what art or charming faculty she had that enabled her
to captivate, as she did, the greatest statesmen, and to give the philosophers occasion to speak so much about her."[3]

But have you heard of this remarkable woman? Despite her
friendships with these great men and her recorded brilliance, is she
ever mentioned in the same breath as Socrates, Plato, or Pericles?
No; what is known about Aspasia, if anything, is that Pericles fell
in love with her and she became his lifelong mistress. The romance
is remembered; the friendships are forgotten.

Jonathan Spence, a professor of history at Yale, kindly directed
me to what he terms "probably the greatest Chinese source on male-
female friendship,"[4] Cao Xueqin's eighteenth-century novel *The Story
of the Stone,* also known as *Dream of the Red Chamber.* In this, the
"most popular book in the whole of Chinese literature" (according
to the translator), the author relates his experiences through the pro-
tagonist Baoyu: "Having made an utter failure of my life, I found
myself one day in the midst of my poverty and wretchedness, thinking about the female companions of my youth. . . . I resolved that
however unsightly my own shortcomings might be, I must not, for
the sake of keeping them hid, allow those wonderful girls to pass
into oblivion without a memorial." But we discover that Baoyu did
not appreciate his female friends as normal human beings; he maintained that "girls are made of water and boys are made of mud,"
and only with girls did he feel "fresh and clean." As impossible as
friendship is when all women are viewed as inferior to all men, it is
no less impossible when women are considered, as they were by this
author, "both morally and intellectually superior."[5]

In his note to me, Spence makes another point: "Though there
are some levels of sexual encounter, basically Baoyu and his female
friends react through conversation and intellectual games." But can

friendship exist between the sexes *without* "some levels of sexual encounter"? Must the interactions of heterosexual women and men always be either trivialized, eroticized, exalted, or qualified by a half dozen "buts"?

But Men and Women Are Too Different to Be Friends

This "but" is the lingering legacy of patriarchal history. Women are *A*, men are *B*. Men do *X*, women do *Y*. Some people still trot out their favorite sex differences to prove that the two sexes were never meant to be friends and shouldn't even try.

In my book *Growing Up Free*, I used hundreds of pages to argue against the notion of inborn differences. I tried to show how females and males are systematically programmed to be different; how, other than our reproductive complementarity, most of our supposedly implacable sex differences are literally "man-made."[6] But I still have questions: Are the differences between the sexes—culturally imposed though they are—going to forever keep us apart? How long before women and men can be friends with each other the way each of us can be friends with someone of our own sex? Before struggling toward some answers, you might want to answer the following questions about the conditions of your own cross-sex friendships.

- If something wonderful happens to you today, which of your friends will you tell first?
- Who do you go to with your most personal problems?
- When you are recuperating in the hospital, what friend do you want to visit you?
- Who would you call if you needed someone to talk to at three o'clock in the morning?

The chances are that the people who came to mind in answer to these questions are women if you are a woman and men if you're a man. Although the two sexes love, live, and work together, when it comes to close friendship, each sex usually turns to its own. Given our society's near obsession with heterosexual relations and our persistent ambivalence about homosexuality, it is surprising how little attention is paid to the fact that, as the preceding chapters have shown, heterosexuals are so homosocial.

Sex Separatism Makes Us Different

Although we are oriented toward the opposite sex for sex, for everything else we are gender loyalists. This is no accident. True friendship is rare between women and men not because we are innately incompatible but because sex separatism is so rigorously ingrained during childhood. Most parents rear male and female children as if preparing them to live in two different worlds—giving them different toys, books, chores, rules, tools, and boundaries and different messages about sex-appropriate emotions. Therefore, before they reach school age, girls and boys *have* become strangers to one another, with incompatible play habits, different ideas of fun, and few grounds for friendship. For a decade or more, says psychologist S. B. Damico, boys and girls establish "separate social systems," have "only limited contact with each other," and act as though "members of the opposite sex are 'horrible' and to be avoided at all costs."

In school, sex enmity can be exacerbated by lining up girls and boys in separate rows, pitting them against each other in spelling bees or dodge ball, and allowing gender ghettos to form in the playground or classroom. Children learn fast that to cross the lines of sex demarcation is to risk the invective "sissy," "tomboy," or worse.

Egalitarian separatism would be bad enough, but boys' exclusivity not only underlines their differences from girls but establishes their superiority. Any sixth-grade teacher knows that the best way to humiliate a boy is to put him wherever the girls congregate. If proximity pollutes, then boy-girl friendship is perilous indeed.

When my twin daughters were 12, they and another girl often dressed up in costumes and improvised scenes with a male classmate who also loved acting. (Eventually the four friends collaborated on a script and produced their own eight-millimeter movie melodrama.) One day the boy confided that he'd been called a "faggot" for playing with girls. He was proud of his answer: "I told the guy, 'If I'm the faggot, how come you're the one who likes boys?' "

It's crazy: To be thought heterosexual, a child must be homosocial, while the child who is heterosocial might be typed as homosexual. That contradiction doesn't seem to bother anyone. Some parents welcome homosocial separatism because they fear that girl-boy friendship could lead to early heterosexual experimentation. Others think mutual scorn between the sexes is cute, harmless, or "only natural." Their idea is that boys should be boyish together, girls should be girlish together, and in due time the call of the wild hormones will bring the sexes together.

But the alienation that accumulates during ten or twelve years of separatism and mutual contempt doesn't just disappear with the first adolescent crush. Future relationships between young men and women are distorted by casting them as strictly sexual. It is difficult to get together as adult friends because sex separatism has labeled friendship and fun homosocial and put only love and sex in the heterosexual column. After a decade of separation and enmity, we cannot just outgrow the feeling that when we are with the other sex, we are, as in our childhoods, in alien territory. That's why so many people continue to rely on members of their own sex for everything *but* sex. That's why the two genders traditionally divide up for conversation, sports activities, and so on. It is rare to find men and women who are not romantically involved who spend time together for fun. People double-date so that when conversation fails the men can talk business or sports and the women can mine the emotional terrain. Women and men sometimes cannot agree on where to vacation because they have diametrically different ideas of recreation and leisure. Many men feel the most relaxed when they're out with the boys.

So, here we are, male and female: reared as strangers, each sex trying to be as opposite from the other sex as possible, believing that to be too much "alike" would mean having "unisex," which is no gender at all. How in the world can two creatures so *invested* in being different ever see the payoff in commonality? How can we enjoy being together if what men and women were taught to enjoy is so different and women's intimacy temperature is thirty degrees higher than men's? How can we become close, given what we know about the way close friendships are formed? (See Chapter 5.)

We know it is *proximity* that lets people get to know each other. But sex separatism prevents that casual overlapping.

We know it is *similarity of values* that brings friends together despite status differences, but what if different values are inculcated in boys along with their cap pistols and in girls along with their Barbie dolls? Or, what if women and men cannot ignore the pre-eminent label of gender long enough to discover they have values in common? Or, what if our discovered similarities threaten our gender identity and cancel out the attraction?

We know *reciprocal liking* is part of the passage to intimacy, but how can we "like" each other if the only alternatives we have experienced are childhood disdain and the sexual teasing of adolescence?

We know *self-disclosure* is the making of a friendship, but how much will we disclose to someone who has been made so alien, so "different"?

Inequality Makes Us Different

To allow "birds of a feather" to find each other under the layers of masculine and feminine posturing, friends have to shed the "opposites attract" ethos of heterosexual sex. And they have to disavow the sexism that props up gender hierarchy. They must see women as full human beings and men as people with feelings before they can see each other as friends. Yet they should not have to be "the same" to have similarities; they must have the freedom to be *different but equal*.

The equality is basic. Without it, there can be no friendship. Sex can flourish between unequals and love can thrive between the powerful and the powerless, between parent and child, between teacher and student, between ruler and subject; but friendship is the one relationship that must be eye to eye. Which is why Aristotle, Cicero, Montaigne, and Confucius concluded that a man (*a fortiori*, a superior) could not be friends with a woman.

For reasons different from theirs, I would have to agree with them. Male-female friendship is still the exception because equality—*social* equality—is still the exception. As the critic Elizabeth Minnich points out, "It is exceedingly difficult to have an unselfconscious mutuality in a friendship when friends are not equal *in the world*."[7]

Friendship must also be not only equal but mutual. Unlike love, it cannot be unilateral or unrequited. Unlike sex, it cannot be forced.

Many contemporary cross-sex friendships are unions not of equal soulmates but of role-players doing sex-stereotyped imitations of classic male-female arrangements. Sociologist Helen Hacker finds that in cross-sex friendships the man calls the shots. He takes more intimacy than he gives. And while a male and female may appear to be confiding as much in one another, they are confiding only information appropriate to their gender: The men reveal their strengths and hide their weaknesses; the women hide their strengths and only show men their helpless side.[8]

Hacker also sees mostly "exchange" relations between cross-sex friends. They help each other decode the behavior of an opposite sex romantic partner; or they use each other as escorts-without-commitment.

Psychologist Susanna Rose, who studied cross-sex friendship among people in their twenties, has found an inequality of exchange within these relationships: Men get acceptance, intimacy, and companionship from their women friends; women get companionship from men but not enough acceptance and intimacy. Rose speculates that women may accept this inequity because they get enough *status* from men to compensate for the other deficiencies.[9]

In my interviews, a few women confessed to preferring men to women friends because of the excitement of allying with the dominant class. "I always felt if I could hold my own with my men friends, I was really smart," says Cynthia, the director of a social service agency. "There were no extra points for being popular with my women friends."

Women learned to devalue their own sex back when boys disdained the company of girls, and girls internalized that view of themselves. Having learned that boys were favored by the whole world and not just by other boys, females accepted male supremacy as a fact. That does not stop women from considering female friendship as important as male friendship, but it does make many women consider women less important than men.

What happens to boys' views of girls once they have been bewitched by adolescent sexual attraction? *They do not change their minds about girls, only their feelings.* While the male libido inspires most boys to overlook what was formerly disdained in girls, it does not necessarily overcome their conditioned belief in female inferiority, which they carry with them into adult life.

Because equality between the sexes has yet to be achieved, true and complete friendship between the sexes is still unusual—except among those who have nontraditional attitudes or nonsexist educational or work experiences, some of whom we will meet at the end of this chapter. Until such new norms become commonplace,

it is no surprise to keep hearing, "But men and women are too
different to be friends."

But There Will Always Be Sexual Tension

I have men friends with whom I do business over lunch or drinks,
other men I know quite well because we have political or professional
interests in common, and men who became friends because they
were my husband's friends or because their wives or lovers are my
friends or colleagues. While we may not routinely exchange intimacies or keep track of one another's lives, I feel comfortable spending time alone with any of these men. But every so often one of the
friendships is skewed by a discordant erotic quotient: Either some
onlooker misinterprets our relationship as an affair (why else would
a man and a woman be having drinks?), which makes us both self-
conscious, or the man himself slips into lust and lechery. Can the
fool really be willing to sacrifice this friendship for a dalliance, I
marvel, as stunned as if I'd invited an old pal to my house for dinner
and he had pocketed the silverware.

Most of the respondents to *PT*'s survey said "sexual tensions
complicate the relationship" between cross-sex friends; yet nearly
half of the respondents "have had a friendship turn into a sexual
relationship, and nearly a third reported having had sexual intercourse
with a friend in the past month."

At several points throughout this book, I have made brief mention
of my feelings on this subject, which can be summarized in three
sentences:

- You can love a friend, and be friends with a lover but that
  does not make love and friendship the same.

- Feeling sexual tension with a friend is as different from actually
  having sex as feeling an awareness of a child's sexuality is from
  commiting incest.

- If you do have sex with a friend, call it what you will, but it
  is no longer "just" friendship.

The Art of Friendship is one of many books that look kindly on
sex within friendship while describing few people who derived long-

term happiness from it.[10] It seems to me that the art of cross-sex friendship is, as I put it in Chapter 2, keeping the apples and oranges separate. To repeat, we need friendship to be an anchor in our lives, different, separate, and apart from all our other relationships. We need it to remain pure—immune to the whiplashes of the libido.

I also have a sociopolitical motive for wanting sex and friendship to remain distinct, and it relates to the preceding discussion. If women are ever to be taken on their merits, as individuals but not a different species, as full persons with minds as well as hearts and bodies, we must be *desexualized in nonsexual contexts*. We must not be seen as The Female when sex and gender are not relevant. We must not allow the word "woman" to be synonymous with carnality; if woman is "made for love," how can she be made for genius, made for power, or made for friendship? And if men and women together are perceived to be automatically, inevitably a sexual unit, how can they see each other as either colleagues or friends?

Keeping sex and friendship separate does not mean giving up friendship's love, which is deep and satisfying unto itself. As Robert Sternburg reported about "the nature of love": the things that matter—feelings, thoughts, motivations, communication, sharing, and support—are the same in both romance and friendship but the "concomitants of love—what goes along with it"—differ in each relationship.[11] You'll also recall Davis and Todd's finding that a major difference between friendship and love is that love is less stable, more conflict-producing, and comes with greater maintenance problems.[12] This is why I can say that love is always enlarged when two lovers have a friendship, while friendship is usually diminished when two friends have sex.

I'm far from the first to say it. Seneca wrote: "Friendship always benefits; love sometimes injures." The contemporary novelist Rita Mae Brown says, "Friendship is love made bearable."[13] And the sociologist Robert Bell confirms that women and men find it easier to have sex without friendship than friendship without sex.[14] In nearly 150 interviews, I found no one who claimed to have mixed sex and friendship successfully or, more precisely, without vastly altering the friendship. Few deny that sexual tension often crackles between a man and a woman who are friends; they just agree from experience that to act on it is usually a mistake.

Sex and the Single Friend

"When two friends go to bed together, the friendship's days are numbered," says Marv, a 28-year-old single man from Michigan. "I've tried it often and it never fails to mess things up. All of a sudden, your friend wants to know where you were last night when she called. Then you can't confide in her any more about the other women in your life. Then you start keeping things from her, and soon you're lying to her. Hell, that's no way to be a friend, so you call it quits. It happens every time."

In her book *Women in College,* Mirra Komarovsky reports that "male insistence on sexual relations frustrates the [women students'] longing for friendship."[15] Nonsexual romance can have as chaotic an effect on friendship as overt sexual acts, according to George Levinger, a social psychologist and an expert on "pair relatedness." When he studied undergraduates at the University of Massachusetts to learn how their friendships differ from their romantic relationships, the students reported that the more romantic an opposite sex friendship is, the more they expect exclusivity, and the more volatile it becomes. They also reported twice as many "ups and down" within romantic friendships over the course of a month as within nonromantic ones.[16]

Michael and Ginger, both 21, had been like brother and sister thoughout high school and college. Then, last summer, "out of nowhere," the sexual element entered their friendship. They'd had a few drinks while talking together as they had done countless times before in the last eight years, but this time "something happened." Ginger reacted to the sexual interlude by becoming very romantic. She now wants more than friendship; she loves Michael and she wants to marry him. The change shocked them both. Michael says marriage is out of the question. "I'm willing to go back to the way we were," he explains. "I'm willing to stop sleeping together and keep on being friends, but Ginger says there's no going back for her. So we're probably going to have to stop seeing each other. We don't know what else to do."

"Men can have sex in friendship and still keep the two components separate," says Linda Sapadin, who is doing her doctoral dissertation on cross-sex friendship. "They can compartmentalize all their relationships. But for many women, unless the friendship turns into a romance after the sex happens, the sex contaminates it. Many women enjoy the *True Confessions* aspect of becoming romantically involved with a male friend. They *use* friendship for romance."[17]

Some women also use friendship with men as a means of confirming their feminine charm. Several told me that, despite their better instincts, they are disappointed when a man friend does not flirt or otherwise show physical interest in them. Harriet, age 25, qualifies that: "I like to feel their interest, but I breathe a sigh of relief once I've made it clear I don't want sex, and we can get on with the friendship." One of the Nonconventional women in Bell's study says she fully expects men's interest to translate into sexual activity: "I rely on my male friends for my sense of sexuality because that self-image is given to me by men. I would be very upset if a man did not find me attractive. So my relationships with my close male friends all have a sexual dimension." While I admire this woman's honesty, the thinking she expresses is all too conventional. I wish she could see that a self-image "given" to her by a man is not a *self*-image. What's more, the same flirtatious behavior sought from male friends cannot then be condemned as sexual harassment when it is expressed by friendly males in the workplace. We have to standardize our criteria for nonsexualized treatment in nonsexual contexts. We can't have it both ways.

Leslie Baeren drives home the point from another direction: "Ironically, I have more male friends than most of my male friends. . . . My lesbianism has defused sexual tension as an issue in my friendships with men. . . . I may seem to provide all the benefits of a woman friend without any of the disadvantages. . . . I am a safer friend than a straight woman—and, of course, my men friends are similarly safer friends for me as well."[18]

Sex with a Married Friend

Many people use friendship as a way to justify becoming sexual with an otherwise inappropriate mate. For instance, says Laurel Richardson, a sociologist and the author of *The New Other Woman,* single women's liaisons with married men often begin with a business friendship.[19] The women can deal with their guilt about the relationship by telling themselves they didn't deliberately plan to have an affair with a married man, it just happened as an extension of their being "friends."

That rationalization works for married people too.

Sally says she felt Fred was such an undemanding friend and "he knew I still loved my husband," so there would be no messy repercussions if she had sex with him. "But it turned out I was the problem," she explains. "Having sex did something to my attitude toward Fred. Suddenly, I thought I deserved more from him. I don't know what I wanted exactly, I just felt entitled to impose on the friendship after we slept together. I wanted to be his Number One friend. I became a clinging vine."

Sophia, 50, tells this story: "Glenn and I have known each other since we were kids. I had a crush on him for about five minutes when I was 14 but I married our mutual friend, Ray, and Glenn married Grace, who also became a good friend of mine. Once we each had our families, we saw each other a few times a week. Our kids grew up together like cousins. For twenty-two years that's how it was; then, about five years ago, Glenn suddenly got seductive. I don't remember what he said, but I remember how I rationalized going along with it. I really needed him during that time because my mother was dying and my husband is basically very passive and uncomfortable with emotion. Glenn gave me what any good friend would—lots of support and a shoulder to cry on. I told myself that making love was nothing more than the ultimate expression of our friendship.

"The affair lasted for two years. I never had trouble looking Grace in the eye because I knew I wasn't going to take Glenn away from her. I was just borrowing him. I still thought of him as *her* husband and my *friend*.

"When she found out, of course, she didn't see it that way. And once *she* knew, I had to tell Ray. Everything ended. The two men's friendship, our couples' friendship, my friendship with Grace, and worst of all, after thirty-five years, my friendship with Glenn. So I gained a lover, lost two friends, then lost the lover, and nearly lost my husband.

"Let me tell you, I was wrong about sex being 'the ultimate expression' of friendship. Sex is an affair, and an affair with a friend can turn into love, and that's very dangerous if the parties are married, and very painful for everyone involved."

Martin has reached the same conclusion. "I had an affair with a woman named Jane, who was my friend and my wife's. We went through all the usual crap about how 'we're not hurting anybody,' but we hurt my wife terribly. She was most upset that Jane could betray her trust. Years later Jane told me that my wife had asked her, 'How could you do this to me?' Jane said she had answered, 'I didn't do it to you, I did it to Martin; I ruined *our* friendship first.' That was true for both of us."

Marrying a Friend

The poet John Gay wrote: "A woman's friendship ever ends in love." If that is true then so does many a man's, since it takes two to tango. I have no problem with two *unattached* friends moving further along the emotional continuum as long as both friends want it and understand the risks for the friendship. Moreover, I'd wager that any friendship that blossoms into love and ends in marriage is probably an especially deep and solid union.

Nickolas Ashford and Valerie Simpson, who wrote such hits as "Solid" and "Closest to Love," were friends for ten years before they married in 1974. "I thought of him as a brother," Simpson says. "We really got to know each other. You know how you try to appear so wonderful in a romance? Well there was never any of that with us." Ashford adds, "We didn't have to play any games."[20]

The marriage of the baseball player Ray Knight and the golfer Nancy Lopez sounds both ridiculous and sexist when she talks about being "dependent on him" and sparing him the laundry or baby-sitting and he says "if you allow her to play golf and be herself, she'll give you everything." Yet Knight speaks winningly about their friendship. They met in 1978 when he was playing with the Cincinnati Reds against a Japanese all-star team and Lopez brought her nephew to the clubhouse to get autographs. After that "we just talked now and then," says Knight. "Mutual respect." Knight was married at the time.

In 1979 Lopez wed a Cincinnati sportscaster. The two couples became friends. Then destiny intervened in the form of some weird coincidences. Knight and his wife got divorced. In 1981 Lopez moved to Houston where her husband had taken a new job. Two months later Knight was traded to the Houston Astros. Lopez and her husband invited him to dinner. Lopez helped him find a house. Then one day she confided in him that her marriage was foundering. "She really didn't have anyone else to talk to, and I'd gone through my divorce the year before," he explains. "It was all on the level. No hanky-panky. . . .

"I look at it as a friendship that turned into a romance. I saw a lot of good things in her before I fell in love with her." They were married in 1982.[21].

From friendship to love is a lovely transformation if the relationship stays honest and the love lasts. But if it doesn't, or if the two friends *do* start playing manipulative games, then, as we've seen, love ends up destroying friendship. This is the possibility that few friends anticipate when they first get into bed together.

Being Friends with a Former Lover

Most men fall *in* love more readily than women, and most women fall *out* of love more readily than men. Psychologist Zick Rubin and his colleagues also found that women coped better than men do with rejection when love affairs end. Men were "hit harder by the breakup; . . . they felt more depressed, more lonely, less happy and less free than did their former girlfriends."[22]

Maybe women are less depressed because they have women friends to turn to, whereas men either don't turn to other men or don't get much nurturing from that quarter. In any case, women cope better with rejection and accept finer gradations of emotion. Thus, a rejected woman is more likely to redefine her relationship with her boyfriend from love to friendship, while "a rejected man may find such a redefinition more difficult to accomplish."

Also, a couple is more likely to stay friends if the man is the one who breaks up or the parting is mutual. It may be hard for a man to segue into friendship with someone who wounded his ego. Women are willing to be friends regardless of who leaves whom. Among Laurel Richardson's test group of single women and married men, friendships that turned into affairs lasted an average of four years. Then, the men wanted a clean break and the women wanted to remain friends.

Two-thirds of Robert Bell's Nonconventional Women say they are maintaining a friendship with a former lover. And in my interviews, several women claimed that friendship with a former lover is the only practicable male-female relationship.

"With ex-lovers, you've already gotten past all the sexual strain that you usually feel with male friends," says Emily, seemingly prescribing a circular solution: Sleep with your men friends to get rid of the sexual tension that makes it so complicated to be friends with

men. But it rarely works out so neatly. For instance, Emily's friendship with her former boyfriend isn't exactly a friendship. He has a
new girlfriend but he's still in love with Emily and *he* is suffering
from a lot more than sexual tension. (Are they friends if one makes
the other suffer?) He buys Emily's idea of friendship, because he'll
keep her in his life any way he can. She, in turn, must be aware of
his love (maybe even enjoys it); why else is she holding back information about her new romance; why won't she ask his advice about
love or sex the way friends do, and why does she occasionally, almost
imperceptibly, sound a note of condescension when she talks about
him? Since she's through with him sexually, maybe that "has-been"
quality has permeated the friendship.

Women who stay friends with their ex-husbands often do so for
the most practical of reasons: to keep the men attached to their
children and cooperative about maintaining child support. But there
are other reasons too. It's possible that women want to stay friends
with an ex-husband or lover to assure themselves that they weren't
being "used." ("See, even without sex, he's still my friend.") Or a
friendship with an ex-lover may protect a woman from facing up to
her own sexuality? ("See, even without sex, I'm still his friend.")

Lorrie Moore has no use for such self-deceptions. When her beau
left her for another woman and then asked "Why can't we be friends?"
Moore said, "Because we are enemies. If we weren't enemies, I
wouldn't be able to get out of bed in the morning and would be
lying there with fuzz on my teeth."

Her advice to ex-lovers: "Someday you will no longer be enemies. Though you will also never be friends. . . . What you have is
a truce that respects what has died between you and doesn't, like
vandals or ghouls, play in the cemetery of it."[23]

Let me summarize all of this. If you are a heterosexual, you can
do one of two things about the sexual component in your male-
female friendships:

- Recognize it and leave it at that. Enjoy the awareness that
  "one of us is a woman and one of us is a man," but don't *do*
  anything about it.
- Allow romance or sex into the friendship but be aware that
  it will most likely *change* the friendship: maybe change it into
  love and marriage, in which case, congratulations; or change

it into something less honest and intimate because of game-playing or unequal commitment; or change it into a duplicitous cabal because you are betraying your lover or spouse while telling yourself it doesn't really count because you're doing it with a friend; or change it into an affair that splits you apart when it's over. And when it's over? Then you're ex-friends who are ex-lovers who want only to be friends.

But My Spouse/Lover Would Be Jealous

Friendship arouses enough varieties of jealousy to provide a soap opera with endless episodes. See if you can follow this: Women are jealous of their women friends' *other* women friends who seem to win more of their confidences. Men are jealous of their men friends' wives or lovers who lure the men away from the revels of male friendship. Men are jealous of their wives' friends' intimacy. Women are jealous of their husbands' friends' camaraderie. Homosexuals are jealous of their lover's friends or their friends' lovers. And straight people are sometimes jealous of the homosexual friends of *their* straight friends. Despite all these permutations, the jealousy aroused by cross-sex friendship was far and away the kind I heard about most. It seems to come in three models: intimacy jealousy, sexual jealousy, and power jealousy. Together they are among the most frequently cited reasons why friendship between women and men "just won't work."

Intimacy Jealousy

"I commute to work every day with a neighbor whose office is near mine," says Judy. "My husband drives me to the train station, he knows the man, he knows I like him, nothing more, but he's jealous of the guy. Actually, he's jealous of the *friendship* because this man and I probably have more concentrated conversation on our way to work than my husband and I do in a month. But I have women friends I talk to that often and it doesn't bother him, so I wonder . . ."

In the "About Men" column in *The New York Times*, Michael McGill described the time his female best friend asked his wife, Janet, "How do you feel about Mick's plans to take next summer off?" Janet glared at Michael and replied icily, "He hasn't said anything to *me* about his plans for next summer." Later, Janet confronted her husband: "Do you know how humiliating it is to hear about what you're doing from another woman? What else have you told her that I don't know?"[24]

I am sympathetic to the discomfort of Judy's husband and Michael's wife. More than that, I am sympathetic to their unspoken question: "Are they talking about *me* behind my back?" However, a person who is sensitive to a beloved's betrayal of intimate information would reasonably feel that way regardless of the sex of the friend hearing the revelation. Judy said her husband doesn't complain about her long conversations with her women friends, and Janet McGill's humiliation was specifically attached to learning information about her husband from "another woman." I confess to being a little more sympathetic to Janet, however. Since male intimacy can be hard to come by, a wife or lover would logically feel entitled to whatever morsels a man is willing to give out. What's more, since Michael's summer plans presumably will affect Janet's plans and their mutual finances, she has reason to expect to be the first to know. We can only ask whether her anger would have been as fierce had she heard about Michael's summer plans from a man.

Sexual Jealousy

In *The Winter's Tale,* King Leontes nearly looses an avalanche of tragedies when he convinces himself that his wife, Queen Hermione, and his lifelong friend Polixenes could not possibly feel only friendship for one another: "Too hot, too hot!" he says. "To mingle friendship far is mingling bloods."

Even without Shakespeare's help, spouses and lovers are still imagining indiscretion where there is only friendship.

"I can't believe I'm letting Evelyn ride around in this squad car for eight hours a day with a guy she calls her partner and best friend," says her boyfriend, Jim, a tavern owner. "She joined the police force against my better judgment in the first place, but she was hell bent to do it; said it was her childhood dream to be a cop. Now she tells me how her and this partner have really gotten to know each other and boy do they have a lot of laughs. Says they trust each other with their lives so why shouldn't they be friends. Now, be *serious:* How long do you think it'll be before they end up in the hay?"

"I know it's my own insecurities, but I get very jealous the minute

my husband starts talking about some 'nice woman' from work,"
says Terry, a postal clerk. "When he's having lunch with one of his
women friends, it ruins my day. My sister keeps telling me 'He's
not your butterfly if he's in a jar, but if you let him go and he comes
back, he's yours.' I know she's right but I still want him in a jar."

In Levittown, says sociologist Herbert Gans, "a woman neighbor
did not visit another [woman] when her husband was home, partly
because of the belief that a husband has first call on his wife's companionship, partly to prevent suspicion that her visit might be interpreted as a sexual interest in the husband. This practice is strongest
among working class women, reflecting the traditional norm that
people of opposite sex come together only for sexual reasons." Gans
suggests there is less eroticization of male-female relations "at higher
class levels; in the upper middle class there are enough shared interests
between men and women to discourage suspicion."[25]

I would question whether "higher" class people are less suspicious
or just less willing to publicly admit their jealousy. And, if there *is*
less sexual jealousy, another kind of jealousy is replacing it.

Power Jealousy

"Allan was threatened by these men, not just because they were
men; they were *my* connections to power, not his," says Mary, a
lawyer married to a lawyer. "When I came out of law school, I was
hired by a more prestigious firm than Allan's and my new friends
were big-shot businessmen and legal minds. Allan couldn't take it.
He made it very uncomfortable for me to see clients or colleagues
after hours, even if we were working on a case. He made it sound
like he was worried about me falling for one of them, but I know
he was jealous because they were very important men and they were
my friends. He's never had that kind of competition in eight years
of marriage."

Americans typically expect a husband's professional universe to
spill homeward and liven up his wife's social life, but it is a rare man
who views his wife's connections to others as a social benefit to him.
One of the rare ones is Robert, who's in finance and is married to a
political lobbyist. Robert says his wife's world interests him and
enriches his social experiences, and she feels the same about his.
"Christina and I joke that we married each other for our friends."

In male-female relations, says psychologist Joseph Pleck, women traditionally have served three functions: Women are "symbols of success," the sexual spoils of men's battles with each other; women are "mediators [who] smooth over men's inability to relate to each other noncompetitively" (when women aren't around to civilize men, as in *Deliverance,* men rape and murder each other); and women serve as a "refuge" from the stressful relations men have with other men.

"If women begin to compete with men and have power in their own right," says Pleck, "men are threatened by the loss of this refuge."[26]

Most women who say "but my husband would be jealous" are referring to the *old* jealousy that assumes a male friend is sexually targeting another man's "symbol of success." (Remember, the Trojan War was started by two men battling over a woman.) But the old jealousy is nothing compared to the seething green monster prowling around the forests of patriarchy now that cross-sex friendship is threatening traditional power dynamics between women and men. This *new* jealousy, which not many men are ready to acknowledge, comes from a fear of change and loss: the loss of the female sex as "mediator" and "refuge" and the fear of changed power relations. When women have men friends, they become men's equals in the eyes of the world. And when men have women friends, they violate the traditional lines of dominance, they break ranks, and they betray the fraternity, the men who gain status from exclusivity and lose it the minute a female becomes a member of their club.

As for women, they too can suffer from power jealousy. Some women are jealous of the women who are their husband's colleagues and friends. And some women are jealous of the women who *have* men friends and are thereby learning the inside dope, the secrets of the old boys' network, the way their minds work.

Meanwhile, many women who are building authentic friendships with men are proving that they do not have to be "one of the boys" to do it. And men who have friendships with women are suddenly seeing the world through the Other's eyes. When one woman and one man are friends, it is hard to consider Woman or Man as a class of adversaries or a faceless blur. He tends not to ignore/mistreat/oppress someone who has become a real person to him. She tends not to fear someone who has shown her his inner self. Cross-sex friendship is humanizing. It is eye-opening. It is life-expanding. It's also very threatening.

Your wife might meet a man who is not "just" the butcher, a neighbor, her boss, or a man on the make; she might meet a man who knows her as a person. *Your* husband might meet a woman who is not "just" his secretary, the kids' pediatrician, a neighbor, or a cocktail waitress; he might meet a woman who interests him as a person. When men and women stop being "just" their roles and start seeing each other as people, their spouses or lovers must match a much more serious competitor rather than rest on the laurels of love or possession—and sexism had better hang onto its britches.

But My Spouse/Lover Is My Best Friend

I've said that line myself. I believe it makes emotional sense for one's mate to be one's closest intimate. I agree with Plato that a lover can be "a divine friend." I agree with Kahlil Gibran that, "among intelligent people, the surest basis for marriage is friendship." I agree with Erica Jong that "sometimes it is worth all the disadvantages of marriage just to have that: one friend in an indifferent world." A lot of people go along with this view: Joel Bloch, a psychologist who surveyed more than 2000 Americans, says 40 percent of all married people consider their spouse their best friend.[27]

On the other hand, we've discussed how the additional elements of love and sex complicate a relationship, so that even if my husband is my best friend, I am aware that ours is a very different kind of friendship; it is not the same as being friends with "one of them." Yet some people use their close friendship with a spouse or lover as a substitute for all other cross-sex relationships—kind of like "I already gave at the office." They act as if they have a finite amount of affection for the opposite sex and if they spend it on a friend there won't be enough left over for their spouse. Maybe that explains why:

- Of the married people studied by Suzanna Rose, 47 percent of the women and 33 percent of the men have *no* cross-sex friendship other than their spouses. (All single men and three out of four single women have at least one.)[28]

- Nicholas Babchuk, a sociologist, finds that, although married people may have couple friendships, half of all husbands and wives do not have even one primary friend (of either sex) independent of their spouse.[29]

Michael McGill goes all the way in the opposite direction. In his column about having a female friend, he wrote: "Wives can answer a man's need for friendship, but I am suspicious of descriptions of wives as a husband's best friend." One of the irate letters published in reponse to his column suggests that McGill might try to explain to his wife "exactly what she is to him. It's fine to have friends of both sexes, but if his wife is not his best friend, what is she? Sex partner? Housekeeper? Child caretaker? What?"[30] If his wife is not his best friend, either she is just a friend like all the others, or they are not friends at all, or she is "a wife," that is, a role not a person.

Martin Simmons provides the sharpest negative view of spousal friendship in his *Essence* article: "What most men seek from women is the fulfillment of relatively mundane, though absolutely critical, needs: sex, physical warmth and touching, love, care for their health, home and children." Men who "say that their best friends are their wives or women are men without strong psychological support."[31] Actually, Simmons couldn't be more wrong. In fact, he has it backwards.

Research with both lower- and middle-class subjects shows that wives offer men the most satisfaction and emotional support of all the relationships in men's lives—more than neighbor, coworker, boss, parent, sibling, or same and opposite sex friends.[32]

In another sample of middle-class respondents, 88 percent of the married men and 78 percent of the married women named their spouses as the person "closest" to them. Of the heterosexual singles, 59 percent of the men and again 78 percent of the women named their betrothed or steady lovers.[33] The nearly thirty-point increase in the male percentages between single and married men testifies to the emotional significance of wives. Unmarried men—still playing the field and largely focused on activities with their men friends— withhold themselves from the experience of total intimacy. But with a wife, they relax and open up as never before, thus naming the loved one as primary. It's almost as though men marry for friendship. This is not true for women.

His and Her Marriage

Sociologist Jessie Bernard has identified a phenomenon she calls "His" marriage and "Her" marriage—two entirely separate experiences that exist within the same marriage—and His marriage is better than Hers.[34] For instance, "when a woman has good news to report her husband is the first to hear," Bernard says, but "when she is depressed, he will be protected—she will share this news with other women."[35]

For decades psychologists and marriage experts have noted that women, especially poor and working-class women, get their support from friends and kin, not from lovers or husbands.[36] Toni Morrison wrote of her character Sula: "She had been looking all along for a friend, and it took her a while to discover that a lover was not a comrade and could never be—for a woman."[37] In the famous phrase of Robert Blood and Donald Wolfe, wives perform the "mental hygiene" function in marriage.[38] Writer Frances Lear put the same thought this way:

> A man brings matter home with him at night. . . . He brings matter home with him because he has to relieve himself of it. . . . So he talks about it to his wife. The usual. The boss and the guys at the office and the bookkeeper and the clients and the backache and the fears. He talks mostly about the fears. He brings his matter home and his wife takes it from him and gets rid of it through the magic of her nurturing. . . . For him without question, there is enough loving going on.[39]

But not for her. Women cannot get from their husbands what most men can get from their female friends, not to mention their wives. In other words, the level of intimacy achieved by all women is so high that a man gets more from a woman friend than most women get from the man who is supposed to be their "other half."

Something one of Linda Sapadin's subjects said strikes me as a curious metaphor for this fact. This man claims he and his late wife were such close friends that he feels her friendship is still inside of him and she is being a friend to his new wife *through* him. With the idea of one wife befriending another from beyond the grave, the husband has made himself a conduit for feelings he thinks appropriate to women but not to men. He is so emotionally intimate with his new wife that he believes he must be occupied by a female spirit.

Many homosexual men have the same need for women as targets of intimacy. Webster and Kurt are gay lovers, each of whom says his best friend is a straight woman. "Mine is my eldest daughter," says Kurt. "She works in my business. I can commiserate with her on anything. Web and I socialize with her and her husband."

"And mine is my ex-wife," Webster laughs. "Kurt and I took the best part of our straight lives with us—the women."

Coupled Togetherness

The occupational hazard for couples who are best friends is that they may become each other's *only* friends. "When my husband died, I realized I must never again put all of my love in one place," says Bonnie, who was widowed at age 27. "We'd spent all our free time together, we even talked to each other at parties. I didn't feel I needed other friends because he was interesting, helpful, loving, a good adviser. He was everything. After he was gone I had nothing and no one. In the five years since, I've made about twenty new friends but not one of them has all of me."

Other married people, perhaps less extreme in their togetherness, are just as exclusive through laziness. "We really should call another couple to go out to dinner with us," says one man. "It's a hassle though, and we have enough fun by ourselves."

Thinking in terms of another *couple* was typical of many of the cross-sex friendships Alan Booth and Elaine Hess found among 800 middle-aged and elderly midwesterners.[40] Other research points up that most middle-class couple friendships are initiated by the husband.[41] Coupled togetherness under the control of men does not constitute authentic cross-sex friendships even though there are two sexes involved.

On the other hand, a memorable three-person friendship existed between Dan Aykroyd, the late John Belushi, and his wife Judy, a graphics designer, who is described as "a warmhearted woman who has the patience and soul of an angel." "It was a wonderful thing," recalls Aykroyd. "Here I had a friendship with this man, but his wife was not excluded at all. . . . I told Judy everything that was going on, and I used to talk her up to him when they were going through their domestics—periods of personality estrangement, alienation, whatever. The woman is often excluded in male-to-male bonding, but it just didn't happen in our case because we would have been shortchanging ourselves, both of us, if we'd done that." About his continuing closeness with Judy since Belushi's death, Aykroyd says: "That's one of the gifts John gave me—a friendship with her that will last forever."[42]

People's attitudes toward coupled friendships vary widely. Nina says she is more timid in a cross-sex group. She lets the husbands do all the talking "about politics, history, and almost anything else." Irwin thinks couple-to-couple sociability is a mask for lack of marital intimacy within each couple. John and Victoria prefer to see Elliot separate from his wife, Ruth. "Elliot's more interesting alone," says John. "When he's with Ruth, he's so possessive and protective of her, it makes us uncomfortable." Martha thinks couple relationships are more trouble than they're worth: "We rarely like both members equally. The conversation always is split by sex and if I prefer the man but have to talk to the woman all night, I'd just as soon pick my own women friends. It's very hard to keep a foursome from realigning into two men and two women."

That reminds me of the old canard about class: Supposedly, when a foursome goes off in a car, the lower-class couples sit one couple in front, one in back; the middle class pairs arrange themselves men in front, women in back; and the upper class couples switch partners—a solution that seems to condemn upper-class marriage more than it proves the superiority of their cross-sex friendships.

But Who Needs It?

Why bother? You're happy with friends of your own sex; you get enough loving from your spouse or lover. Who needs cross-sex friendship and all its complications? And who says it's so desirable?

Now, you have a point.

In her book *The Men in Our Lives,* Elizabeth Fishel includes chapters on fathers, lovers, husbands, and mentors but none on friends.[43] And for all the love interest in Shakespeare's plays, as my daughter Abigail points out, connections between men and women are relatively superficial. "Bonding within the sexes, however, is much stronger, substantiated usually by long histories of friendship and intimacy." Most friendship scholars concede that at all ages both sexes prefer same-sex friends and get less help, loyalty, intimacy, stability, and support from their cross-sex friendships.

But there is one dissenting vote. Nan Lin, a sociologist who recently completed a three-year survey of 1000 adults to see what makes people mentally healthy, found that the people who have close confiding friendships are less anxious and depressed than those who don't—and those with the fewest negative symptoms have a confidant of the opposite sex. Lin says cross-sex friendship is beneficial because "women are usually better at communicating than are men, and so when their male friends are depressed they are more likely to get the men to express their feelings than are men's male friends. Men are generally more practical. When they are depressed, they go out and do things, which is what they tell their depressed women friends to do."[44]

My first impulse is to object to a formula for male-female friendship that prescribes sex-stereotyped behavior from each sex. But on second thought, how will we ever blend and distill our sex-specific strengths unless we teach them to each other? Maybe it's important at this point in human history to make the most of the talents we've acquired in our gender ghettos; pool them, share them, and say outright that we need each other for our mental health and well-being. Which leads me to a third thought: Wait a minute, you can't equate what women do with what men do in those friendships. Behind that word "communicating" is women's lifesaving, nerve-calming, heartwarming talent for nurture that no amount of men's telling people to "go out and do things" can match.

The trade-off is not the same for both sexes—not yet anyway. For now, when we promote cross-sex friendship, what we're really saying is that *men need women*. For men's sake and for the good of society. You don't have to go as far into depravity as *Deliverance* to see that men often do better when women are around. Police officials have found that women on patrol with men tend to defuse violent situations better than all-male teams.[45] Space scientists have discovered that in the cramped conditions of a capsule "the whole work atmosphere and the mood in a crew of men and women are better than in men-only ones. Somehow, the women elevate relationships in a small team, and this helps to stimulate its capacity for work."[46]

Yet, women's so-called civilizing effect upon men has been ridiculed more often than praised. In his essay "Men, Boys and Wimps," George Stade, an English professor, reminds us of America's glorious literary tradition of boy heroes who had to cut the apron strings before they could grow up and of men who had to leave women behind before they could have any fun. Longing for the old-style adventure stories that fueled male fantasies, he regrets that publishers' lists are now dominated by what Alice Walker calls "womanist" fiction. "There is no relief from this sort of thing anywhere," he cries, "—not even in hard-boiled detective fiction, once the preserve of manly men strong enough to go their ways without women."[47]

But what we are discovering is that men who go their ways without women frequently make a mess of things and, more important, aren't as happy as men who have meaningful women in their lives. Statistical evidence proves that married men are happier, healthier, and live longer than single men, and, as we've seen, men with close women friends are the least lonely; men gain intimacy in cross-sex friendship, and lose it in their same-sex pairs; and the more women friends a man has, the higher his self-esteem. Women do not gain any boosts from their friendships with men. Linda Sapadin's findings suggest that men feel closer, more nurtured, more important, more excited, and less competitive with their women friends, while women feel less close, less enjoyment, less understanding, less excitement, and more competitive with their men friends.

The question one might more logically pose—Stade, Hemingway, and Mailer, to the contrary—is why shouldn't women go their ways without men?

Women of every age seem to have reached the same conclusion. Twenty-three-year-old Marissa says: "I expect very little from my men friends and I'm disappointed; they expect a great deal from me and they get it."

Caroline, 48, grumbles: "I've stopped putting out for my men friends. I nurse them through divorces, then they get themselves together and they're not around when I need them."

Stella, 34, comments: "When my male friends are happy they want me to treat them like men, which means sexually. When they're in pain, they want me to treat them like women, which means therapeutically. I've decided it's easier to be friends with a child." And 15-year-old Stacey says: "Boys don't like it when we talk, they only like it when *they* talk."

My friend Margaret Stern sums it up: "There's still only one sex that listens."

So the question "But who needs it?" should be restated: "But do women need it?" And the answer is maybe women don't need men the way men need women, but some women and men have a great friendship anyway.

But I Already Have It

More often than not, those who already have satisfying cross-sex friendships also have something unique about themselves or their situation that explains it. For example, in contrast to sex-role conformists, the Nonconventional women and men in Robert Bell's study have more cross-sex friends and feel as close to them as to their own gender.[48] In Booth and Hess's group of 800 middle-aged midwesterners, the women who have men friends are in the younger end of the age range, work outside the home, belong to professional organizations, and are married to white-collar men—all factors that give them access to men with whom to establish a friendship. In her study of fifty outstanding career women, psychologist Marilyn Ruman found that they all had male friends in their adolescence who gave them insights into the male world, which both contributed to their present success and kept them involved with men friends: "Unlike other women, they learned to approach men as people, not as potential dates and husbands," says Ruman.[49]

In short, people with satisfying cross-sex friendships probably answer to this description:

- They have lived close enough to members of the other sex to see them as "regular" human beings.
- They met through their work or outside interests or in a context that allowed them to perceive one another as equals.
- At least one of them is a sex-role nonconformist.
- They don't have sex together.

You'll recognize these factors in each of the following excerpts from published accounts of pleasure-giving male-female friendship.

"She is my best and oldest friend," says Tim Lovejoy, a painter, who calls Frederica von Stade by the nickname Flicka, even though she is now a world-famous opera singer. "I began as her brother's playmate. She was three when we met. I was five. They lived up the road, and I spent most of my childhood in that house. . . . Her mother once said to me when I was very young and we were obviously very close, 'I would kill you if you ever fell in love with Flicka. Lovers are easy to find. Friends are impossible to find.' There are people who are bonded because of their trauma and there are people who are bonded because they laugh together. I think we have always brought the good times to one another."[50]

"My best friend, Bill, identifies with my career," says Rita Mae Brown, a novelist and screenwriter. "If I take a beating on a book, Bill is right by my side. He's on my team. He'll threaten to punch out a critic or he'll say, 'Come on, let's ride up in the Blue Ridge and forget these turkeys.' " Rita Mae explains what she gets from all her men friends: "They will go out of their way to introduce me to people they think could help me. I try to return the favor. Most of them are able to draw closer to me through an activity. In other words, we usually don't sit and chat, we do something. Maybe we'll ride horses or plant azalea bushes and we talk while we're working/playing. . . . I need my men friends. I learn something from them that I can't learn from women, namely, what it is like to be a man."[51]

Katie Trieller, a coordinator of adolescent health services for a hospital, and Barry Wilansky, a psychologist, met through their work. Katie is married to a lawyer; Barry is divorced. "Barry is the kind of person you can talk with as freely as with any girlfriend because he's plugged into the 'feeling side' of life," says Katie. "In that sense, psychologists have an edge over many men."[52]

Elaine Dolling, a widow for ten years, and Isaac Rodriguez, the owner of a dry cleaners who is separated from his wife, met at a meeting of Parents Without Partners. "Because I'm not interested in marrying again, it has become important to me to have stable on-going relationships with women as friends," says Isaac. "In a way they are freer with you because you relate to them just as they are, not only as sexual objects."

"He makes me feel good and see myself in a different perspective," offers Elaine. "If you asked me five years ago, I'd have said I don't believe in platonic relationships. Today I certainly do."[53]

James Brooks, the writer-director of the movie *Terms of Endearment* and the creator of such television series as *Room 222*, *The Mary Tyler Moore Show*, and *Taxi*, became friends with Pat Nardo when she was a secretary on one of his shows. "My relationship with Jim is the most intense, complicated, painful relationship I've ever had with a human being I wasn't sleeping with," says Pat, who is now a television producer and writer. "I'd tell him what I'd tell a girl-friend. You never do that with a man."[54]

Student JoAnne Flynn has one "boyfriend" but several men friends who share her enthusiasm for weight training and muscle develop-ment. Of the men who matter to her in the weight room at the University of California at Berkeley, she says: "We relate less as male to female and more as friend to friend."[55]

Columnist Liz Smith and screenwriter and director Robert Ben-ton *(Bonnie and Clyde, Places in the Heart)* have been friends since they worked together on the University of Texas humor magazine.

"I think our perceptions of each other are mysterious and would be very surprising to each other," says Liz. "But I think we've always had some deep-seated sexual attraction without ever doing anything about it. And it's sort of like having a wonderful secret—or money in the bank. I find I respond to him very much on the level of his being this terrific male person who really loves women—he's not one of those macho guys. He would burst into tears before he would do anything mean. He's just a lovely person without being a wimp. It's great to have a friend you feel that way about."[56]

Emily Prager and her friend Bill lived together after graduation in a time when "living together without sleeping together was dis-tinctly perverse," she recalls. "What we were about was compan-ionship, someone to come home to, to eat dinner with, to discuss the day. What we were not about were emotional ups and downs, power plays and games, tears, shouting and recriminations, euphoria or despondency—feelings that we then associated with a relationship that included sex."

After three years, they established separate residences, but Emily continued to keep her off-season clothes at Bill's house because he had more storage space. The changing of her wardrobe every spring and fall are "seasonal rites, symbolic renewals of a tie between us," she says. "We still spend Thanksgiving and Christmas together and probably always will."[57]

Nowadays, many college students consider it part of their edu-cation to see how the "other half" lives. "We all look like derelicts in the morning, but that's reality," says Peter Conte, who shared Apt. #1 at Vassar College with two women and another man. "There were no pretenses here. I now feel I can live with anybody anywhere under any circumstances."

"You begin to realize men are just other people," says Laura Flinchbaugh, another apartment mate.[58]

The same year, Suite 22 at Barnard College was shared by two women, an Orthodox Jew and an Irish Catholic, and two men, a Lebanese Christian and an atheist. Monica Marks, the Jewish woman, says, "I was worried more about the idea of living with someone from Lebanon than I did about living with two men." But she and Stephen Donelia of Beirut got along fine.

"It's just more relaxed than when you're in a single-sex living situation," says Alex White. "There's no competition, and the conversation is not always about sex, sports, and women. We sometimes talk about those things too, but it doesn't get sleazy. . . . These people are your friends, the people you eat breakfast with, the people you take phone messages for. You don't want to get involved with them sexually."

"I got a lot of insight into men I never had before, such as learning that they, too, can clean bathtubs and toilets," adds Jennifer Miletta. "It's more like the real world. In the real world, you have friends of both sexes."[59]

Maybe in the world these young people are making that statement will be more true than it is today.

Chapter 16

❧ ——————————— ❧

Friends for Life

How Friendships Change from Infancy to Old Age

Someone had put sand in the lawnmower gas tank, ravaged the tomato patch, broken a dozen eggs on the bed, sprayed the black dog with white paint, taken the wet clothes off the line and scattered them in the dirt, and given the baby a punk haircut.

Who could have done such things?

According to 3-year-old Ben, the perpetrator of these crimes was a playmate of indeterminate species named Julie.

"What does Julie look like anyway?" Ben's mother asked, fighting tears as she surveyed the carnage in the house and yard.

"Ohhhh, he's really, really big," Ben's hands stretched over his head, and he looked to the sky. "And he's FOUR YEARS OLD!" With further probing, Ben revealed that Julie stomps about in "bii-i-g boots," eats dog food and gum, barks and runs up trees, and doesn't wear diapers like *some* people. "He wears underwear with holes because he's a really, really big boy!"

While claiming that his giant friend attends Sunday school "every day," Ben had to agree with his Mom that Julie could be quite naughty at times.

"But he's gone now," said Ben, sadly.

"You mean forever?" said his mother, repressing her joy.

As soon as Ben went out to play, his mother called her neighbor across the street to announce Big Julie's departure.

"Is that right?" said the neighbor after a pause. "Then would you mind telling me who that is hosing out the inside of your car?"[1]

Most of us would love to have a friend like Julie—invisible, powerful, irrepressible, and absolutely our own; a toilet-trained, Sunday-school type who takes the rap for our worst impulses while epitomizing our best selves. If not Julie, then Laughing Tiger: "He doesn't roar. He never scares children," says 2-year-old Jan. "He doesn't bite. He just laughs." This agreeable beast also allows himself to be scolded or sat upon by grown-ups who are unaware of his reserved place at the dinner table. Four-year-old Missy keeps "an Indian looking over my shoulder." Donna, age 4, has five imaginary husbands who accompany her on the school bus. And Tony's mouse pal Hubert stays under the table and obediently eats Tony's mealtime rejects.[2]

Up to two-thirds of all children between the ages of 3 and 10 invent such companions. Rather than greeting the phenomenon with alarm, psychologists now believe that the child who conjures up a fantasy friend is "smarter, more creative and better adjusted than children who do not have such vivid fantasies." Usually a firstborn or only child, he or she generally exhibits better than average concentration, a warmer, nonaggressive personality, advanced language skills, and often grows up to be a high literary achiever.[3]

If imaginary friends do not become obsessions and if they are outgrown in a reasonable time, these phantasmagoric creations can do good work while they're in residence: They allow kids to safely explore the unfamiliar; they absorb fears, guilt, and anger and compensate for defects in the child's reality; they offer uncritical support, and above all, they *listen*.

When you think about it, those are the very qualities we look for in a friend until the end of our days. Symbolically, then, the imaginary friend is not just a phenomenon of childhood but the personification of a universal, lifelong yearning for safety through a soulmate.

The coming and going of the imaginary friend also could symbolize a main theme of this book: the need for idealized notions of friendship (that "what am I missing?" feeling described in Chapter 1) to be displaced by mature, realistic expectations. Like the child's benevolent giant—comforting for a time but healthiest in its demise—the adult fantasy of an Ideal Friend inspires us at the outset but distorts our social self if it overstays its welcome. Inevitably, both the imaginary friend and the Ideal Friend must retreat in favor of human interaction, warts and all.

In this final chapter, I will identify friendship phenomena as unique to other stages of development as the imaginary friend is to early childhood. In tracing the increasing sophistication of the social organism from infancy to old age, we'll see how friends serve different purposes at every stage of life, how each new phase of interpersonal competency builds upon the preceding one, and how our definition of friendship changes almost year by year as we grow up.

It's not too glib to say that as we travel across the life span, *we make friends and friends make us.* While social science has plumbed the depths of the family, only in the last ten or fifteen years have peer relations been studied with an eye to discerning who we like, why we like them, and what we do with them—as well as what it means to us and what it does *for us* to be "among friends" at each stage of the life span.[4] (As you read, bear in mind that all age categories and developmental generalizations are subject to individual variations.)

Infants and Toddlers: Precursors of Adult Friendship

Until they are around 10 months old, babies view each other as objects, less interesting than a wind-up toy but more diverting than a stuffed animal. A "play date" between two infants who can sit and crawl is actually a social experience for the babies' parents who visit together while their offspring engage in parallel but separate activities in the same room. The babies handle toys, throw things, and vocalize into the air but rarely interact beyond an occasional grab at each other's nose or a toy takeover, which invariably ends in tears.

Babies first experience a rudimentary form of friendship when they discover *the fun of feedback:* "I put my nice blanket over my head. You laugh." They also begin to get an inkling of their *mutual separateness:* "I want you to stack my plastic bagels like a pyramid; you insist on using them for teething rings. I notice that you are not as obliging as Mom and Dad who always manage to understand my gestures and play with me as I dictate. You defy my wishes and continue to rub your gums while I am clearly interested in stacking. Can it be you are a separate person with a mind of your own? I put a plastic bagel in my mouth. Maybe if I suck now, you will stack later. Since you're fun to be with and I want to play with you, I suppose I will have to give as well as take."

That's the way I imagine babies experience their earliest social epiphanies. But however it really happens, psychologist Zick Rubin says, "Once this awareness emerges, it develops at a rapid pace through the second and the early part of the third year. By the time children are two and a half years old, they are able to manage interactions with one another that contain, in fledgling form, all the basic features of social interaction among older children or adults— sustained attention, turn-taking, and mutual responsiveness."

Several other characteristics of babies' fledgling social relations are direct antecedents of the adult friendship behaviors commented on in italics below. You can refresh your recollection of the adult behaviors by referring to the chapters cited in parentheses.

- When babies begin to initiate relationships, they signify interest in another child by thrusting out a friendship offering such as a pacifier, rattle, or a fistful of banana. *Altruism and generosity forever remain hallmarks of friendship* (Chapter 4). *Or, from the negative side, some people never outgrow the habit of luring friends with possessions or other attractions* (Chapters 2, 3).

- Babies often interact around the catalyst of play equipment, but toys can also distract infants from interpersonal relations. *Remember the "pals"—usually men—who need an activity to bind them? For them, too, physical diversions can be an escape from intimacy* (Chapters 3, 13). In the second year of life, children are able to enjoy each other without toys. They toddle away and back, hug and laugh, climb on one another, make sounds and funny faces. *Their joy in just being together reminds us of the "person qua person" pleasure of adult communal friendship* (Chapters 3, 5).

- Babies play favorites. As early as 8 months of age, one baby in a play group was approached more than the other four and one baby was consistently avoided. (Adult observers agreed that the popular baby was the most responsive and reciprocal.) By the age of 14 months, infants show very definite preferences in their companions. They also pick up cues from their parents about which playmates are more or less acceptable. *Adults continue "falling in like" with a select few—and sometimes absorb the biases of others in making those "choices"* (Chapters 4, 9, 10).

- From the age of 1 on, toddlers prefer friends who are age-mates. *So do we all* (Chapters 5, 11).

- By the end of the second year, many children show the capacity to miss their friends. They suffer over separations and rejoice at reunions. Permanent leave-takings, for example, when a playmate moves away, can cause depression and sadness. A child's distress may not be articulated, but *it is as obvious as adults' emotional reactions to friendship's exits and endings* (Chapter 7).

- When they begin to talk, at around 18 months, babies exchange one-word sentences as if they were gifts. "Ap-poo," says Terry, brandishing his apple. With a logic known only to him, Ray answers, "Piwowe" and puts his head on a pillow. *How many times has a 30-year-old's response to something you've said seemed nearly as disconnected?* With cognitive growth and experience, children's conversational facility flowers. They use talk as sound play, experimenting together with nonsense words, repetition, and odd rhythms and breaking each other up with "dirty" words like sissy, doody, ka-ka, and poo-poo. They use talk to get acquainted and chatter accompanies their activities. I've often watched 3-year-olds jabber away together while playing "house" or "space station": assigning roles ("I'm the mommy, you're the baby"); giving orders ("Go put out the fire!"); attending to the injured ("I kiss the boo-boo"), and excluding unwanted peers ("No more room on the rocket!"). *As we age, we increase our vocabulary and add a few subtleties, but we continue to use language to play "friendship": to meet people, woo our select few, become enmeshed, kid around, comfort, manipulate, reveal, explain ourselves, argue, love them or leave them* (Chapters 5, 6, 7).

- Infants and toddlers make friends one-on-one. They also show little preference for one sex or another. But by the age of 3 or 4, if they have been regularly exposed to other children, they begin to feel comfortable in groups, and they start gravitating toward friends of their own sex. This "preference" develops with more than a little help from the surrounding culture: sex-typed media, parents who encourage kids to seek

same-sex playmates or show concern if their child has a best
friend of the opposite sex, and teachers who assign children
to gender groupings and "sex-appropriate" activities. Not surprisingly, from age 4 on, most boys play at such group activities as climbing, building, running, and jumping, *as if training
for the action-centered, competitive male friendships of later life* (Chapter
13), while most girls cluster in pairs and engage in small-scale
domestic role-playing, dress-up, drawing, talking, and other
*social activities that mirror the culture's feminine ideal and foster the
intimate twosomes so typical of female friendship* (Chapter 14).
Inevitably, the gender camps become barricaded—with pun-
ishment for crossover—and cries of "No girls allowed" or
"Boys can't play" resound through the playground. *All this
presages adults' homosocial friendship networks and the estrangement
that women and men feel on the turf of the other sex* (Chapter 15).

Age 3 to 10: Solidifying the Social Self

From about 3 to 6, children become less egocentric, more aware
of the emotions of others, and more willing to share. They choose
their playmates on the basis of similarity, physical attractiveness,
possessions, and mutual activity rather than mere availability. But
they are socially erratic: tender and generous one minute, demanding
and hurtful the next; best friends on Monday, enemies on Tuesday,
and capable of banishing a pal from their rocket without a thought.

Around the age of 6, children begin to take the perspective of
another person, a giant leap for friendship. They learn that tactics
acceptable in the family may not pass muster with peers. They make
"social accommodations," recognize that different people may see
the same event differently, distinguish between intent and action
("Pammy didn't *mean* to hurt me"). They also try to put down others
to enhance their own popularity.

Between 8 and 10, "being with one's friends is a major motive
for going to school." This is when youngsters start forming sex-
segregated cliques, exchanging vows to always wear green on
Wednesdays, or "nevernevernever" betray a secret. Two kids who
really like each other forge tight "chumships," help solve each other's
problems, share feelings, take into account the friend's opinions of

them ("If I talk behind Teddy's back, he won't like me anymore"), and care about making the chum happy.

At this stage, having good friends begins to yield major developmental rewards. Kids with chums have significantly higher self-esteem than those without (and grow up to enjoy more intimate friendships in later life). Peers contribute considerably to the development of moral attitudes that are enlarged in later adolescence: justice, cooperation, equal treatment, and mutual respect. Yet along with their capacity for moral behavior, empathy, and fairness, children of this age also have learned to lie, disguise their real feelings, and manipulate others. There is a marked upsurge in teasing, bullying, and scapegoating. In short, by the end of the preadolescent period, the child is no stranger to the best and worst of friendship.

Age 11 to 17: Balancing Belonging and Independence

Young adolescent friendships may change week by week—or start now and last a lifetime. Most of the respondents to *Psychology Today*'s friendship survey said their closest friends were people they met when they were kids, and the majority of men in another national study said they've never again had "an intimate male friend of the kind they recall fondly from boyhood or youth."[5]

There are two reasons why these unions often are so lasting and meaningful. First, "they are formed when the lack of strong boundaries to the self permits one to become deeply emotional and to express one's deepest sense of self to others who, having similar vulnerabilities, cannot be considered agents of a hostile world."[6] Second, the friendships of adolescence are good enough to last because by this stage youngsters have all the necessary tools of social competence and "social cognition."[7]

However, what they have yet to manage is the intensity of it all. Teenagers suffer very high rates of loneliness not because they have fewer friends but because they are so easily alienated and so deeply concerned about acceptance and social integration.[8] They need more experience in connecting, disconnecting, and bouncing back to center after social experimentation and wild extremes of feeling.

Gender issues add to the volatility. Although today's youths have more nonerotic male-female friendships than any other generation, they, like their parents, show a strong preference for friends of their own sex, and, like adults, heterosexual teens use cross-sex friends as "informers"—spies in the ranks of the other sex. (Some kids may develop a romantic crush on a friend of the same sex. Whether this is a temporary burst of overzealous admiration or a signal of homosexual orientation is something they themselves may not know for sure and probably wouldn't tell you if they do.)

Adolescents exhibit sex differences similar to those we found in adult friendships (Chapters 13 and 14): The girls tend to be more intense, affectionate, confiding, exclusive, and nurturant; the boys are more open to newcomers and emphasize similar interests, competitiveness, and having fun together.

"These five girls hug and kiss each other every morning, put their arms around each other, and chum it up, but when one of them goes off to class, all the others attack her," says Rob Steinman, 17. "Boys do a lot of backstabbing, too, but at least we don't pretend to be best friends."

Teenagers of both sexes are convinced that their social lives can be annihilated by a "gross" word or the "wrong" outfit. If their friends are wearing bowling shirts and six earrings, that image is a MUST and they won't leave home without it. They may look like rebels to us, but in actuality most of them are slavish conformists trying to keep up with whatever dress and language is required by their chosen teen culture.

Even the smallest school has its jocks, brains, computer nerds, punks, preppies, actors, drinkers, druggies, chewers (of tobacco), motorheads (car nuts), and so on.[9] "As you change cliques, you change friends," says Nick Stern, a high school senior. "One guy I used to be friends with wasn't able to merge with my big group. He was kind of short and soft-spoken and the guys didn't think he was cool. Maybe he was too nice."

Peer group judgments can be harsh and painful, but moving with the crowd is normal. In one survey, the majority of high school achievers admitted being vulnerable to peer pressure in social activities, appearance, social behavior, dating, life-style, school performance, drinking, drugs, music, sex, studying, and college plans.[10] Although few parents imagine their children's friends to be a positive influence on any of these issues, in fact they very often are. Friends help each other adjust to school strains and reduce the harmful effects of stress. Their grades and achievement orientation improve when their friends are higher scoring than they (and decline when they have lower scoring friends).[11] Intimacy, generosity, cooperation, and helpfulness blossom during these years. And when kids are unselfish with their friends they tend to be more altruistic toward others too.

I think of the adolescent friendship network as the underground railway that transports the social self from childhood dependence to mature relationships. Kids use friends to help them detach from their parents, just as they use an accepting family to help them when peer pressure is unbearable. Chums are invaluable too for compare-and-contrast checkups ("Is what's happening to me happening to you?" "Am I normal?"). Like talking mirrors, they reflect and interpret one another's changing bodies and dress rehearsal identities. Their self-esteem soars when a friend seeks their advice or validates their tastes. They care desperately about being well-liked, ranking their worries about losing their friends way up there with concern about their looks, grades, their parents' safety, world hunger, poverty, and violence. As we've seen, many adults keep right on worrying about being liked and not losing their friends—worries they too place on a par with all the great issues.

In sum, between sexual maturation and the assumption of adult roles, friends are the most important part of a person's life—more psychologically important than parents, romantic partners, wide popularity, or good grades, and more developmentally important with each passing year. As my son, David, wrote when he was a junior in high school: "Friendship is a key factor in an adolescent's sanity. I would be a seriously disturbed kid if my social life wasn't secure. (You might say it's my social security.) I used to depend on my parents for company, learning, entertainment, and problem-solving. Now they are mostly just there for loving. My friends are the building blocks of my independence and self-satisfaction."

When asked about their major life goals, a national sample of high school seniors put "close friendship" second only to "a good marriage and family life."

Age 18 to 39: Balancing Friendship and Everything Else

Surveys show that of all age groups, college students and people in their twenties have the largest number of friends but also very high rates of loneliness. College students often find it hard to maintain their high school friends; some may have to make new friends for the first time since kindergarten.

Nevertheless, many people describe college as an ideal environment for friendship—a place where all kinds of people are brought together with the equalizing identity of "student" at a time of life when they are no longer children but don't yet have a full load of adult responsibilities. College gives them the luxury of all-night sessions on Homer, Hegel, hypocrisy, or the scourge of acne. When else can friends read novels together, play beer-drinking games without feeling silly, shamelessly seek each other's advice on whether to work on Wall Street or lobby for the homeless? When, if ever again, can we balance friendship against everything else we do and give it better than equal time?

After describing three adored college friends, Abby, age 21, says wistfully, "I know I'm going to look back on all this as a dream."

College also gives some people dream roommates.[12] My interview with four young women who share a suite proves that roommates are to friendship what microwave ovens are to cooking—a miracle of high-speed intensity.

"We know each other totally and we're conscious of how special we are as a foursome," says Robin. "Since I admire each of them and the time we spend together is fascinating and fun and never seems wasted, there's nothing motivating me to make other friends."

"We've been labeled 'exclusive' because we get along so well," explains Kathy. "I have a few friends outside the room but when I try to blend them in, it doesn't work."

"The trouble is, when you spend time with an outside friend, you lose time with your roommates," adds Jen. "And I never want to miss anything."

Of course it's not *all* peaches and cream.

"Each of us has felt aligned against by the others," Jen continues.

"When you leave the room, you want to put your ear to the door to hear if anyone is talking about you."

"Most of those problems are situational," says Joan, the fourth suite mate. "We complain when one of us is on the phone too long, or is too uptight about her work, or freaks out about sharing the computer, or makes noise when the others want to sleep. You have to expect *some* tension when four people live in so little space."

"Still," Robin puts in, "when we're all scattered during school vacations I miss the sharing."

"Me too," says Joan. "And I worry about how we'll stay close when we're leading our separate lives."

"Yeah," nods Kathy. "After graduation we'll have no common ground. You don't return to your dorm for Thanksgiving."

Competing Interests

As life becomes crowded with family, work, and community interests, where does friendship fit in?

From age 20 to 40, according to psychoanalyst Erik Erikson, humanity's main psychological task is to develop a mature capacity for intimacy, in friendship as well as in love relationships—and, indeed, research shows that people in their twenties spend more time with friends than does any other age group except the over-seventies.

Actually, it is not so much age but career attitudes and parental status that dictate the time we have available for friendship: Old people have the most free time (forty-three hours per week), childless singles and marrieds come next, then parents with no kids at home, and, finally, single or married people doing active parenting who average up to twenty *fewer* leisure hours per week than the childless. Men, and increasingly women, who give their primary attention to their jobs during these "empire-building" years obviously have less time for friendship. Likewise, mothers have fewer friends than fathers because the sexual division of labor still puts more child-rearing demands on Mom; when the kids are grown, however, it is women who have more friends than men.

The attractive up-scale clique in *The Big Chill* makes it look easy to have career success, marriage, and maybe even a child or two and still maintain complex friendships. Commercials showing attractive young friends cavorting on the beach suggest that good times needn't disappear after high school or college. In real life though, as we take on adult roles, we have to reorder our priorities and make choices. Until we become experienced at balancing many competing interests, serious clashes may result. Chapter 6 reviewed how a spouse can come between friends; in her book *Married People,* Francine Klagsbrun warns of the dangers when a friend comes between spouses and

> when the side with the friend confides everything that is going on in the marriage to that friend—all the fights, all the sexual difficulties, all the in-law quarrels. Once the doors to a marriage have been opened in that way, they are hard to shut again. . . . Unfortunately, friends have a way of becoming too sympathetic, too willing to take sides and urge partners to actions they may not really want.[13]

Part of growing up is accepting that each couple must make its own rules, mark off where the door closes on the marriage and where it opens to our friends, where we draw the lines of loyalty and secrecy, how to juggle time for us and time for outsiders, what to do if we feel jealous of a spouse's cross-sex friend or if we like only one member of a couple.

As we move through our twenties and thirties, we take on friends who match our stage of personal development as well as our marital status, class, age, and so on. And we also learn that it is normal to leave some friends behind. Some of us retreat from childhood associates because they remind us of our own immaturity—not to mention our carefree years. Some of us become estranged from friends whose life is unchanged. One study found, for example, that many men who become fathers abandon their boyhood pals in preference for their current neighbors and coworkers.[14] "If a friendship validates our sense of what we *were* and does not validate our sense of what we are now, then it can become untenable," says psychiatrist Michael Milano. "You can be nostalgic and evoke the time when you were the same but because you no longer are the same there is no forward momentum in the friendship."[15]

Whether we keep old pals or make new ones, it is ironic that we have the least time for friendship when we have the most need for friends. In the years when we're establishing ourselves and our families we need friends to give us help moving furniture, painting the house, making decisions, borrowing necessities, minding the children; more important, we need them to get us through stressful events.[16] Not only does having a close confidant make people better able to cope with marital disruption, money problems, failure, illness, or death, but, interestingly, children also reap the benefits when their parents have close, dependable friends to call on in a crisis. Such children seem to be happier in their families, in their own friendships, and in school. What is the connection between *your* friendships and your child's well-being?[17] Parents with a solid support system are happier and less easily defeated by the hectic routines of family life and therefore more available to the pleasures of child-rearing.

It is uncanny how closely the friendships of each stage of life fit our private psychological needs. Adolescent friends help us detach from our parents; adult friends help us *be* better parents. The chums of youth help in our search for identity, but once we know who we are, we want friends who are like us. We no longer define ourselves through others—we *refine* ourselves by seeking companions who mirror the most pleasing parts of our self-image. In this search, we make and drop new friends frequently. We alternate between judgmental inflexibility and no standards at all. Some people devote the young adult years to social climbing because their need for status outweighs their need for social authenticity. Others pursue short-lived enthusiasms—the witty young woman in the sales department, the couple with all those books who moved in down the block, the nice man who picked up his daughter at our son's birthday party and stayed for hours—the many bright soulmate possibilities who for one reason or another grew dull.

On the cusp of 40, when we're up to our eyebrows in existential angst, we take a new look at the friends who've been there all along, the ones who witnessed our poverty, pregnancies, and peccadilloes; collaborated with us on diets, vacations, and mutual paranoia; survived fallings-out, comings-out, changed jobs, changed spouses, separations and reunions; watched our children grow from chubby cherubs to teenagers who are the same age now as some of us were when we first met. As we tote up the years, savor the memories, and review the shared history, suddenly we look at this person and think, "Gee, we're *old friends,*" and we know that, no matter how many exciting new people may come into our lives, we two will be special to one another.

Age 40 to 64: Consolidating Gains, Cutting Losses

"After the age of forty there isn't much to live for except friend-ship," says a character in Francine du Plessix Gray's *World Without End*.

Although middle age is when we spend the least time with friends and our friendships tend to be fewer and less intense, it is also when our relationships are more selective and stable (most studies are based on a white middle-class sample). If we have been successful at inti-macy in the young adult decades, Erikson says we move on to the stage he calls "generativity," roughly between 40 and 65, when we look beyond our own lives, care about the larger social family, and want to leave a better world for those who come after us. Supposedly, even men who've been workaholics become "more affiliative"—they try to make up for lost time with their wives and children and with friends if they can.

Other psychologists say just the opposite: That this is a period of concentration on career, not family *or* friends; that most people see these years as the shank of their lives, their last chance to make a success of themselves. This is when most people reach the top of their earning powers. Unless they're in the low-income category, this is when they can afford to buy services rather than rely on friends for an exchange of favors. They're as self-sufficient now as they'll ever be.

Supposedly, mid-life is also the stage when people confide in relatives more than friends. It's when marriages break up and take couple-friends on the rocks with them. It's when the kids leave home and friendships that were centered on interfamily activities fade away. It's when we get tired of old friends but find it hard to make new ones. Toward the end of this stage, psychologists say, we start losing interest in others as part of a "normal" process of "disengagement" that prepares us for old age and death.

My interviews tell me these findings are true and not true. True for some working people who say they can't worry about friendship until they retire. (I'm thinking of an international banker who has promised his wife that on January 1, 2000, they will take off for a year to visit their friends around the world.) But not true for many other mid-life people who are down-shifting from career over-drive and making time for friends *now* (Chapter 8).

Sure, plenty of people are bored by the predictability of old friends

("I've grown too cynical for her starry-eyed view of life," says a newspaperwoman about a longtime friend). But at least as many others say they've just begun to appreciate pals they'd taken for granted. And as Chapter 6 detailed, it's always possible to see an old friend in a flattering new light.

On the question of "disengagement," a number of older middle-aged folks countered that they'd grown *more* socially active not less as their family concerns diminished and they've become more economically secure. Many interviewees told me they were particularly interested in making new friends. "I'm not the same person I was twenty years ago," says one 50-year-old. "I need fresh troop reinforcements to complement who I am now." And as for those in this age group with an off-track timetable for childbearing and career advancement, their friendship attitudes were more in sync with people ten and twenty years younger.

It seems that the stage between 40 and 65 is one of multiple contradictions as people reassess the meaning of their lives and particularly the value of friends and family. A few of these reassessments carried the force of epiphany:

You won't always have your family.   It's common for people in this age group to complain about caring for aging parents, but Rayna Rapp had the opposite problem. "When my parents retired and moved to California, I was stunned to realize that they didn't need me," she says. "They preferred to make a commitment to their own peers." In giving up her status as her parents' child (the good daughter who was ready to parent *them*), she also more clearly saw herself as an adult who needed age-mates of her own. "It made me see how important friends are to *everyone's* independence."

What Rapp saw as a middle-aged adult whose parents moved away can be said even more emphatically of people whose adult children leave home. A perceptive friend suggests that I've chosen to write a book on friendship at this point in my life because (1) I now have an empty nest and I'm compensating by turning to friends, and (2) a merger of family and friendship is required to formally include my children, who are too old to be mothered but old enough to be friends, in my social circle. Both interpretations ring true.

A new awareness of mortality increases the value of our human attachments.   Incapacity, illness, disease, and death intrude upon the middle years and remind us of the fragility of life. This is when most people first experience the death of a friend that is not accidental: a healthy 45-year-old has a heart attack, a tennis partner dies of lung cancer, an old friend is rendered mute by a stroke; it stuns. "I've really started cherishing my friends in a conscious way," says a 48-year-old New Yorker who lost her best friend to cancer. "I can no longer behave as if we have all the time in the world." Others told me they now catch themselves staring lovingly at a friend, drinking in his or her face, or worrying about a dear friend's health. They don't postpone get-togethers as blithely as they once did. "It's not that I'm morbid," says a man of 55. "I'm just aware that we're not going to live forever."

It's more important to preserve a friendship than to express "honesty at all costs."   Mid-life men still tend to prefer friends who agree with them on issues and activities, while women prefer friends with whom they're emotionally compatible. As they move into their forties and fifties, however, men become more like women in their deepening realization of the meaning of friends, and women become more like men in their willingness to let differences pass rather than hash over every nuance of feeling. Both sexes show a growing desire to avoid argument, to protect the friendship rather than let it all hang out in the more confrontational style of their younger years.

You need different kinds of friends to provide different kinds of support in different situations.   "One of the things I've noticed is how many more lives I intersect as I get older," says a man of 58. "It's a great perk of middle-age to have friends from all walks of life all over the place who I can turn to for help and support."

Friendship diversity is especially important during the stressful events of the mid-life period. Just as job pressures can be minimized by friends who understand your working conditions, in other life circumstances certain friends are more morale-building than others (Chapter 6). Take widowhood for example. Research shows that widows with a lot of family support don't do as well as widows with a lot of friends—specifically, *married* friends. Their support is more important in the early stages of grief, while single or widowed friends become more useful later when the widow is ready to embark upon single life.[18]

A woman in her forties claims that during periods of strife, her network of couple-friends has helped keep her marriage together. "I might have walked out many times, but it was easier to keep working at my marriage than to risk losing my friends," she says. "Because of the other couples, I've avoided divorce in favor of tolerance. Their marriages have taught me to compromise. Besides, with friends like these who needs a perfect husband?"

Friends can rejuvenate a mid-life slump. Martin Edelston told me about a man who went to the wisest counselor he could find and said, "Life has become boring with my wife. What should I do?" The sage's advice came in the form of a question: "What kind of friends do the two of you have?"

I wouldn't go so far as to say that a dead marriage can be resuscitated by a lively outsider, but I do agree that an active social life prevents stagnation, married or not.

In *Best Friends* (original title: *Men and Friendship*), psychologist Stuart Miller concluded his long search with the statement: "It is *not easy* to go out and make real friends after the age of 35." This may be true of men in general, given their socialization to avoid intimacy; it may also be true of people who don't go out to work, don't belong to groups, or don't move outside their circumscribed worlds. But it isn't true of everyone.

"We met this terrific couple last year on a cruise," says Warren, 51. "The trip turned out to be a big bust but it was worth it because we found these people. We vowed never to set foot on another ship, but this summer the four of us are going on a photo safari together."

Violet discovered a new person in an old familiar place: "This woman sat down next to me at the hairdresser, looked at herself in the mirror, pronounced her hair a 'plate of spaghetti' and asked me, 'Is there any hope for this mess?' I suggested a pixie style and she actually had the beautician cut her hair to my specifications. That's the sort of impetuous nut she is. She's had me standing on rooftops looking for Halley's comet. She calls at 2 a.m. to sing me a song or to get me to write letters to the editor about saving whales and sea lions. I'm 44, but since I met her I feel half my age."

Walter, age 60, says of his new friend: "I'd seen the guy a million times on the train but we'd never spoken. Then, on the day the NASA shuttle exploded, we started talking about it during the ride home. His open way of dealing with his feelings helped me cope with my own emotions about the tragedy. We became friends because he revealed his inner self."

Olivia, divorced and 55, traded wisecracks with a young man at her office, then impulsively invited him and his wife to her New Year's party. She's been a friend of theirs ever since.

Forty-year-old Craig had a textbook experience: He and another man spent three hours trapped in a stalled elevator. By the time they were freed, they were friends.

Sometimes the new friends people are so excited about are their own grown children. They've gotten to know each other as equals partly because children of the affluent, like their poorer counterparts, now stay longer under their parents' roofs, and partly because education and shared values have narrowed the generation gap (Chapter 11). We've seen that the working class and certain ethnics have always made family into friends, but among the middle class, the closeness between parents and their young adult offspring is a spirited new trend (Chapter 3).

Another striking middle-class, middle-aged phenomenon is the long-term multi-family friendship—a group of couples who have been closely involved since they first married and started having babies and who still maintain rituals of collective reunion. In single-sex clusters, they play sports or meet for lunch. Their kids, now off at college or recently graduated, still keep in touch. While the families no longer rent summer houses cheek by jowl, they reunite for anniversaries, birthdays, holidays, or vacation trips. They lead parallel lives and like it.

A dozen couples in Peekskill, New York, founded the Round Robin Nursery Group when their children were toddlers. For twelve years the twelve families had fun together, helped each other cope, and celebrated each other's milestones. Although Betty and Bernard Miller left Peekskill in 1960, they and the six remaining couples have continued to meet periodically and relish the latest news about their respective offspring, now in their thirties. "We've had many friends since then, but none compare to the Round Robin people," says Betty. "Those families were our family."

Age 65 Plus: Realities and Surprises of the Later Years

Item: Your children are gone, you've retired, maybe you've moved to a senior citizens' development. Do these changes make you think, "Now I'm useless" or "For the first time in my life, I'm free to be a friend"?

Item: Some older people have a mate; others are widowed or single. If you're over 65 and alone, do you retreat into self-pity and afternoon naps or do you reinvest in friends?

Item: Some oldsters have their health, savings accounts, and comfortable pensions; most live with some infirmity or financial worries. Do you let health and money problems dominate your thoughts or are you making a positive contribution to your social network within your limitations?

In other words, what effect does aging have on friendship and what effect do friends have on people as they grow old? The answers are surprising.

Friends are not monolithic. Some people are better than others at providing the essential things old folks need: emotional companionship, goods and services, and special help during a crisis.[19] We can give love at any age but the older we get, the less we're able to provide our friends with physical, practical benefits. These must come from younger people, family members, and health care institutions.

I find it unexpectedly tidy that communal relations (emotional companionship) should surface at the close of life as the elemental distillation of friendship, while exchange relations (goods, services, help, palships) fall by the wayside along with the other competencies of youth (Chapter 3).

Friendship cliques add up to more than the sum of their members. It's unusual to find old men running in packs as young men do, or old women going to the theater as a group; most elders' friendships are one-to-one. And yet, group friendship has been found to be far more beneficial. Being part of a clique gives old people a sense of belonging and an opportunity to share resources, help each other adapt to the aging process, and enhance their low self-image.[20] In the substitute society of the senior citizens clique, they can gain status and exercise leadership that is no longer available to them in the larger world.

People are less lonely after age 70 than at any other stage of the life span.   Experience has taught them to take ambiguities in their stride. They know no one person is going to provide everything they need. Instead of being bound together by activities or demanding reciprocal exchanges, most elders have learned to take comfort in the pure pleasure of caring and being cared about. They know it's not the worst thing in the world to disagree with a friend or to be disappointed in someone or to spend the evening alone. They're not afraid of solitude.

"Older people become more self-sufficient and their lives are simpler," explains psychologist Anne Gerson. "They have a better idea than younger people do of what to expect from relationships."

Sex differences in friendship hit men hardest in old age.   Over the age of 70, surveys show, two out of five men and three out of five women have at least one intimate friend.[21] Men of this age have fewer friends than do women and are somewhat more prone to loneliness because men are used to having friendships develop around their work. Without that focal point, they don't have the knack of making connections. Also, since men typically see friends as partners in activity, the less they're physically able to do, the more they're at loose ends. As their old friends die, they don't seem to know how to strike up new pals unless there's a card game or hobby to bridge the gap that women fill with talk. When a man has no friends, he often relies on his wife for company, monopolizing her time so much that *her* friendships suffer.

The effects of gender are especially disturbing at this stage because friends are so important to old people's health and well-being: Involvement in social relations has been found to predict a better adjustment to their retirement, infirmity, or the death of their loved ones. When asked, "Do you have someone to talk over personal problems with?" most older men name their wives, while women name close friends or their children. Men whose wives were their best friend suffer the most mental illness after their wives die. Without her and without his coworkers, a man may be newly unwillingly dependent on relatives or utterly alone.

Although the death of a spouse usually takes a greater emotional toll on men who lack the back-up support of comforting friends, older men are sought after as marriage partners almost immediately. Seventy percent of women and 30 percent of men are widowed or single by age 65; widows outnumber widowers four to one. My hunch is that many old men marry to have a friend of their own (as well as the continuation of domestic services to which they've become accustomed).

Older widows usually find that the size of their social circle decreases, but the *importance* of friends increases. In fact, the average widow gets more help and support from her friends than do married women of the same age.[22] Women friends surround her with camaraderie to make up for her loss.

Friends are more psychologically important than relatives. As noted in Chapter 11, friends have a greater impact on old people's morale than family members do. Contrary to their adult children's instincts (or guilt feelings), most elderly people prefer to live near well-liked age-mates rather than to be "taken in" by their children. Frequent interaction with close friends, but not with relatives, helps the aged adjust to role changes and adds to their general life satisfaction.[23] Among elderly women, believe it or not, the ones who are most contented and have the least death anxiety are those with many friends and few offspring living near them.[24]

People's age-mates keep them young because friends grow old with them, whereas offspring remind them of the past when they were more functional and respected. For all their good intentions, relatives may encourage dependency, infantilize the elderly, and make them feel burdensome. Friends are more apt to foster self-sufficiency and treat one another as equals. Assistance from a friend is more acceptable for being voluntary. And old people gain self-respect in the act of helping each other.

Old People Need to Be Needed. It's especially hard for old people to feel useful in a society that disregards anyone who doesn't work for money. (Children and housewives suffer the same ill-treatment.) They are reluctant to label themselves as elderly not just because of the youth and beauty bias of this culture but because being old is associated with uselessness and helplessness. Although they may need help, oldsters want more than caretakers; they want friends just like everyone else, and, mostly, they want to feel needed themselves.

Nowhere is this better understood than at the Daughters of Jacob Geriatric Center where the residents have a large part in running the place. (Their Hadassah chapter president is 93 years old.) One of the center's most successful programs is Bikur Cholim, friendly visiting, an organized round of social visits complete with flowers, candy, cookies, and conversation, during which volunteers create friendship where there would be emptiness. They pop in on residents who rarely have visitors because, at an average age of 88, their children are either living in retirement themselves or have died before their parents.

Friendship is a vital compensation for the many losses experienced by the elderly: the loss of loved ones and meaningful roles at work, in the family, and in the neighborhood; the loss of health, physical capacity, and financial security. Many old people also reaffirm their ethnic and religious ties in these years to fill the yawning gaps in their identity and to connect with friends who may give them points for being a senior member of the tribe.

Their need for status, prestige, and self-esteem shows up sometimes in a surprisingly overt fashion.[25] Many say they like being seen with friends who make them feel important: "Others look up to me because I know this person," they confide. A 79-year-old man wants you to know that his friend, the doctor, once had movie stars among his patients. A woman of 67 brags about a slightly younger friend who is still employed—"and she can get it for you wholesale."

When having prestigious friends isn't feasible, old people often try to gain status by competing with their "ordinary" friends as to who has the best children. One elderly woman is the celebrity of her group because her granddaughter is a soap opera star. Two friends in their seventies, one with a lawyer son and one with a lawyer daughter, parry indirect blows. "Of course, my daughter isn't interested in making tons of money," says one, apropos of nothing. The other woman, feeling that this is a veiled attack on her son's ethical purity, becomes defensive about his success. They never argue outright. They just drop innuendos into each other's placid life, like torpedoes.

Last February, at a Miami Beach condominium populated mostly by senior citizens, I overheard the following exchange between three old men playing shuffleboard:

First Man: "So, did you get any Valentine's Day cards?"

Second Man: "Are you kidding? I got from my son a card, and from my two grandchildren I got hand-mades with doilies."

First Man: "Me, I got a huge box of candy. Every year they remember me with something nice."

Third Man: "My son sent me a Valentine's check. My daughter sent me a plane ticket back home. Such generous kids."

First Man: "My son is bringing his family down to visit me next month."

Second Man: "Did you hear, Sidney didn't get nothing for Valentines? Some people's children don't care about them."

Third Man: "It's a shame."

First Man: "A real shame."

Only 8 percent of the elderly live with their children and grandchildren; about a fourth live with an adult child; most live alone or with unrelated age-mates in retirement communities or nursing homes.

Because of their need to feel needed, for this age group more than any other, place of residence is critical.[26] Although theoretically we may favor age-integrated communities, as we've seen, what most fosters individual satisfaction and friendship is age-segregated housing. When the old are dispersed among families or singles, they tend to be the most isolated from each other and detached from the larger society. In single-room-occupancy hotels, people respond to one another only in emergencies. In communities organized especially for the aged, on the other hand, old people can be independent yet know there is help at hand; their social life is part of their daily life. And when there are no younger people around, they fill the authority roles denied them in an age-integrated society. They feel useful and appear competent in the eyes of their friends.

Dr. Charles Longino, Jr., director of the Center for Social Research and Aging at the University of Miami, says the average age of people living in retirement communities is much older than ever before, yet they "have significantly fewer problems of loneliness and social isolation, and more positive self-regard and they exhibit evidence of gerontophilia (a pride in and desire to associate with their age group)."[27]

Balancing Old Friends and New Friends

It takes a long time to grow an old friend.

John Leonard, critic

If a man does not make new acquaintances as he advances through life he will soon find himself left alone.

Samuel Johnson

"We go back a lot of years together," says an 82-year-old of a friend with whom he went to elementary school. "He knew me long before I could shave. He knows that I used to be able to run rings around most guys. I don't have to tell him what I did with my life. He knows."

Old friends become more important as we age, and very often our best friends are our oldest friends. More than a fifth of the respondents to *PT*'s friendship survey said their closest friend was someone they'd known for twenty years or more. Old friends validate one another in a historical sense, not just in the here and now. Each carries an image of the other's younger self, the self that still lives behind every wrinkled face.

In a 1984 interview, the British poet Stephen Spender, 75, said of the writer Christopher Isherwood: "Christopher and I have always had exactly the same kind of relationship since we first met and that was in Berlin fifty-three years ago. So that we very much have the sense that we are play-acting, that we are still the same people that we were when we were young. Only now we are got up to play the parts of these old fellows talking to each other. . . . the point was that we were both disembodied voices, that we had both somehow got lodged in these old bodies."[28]

Mildred and Bob Kent and Esther and Harry Katz, two couples in their seventies, have been friends for thirty-eight years. Is your friendship based on shared nostalgia? I ask.

"Some of it is," Mildred admits. "But we have enough in common even without the memories."

"Actually, the Kents are our *newest* friends," laughs Esther. "They're babies compared to a girlfriend I've had since I was 12."

"Or the guy I've known for seventy years," chimes in Harry.

The longer friends know each other, it seems, the less time they need to spend together to maintain their closeness. Intimacy may be cumulative. Or perhaps friends come to assume that someone who's been there for so long will be there always. But of course, that's not the case, especially when we start reading the obituary page with tears in our eyes. Therefore, people balance the keeping of old friends with ongoing efforts to make new friends, especially friends of varying ages and interests. Unless their ages are staggered, our friends tend to die off all at once. Unless they are diverse, we might be left with companions who like to sit and talk but no one to travel with; friends who like to play cards but no one strong enough to drive us to the doctor's; friends who still care enough to complain about the national economy but no one able to loan us twenty dollars.

Janet Barkas describes a strategy for introducing new blood into a social circle. "Once a month a couple who are semi-retired university professors have Saturday dinner with several other couples. The host couple of the month must invite one couple unknown to the others. In that way, all the friends, whose age differences span a few decades, try to make new friends while reinforcing their old friendships."[29]

This option may not suit everyone. Uncoupled people and those with less education or fewer private resources find new friends in voluntary organizations whose membership is based on skills and interests, not age. Eighty percent of the elderly participate in church, fraternal, ethnic, or veterans groups, and up to 22 percent are regularly active in volunteer work. More and more senior citizens' summer camps are attracting the socially inclined, and VASCA (Vacations and Senior Centers Association, 275 Seventh Avenue, New York, N.Y. 10001) provides "scholarships" for those who can't afford the fees. Old people need transportation, expense reimbursement, and safe surroundings before they can get involved, but once they're out and about, new relationships come in due course.

Elders who live in senior villages meet new people over golf, on the first-aid rescue team, while doing pottery, photography, or poll-watching, at Bingo, AA meetings, or on any of the committees that organize the social and cultural life of their community. Arlie Hochschild describes one such community in San Francisco whose residents interacted constantly while performing such jobs as serving on the Flower Committee or the Secret Pal project (which made sure everyone got a birthday present) or being treasurer or vice president of *something*. Furthermore, she says, "For friends lost through death, there were replacements. Whenever an apartment was vacated, it was immediately filled by the first on a long list of applicants."

It's easy to criticize age-segregated communities: They take old people out of the mainstream; they create a science-fiction world in which children and young people are almost nonexistent; they try to cheat death of its impact. But those objections seem coldly intellectual compared to the conviviality so many old people claim to find in a society of their peers.

"The fellowship here is very close," says Dorothy Clark of a trailer park for the elderly. "We're so close to everybody here now, to our friends, that we couldn't live anywhere else."[30]

Still, there are oldsters who won't live in a retirement community, don't need a nursing home, and yet have trouble finding a social niche for themselves. That's the situation for Emma, 75, who spends most of the year up North in the home in which she reared her family and goes to Florida for three months in winter. "What do you do when you're bored by most people your own age, but you haven't the energy to keep pace with younger people?" she asks. She wants to be part of her peer group but at the same time she tries to differentiate herself from them because she has absorbed society's disdain for the aged.

She's also caught in a dilemma between new and old friends. New friends offer full attention and genuine interest in her experiences. She lights up like a lamp when she can tell her life story to virgin listeners. But she confuses them; she meanders off the point or speaks in a shorthand new friends can't always understand. Old friends, on the other hand, have the advantage of knowing the stars of her continuing family saga: her children, sisters and brothers and everyone in *their* families, her first husband who died when she was in her forties and her second husband who died about fifteen years ago. And some *old* old friends even knew her parents. But old friends stop her with, "Emma, not again. We've heard that one a million times." New friends are a romance, old friends, a marriage. Emma wants both but sometimes she has no patience for either.

Obviously there's something to be said for both longevity and freshness. However, most of what's been said is a paean to long-term friendship. There's the proverb: "The best mirror is an old friend." Ecclesiastes and Cicero, among others, equated good friends with good wine, contending both improve with age. Close friendship "is the fruit of years and of work," said William James. And, mused Oliver Wendell Holmes: "There is no friend like an old friend, Who has shared our morning days . . ."

But it is a lesser-known poet, Joseph Parry, who is most realistic and thus more evenhanded:

> Friendships that have stood the test—
> Time and change—are surely best . . .
> But old friends, alas! may die,
> New friends must their place supply.
> Cherish friendship in your breast—
> New is good but old is best;
> Make new friends, but keep the old;
> Those are silver, these are gold.

My Friends, in Closing . . .

This book began with contradictions and it ends with a contradiction: We need old friends to help us grow old and new friends to help us stay young.

Throughout these pages I have resolved many other issues by accepting the paradoxes involved—by synthesizing dualities, opposites, and logical incongruities and arguing that the truth about friendship *is* its contradictions.

Even the act of creating this book was a contradiction: I had to leave my friends in order to write about them. I had to be solitary in order to honor friendship.

I've suggested many other paradoxes that are both reassuring and instructive:

- Modern society is not conducive to friendship, yet millions of us are defying depersonalization, disavowing competition, making connections, and seeking friends as never before.

- Many people think they are inadequate friends but, despite sex-role conditioning and the culture of calibration, most of us seem to have at least one or two quite wonderful friendships.

- Acquaintances, neighbors, confederates, pals, kin, and co-workers aren't in the category of "friends"—unless they're *your* friends. What counts is not where or how you met but what you feel and do about it.

- Friends may mollify our discontents and distract us from the rest of the world; they may also empower us, energize us, and help us to change our lives.

- Liking people who are like us may be a symptom of bigotry— but also of our impulse toward equality.

- Two close friends can simultaneously be the same and never-quite-the-same; friends from different cultures open new doors for each other, but they also know when to knock.

- Small towns are great for friendship; so are suburbs and cities.

- Men's friendships are usually superficial but fun; women's friendships are usually intimate but not always beneficial. Each gender would benefit from some of the other's ways.

- Because of sexism, men and women can't be friends. Because of sexism, men and women *must* be friends.

- It's smart to be friends with one's sex partner but dumb to have sex with one's friends.

- No friend is perfect, but some imperfections are violations, some advice is an assault, some betrayals are unforgivable; no friendship is ideal, but some are so fatally flawed they deserve to be put out of their misery.

- In the trinity of human priorities, friendship usually stands behind love and family. Yet, in old age, when new lovers are rare, new children rarer, and the family dwindling, there is, still and always, the possibility of a new friend.

Finally, although centuries of wisdom have yielded the scores of friendship criteria detailed in the foregoing chapters, in the last analysis, friendship is what you say it is.

This is not double-talk. All these contradictions define the essence of a relationship that is itself the ultimate contradiction, for it offers freedom *and* fusion balanced as you wish with whomever you like, for whatever your reasons, with as many as you choose, whenever and however you want it. We break no laws if we abandon a friend, but few of us give up a friendship easily. No one forces us to make the commitment. But we do it anyway. We elect the "burden" of intimacy because only with it do we outwit the fundamental isolation of existence. Our lives are full of things to do and people we already care about but still we choose to deepen old friendships and make new ones. No wonder we get confused. No wonder we're not sure if we're "doing it right." And no wonder it took a full-length book to conclude that there are no hard and fast rules. From the rocking horse to the rocking chair, friendship keeps teaching us about being human. No wonder we care so much and no wonder we spend so much of our lives among friends.

Notes

Chapter 1: The Dinner Party

1. The motion picture eventually became *The Four Seasons*, written and directed by Alan Alda, produced by Martin Bregman, and released by Universal Pictures.

Chapter 2: Contradictions

1. P. Ariès, *Centuries of Childhood: A Social History of Family Life*, Random House, 1965.
2. *Forbes*, January 14, 1985, p. 12. See Also, *"Where Does the Time Go?" United Media Enterprises Report on Leisure in America*, Newspaper Enterprise Associates, 1983; G. Godbey, *Leisure in Your Life: An Exploration*, Pennsylvania State University Press, 1985.
3. S. J. Ball-Rokeach and M. Rokeach, *The Great American Values Test: Influencing Behavior and Belief Through Television*, Free Press, 1984.
4. *The Connecticut Mutual Life Report on American Values in the '80s: The Impact of Belief*, Research & Forecasts, 1981.
5. C. S. Fischer, *To Dwell Among Friends: Personal Networks in Town and City*, University of Chicago Press, 1982.
6. J. G. Williams and C. H. Solano, "The Social Reality of Feeling Lonely: Friendship and Reciprocation," *Personality and Social Psychology Bulletin*, June 1983. See also L. A. Peplau and D. Perlman, eds., *Loneliness: A Sourcebook of*

Current Theory, Research, and Therapy, Wiley-Interscience, 1982; D. Perlman and L. A. Peplau, "Toward a Social Psychology of Loneliness," in S. Duck and R. Gilmour, eds., *Personal Relationships,* vol. 3: *Personal Relationships in Disorder,* Academic Press, 1981; Z. Rubin, "Seeking a Cure for Loneliness," *Psychology Today,* October 1979.

7. R. S. Weiss, *Loneliness: The Experience of Emotional and Social Isolation,* MIT Press, 1974.

8. D. Yankelovich, *New Rules: Searching for Self-Fulfillment in a World Turned Upside Down,* Random House, 1981.

9. D. Riesman, R. Denney, and N. Glazer, *The Lonely Crowd: A Study of the Changing American Character,* Yale University Press, 1950.

10. A. Toffler, *Future Shock,* Bantam Books, 1970, p. 383.

11. C. Rubenstein and P. Shaver, *In Search of Intimacy: Surprising Conclusions from a Nationwide Survey on Loneliness and What to Do about It,* Delacorte Press, 1982. See also, K. A. Franck, "Friends and Strangers: The Social Experience of Living in Urban and Non-Urban Settings," *Journal of Social Issues,* Summer 1980.

12. "Post-30 Group of Unmarrieds Found in Big Rise by Census," *New York Times,* May 21, 1984; "Americans Marrying Later," *New York Times,* July 6, 1984.

13. "Single Living: The Growing Population of Women Who Are Changing Our Attitudes and Our Lives," *Ms.,* November 1984. See also, "Adapting to the High Cost of Housing," *New York Times,* February 3, 1985, and "More Turn to Sharing to Cover Rising Rents," *New York Times,* August 25, 1985; P. Parmalee and C. Werner, "Lonely Losers: Stereotypes of Single Dwellers," *Personality and Social Psychology Bulletin,* no. 4 (1978).

14. F. Dickson-Markman, "Self-Disclosure Among Friends and Lovers: An Investigation of the Role of Friendship Patterns and Social Support in Marital Satisfaction," *Dissertation Abstracts International,* vol. 43, no. 7 (January 1983), p. 2388-B.

15. J. S. McIlwee, "Women's Survival in Nontraditional Blue-Collar Occupations," *Frontiers,* vol. 6, no. 1 (1981).

Chapter 3: Soul-Searching

1. G. Simmel, *The Sociology of Georg Simmel,* Free Press, 1950.

2. G. A. Allan, *A Sociology of Friendship and Kinship,* Allen & Unwin, 1979.

3. R. Brain, *Friends and Lovers,* Basic Books, 1976.

4. P. H. Wright, "Self-Referent Motivation and the Intrinsic Quality of Friendship," *Journal of Social and Personal Relationships,* vol. 1 (1984).

5. M. S. Clark, "Noncomparability of Benefits Given and Received: A Cue to

the Existence of Friendship," *Social Psychology Quarterly*, vol. 44 (1981).

6. L. B. Rubin, *Worlds of Pain: Life in the Working-Class Family*, Basic Books, 1976.

7. L. M. Verbrugge, "Multiplexity in Adult Friendships," *Social Forces*, June 1979.

8. C. Rubenstein and P. Shaver, *In Search of Intimacy: Surprising Conclusions from a Nationwide Survey on Loneliness and What to Do about It*, Delacorte Press, 1982, p. 157.

9. *The Connecticut Mutual Life Report on American Values in the '80s: The Impact of Belief*, Research & Forecasts, 1981.

10. A. Toffler, *Future Shock*, Bantam Books, 1970, pp. 104–05.

11. E. Maxwell, *I Married the World*, Heinemann, 1955.

12. C. Werner and P. Parmalee, "Similarity of Activity Preferences Among Friends: Those Who Play Together Stay Together," *Social Psychology Quarterly*, March 1979.

13. C. B. Stack, *All Our Kin: Strategies for Survival in a Black Community*, Harper & Row, 1974.

Chapter 4: A Friend Is Someone Who . . .

1. J. W. Anglund, *A Friend Is Someone Who Likes You*, Harcourt Brace Jovanovich, 1958.

2. D. Goleman, "Great Altruists: Science Ponders Soul of Goodness," *New York Times*, March 5, 1985.

3. L. A. Blum, *Friendship, Altruism and Morality*, Routledge & Kegan Paul, 1980.

4. A. Beatts, "Women, Friendship and Bitchiness," *Vogue*, August 1981.

5. C. S. Lewis, *The Four Loves*, Harcourt Brace Jovanovich, 1971.

6. E. M. Forster, quoted in M. Walzer, *Obligations: Essays on Disobedience, War and Citizenship*, Harvard University Press, 1970, p. 14.

7. I. N. Sandler, "On Buffers and Boosters: Social Support for Negative and Positive Life Events." Paper presented at the annual convention of the American Psychological Association, August 1981.

8. N. Luhmann, *Trust and Power*, Wiley, 1980.

9. B. Barber, *The Logic and Limits of Trust*, Rutgers University Press, 1983.

10. K. Lindsey, "Rx for Depression: One Friend Every 4 Hours," *Ms.*, June 1979.

11. J. B. Rotter, "Interpersonal Trust, Trustworthiness and Gullibility," *American Psychologist*, January 1980.

12. *The Connecticut Mutual Life Report on American Values in the '80s: The Impact of Belief*, Research & Forecasts, 1981.

13. L. A. DeSalvo, "Lighting the Cave: The Relationships Between Vita Sackville-West and Virginia Woolf," *Signs*, Winter 1982.

14. A. Rich, untitled poem in *Poems: Selected and New, 1950–1974*, Norton, 1975.

15. D. Brissett and R. Oldenburg, "Friendship: An Exploration and Appreciation of Ambiguity," *Psychiatry*, November 1982.

16. C. H. Solano, P. G. Batten, and E. A. Parish, "Loneliness and Patterns of Self-Disclosure," *Journal of Personality and Social Psychology*, September 1982.

17. L. F. Berkman and L. Breslow, *Health and Ways of Living: The Alameda County Study*, Oxford University Press, 1983.

18. Studies described in T. Voss, "Good Friends and Good Health Go Hand in Hand," *Prevention*, March 1981.

19. D. Goleman, "Confiding in Others Improves Health," *New York Times*, September 18, 1984.

Chapter 5: The Passage to Intimacy

1. M. T. Hallinan, "Structural Effects on Children's Friendships and Cliques," *Social Psychological Quarterly*, vol. 42, no. 1 (1979).

2. A. S. Ross, "A Cohort Analysis of Loneliness and Friendship in the First Year of University." Paper presented at the annual convention of the American Psychological Association, September 1979. See also, M. R. Fondacar et al., "Development of Friendship Networks as a Prevention Strategy in a University Megadorm," *Personnel and Guidance Journal*, May 1984.

3. R. L. Null, "Student Perceptions of the Social and Academic Climates of Suite Living Arrangements," *Journal of College and University Student Housing*, Summer 1981.

4. R. Sommer and M. Horner, "Social Interaction in Co-ops and Supermarkets," *Communities*, vol. 20 (1981); R. S. Ulrich and D. L. Addoms, "Psychological and Recreational Benefits of a Residential Park," *Journal of Leisure Research*, vol. 13 (1981).

5. G. Collins, "Disabled and Able Children," *New York Times*, June 24, 1985.

6. M. Pilisuk and M. Minkler, "Supportive Networks: Life Ties for the Elderly," *Journal of Social Issues*, vol. 36 (1980).

7. P. F. Lazarsfeld and R. K. Merton, "Friendship as a Social Process," in M. Berger, T. Abel, and C. H. Page, eds., *Freedom and Control in Modern Society*, Van Nostrand, 1954. See also, M. Prisbell and J. F. Andersen, "The Importance of Perceived Homophily, Level of Uncertainty, Feeling Good, Safety, and Self-Disclosure in Interpersonal Relationships," *Communication Quarterly*, vol. 28, no. 3 (Summer 1980).

8. L. M. Verbrugge, "The Structure of Adult Friendship Choices," *Social Forces*, vol. 56, no. 2 (1977).

9. S. W. Duck and R. G. Craig, "Personality Similarity and the Development of Friendship," *British Journal of Social and Clinical Psychology*, 1978.

10. S. L. Feld, "Social Determinants of Similarity Among Associates," *American Sociological Review*, December 1982.

11. M. Lea and S. Duck, "A Model for the Role of Similarity of Values in Friendship Development," *British Journal of Social Psychology*, November 1982.

12. L. C. Pogrebin, "The Power of Beauty," *Ms.*, December 1983.

13. E. Bercheid and E. Walster, "Physical Attractiveness," *Advances in Experimental Social Psychology*, vol. 7 (1974).

14. G. Smith, "Gender and Attractiveness Related to Preschool Peer Interactions." Paper presented at the annual meeting of the Midwestern Psychological Association, May 1982.

15. J. D. Corrigan, "Salient Attributes of Two Types of Helpers," *Journal of Counseling Psychology*, vol. 26, no. 6 (1978).

16. D. Bar-Tel and L. Saxe, "Physical Attractiveness and Its Relationship to Sex Role Stereotyping," *Sex Roles*, vol. 2, no. 2 (1976). See also, study by W. Goldman and P. Lewis described in "Good Looking People Are Likable Too," *Psychology Today*, July 1977; L. W. Banner, *American Beauty*, Knopf, 1983; R. Lakoff and R. Scherr, *Face Value: The Politics of Beauty*, Routledge & Kegan Paul, 1985; R. M. Jones and G. R. Adams, "Assessing the Importance of Physical Attractiveness Across the Lifespan," *Journal of Social Psychology*, October 1982.

17. R. W. Emerson, "Friendship," in *For Friendship's Sake*, Dodge, 1900, p. 14.

18. K. E. Davis and M. J. Todd, "Friendship and Love Relationships," *Advances in Descriptive Psychology*, vol. 2 (1982). See also, K. E. Davis, "Near and Dear: Friendship and Love Compared," *Psychology Today*, February 1985.

19. P. H. Wright and Paula Berghoff, "The Acquaintance Form and the Study of Relationship Differentiation." Paper presented at the Second International Conference on Personal Relationships, July 1984.

20. R. J. Sternburg, "Measuring Love." Paper, Yale University, Department of Psychology, n.d.

21. W. K. Rawlins, "Negotiating Close Friendship: The Dialectic of Conjunctive Freedoms," *Human Communication Research*, Spring 1983. See also W. K. Rawlins, "Openness as Problematic in Ongoing Friendships: Two Conversational Dilemmas," *Communication Monographs*, March 1983.

22. J. Bensman and R. Lilienfeld, "Friendship and Alienation," *Psychology Today*, October 1979.

23. Ibid.

24. F. Bacon, "The Fruit of Friendship," in *For Friendship's Sake*, Dodge, 1900, pp. 83–84.

Chapter 6: Flashpoints

1. M. Argyle and A. Furnham, "Sources of Satisfaction and Conflict in Long-Term Relationships," *Journal of Marriage and the Family*, August 1983.

2. A. L. Sillars, "Attribution and Communication in Roommate Conflicts," *Communication Monographs*, August 1980.

3. L. Bernikow, *Among Women*, Harper & Row, Colophon Books, 1981.

4. Z. Rubin, "Friends and Lovers," *Psychology Today*, October 1982.

5. J. Barkas, quoted in M. Slade, "Marriage of Friend: Mixed Blessing," *New York Times*, December 31, 1984.

6. B. Sabol, "Three Is Company," *Mademoiselle*, December 1982.

7. J. Moussaieff Masson, trans. and ed., *The Complete Letters of Sigmund Freud to Wilhelm Fliess, 1877–1904*, Harvard University Press, Belknap Press, 1985.

8. P. Mahony, "Friendship and Its Discontents," *Contemporary Psychoanalysis*, January 1979.

9. V. Woolf, *The Diary of Virginia Woolf, 1920–24*, ed. A. O. Bell, Harcourt Brace Jovanovich, 1977, pp. 225–26.

10. J. A. Levy, "Re-entry Women on the College Campus," in H. Z. Lopata and D. Maines, eds., *Research in the Interweave of Social Roles: Friendship*, vol. 2 (1981).

11. R. C. Tripathi et al., "Accepting Advice: A Modifier of How Social Support Affects Well-Being," *Journal of Social & Personal Relationships*, 1984.

12. D. R. Lehman et al., "Social Support for the Bereaved: Recipients' and Providers' Perspectives on What Is Helpful." Paper, University of Michigan Institute for Social Research, 1985. See also, M. Davidowitz and R. D. Myrich, "Responding to the Bereaved: An Analysis of 'Helping' Statements," *Research Record*, vol. 1 (1984); C. B. Wortman and T. L. Conway, "The Role of Social Support in Adaptation and Recovery from Physical Illness," in S. Cohen and L. Syme, eds., *Social Support and Health*, Academic Press, 1985.

13. S. Rimer, "Volunteers Comfort Lonely AIDS Children," *New York Times*, February 27, 1986; G. Dullea, "Ill Children and Pain of Isolation," *New York Times*, January 21, 1985; S. B. Johnson, "Peer Relationships Among Chronically Ill Children." Paper presented at the annual meeting of the Southeastern Psychological Association, 1981; "Cancer: The Psychosocial Effects," a report on the study conducted by R. Heinrich et al., *Psychology Today*, April 1985.

14. N. Brozan, "Young Cancer Patients Share Experiences," *New York Times*, July 2, 1984.

15. "Friends for Teen-Age Patients," *New York Times*, August 12, 1985.

16. S. Linscott, "Are Friends Still Friends in Adversity?" *New York Times*, August 29, 1984.

17. "To Manuel Garcia, Love Is a Shaved Head," *New York Times*, July 20, 1985.

18. S. Wainright, *Stage V: A Journey Through Illness*, Acacia, 1984.

19. C. Ascher, "It's All Right to Be Honest: How One Friend Survived an Incurable Illness," *Ms.*, April 1985.

20. D. Goleman, "Emotional Support Has Its Destructive Side," *New York Times*, August 27, 1985.

21. M. Bender, "Two for the Road," *New York Times*, December 2, 1984.

22. S. Halling, "Surprised By the Other: Choice Points in Relationships." Paper presented at the annual convention of the American Psychological Association, 1981.

23. Quoted in A. Rossi, "A Feminist Friendship," *Ms.*, January 1974.

24. P. A. M. Spacks, *Gossip*, Knopf, 1985.

25. B. Hodges, "Effect of Valence on Relative Weighting in Impression Formation," *Journal of Personality and Social Psychology*, vol. 30 (1974). See also, D. Hamilton and M. Zanna, "Differential Weighting of Favorable and Unfavorable Attributes in Impression of Personality," *Journal of Experimental Research in Personality*, vol. 6 (1972); M. Richey et al., "Relative Influence of Positive and Negative Information in Impression Formation and Persistence," *Journal of Personality and Social Psychology*, vol. 5 (1967).

26. K. Rook, "Nonsupportive Aspects of Social Relationships." Paper presented at annual meeting of the American Psychological Association, August 1985. See also, K. Rook, "The Negative Side of Social Interaction: Impact on Psychological Well-Being," *Journal of Personality and Social Psychology*, vol. 46, no. 5 (1984).

27. A. Abbey and M. Rovine, "Social Conflict: The Negative Aspect of Social Relations." Paper presented at annual meeting of the American Psychological Association, August 1985.

Chapter 7: Exits and Endings

1. W. Smith, "Lynne Sharon Schwartz," *Publishers Weekly*, August 3, 1984.

2. M. S. Davis, *Intimate Relations*, Free Press, 1973.

3. S. Miller, *Men & Friendship*, Houghton Mifflin, 1983, pp. 56–57. (Reprinted as *Best Friends*, Gateway Books, 1985.)

4. E. Coleman and B. Edwards, *Brief Encounters: How to Make the Most Out of Relationships That May Not Last Forever*, Doubleday, Anchor Press, 1980.

5. M. L. Knapp, *Social Intercourse: From Greeting to Goodbye*, Allyn & Bacon, 1978.

6. L. A. Baxter, "Strategies for Ending Relationships: Two Studies," *Western Journal of Speech Communication*, Summer 1982. See also, S. Duck and D. Allison, "I Liked You but I Can't Live with You: A Study of Lapsed Friendships." Paper, Department of Psychology, University of Lancaster, England.

7. J. M. Lewis, "Dying with Friends," *American Journal of Psychiatry*, March 1982.

8. J. Spence, *The Memory Palace of Matteo Ricci*, Viking, Penguin, 1984, p. 150.

9. D. Metzger, "The Story of Friendship"; available from the author, 20666 Callon Drive, Topanga, Calif. 90290.

Chapter 8: Living the Social Life

1. S. Salmans, "Busy Night Out for Networking," *New York Times*, September 17, 1985.

2. Rudolf Nureyev, quoted in "The Evening Hours," *New York Times*, November 2, 1984.

3. Research by W. Jones and D. Russell reported in D. Goleman, "Social Anxiety: New Focus Leads to Insights and Therapy," *New York Times*, December 18, 1984.

4. J. Huizinga, *Homo Ludens: A Study of the Play-Element in Culture*, Beacon Press, 1950, p. 205.

5. S. V. Levine, *Radical Departures: Desperate Detours to Growing Up*, Harcourt Brace Jovanovich, 1984.

6. L. Wolfe, "Friendship in the City," *New York*, July 18, 1983.

7. D. Jerome, "Lonely Women in a Friendship Club," *British Journal of Guidance and Counseling*, January 1983.

8. K. Anderson, "Friends," *Denver Post*, September 15, 1985.

9. S. G. Freedman, "The Gritty Eloquence of David Mamet," *New York Times Magazine*, April 12, 1985.

10. The National Organization for Changing Men, Box 93, Charleston, Ill. 61920.

11. Red Cross Telephone Club, (212) 787-1000.

12. J. L. Barkas, *The Help Book*, Scribners, 1979; n.a., *The Source Book, 1984–1985*, UNIPUB, 1985.

13. "New York City Tries to Reduce Number of Jail Suicides," *New York Times*, July 21, 1985.

14. N. Brozan, "Friendship in Patients' Last Days," *New York Times*, October 28, 1985.

15. L. Bernikow, *Among Women*, Harper & Row, Colophon Books, 1981.

16. E. Nemy, "Lunch for Women: Food and Ideas," *New York Times*, April 6, 1983.

17. Wolfe, "Friendship in the City."

18. L. Van Gelder, "Inventing Food-Free Rituals," *Ms.*, December 1982.

19. F. Kandel and M. Heider, "Friendship and Factionalism in a Tri-Ethnic Hous-

ing Complex for the Elderly in North Miami," *Anthropological Quarterly*, vol. 52, no. 1 (1979).

20. Personal communication, Melanie Howard, National Association of Greeting Card Publishers, April 1985; L. Belkin, "Greeting Cards for No Occasion," *New York Times*, August 17, 1985.

21. F. Ferretti, "When Life Is Too Busy to Be Impromptu," *New York Times*, November 14, 1985.

22. B. Ehrenreich, "Hers," *New York Times*, February 21, 1985.

23. "Leaving the Office Behind," *Publishers Weekly*, February 8, 1985.

24. "Metropolitan Diary," *New York Times*, May 16, 1984.

25. J. L. Barkas, *Friendship: A Selected, Annotated Bibliography*, Garland, 1985.

26. J. Leonard, Introduction, in B. P. Wolff, *Friends and Friends of Friends*, Dutton, 1978.

27. E. Abel, "(E)merging Identities: The Dynamic of Female Friendship in Contemporary Fiction by Women," *Signs*, vol. 6, no. 3 (1981).

28. V. Woolf, *A Room of One's Own*, Harcourt, 1963.

29. L. C. Pogrebin, "One Step Forward: Women's Friendship," *Ms.*, September 1981.

30. "Letters to the Editor," *New York Times*, July 4, 1985.

31. Z. Rubin, "Friends in Need (of Votes)," *Baltimore Sun*, July 11, 1984.

32. J. P. Flanders, "Paradigms to Study and Control Loneliness." Paper presented at UCLA Research Conference on Loneliness, May 1979.

33. Forget-Them-Not, P.O. Box 1596, Rockefeller Center Station, New York, N.Y. 10185.

34. Friend Finders International, P.O. Box 680, Poulsbo, Wash. 98370.

35. L. Van Gelder, "The Strange Case of the Electronic Lover," *Ms.*, October 1985.

36. S. Turkle, *The Second Self: Computers and the Human Spirit*, Simon & Schuster, 1984.

Chapter 9: A Sense of Place, A Touch of Class

1. M. Berg and E. A. Medrich, "Children in Four Neighborhoods: The Physical Environment and Its Effect on Play and Play Patterns," *Environment and Behavior*, vol. 12 (1980).

2. F. J. Ianni et al., "A Field Study of Culture Contact and Desegregation in an Urban High School," Educational Resources Information Center (ERIC), ED 160 672, 1979.

3. J. E. Blackwell and P. S. Hart, *Cities, Suburbs, and Blacks: A Study of Concerns, Distrust, and Alienation*, General Hall, 1982.

4. C. Kirschenbaum, "Instant Activism: A Moment of Truth for Austin's Gays," *Ms.*, October 1985.

5. S. H. Anderson and D. W. Dunlap, "Welcome Program for Homosexuals," *New York Times*, September 19, 1985.

6. L. Erdrich, "Where I Ought to Be: A Writer's Sense of Place," *New York Times Book Review*, July 28, 1985.

7. A. Dobrin, "New Tongues in the Neighborhood," *New York Times*, July 21, 1985.

8. B. H. Gelfant, "Grace Paley: Fragments for a Portrait in Collage," in B. H. Gelfant, *Women Writing in America: Voices in Collage*, University Press of New England, 1984.

9. E. B. Fein, "For Goetz Victim's Mother, Worry and Self-Doubt," *New York Times*, January 12, 1985.

10. R. G. Genovese, "A Women's Self-Help Network as a Response to Service Needs in the Suburbs," *Signs*, vol. 5, no. 3 (1980).

11. R. Seidenberg, *Corporate Wives—Corporate Casualties?* Doubleday, Anchor Press, 1975.

12. H. Varenne, *Americans Together, Structured Diversity in a Midwestern Town*, Teachers College Press, 1977.

13. B. Adelman, *Down Home: Camden, Alabama*, Times Books, Quadrangle, 1972.

14. C. Rubenstein and P. Shaver, *In Search of Intimacy: Surprising Conclusions from a Nationwide Survey on Loneliness and What to Do about It*, Delacorte Press, 1982.

15. B. Robey, *The American People: A Timely Exploration of a Changing America and the Important New Demographic Trends around Us*, Dutton, 1985.

16. C. S. Fischer, "The Public and Private Worlds of City Life," *American Sociological Review*, June 1981; J. C. Horn, "In Cities Fast Friends Come Slowly," *Psychology Today*, April 1981.

17. A. Harmetz, "Images Served at Hollywood Parties," *New York Times*, November 20, 1985.

18. Meg Greenfield, "Friendship in Washington," *Newsweek*, July 25, 1983.

19. M. Cochran et al., "The Ecology of Urban Family Life: A Summary Report," Cornell University, Department of Human Development and Family Studies, June 1982.

20. Ibid.

21. R. Horowitz, *Honor and the American Dream: Culture and Social Identity in a Chicano Community*, Rutgers University Press, 1983.

22. J. B. Gurdin and H. Hutter, "Some of My Best Friends Are . . . The Relationship of Ethnicity to Close Friendship in Montreal," *Quebec Studies*, vol. 3 (1985).

23. L. M. Verbrugge, "The Structure of Adult Friendship Choices," *Social Forces*, vol. 56, no. 2 (1977).

24. M. di Leonardo, *The Varieties of Ethnic Experience: Kinship, Class, and Gender Among California Italian-Americans,* Cornell University Press, 1984.

25. G. Allan, "Class Variations in Friendship Patterns," *British Journal of Sociology,* September 1977.

26. J. Gustfield, J. Kotarba, and P. Rasmussen, "The Public Society of Intimates: Friends, Wives, Lovers and Others in Drinking-Driving Drama," in H. Z. Lopata and D. Maines, eds., *Research in the Interweave of Social Roles: Friendship,* vol. 2 (1981).

27. C. S. Fischer, "The Friendship Cure-All," *Psychology Today,* January 1983, p. 74.

28. S. G. Freedman, "How 'Big River,' a Story Begun in a Car, Made It to Broadway," *New York Times,* July 16, 1985.

29. R. P. Coleman and L. Rainwater, *Social Standing in America: New Dimensions of Class,* Basic Books, 1978.

30. H. Gans, *The Levittowners: Ways of Life and Politics in a New Suburban Community,* Pantheon Books, 1967.

31. L. B. Rubin, *Worlds of Pain: Life in the Working-Class Family,* Basic Books, 1976.

32. J. Balkin and J. A. Donaruma, "Contributions of Family and Friends to Fear of Success in Men," *Journal of Psychology,* November 1978.

33. G. Collins, "Celebrity Families: Problems of Success," *New York Times,* September 23, 1985.

34. E. Newton, "Sex and Sensibility: Social Science and the Idea of Lesbian Community." Paper, State University of New York at Purchase, N.Y., 1985.

35. F. Bacon, "The Fruit of Friendship," in *For Friendship's Sake,* Dodge, 1900.

Chapter 10: Our Own Kind

1. M. L. Clark, "Gender, Race and Friendship Research." Paper presented at the annual meeting of the American Educational Research Association, April 1985.

2. W. M. Usui, "Homogeneity of Friendship Networks of Elderly Blacks and Whites," *Journal of Gerontology,* vol. 39, no. 3 (1984).

3. C. S. Fischer, *To Dwell Among Friends: Personal Networks in Town and City,* University of Chicago Press, 1982.

4. F. Hayes, "Gesticulation: A Plan of Classification." Paper presented at the meeting of the American Association of Teachers of Spanish and Portuguese, December 28, 1975.

5. E. T. Hall, *The Hidden Dimension,* Doubleday, 1966.

6. R. Birdwhistell, quoted in B. Schaffner, ed., *Group Processes,* Josiah Macy Jr. Foundation, 1959, p. 184.

7. E. T. Hall, "The Anthropology of Manners," *Scientific American,* April 1955.

8. J. Noesjirwan, "A Laboratory Study of Proxemic Patterns of Indonesians and Australians," *British Journal of Sociology and Clinical Psychology,* November 1978.

9. T. S. Jones and M. S. Remland, "Cross-Cultural Differences in Self-Reported Touch Avoidance," Educational Resources Information Center (ERIC) ED 214 206, 1981.

10. Hall, *Hidden Dimension.*

11. E. Goffman, *Behavior in Public Places: Notes on the Social Organization of Gatherings,* Free Press, 1963.

12. R. Horowitz, *Honor and the American Dream: Culture and Social Identity in a Chicano Community,* Rutgers University Press, 1983.

13. A. Helms, "Cultures in Conflict: Arab Students in American Universities." Paper presented at annual meeting of the Southwestern Anthropological Association, March 1978.

14. J. Walz, "A Mini-Film on French Kinesics." Paper presented at Indiana University Conference on Foreign Languages, February 1975.

15. N. Darnton, "Style Around the World," *New York Times Magazine,* August 25, 1985.

16. Hall, *Hidden Dimension.*

17. S. E. Keefe, "Personal Communities in the City: Support Networks Among Mexican-Americans and Anglo-Americans," *Urban Anthropology,* Spring 1980.

18. S. J. Morse, "Requirements for Love and Friendship in Australia and Brazil," *Australian Journal of Psychology,* December 1983.

19. M. L. Knapp et al., "Compliments and Cultures," *Psychology Today,* August 1985.

20. H. L. Nostrand, "Culture-Wide Values and Assumptions as Essential Pedagogical Content." Paper presented at 82nd annual meeting of the Modern Language Association, December 1967.

21. D. L. Williams, "Thai Ways and My Ways," Educational Resources Information Center (ERIC), ED 231 183, 1983.

22. F. Bekata, "The Natural History of Friendship: A Cross-Cultural Study," *Dissertation Abstracts International,* vol. 41, no. 7 (1981), p. 2811-B.

23. M. L. Clark and M. Ayers, "Race, Gender and Reciprocity: Effects of Friendship Similarity During Early Adolescence." Paper presented at the annual meeting of the American Educational Research Association, April 1985.

24. R. P. Coleman and L. Rainwater, *Social Standing in America: New Dimensions of Class,* Basic Books, 1978.

25. C. B. Stack, *All Our Kin: Strategies for Survival in a Black Community,* Harper & Row, 1974.

26. P. Giddings, *When and Where I Enter: The Impact of Black Women on Race and Sex in America,* Morrow, 1984.

27. U. Hannerz, *Soulside: Inquiries into Ghetto Culture and Community,* Columbia University Press, 1969.

28. Ibid.

29. R. F. Kandel and M. Heider, "Friendship and Factionalism in a Tri-Ethnic Housing Complex for the Elderly in North Miami," *Anthropological Quarterly,* vol. 52, no. 1 (1979).

30. C. E. Hill, "Ethnicity as a Factor in Urban Social Change in a Southern City," Educational Resources Information Center (ERIC), ED 138 688, 1977.

31. Hohri's view of generational differences is corroborated in research done among Japanese in Chicago and Minneapolis/St. Paul; see M. D. Albert, "Japanese American Communities in Chicago and the Twin Cities," *Dissertation Abstracts International,* vol. 41, no. 7 (January 1981), p. 3260-A.

32. R. G. Monson, *Jewish Campus Life,* American Jewish Committee, Institute of Human Relations, 1984.

33. M. di Leonardo, *The Varieties of Ethnic Experience: Kinship, Class, and Gender Among California Italian-Americans,* Cornell University Press, 1984.

34. B. Robey, *The American People: A Timely Exploration of a Changing America and the Important New Demographic Trends around Us,* Dutton, 1985.

35. These points have been distilled from conversations with Micaela di Leonardo.

Chapter 11: The Same and Different

1. L. Rohter, "Immigrant Factory Workers Share Dream, Luck and a Lotto Jackpot," *New York Times,* August 23, 1985.

2. G. Allport, *The Nature of Prejudice,* Doubleday, Anchor Press, 1958.

3. J. Provinzano, "Settling Out and Settling In." Paper presented at annual meeting of the American Anthropological Association, November 1974.

4. D. Riesman, R. Denney, and N. Glazer, *The Lonely Crowd: A Study of the Changing American Character,* Yale University Press, 1950.

5. B. M. Campbell, "Friendship in Black and White," *Ms.,* August 1983.

6. S. Bockner, "Friendship Patterns of Overseas Students," *Journal International de Psychologie* (English translation provided), vol. 12, no. 4 (1977).

7. S. Ting-Toomey, "Ethnic Identity and Close Friendship in Chinese-American College Students." Paper presented at the annual meeting of the International Communication Association, May 1980.

8. R. W. Brislin, "Interaction Among Members of Nine Ethnic Groups and Belief-Similarity Hypothesis," *Journal of Social Psychology,* December 1971. See also S. G. Cole and K. Davenport, "Reported Friendliness Toward Mexican-Americans as a Function of Belief Similarity and Race," Educational Resources Information Center (ERIC), ED 082 076, 1972; D. Koulack and D. Cumming,

"Acceptance and Rejection as a Function of Ethnicity and Belief Intensity," *Journal of Social Psychology*, December 1973.

9. J. Spangenberg and E. M. Nel, "The Effect of Equal Status Contact on Ethnic Attitudes," *Journal of Social Psychology*, December 1983.

10. H. J. Gans, *The Urban Villagers: Group and Class in the Life of Italian-Americans* (revised), Free Press, 1982.

11. E. H. Robbins, "Class and Ethnicity: Social Relations in Wabash, Newfoundland-Labrador," Ph.D. dissertation, University of Michigan, 1975.

12. B. T. Dill, "Race, Class and Gender: Prospects for an All-Inclusive Sisterhood," *Feminist Studies*, Spring 1983.

13. B. Adelman, *Down Home: Camden, Alabama*, Times Books, Quadrangle, 1972.

14. R. Atsumi, "Tsukiai—Obligatory Personal Relationships of Japanese White Collar Employees," *Human Organization*, vol. 38, no. 1 (1979).

15. F. Douglass, *Narrative of the Life of Frederick Douglass, an American Slave*, New American Library, Signet, 1968.

16. B. Hooks, *Ain't I a Woman: Black Women and Feminism*, South End Press, 1981.

17. P. M. Palmer, "White Women/Black Women: The Dualism of Female Identity and Experience in the United States," *Feminist Studies*, Spring 1983.

18. M. Margolis, "Black/White Friendship," *Seventeen*, March 1982.

19. M. di Leonardo, *The Varieties of Ethnic Experience: Kinship, Class, and Gender Among California Italian-Americans*, Cornell University Press, 1984.

20. C. E. Hill, "Ethnicity as a Factor in Urban Social Change in a Southern City," Educational Resources Information Center (ERIC), ED 138 688, 1977.

21. J. B. Gurdin and H. Hutter, "Some of My Best Friends Are . . . The Relationship of Ethnicity to Close Friendship in Montreal," *Quebec Studies*, vol. 3 (1985).

22. S. O. Murray, "The Institutional Elaboration of a Quasi-Ethnic Community," *International Review of Modern Sociology*, vol. 9, no. 2 (1979).

23. J. C. Albro and C. Tully, "A Study of Lesbian Lifestyles in the Homosexual Micro-Culture and the Heterosexual Macro-Culture," *Journal of Homosexuality*, vol. 4, no. 4 (1979).

24. A. P. Bell and M. S. Weinberg, *Homosexualities: A Study of Diversity Among Men and Women*, Simon & Schuster, 1978.

25. J. Malone, *Straight Women/Gay Men: A Special Relationship*, Dial Press, 1980.

26. R. Nahas and M. Turley, *The New Couple: Women and Gay Men*, Seaview Books, 1979.

27. P. Black, "When a Friend Tells You She's Gay," *Mademoiselle*, March 1983.

28. E. Newton and S. Walton, *Womenfriends*, Friends Press (520 W. 110 Street, New York, N.Y. 10025), 1976.

29. Nahas and Turley, *New Couple*.

30. Ibid.

31. L. M. Shears and C. J. Jensema, "Social Acceptability of Anomalous Persons," *Exceptional Children,* October 1969.

32. R. K. Jantz et al., *Children's Attitudes Toward the Elderly,* University of Maryland Press, 1976.

33. A. G. Cryns and A. Monk, "Attitudes of the Aged Toward the Young," *Journal of Gerontology,* vol. 1 (1972); see also, C. Seefeld et al., "Elderly Persons' Attitude Toward Children," *Educational Gerontology,* vol. 8, no. 5 (1982).

34. K. L. Woodward and A. Kornhaber, *Grandparents, Grandchildren: The Vital Connection* (Doubleday, Anchor Press, 1981), quoted in "Youth Is Maturing Later," *New York Times,* May 10, 1985.

35. L. J. Hess and R. Hess, "Inclusion, Affection, Control: The Pragmatics of Intergenerational Communication." Paper presented at the Conference on Communication and Gerontology of the Speech Communication Association, July 1981.

36. V. Secunda, *By Youth Possessed: The Denial of Age in America,* Bobbs-Merrill, 1984.

37. J. Bingham, "Old, Young and the Labor of Love," *New York Times,* September 1, 1985.

38. P. Rosser and M. Cohen, "Skip-a-Generation Friendships," *Ms.,* August 1980.

39. D. Klosky and W. Howard, "Family Affair," *Yale Daily News,* October 4, 1985.

40. S. Jacoby, "My Life as a Confidante: The Real Pleasures of Friendship with Other People's Children," *Vogue,* August 1983.

Chapter 12: Friends at Work

1. D. Carnegie, *How to Win Friends and Influence People,* Simon & Schuster, Pocket Books, 1937, rev. ed. 1982.

2. L. M. Verbrugge, "Multiplicity in Adult Friendships," *Social Forces,* June 1979.

3. R. Baker, "Clinging to Social Antiquity," *New York Times,* May 12, 1984.

4. R. Little, "Friendships in the Military Community," in H. Z. Lopata and D. Maines, eds., *Research in the Interweave of Social Roles: Friendship,* vol. 2 (1981).

5. P. Zavella, "Abnormal Intimacy: The Varying Work Networks of Chicana Cannery Workers," *Feminist Studies,* Fall 1985.

6. C. S. Fischer, *To Dwell Among Friends: Personal Networks in Town and City,* University of Chicago Press, 1982.

7. L. Lamphere, "Bringing the Family to Work: Women's Culture on the Shop Floor," *Feminist Studies,* Fall 1985.

8. A. R. Hochschild, *The Unexpected Community: Portrait of an Old Age Subculture,* University of California Press, 1983.

9. H. Wong, "Typologies of Intimacy," *Psychology of Women Quarterly*, Spring 1981.

10. *Miller Lite Report on American Attitudes Toward Sports*, Research & Forecasts, 1983.

11. M. Goldfischer, "My Say," *Publishers Weekly*, December 7, 1984.

12. M. Greenfield, "Friendship in Washington," *Newsweek*, July 25, 1983.

13. R. M. Kanter, *Men and Women of the Corporation*, Basic Books, 1977.

14. Report of Right Associates, New York, a national outplacement and human resources firm, cited in *Women in Business*, March/April 1985.

15. D. R. Kaufman, "Associational Ties in Academe: Some Male and Female Differences," *Sex Roles*, vol. 4 (1978); P. B. Forsyth, "Toward an Understanding of Interaction and Work Alienation Among Male and Female Educators," *Journal of Educational Equity and Leadership*, Winter 1981.

16. J. R. Lincoln and J. Miller, "Work and Friendship Ties in Organizations: A Comparative Analysis of Relational Networks," *Administrative Science Quarterly*, June 1979.

17. M. R. Rueschemeyer, "Personal Life and the Demands of Work: An Exploratory Study of Professional Men and Women in the United States and Two Socialist Societies," *Dissertation Abstracts International*, vol. 38, no. 12 (June 1978), p. 7599-A.

18. D. Jacobson, "Fair-Weather Friend: Label and Context in Middle-Class Friendship," *Journal of Anthropological Research*, vol. 31 (1975).

19. F. Rosenberg, "Women Doctors Speak Out," *New Directions for Women*, July/August 1985.

Chapter 13: Men's Togetherness

1. J. Lipman-Blumen, "Toward a Homosocial Theory of Sex Roles: An Explanation of the Sex-Segregation of Social Institutions," in M. Blaxall and B. Reagan, eds., *Women and the Workplace: The Implications of Occupational Segregation*, University of Chicago Press, 1976.

2. L. Tiger, *Men in Groups*, Random House, 1969.

3. J. H. Pleck, "Man to Man: Is Brotherhood Possible?" in N. Glazer-Malbin, ed., *Old Family/New Family: Interpersonal Relationships*, Van Nostrand, 1975.

4. M. Gibbs, D. Auerbach, and M. Fox, "A Comparison of Male and Female Same-Sex Friendships," *International Journal of Women's Studies*, May 1980.

5. E. Aries, "Male-Female Interpersonal Styles in All Male, All Female and Mixed Groups," in A. G. Sargent, ed., *Beyond Sex Roles*, 2nd ed., West Publishing, 1985.

6. R. R. Bell, "Friendships of Women and of Men," *Psychology of Women Quarterly*, Spring 1981.

7. A. P. Bell and M. S. Weinberg, *Homosexualities: A Study of Diversity among Men and Women*, Simon & Schuster, 1978.

8. S. Miller, *Men & Friendship*, Houghton Mifflin, 1983. (Reprinted as *Best Friends*, Gateway Books, 1985.)

9. D. J. Levinson et al., *The Seasons of a Man's Life*, Knopf, 1978.

10. M. E. McGill, *The McGill Report on Male Intimacy*, Holt, Rinehart & Winston, 1985.

11. M. Komarovsky, *Dilemmas of Masculinity: A Study of College Youth*, Norton, 1976.

12. J. LaBonte, "Peaches and Men: A Story from Prison," in J. H. Pleck and J. Sawyer, eds., *Men and Masculinity*, Prentice-Hall, Spectrum Books, 1974.

13. Miller, *Men & Friendship*, pp. 139–40.

14. H. Gold, "In Each Other's Company," *New York Times Magazine*, August 19, 1984.

15. R. A. Lewis, "Emotional Intimacy among Men," *Journal of Social Issues*, vol. 34, no. 1 (1978).

16. M. Rothstein, "The Origin of the Universe, Time and John Updike," *New York Times*, November 21, 1985.

17. S. Tesich, "Focusing on Friends," *New York Times Magazine*, December 4, 1983.

18. J. Leonard, Introduction, in B. P. Wolff, *Friends and Friends of Friends*, Dutton, 1978.

19. L. R. Davidson and L. Duberman, "Friendship: Communication and Interactional Patterns in Same-Sex Dyads," *Sex Roles*, August 1982. See also, S. Weitz, "Sex Differences in Nonverbal Communication," *Sex Roles*, February 1976; R. Rosenthal et al., "Body Talk and Tone of Voice: The Language Without Words," *Psychology Today*, vol. 8, no. 4 (1974).

20. P. Feinberg, *Friends: The Special Qualities of Friendships*, Quick Fox, 1980.

21. McGill, *McGill Report*.

22. M. Carroll, "Here's How It Really Is Between Men," *50 Plus*, March 1985.

23. A. Brooks, "When Older Men Divorce," *New York Times*, October 12, 1984.

24. M. F. Fasteau, *The Male Machine*, McGraw-Hill, 1974.

25. D. H. Bell, *Being a Man: The Paradox of Masculinity*, Harcourt Brace Jovanovich, 1984.

26. Davidson and Duberman, "Friendship."

27. E. J. Aries and F. L. Johnson, "Close Friendship in Adulthood: Conversational Content between Same-Sex Friends," *Sex Roles*, December 1983.

28. E. J. Aries, "Interaction Patterns and Themes of Male, Female and Mixed Groups," *Small Group Behavior*, vol. 7 (1976).

29. A. Haas, "Partner Influences in Sex-Associated Spoken Language of Children," *Sex Roles*, vol. 7, no. 9 (1981); F. L. Johnson and E. J. Aries, "Conversational

Patterns Among Same-Sex Pairs of Late Adolescent Close Friends," *Journal of Genetic Psychology*, June 1983.

30. Aries, "Interaction Patterns."

31. J. Levin and A. Arluke, "An Exploratory Analysis of Sex Differences in Gossip," *Sex Roles*, February 1985.

32. Aries, "Interaction Patterns."

33. Aries and Johnson, "Close Friendship."

34. Jake, "A Man's Opinion," *Glamour*, November 1980.

35. M. Simmons, "My Main Man: The Truth About Male Friendship," *Essence*, November 1981.

36. C. W. Franklin II, "The Black Male Urban Barbershop as a Sex-Role Socialization Setting," *Sex Roles*, May 1985.

37. E. E. LeMasters, *Blue-Collar Aristocrats: Life-Styles at a Working-Class Tavern*, University of Wisconsin Press, 1975.

38. "Voices from the Tombs Speak: Yale's Three All-Male Societies Shroud Themselves in Ritual," *Yale Daily News*, April 17, 1985.

39. K. Anderson, "Friends: William Howarth and Bill Gunesch," *Denver Post*, September 15, 1985.

40. Leonard, Introduction.

41. T. Powers, "Can Friendship Survive Success?" *Ms.*, January 1975.

42. Feinberg, *Friends*.

43. M. A. Fitzpatrick and A. Bochner, "Perspectives on Self and Other: Male-Female Differences in Perceptions of Communication Behavior," *Sex Roles*, May 1981.

44. L. Wheeler et al., "Loneliness, Social Interaction and Sex Roles," *Journal of Personality and Social Psychology*, vol. 45, no. 4 (1983).

45. J. L. Fischer and L. R. Narus, Jr., "Sex Roles and Intimacy in Same Sex and Other Sex Relationships," *Psychology of Women Quarterly*, Spring 1981; J. P. Lombardo and L. O. Lavine, "Sex Role Stereotyping and Patterns of Self-Disclosure," *Sex Roles*, April 1981.

46. D. Michaelis, *The Best of Friends: Profiles of Men & Friendship*, Morrow, Quill, 1983.

47. R. Brain, *Friends and Lovers*, Basic Books, 1976. See also, S. N. Eisenstadt, "Ritualized Personal Relations: Blood Brotherhood, Best Friends, Compadre, etc.: Some Comparative Hypotheses and Suggestions," *Man*, July 1956.

48. J. K. Ehrhart and B. R. Sandler, *Campus Gang Rape: Party Games?* Project on the Status and Education of Women, Association of American Colleges, 1818 R St. N.W., Washington, D.C. 20009.

49. A. Merton, "Return to Brotherhood," *Ms.*, September 1985.

50. "L.I. Case Is First Test of State's New Hazing Law," *New York Times*, September 9, 1984.

51. D. H. Lawrence, *Studies in Classic American Literature,* Viking, 1964, p. 169.

52. W. Broyles, Jr., "Why Men Love War," *Esquire,* November 1984.

53. R. Little, "Friendships in the Military Community," in H. Z. Lopata and D. Maines, eds., *Research in the Interweave of Social Roles: Friendship,* vol. 2 (1981).

54. Feinberg, *Friends.*

55. Ibid.

56. R. R. Bell, "Friendships of Women and Men," *Psychology of Women Quarterly,* Spring 1981.

57. P. H. Wright, "Men's Friendships, Women's Friendships and the Alleged Inferiority of the Latter," *Sex Roles,* January 1982.

Chapter 14: Women Friends

1. N. Chodorow, *The Reproduction of Mothering: Psychoanalysis and the Sociology of Gender,* University of California Press, 1978.

2. J. Piaget, *The Moral Judgment of the Child,* Free Press, 1965.

3. C. Gilligan, *In a Different Voice: Psychological Theory and Women's Development,* Harvard University Press, 1982.

4. J. B. Miller, *Toward a New Psychology of Women,* Beacon Press, 1976.

5. "Psychology Revising Its View of Women," *New York Times,* March 20, 1984.

6. E. Lenz and B. Myerhoff, *The Feminization of America: How Women's Values Are Changing Our Public and Private Lives,* Tarcher, 1985.

7. B. B. Hess, "Friendship and Gender Roles Over the Life Course," in P. J. Stein, ed., *Single Life: Unmarried Adults in Social Context,* St. Martin's Press, 1981.

8. D. W. Winnicott, *The Maturational Process and the Facilitating Environment: Studies in the Theory of Emotional Development,* International Universities Press, 1965; and D. W. Winnicott, *The Family and Individual Development,* Basic Books, 1965.

9. M. I. Barreno, M. T. Horta, and M. V. da Costa, *The Three Marias,* Doubleday, 1975, p. 119.

10. J. L. Barkas, "Friendship Patterns among Young Urban Single Women," Ph.D. thesis, City University of New York, 1983.

11. R. Horowitz, *Honor and the American Dream: Culture and Social Identity in a Chicano Community,* Rutgers University Press, 1983.

12. B. Hooks, *Ain't I a Woman: Black Women and Feminism,* South End Press, 1981.

13. S. de Beauvoir, *The Second Sex* (1952), Knopf, 1968.

14. L. Bernikow, *Among Women,* Harper & Row, Colophon Books, 1981.

15. V. Miner, "Rumors from the Cauldron: Competition Among Feminist Writers," *Women's Studies International Forum,* vol. 8, no. 1 (1985).

16. M. Adams, "The Single Woman in Today's Society," *American Journal of Orthopsychiatry*, October 1971.

17. R. Pogrebin, "Looking at Brotherhood from the Outside," *Yale Daily News*, November 12, 1985.

18. L. B. Rubin, *Worlds of Pain: Life in a Working-Class Family*, Basic Books, 1976.

19. E. D. Genovese, "Life in the Big House," in N. F. Cott and E. H. Pleck, eds., *A Heritage of Her Own: Toward a New Social History of American Women*, Simon & Schuster, 1979.

20. C. Smith-Rosenberg, "The Female World of Love and Ritual: Relations between Women in 19th Century America," *Signs*, vol. 1 (1975).

21. C. N. Degler, *At Odds: Women and the Family in America from the Revolution to the Present*, Oxford University Press, 1980.

22. S. Shapiro, "What Is Romantic Friendship?" *Sojourner*, October 1983.

23. L. Faderman, *Surpassing the Love of Men: Romantic Friendship and Love between Women from the Renaissance to the Present*, Morrow, 1981.

24. A. Rich, "Compulsory Heterosexuality and Lesbian Existence," *Signs*, vol. 5, no. 4 (1980).

25. V. A. Vetere, "The Role of Friendship in the Development and Maintenance of Lesbian Love Relationships," *Journal of Homosexuality*, Winter 1982.

26. M. Krance, "A Recipe for Friendship. Nela and Fela: Two for the Book," *Chicago Tribune*, December 27, 1983.

27. M. di Leonardo, "The Female World of Cards and Holidays: Women, Families and the Work of Kinship," *Signs*, Spring 1986.

28. C. B. Stack, *All Our Kin: Strategies for Survival in a Black Community*, Harper & Row, 1974.

29. S. J. Yanagisako, "Women-Centered Kin Networks in Urban Bilateral Kinship," *American Ethologist*, vol. 4, no. 2 (1977).

30. L. Harris, *Holy Days: The World of a Hasidic Family*, Summit Books, 1985.

31. R. Giallombardo, "Social Roles in a Prison for Women," *Social Problems*, Winter, 1966.

32. B. W. Cook, "Female Support Networks and Political Activism," in Cott and Pleck, *A Heritage of Her Own*.

33. N. Sahli, "Smashing: Women's Relationships Before The Fall," *Chrysalis*, vol. 8 (1979).

34. L. J. Rupp, "Imagine My Surprise: Women's Relationships in Historical Perspective," *Frontiers*, vol. 5, no. 3 (1981).

35. N. B. Maglin, "Vida to Florence: Comrade and Companion," *Frontiers*, vol. 4, no. 3 (1979).

36. E. Power, *Medieval Women*, Cambridge University Press, 1975.

37. R. Curb and N. Manahan, *Lesbian Nuns: Breaking Silence*, Naiad Press, 1985.

38. M. Turk, *The Buried Life: A Nun's Journey*, World, 1971.

39. E. Freedman, "Separatism as Strategy: Female Institution Building and American Feminism, 1870–1930," *Feminist Studies*, Fall 1979.

40. E. K. Minnich, "Friendship between Women: The Act of Feminist Biography," *Feminist Studies*, Summer 1985.

41. E. C. Stanton, *Eighty Years and More*, 1898; reprinted, Schocken, 1971.

42. J. L. Surrey, "Self-in-Relation: A Theory of Women's Development," Stone Center for Development Services and Studies, Wellesley College, in preparation.

43. C. L. Hejinian, "An Exploration of the Role of Same-Sex Close Friendship in Women's Adult Development," *Dissertation Abstracts International*, vol. 42, no. 12 (June 1982), p. 4970-B.

44. M. Daly, *Gyn/Ecology: The Metaethics of Radical Feminism*, Beacon Press, 1978.

45. A. Seiden and P. Bart, "Woman to Woman: Is Sisterhood Powerful?" in N. Glazer-Malbin, ed., *Old Family/New Family: Interpersonal Relationships*, Van Nostrand, 1975.

46. R. R. Bell, "Friendships of Women and of Men," *Psychology of Women Quarterly*, Spring 1981.

47. J. Acker, K. Barry, and J. Esseveld, "Feminism, Female Friends and the Reconstruction of Intimacy," in H. Z. Lopata and D. Maines, eds., *Research in the Interweave of Social Roles: Friendship*, vol. 2 (1981).

48. R. Green, "Magnolias Grow in Dirt: The Bawdy Lore of Southern Women," *Southern Exposure*, Winter 1977.

49. Bernikow, *Among Women*.

50. K. Anderson, "Friends," *Denver Post*, September 15, 1985.

51. Ibid.

Chapter 15: Can Women and Men Be Friends?

1. *Oxford Classical Dictionary*, Oxford University Press, 1977.

2. Plato, *Menexenus*, Loeb Classical Library, 1929.

3. *Plutarch's Lives*, Morris, n.d.

4. Personal communication, August 1985.

5. Cao Xueqin, *The Story of the Stone*, trans. David Hawks, Penguin Classics, 1973.

6. L. C. Pogrebin, *Growing Up Free: Raising Your Child in the '80s*, McGraw-Hill, 1980.

7. E. K. Minnich, "Friendship between Women: The Act of Feminist Biography," *Feminist Studies*, Summer 1985.

8. H. H. Hacker, "Blabbermouths and Clams: Sex Differences in Self-disclosure

in Same-Sex and Cross-Sex Friendship Dyads," *Psychology of Women Quarterly*, Spring 1981.

9. S. M. Rose, "Same and Cross-Sex Friendship and the Psychology of Homosociality," *Sex Roles*, vol. 12, no. 1/2 (1985).

10. C. Leefeldt and E. Callenbach, *The Art of Friendship*, Pantheon Books, 1982.

11. R. J. Sternburg, "Measuring Love." Paper, Yale University, Department of Psychology, n.d.

12. K. E. Davis and M. J. Todd, "Friendship and Love Relationships," *Advances in Descriptive Psychology*, vol. 2 (1982). See also, K. E. Davis, "Near and Dear: Friendship and Love Compared," *Psychology Today*, February 1985.

13. R. M. Brown, "Some of My Best Friends Are . . . Men," *Ms.*, September 1985.

14. R. R. Bell, *Worlds of Friendship*, Sage, 1981.

15. M. Komarovsky, *Women in College: Shaping New Feminine Identities*, Basic Books, 1985.

16. G. Levinger, "Toward the Analysis of Close Relationships," *Journal of Experimental Psychology*, vol. 16 (1980).

17. L. Sapadin, "Cross-Sex Friendships: Their Emergence, Character and Value," Dissertation in preparation, City University of New York. (Linda Sapadin, Relationship Institute of America, 19 Cloverfield Rd., Valley Stream, N.Y. 11581.)

18. L. G. Baeren, "Can Women and Men Really Be Friends," *Sojourner*, October 1983.

19. L. Richardson, *The New Other Women: Contemporary Single Women in Affairs with Married Men*, Free Press, 1985.

20. J. Klemesrud, "Ashford & Simpson: Living Their Love Songs," *New York Times*, March 23, 1985.

21. J. Durson, "Knight and Lopez Keep Home and Heart in Play," *New York Times*, March 31, 1985.

22. Z. Rubin, "Loving and Leaving: Sex Differences in Romantic Attachments," *Sex Roles*, August 1981.

23. L. Moore, "Let's Be Friends: A How-Not-To," *Ms.*, September 1985.

24. M. McGill, "About Men: A Female Best Friend," *New York Times Magazine*, March 24, 1985.

25. H. Gans, *The Levittowners: Ways of Life and Politics in a New Suburban Community*, Pantheon Books, 1967.

26. J. Pleck, "Power and Patriarchy," *Brother*, Summer 1984. (Order from Brother, 1900 Fruitvale Avenue, Oakland, Calif. 94601.)

27. J. D. Bloch, *Friendship*, Macmillan, 1980.

28. Rose, "Same and Cross-Sex Friendship."

29. N. Babchuk, "Primary Friendship and Kin: A Study of the Associates of Middle Class Couples," *Social Forces*, vol. 43 (1965).

30. L. France, "Letters to the Editor: A Female Best Friend," *New York Times Magazine,* May 5, 1985.

31. M. Simmons, "Male Friendship," *Essence,* November 1981.

32. M. Argyle and A. Furnham, "Sources of Satisfaction and Conflict in Long-Term Relationships," *Journal of Marriage and the Family,* August 1983.

33. J. L. Fischer and L. R. Narus, Jr., "Sex Roles & Intimacy in Same Sex and Other Sex Relationships," *Psychology of Women Quarterly,* Spring 1981.

34. J. Bernard, *The Future of Marriage,* Bantam Books, 1973.

35. J. Bernard, *The Female World,* Free Press, 1981.

36. D. L. Gillespie, "Who Has the Power? The Marital Struggle," *Journal of Marriage and the Family,* vol. 33 (1971).

37. T. Morrison, *Sula,* Bantam Books, 1973.

38. R. O. Blood and D. M. Wolfe, *Husbands and Wives,* Free Press, 1960.

39. F. Lear, "Love between Grown-Ups," *Ms.,* December 1983.

40. A. Booth and E. Hess, "Cross-Sex Friendship," *Journal of Marriage and the Family,* February 1974.

41. N. Babchuk and A. P. Bates, "The Primary Relations of Middle Class Couples: A Study in Male Dominance," *American Sociological Review,* June 1963.

42. D. Michaelis, *The Best of Friends: Profiles of Men & Friendship,* Morrow, Quill, 1983.

43. E. Fishel, *The Men in Our Lives: Fathers, Lovers, Husbands, Mentors,* Morrow, 1985.

44. N. Lin, quoted in S. Johnson, "Friendship Between the Sexes," *New York Times,* October 8, 1984.

45. L. Pogrebin, "Do Women Make Men Violent?" *Ms.,* November 1974.

46. Y. Clearwater, "Intimacy in Space," *Psychology Today,* July 1985.

47. G. Stade, "Men, Boys and Wimps," *New York Times Book Review,* August 12, 1984.

48. R. R. Bell, "Friendships of Women and of Men," *Psychology of Women Quarterly,* Spring 1981.

49. M. Ruman quoted in S. Johnson, "Friendship between the Sexes," *New York Times,* October 8, 1984.

50. H. Johnson, "Best Friends," *Vogue,* July 1984.

51. Brown, "Some of My Best Friends Are."

52. N. Rubin, "A More Tolerant Time for Cross-Gender Friendships," *Newsday,* October 23, 1984.

53. Ibid.

54. A. Harmetz, "Coming to Terms with Success," *New York Times,* April 8, 1984.

55. R. Derieux, "The Weight Room: Building Strong Friendships," *Ms.*, October 1985.

56. Johnson, "Best Friends."

57. E. Prager, "Roommates, but Not Lovers," *Ms.*, April 1979.

58. J. Klemesrud, "Learning to Share: Co-ed Suites on Campus," *New York Times*, May 10, 1985.

59. Ibid.

Chapter 16: Friends for Life

1. D. Aufderheide, "A Friend We Love from Afar," *Christian Science Monitor*, October 22, 1981.

2. S. Fraiberg, *The Magic Years: Understanding and Handling the Problems of Early Childhood*, Scribners, 1968; M. R. Jalongo, "Imaginary Companions in Children's Lives and Literature," *Childhood Education*, January/February 1984; M. Pines, "Invisible Playmates," *Psychology Today*, September 1978.

3. K. Berger, *The Developing Person*, Worth, 1980. See also, C. E. Schaefer, "Imaginary Companions and Creative Adolescents," *Developmental Psychology*, vol. 1, no. 6 (1969).

4. The following sources have informed my review of friendship behavior during each stage of human development: T. J. Berndt, "The Features and Effects of Friendship in Early Adolescence," *Child Development*, December 1982; B. J. Bigelow and J. J. LaGaipa, "The Development of Friendship Values and Choice," in H. C. Foot, A. J. Chapman, and J. R. Smith, eds., *Friendship and Social Relations in Children*, Wiley, 1980; B. B. Brown, "A Life-Span Approach to Friendship," in H. Z. Lopata and D. Maines, eds., *Research in the Interweave of Social Roles: Friendship*, vol. 2 (1981); W. J. Dickens and D. Perlman, "Friendship Over the Life Cycle," in S. Duck and R. Gilmour, eds., *Personal Relationships*, vol. 2: *Developing Personal Relationships*, Academic Press, 1981; E. Douvan and J. Adelson, *The Adolescent Experience*, Wiley, 1966; C. O. Eckerman and J. L. Whatley, "Toys and Social Interaction Between Infant Peers," *Child Development*, vol. 48 (1977); D. Eder and M. T. Hallinan, "Sex Differences in Children's Friendship," *American Sociological Review*, April 1978; W. Furman and K. L. Bierman, "Developmental Changes in Young Children's Conceptions of Friendship," *Child Development*, June 1983; C. Garvey, *Children's Talk*, Harvard University Press, 1984; S. Haupert, "Men and Friendship in the Fourth Decade of Life," Master's thesis, Smith College, School for Social Work, 1981; B. B. Hess, "Friendship and Gender Roles Over the Life Course," in P. J. Stein, ed., *Single Life: Unmarried Adults in Social Context*, St. Martin's Press, 1981; C. Howes, "Patterns of Friendship," *Child Development*, August 1983; F. T. Hunter and J. Youniss, "Changes in Functions of Three Relations During Adolescence," *Developmental Psychology*, November 1982; P. M. Keither et al., "Confidants and Well-Being: A Note on Male Friendship

in Old Age," *Gerontologist,* June 1984; M. G. Lewis et al., "The Beginning of Friendship," in M. Lewis and L. A. Rosenblum, eds., *Friendship and Peer Relations,* Wiley, 1975; M. F. Lowenthal, M. Thurnher, and D. Chiriboga, eds., *Four Stages of Life,* Jossey-Bass, 1975; J. Oden, "Peer Relationship Development in Childhood," in L. G. Katz, ed., *Current Topics in Early Childhood Education,* vol. 4 (1982); H. S. Perry and M. L. Gavel, eds., *The Collected Works of Harry Stack Sullivan,* vol. 1, Norton, 1953; A. Rossi, "Life-Span Theories and Women's Lives," *Signs,* Autumn 1980; Z. Rubin, *Children's Friendships,* Harvard University Press, 1980; N. Shulman, "Life-Cycle Variations in Patterns of Close Relationships," *Journal of Marriage and the Family,* November 1975; S. A. Tesch, "Review of Friendship Development Across the Life Span," *Human Development,* September/October 1983; G. E. Vaillant, *Adaptation to Life,* Little, Brown, 1977; J. Youniss, "Friendship in Moral Development," *Momentum,* May 1982.

5. D. J. Levinson et al., *The Seasons of a Man's Life,* Knopf, 1978.

6. J. Bensman and R. Lilienfeld, "Friendship and Alienation," *Psychology Today,* October 1979.

7. R. E. Muus, "Social Cognition: Robert Selman's Theory of Role Taking," *Adolescence,* Fall 1982; G. R. Adams, "Social Competence During Adolescence," *Journal of Youth and Adolescence,* June 1983; K. D. McGuire and J. R. Weisz, "Social Cognition and Behavior Correlates of Preadolescent Chumship," *Child Development,* December 1982.

8. R. A. Goswick, "Components of the Lonely Experience in Adolescents and Young Adults." Paper presented to the Southwestern Psychological Association, April 1981.

9. J. Cohen, "High School Subcultures and the Adult World," *Adolescence,* Fall 1979. See also, M. H. Leona, "An Examination of Adolescent Clique Language in a Suburban Secondary School," *Adolescence,* Fall 1978.

10. *1985 Survey of High Achievers: Attitudes and Opinions from the Nation's High Achieving Teens* (Who's Who Among American High School Students, 721 N. McKinley Rd., Lake Forest, Ill. 60045). See also J. O. G. Billy et al., "Adolescent Sexual Behavior and Friendship Choice," *Social Choices,* March 1984; W. J. Liccione, "The Relative Influence of Significant Others on Adolescent Drinking," *Journal of Alcohol and Drug Education,* Fall 1980; G. J. Huba et al., "Beginning Adolescent Drug Use and Peer and Adult Interaction Patterns," *Journal of Consulting and Clinical Psychology,* April 1979; A. V. Wister and W. R. Avison, "Friendly Persuasion: A Social Analysis of Sex Differences in Marijuana Use," *International Journal of the Addictions,* vol. 17, no. 3 (1982); D. B. Kandel, "Homophily Selection and Socialization in Adolescent Friendship," *American Journal of Sociology,* September 1978.

11. J. L. Epstein, "Friends in School: Patterns of Selection and Influence in Secondary School." Paper, Johns Hopkins University, Center for Social Organization of Schools, November 1978.

12. J. H. Berg, "Development of Friendship between Roommates," *Journal of Personality and Social Psychology,* vol. 46, no. 2 (1984).

13. F. Klagsbrun, *Married People: Staying Together in the Age of Divorce*, Bantam Books, 1985.

14. C. A. Stueve and K. Gerson, "Personal Relations Across the Life Cycle," in C. S. Fischer, ed., *Networks and Places: Social Relations in the Urban Setting*, Free Press, 1977.

15. O. Evans, "When Friends Drift Apart," *New York Times*, April 16, 1984.

16. R. A. Caldwell, "Social Support: Its Structure and Impact on Marital Disruption," *American Journal of Community Psychology*, December 1982. See also, B. B. Brown, "The Impact of Confidants on Adjusting to Stressful Events in Adulthood." Paper presented to the Gerontological Society, November 1980.

17. R. Homel and A. Burns, "Parental Social Networks and Child Development." Paper presented to International Society for the Study of Behavior Development, August 1981. See also, T. G. Power and R. D. Parke, "Social Network Factors and the Transition to Parenthood," *Sex Roles*, November 1984.

18. E. A. Bankoff, "Effects of Friendship Support on the Psychological Well-Being of Widows," in Lopata and Maines, *Research in the Interweave of Social Roles*.

19. G. J. Wentowski, "Old Age in an Urban Setting: Coping Strategies, Reciprocity and Personal Networks." Paper presented to Gerontological Society, November 1979.

20. H. A. Nall, "Just Like Brothers: An Ethnographic Approach to the Friendship Ties of an Urban Group of Elderly Black Men," *Dissertation Abstracts International*, vol. 43, no. 7 (January 1983), p. 2390-A.

21. E. A. Powers and G. L. Bultena, "Sex Differences in Intimate Friendships of Old Age," *Journal of Marriage and the Family*, vol. 38, no. 4 (1976).

22. K. A. Roberto, "Friendship Patterns Among Older Women," *International Journal of Aging and Human Development*, vol. 19, no. 1 (1985). See also, C. J. Barrett, "Sex Differences in the Experience of Widowhood." Paper presented to the American Psychological Association, August 1978; H. Lopata, *Widowhood in an American City*, Schenkman, 1973; M. F. DeMellier, "Intimate Friendship and Adaptation to Life Stress in Older Adult Females," *Dissertation Abstracts International*, vol. 42, no. 10 (April 1982), p. 4221-B.

23. V. Wood and J. F. Robertson, "Friendship and Kinship Interaction: Differential Effect on the Morale of the Elderly," *Journal of Marriage and the Family*, vol. 40 (1978).

24. L. A. Tate, "Life Satisfaction and Death Anxiety in Aged Women," *International Journal of Aging and Human Development*, vol. 15, no. 4 (1982).

25. S. G. Candy et al., "A Developmental Exploration of Friendship Functions in Women," *Psychology of Women Quarterly*, Spring 1981.

26. F. J. Nussbaum, "The Interaction Behavior of Elderly Individuals Across Three Living Environments." Paper presented to the Speech Communication Association, June 1981.

27. C. Longino, quoted in F. Ferretti, "Elderly Choose Retirement Community Living," *New York Times,* April 5, 1984.

28. J. Gross, "The Inner Age of Stephen Spender," *New York Times Book Review,* February 26, 1984.

29. J. L. Barkas, *Friendship Throughout Life,* Public Affairs Committee, 1983.

30. F. Ferretti, "Retirement Life Varies in Three Communities," *New York Times,* April 12, 1986.

Selected Bibliography

The numbers in parentheses at the ends of entries indicate the chapter(s) in which the primary discussion of the topic will be found.

Adato, A., "Leave-Taking: A Study of Commonsense Knowledge of Social Structure," *Anthropological Quarterly*, vol. 48 (1975). (7)

Amir, Y., "Contact in Ethnic Relations," *Psychological Bulletin*, vol. 71 (1969). (11)

Argyle, M., and Furnham, A., "Sources of Satisfaction and Conflict in Long-Term Relationships," *Journal of Marriage and the Family*, August 1983. (3)

Aristotle, *The Nicomachean Ethics*, Harvard University Press, 1962. (3)

Asch, A., "Lives Without, Lives Within: Autobiographies of Blind Women and Men," *Journal of Visual Impairment and Blindness*, June 1983. (11)

Bacon, F., "The Fruits of Friendship," in *For Friendship's Sake*, Dodge, 1900. (3)

Baker, P. M., "The Friendship Process: A Developmental Model of Interpersonal Attraction," *Sociological Spectrum*, vol. 3, no. 3–4 (1983). (5)

Ball, R. E., et al., "Friendship Networks: More Supportive of Low-Income Black Women?" *Ethnicity*, March 1980. (9)

Balswick, J., and Peek, C., "The Inexpressive Male: A Tragedy of American Society," *Family Coordinator*, vol. 20 (1971). (13)

Barkas, J. L., *Friendship Throughout Life*, Public Affairs Committee, 1983. (16)

Barnhart, E., "Friends and Lovers in a Lesbian Counterculture Community," in N. Glazer, ed., *Old Family/New Family*, Van Nostrand, 1970. (11)

Baxter, L. A., "Self-Disclosure as a Relationship Disengagement Strategy," *Human Communication Research*, Spring 1979. (7)

—— and Philpott, Jr., "Communicator Age & Sex Role Orientation Differences in Preferred Relationships Termination Strategies." Paper presented at the annual meeting of the Speech Communication Association, November 1981. (7)

Bell, R. R., *Worlds of Friendship*, Sage, 1981. (13, 14)

Benedict, E., *Slow Dancing*, Knopf, 1985. (8)

Berger, C. R., and Calabrese, R. J., "Some Explorations in Initial Interaction and Beyond," *Human Communication Research*, vol. 1 (1975). (5)

Berger, R. M., "Realities of Gay and Lesbian Aging," *Social Work*, vol. 29, no. 1 (1984). (16)

Bernard, J., *The Female World*, Free Press, 1981. (14)

Best, R., *We've All Got Scars: What Boys and Girls Learn in Elementary School*, Indiana University Press, 1983. (16)

Bigelow, B., "Children's Friendship Expectations: A Cognitive Developmental Study," *Child Development*, vol. 48 (1977). (16)

Blackwell, J. E., and Hart, P. S., *Cities, Suburbs, and Blacks: A Study of Concerns, Distrust, and Alienation*, General Hall, 1982. (9, 11)

Block, J. D., *Friendship: How to Give It, How to Get It*, Macmillan, 1980. (8, 13)

Bohannan, P., "The Six Stages of Divorce," in P. Bohannan, ed., *Divorce and After*, Doubleday, 1970. (6)

Booth, A., "Sex and Social Participation," *American Sociological Review*, vol. 37 (1972). (13)

Bruner, J., "Interaction, Communication and Self," *Journal of the American Academy of Child Psychiatry*, January 1984. (10)

Caldwell, M. A., and Peplau, L. A., "Sex Differences in Same Sex Friendship," *Sex Roles*, July 1982. (13, 14)

Campbell, A., *The Sense of Well-Being in America: Recent Patterns and Trends*, McGraw-Hill, 1981. (4)

Cannon, L. W., "Trends in Class Identification among Black Americans from 1952 to 1978," *Social Science Quarterly*, March 1984. (9)

Carnegie, D., *How to Win Friends and Influence People*, Simon & Schuster, Pocket Books, 1937, rev. ed. 1982. (8)

Carrillo, A. P., et al., *No More Stares*, Disability Rights Education and Defense Fund (2032 San Pablo Avenue, Berkeley, Calif. 94702), 1982. (11)

Chappell, N. L., "Re-examining Conceptual Boundaries: Peer and Intergenerational Relations," *Essence: Issues in the Study of Ageing, Dying and Death*, vol. 4, no. 3 (1980). (11)

Charlesworth, R., and Hartup, W. W., "Positive Social Reinforcement in the Nursery School Peer Group," *Child Development*, vol. 38 (1967). (16)

Chesler, M. A., and Barbarin, O. A., "Dilemmas of Providing Help in a Crisis: The Role of Friends with Parents of Children with Cancer," *Journal of Social Issues*, vol. 40, no. 4 (1984). (6)

Chodorow, N., "Family Structure and Feminine Personality," in M. Z. Rosaldo and L. Lamphere, eds., *Woman, Culture, and Society*, Stanford University Press, 1974. (14)

Cicero, "De Amicitia," in *The Joys of Friendship*, Foulis (London), n.d. (3)

Clark, M. L., "Gender, Race and Friendship Research." Paper presented at the annual meeting of the American Educational Research Association, April 1985. (11)

—— and Ayers, M., "Race, Gender and Reciprocity: Effects of Friendship Similarity During Early Adolescence." Paper presented at the annual meeting of the American Educational Research Association, April 1985. (11)

Cohen, J., et al., "Cross-Sex Friendship in Children," *Psychology in the Schools*, October 1980. (15)

Creecy, R., "Environmental and Structural Effects on Friendship in Old Age," *Gerontologist*, vol. 15, no. 5 (1975). (11)

Davey, A., "Pride and Prejudice in the Primary School," *Education*, Fall 1981. (10)

David, D. S., and Brannon, R., *The Forty-Nine Percent Majority: The Male Sex Role*, Addison-Wesley, 1976. (13)

Davidson, L. R., and Duberman, L., "Friendship: Communication and Interactional Patterns in Same-Sex Dyads," *Sex Roles*, August 1982. (14)

Davidson, S., and Packard, T., "The Therapeutic Value of Friendship Between Women," *Psychology of Women Quarterly*, Spring 1981. (14)

Diaz, R. M., and Berndt, T. J., "Children's Knowledge of a Best Friend: Fact or Fancy?" *Developmental Psychology*, vol. 18, no. 6 (1982). (16)

Didion, J., *A Book of Common Prayer*, Simon & Schuster, 1977. (8)

Dowd, M., "Horrors of Hors d'Oeuvres Circuit," *New York Times*, March 1, 1985. (9)

Dubois, E., "The Gratuitous Act: An Introduction to the Comparative Study of Friendship Patterns," in E. Layton, ed., *The Compact: Selected Dimensions of Friendship*, University of Toronto Press, 1974. (16)

Duck, S., *Friends for Life: The Psychology of Close Relationships*, St. Martin's Press, 1983. (5)

——, *The Study of Acquaintance*, Gower Press (Hampshire, England), 1977. (5)

Dunkel-Schetter, C., "Social Support and Cancer: Findings Based on Patient Interviews and Their Implications," *Journal of Social Issues*, vol. 40, no. 4 (1984). (6)

Durojaiye, M. O. A., "Patterns of Friendship in an Ethnically Mixed School," *Race*, vol. 12, no. 2 (1970). (11)

——, "Patterns of Friendship and Leadership Choices in a Mixed Ethnic Junior School," *British Journal of Educational Psychology*, vol. 39, no. 1 (1969). (10)

Edgar, T. M., "Homophobia and Intimate Self-Disclosure: Why Aren't Men Talking?" Paper presented at the annual meeting of the International Communication Association, May 1983. (13)

Elder, G., "Appearance and Education in Marriage Mobility," *American Sociological Review,* vol. 34 (1969). (9)

Emerson, R. W., "Friendship," in *For Friendship's Sake,* Dodge, 1900. (3)

Epstein, J. L., *Choice of Friends Over the Life Span: Developmental and Environmental Influence,* Johns Hopkins University, Center for Social Organization of Schools, July 1983. (16)

Erikson, E., "Identity and the Life Cycle," *Psychological Issues,* vol. 1, no. 1 (1959). (16)

Fillmer, H. T., "Sex Stereotyping of the Elderly by Children," *Educational Gerontology,* vol. 8, no. 1 (1982). (11)

Fine, M., and Asch, A., "Disabled Women: Sexism without the Pedestal," in M. J. Deegan and N. A. Brooks, eds., *Women and Disability: The Double Handicap,* Transaction Books, 1985. (11)

Fischer, C. S., *To Dwell Among Friends: Personal Networks in Town and City,* University of Chicago Press, 1982. (2, 3, 8, 9)

———, "The Public and Private Worlds of City Life," *American Sociological Review,* June 1981. (3)

———, "What Do We Mean By 'Friend': An Inductive Study," *Social Network,* no. 3 (1982), pp. 287–306. (2)

Fisher, B., and Galler, R., "Friendship and Fairness: How Disability Affects Friendship between Women," in A. Asch and M. Fine, eds., *Disabled Women: Psychology from the Margins,* Temple University Press, to be published in 1987. (11)

Foa, U. G., and Foa, E. B., *Societal Structures of the Mind,* Thomas, 1974. (3)

Fox, M., et al., "Age and Gender Dimensions of Friendship," *Psychology of Women Quarterly,* December 1985. (16)

"Friendship: An Inquiry," *Psychology Today,* March 1979. (2)

"The Friendship Bond: Survey Report on Friendship in America," *Psychology Today,* October 1979. (2, 3)

Gamarekian, B., "One's Kingdom for a Good Seat," *New York Times,* July 19, 1984. (9)

Gans, H., *The Levittowners: Ways of Life and Politics in a New Suburban Community,* Pantheon Books, 1967. (9)

Garfinkel, P., *In a Man's World: Father, Son, Brother, Friend, and Other Roles Men Play,* NAL Books, 1985. (13)

Gliedman, J., and Roth, W., *The Unexpected Minority: Handicapped Children in America,* Harcourt Brace Jovanovich, 1980. (11)

Godwin, G., *The Finishing School,* Viking, 1984. (8)

Goebel, J. B., and Cole, S. G., "Mexican-American and White Reactions to Stimulus Persons of Same and Different Race: Similarity and Attraction as a Function of Prejudice," *Psychological Reports,* June 1975. (11)

Goffman, E., *Stigma: Notes on the Management of Spoiled Identity,* Prentice-Hall, 1963. (11)

Goist, D. F., "Will You Still Need Me? Will You Still Feed Me? When I'm 84," *Dissertation Abstracts International*, vol. 41, no. 3 (September 1980), p. 1119-A. (16)

Goleman, D., "Emotional Support Has Its Destructive Side," *New York Times*, August 27, 1985. (6)

——, "Saying Goodbye Speaks Volumes," *New York Times*, April 3, 1984. (7)

Gottman, J., *How Children Become Friends*, University of Chicago Press, Monographs of the Society for Research in Child Development, vol. 48, no. 3 (1983). (16)

Goudy, W. J., et al., "Social Ties and Life Satisfaction of Older Persons," *Journal of Gerontological Social Work*, Fall 1981. (16)

Gould, R. E., et al., "Do Men Have Better Relationships with Each Other than Women Do with Other Women?" *Medical Aspects of Human Sexuality*, vol. 13, no. 9 (1979). (13)

Gray, F. du Plessix, *World Without End*, Berkley, 1982. (8)

Greenberg, J., *In This Sign*, Holt, Rinehart and Winston, 1970. (11)

Grunebaum, H., and Solomon, L., "Toward a Theory of Peer Relationships," *International Journal of Group Psychotherapy*, July 1982. (16)

Guinzburg, S., "Kindergarten Segregationists," *Psychology Today*, November 1983. (10)

Hacker, H. H., "Blabbermouths and Clams: Sex Differences in Self-disclosure in Same-Sex and Cross-Sex Friendship Dyads," *Psychology of Women Quarterly*, Spring 1981. (13)

Hartup, W. W., "The Origins of Friendship," in M. Lewis and L. A. Rosenblum, eds., *Friendship and Peer Relations*, Wiley, 1975. (16)

Hatfield, E., and Traupmann, J., "Intimate Relationships: A Perspective from Equity Theory," in S. Duck and R. Gilmour, eds., *Personal Relationships*, vol. 1: *Studying Personal Relationships*, Academic Press, 1981. (3)

Hayes, D. S., "Cognitive Bases for Liking and Disliking among Preschool Children," *Child Development*, vol. 49 (1978). (16)

Hess, B. B., "Aging, Gender Role and Friendship," *Educational Horizons*, Summer 1982. (16)

——, "Friendship," in M. W. Riley and A. Foner, eds., *Aging and Society*, vol. 3: *A Sociology of Age Stratification*, Russel Sage Foundation, 1972. (16)

Hickey, T., and Kalish, R. A., "Young People's Perceptions of Adults," *Journal of Gerontology*, vol. 23 (1968). (11)

Hinde, R. A., *Towards Understanding Relationships*, Academic Press, 1979. (3)

Hochschild, A. R., *The Unexpected Community: Portrait of an Old Age Subculture*, University of California Press, 1983. (16)

Huckfeldt, R. R., "Social Contexts, Social Networks, and Urban Neighborhoods: Environmental Constraints on Friendship Choice," *American Journal of Sociology*, vol. 89, no. 3 (1983). (9)

Hunter, M. S., et al., "Female Friendship: Joint Defense Against Situational Power Inequity," *Psychology*, vol. 20, no. 1 (1983). (14)

Huston, T. L., and Levinger, G., "Interpersonal Attraction and Relationships," *Annual Review of Psychology*, vol. 29 (1978). (5)

Israeloff, R., "How to Keep Marriage from Spoiling Friendships with Single Friends," *Glamour*, October 1983. (6)

Jacklin, C. N., and Maccoby, E. E., "Social Behavior at 33 Months in Same-Sex and Mixed-Sex Dyads," *Child Development*, vol. 49 (1978). (15)

Jecker, J., and Landy, D., "Liking a Person as a Function of Doing Him a Favor," *Human Relations*, vol. 22 (1969). (4)

Jelinek, M. M., and Brittan, E. M., "Multiracial Education: 1. Inter-ethnic Friendship Patterns," *Educational Research*, vol. 18, no. 1 (1975). (10)

Jordan, J. V., "Empathy and Self Boundaries," Stone Center for Developmental Services and Studies, Wellesley College, 1984. (14)

Kelley, H. H., and Thibaut, J. W., *Interpersonal Relations: A Theory of Independence*, Wiley, 1978. (3)

Kim, Y. Y., "Acculturation and Patterns of Interpersonal Communication Relationships: A Study of Japanese, Mexican and Korean Communities in the Chicago Area." Paper presented at the annual meeting of the Speech Communication Association, November 1978. (11)

Knapp, M. L., *Social Intercourse: From Greeting to Goodbye*, Allyn & Bacon, 1978. (5, 7)

——, et al., "The Rhetoric of Goodbye: Verbal and Nonverbal Correlates of Human Leave-Taking," *Speech Monographs*, vol. 40 (1973). (7)

Kolman, A. S., "Self-Disclosure Patterns of Male and Female College Students: Change Over Time," Educational Resources Information Center (ERIC) ED 162 944, 1978. (13)

Kourvetaris, G. A., and Dobratz, B. A., "An Empirical Test of Gordon's Ethnoclass Hypothesis among Three Enthnoreligious Groups," *Sociology and Social Research*, vol. 61, no. 1 (1976). (10)

Kurdek, L. A., and Krile, D., "A Developmental Analysis of the Relationship between Peer Acceptance and Both Interpersonal Understanding and Perceived Social Self-competence," *Child Development*, December 1982. (16)

Ladd, G. W., "Social Networks of Popular, Average and Rejected Children in School Settings," *Merrill Palmer Quarterly*, July 1983. (16)

La Gaipa, J. J., "A Systems Approach to Personal Relationships," in S. Duck and R. Gilmour, eds., *Personal Relationships*, vol. 1: *Studying Personal Relationships*, Academic Press, 1981. (3)

——, "Testing a Multidimensional Approach to Friendship," in S. Duck, ed., *Theory and Practice in Interpersonal Attraction*, Academic Press, 1977. (5)

LaPatra, J., *The Age Factor: Love, Sex and Friendship in Age Different Relationships*, Evans, 1980. (11)

Lee, L. C., "Social Encounters of Infants: The Beginnings of Popularity." Paper presented to the International Society for the Study of Behavioral Development, 1973. (16)

Leefeldt, C., and Callenbach, E., *The Art of Friendship*, Pantheon Books, 1982. (8)

Levinger, G., "Toward the Analysis of Close Relationships," *Journal of Experimental Social Psychology*, vol. 16 (1980). (5)

Levinson, D. J., et al., *The Seasons of a Man's Life*, Knopf, 1978. (15)

Liebow, E., *Tally's Corner: A Study of Negro Streetcorner Men*, Little, Brown, 1967. (9)

Lindenbaum, J. P., "The Shattering of an Illusion: The Problem of Competition in Lesbian Relationships," *Feminist Studies*, Spring 1985. (14)

Lindsey, K., *Friends as Family*, Beacon Press, 1981. (8)

Longino, H., and Miner, V., eds., *Competition among Women: A Feminist Analysis*, Feminist Press, to be published in 1987. (14)

Machlowitz, M., *Whiz Kids: Success at an Early Age*, Arbor House, 1985. (12)

——, *Workaholics: Living with Them, Working with Them*, Addison-Wesley, 1980. (12)

Mannarino, A. P., "Friendship Patterns and Self-Concept Development in Preadolescent Males," *Journal of Genetic Psychology*, vol. 133, no. 1 (1978). (16)

Mayer, T. F., "Parties and Networks," *Journal of Mathematical Sociology*, May 1984. (8)

McDuffie, W. G., "You Don't Have to Be My Grandparent to Be My Good Friend." Paper presented at the annual meeting of the National Association for the Education of Young Children, November 1979. (11)

McTavish, D. G., "Perceptions of Old Age," *Gerontologist*, vol. 11 (1971). (11)

Mendoza, R. H., "Information Processing Styles: A Cross-Cultural Study," *Dissertation Abstracts International*, vol. 41, no. 10 (April 1981), p. 3935-B. (11)

Miller, L. D., "Attraction and Communication Style: Perceptual Differences between Friends and Enemies as a Function of Sex and Race." Paper presented at the annual meeting of the International Communication Association, April 1978. (10).

Mills, J., and Clark, M. S., "Exchange and Communal Relationships," in L. Wheeler, ed., *Review of Personality and Social Psychology*, Sage, 1982. (3)

Montaigne, "Of Friendship," in *Essays*, Penguin Classics, 1958. (3)

Morrison, T., *Sula*, Bantam Books, 1973. (8)

Murray, R. M., "Patterns of Adult Friendships," *Dissertation Abstracts International*, vol. 43, no. 5 (November 1982), p. 1638-B. (4)

Naylor, G., *The Women of Brewster Place*, Viking, 1982. (8)

Newcomb, A. F., and Brady, J. E., "Mutuality in Boys' Friendship Relations," *Child Development*, vol. 53 (1982). (16)

Newman, M. A., et al., "Ethnic Awareness in Children: Not a Unitary Concept," *Journal of Genetic Psychology*, September 1983. (10).

Oates, J. C., *Solstice,* Dutton, 1985. (8)

Off Our Backs, Special Issue on Women and Disability, May 1981. (11)

Olstad, K., "Brave New Men," in J. Petras, ed., *Sex: Male/Gender: Masculine,* Alfred, 1975. (13)

Paley, G., *Later the Same Day,* Farrar, Straus & Giroux, 1985. (8)

Parham, W. D., and Tinsley, H. E. A., "What Are Friends For? Students' Expectations of the Friendship Encounter," *Journal of Counseling Psychology,* September 1980. (4)

Parmalee, P., and Werner, C., "Lonely Losers: Stereotypes and Single Dwellers," *Personality and Social Psychology Bulletin,* no. 4 (1978). (2)

Phillips, G. M., and Wood, J. T., *Communication and Human Relationships: The Study of Interpersonal Communication,* Macmillan, 1983. (14)

Piercy, M., *Small Changes,* Fawcett, Crest, 1978. (8)

Pilisuk, M., and Minkler, M., "Supportive Networks: Life Ties for the Elderly," *Journal of Social Issues,* vol. 36 (1980). (8)

Plutzik, R., and Plutzik, L. M., *The Private Life of Parents: How to Take Care of Yourself and Your Partner While Raising Happy, Healthy Children: A Complete Survival Guide,* Dodd, Mead/Everest House, 1983. (6)

Pogrebin, L. C., "Alan Alda Talks about Love, Friendship, Sex, Envy, Food and a Few Not So Deadly Sins," *Ms.,* June 1981. (6)

——, *Growing Up Free,* McGraw-Hill, 1980; chapters 17, 18. (16)

——, "Competing with Women," *Ms.,* July 1972. (14)

Pramuk, G., and Danner, F., "Developmental Patterns of Self-disclosure." Paper presented to American Educational Research Association, March 1982. (16)

Reisman, J. M., and Schorr, S. I., "Friendship Claims and Expectations Among Children and Adults," *Child Development,* vol. 49, no. 3 (1978). (2)

Richey, M. H., and Richey, H. W., "The Significance of Best-Friend Relationships in Adolescence," *Psychology in the Schools,* October 1980. (13, 16)

Rook, K. S., "Promoting Social Bonding: Strategies for Helping the Lonely and Socially Isolated," *American Psychologist,* December 1984. (4)

Rose, P. I., *Strangers in Their Midst: Small-Town Jews and Their Neighbors,* Richwood, 1977. (10)

Rosenfeld, L. B., "Self-Disclosure Avoidance: Why I Am Afraid to Tell You Who I Am," *Communication Monographs,* March 1979. (13)

Rossi, A., "Life-Span Theories and Women's Lives," *Signs,* Autumn 1980. (12)

Rubin, L. B., *Just Friends,* Harper & Row, 1985. (11)

Rubin, Z., "Breaking the Age Barrier to Friendship," *Psychology Today,* March 1980. (11)

——, *Children's Friendships,* Harvard University Press, 1980. (8)

——, *Liking and Loving: An Invitation to Social Psychology,* Holt, Rinehart and Winston, 1973. (2)

Ryff, C. D., and Migdal, S., "Intimacy and Generativity: Self-perceived Transitions," *Signs,* vol. 9, no. 3 (1984). (16)

Safilios-Rothschild, C., "Toward a Social Psychology of Relationships," *Psychology of Women Quarterly,* Spring 1981. (2)

Santmyer, H. H., . . . *And Ladies of the Club,* Berkley, 1985. (8)

Savin-Williams, R. C., and Knipp, C. J., "Nominated and Observed Adolescent Friendship: A Comparison of Findings." Paper presented at the annual convention of the American Psychological Association, August 1983. (16)

Scanzoni, J., "Social Exchange and Behavioral Interdependence," in R. L. Burgess and T. L. Huston, eds., *Social Exchange in Developing Relationships,* Academic Press, 1979. (3)

Selman, R. L., *The Growth of Interpersonal Understanding: Developmental and Clinical Analysis,* Academic Press, 1980. (5, 16)

Serbin, L. A., "Sex Stereotyped Play Behavior in the Preschool Classroom." Paper presented to the Society for Research in Child Development, March 1977. (15)

Simon, R. J., et al., "An Empirical Note about Married Women and Their Friends," *Social Forces,* vol. 48 (June 1970). (9)

Spenkle, D. H., and Cyrus, C. L., "Abandonment: The Stress of Sudden Divorce," in C. R. Figley and H. I. McCubbin, eds., *Stress and the Family,* vol. 2: *Coping with Catastrophe,* Brunner/Mazel, 1983. (6)

Stueve, A., *The Elderly as Network Members,* Haworth Press, 1983. (16)

—— and Gerson, K., "Personal Relations Across the Life Cycle," in C. S. Fischer, ed., *Networks and Places: Social Relations in the Urban Setting,* Free Press, 1977. (3)

Sullivan, H. S., *The Interpersonal Theory of Psychiatry,* Norton, 1953. (16)

Sundstrom, E., and Sundstrom, M. G., *Work Places: Psychology of the Physical Environment,* Cambridge University Press, 1986. (12)

Suttles, G., "Friendship as a Social Institution," in G. J. McCall, ed., *Social Relationships,* Aldine, 1970. (3)

Swain, S., "Covert Intimacy: Closeness in Men's Same-Sex Friendships," Center for Research on Women, Wellesley, Mass. 02181. (13)

Swartz, M., "When a Close Friend Marries," *Glamour,* June 1982. (6)

Temme, L. V., and Cohen, J. M., "Ethnic Differences in High School Friendship," *Sociology of Education,* vol. 43, no. 4 (1970). (10)

Thomas, E. C., and Yamamoto, K., "Attitude Toward Age: An Exploration in School Age Children," *International Journal of Aging and Human Development,* vol. 6 (1975). (11)

Thomas, K. C., "The Influence of Race on Adolescent Friendship Patterns," *Educational Studies,* vol. 8, no. 3 (1982). (11,16)

Ting-Toomey, S., "Ethnic Identity and Close Friendship in Chinese-American College Students." Paper presented at the annual meeting of the International Communication Association, May 1980. (10)

Toffler, A., *Future Shock,* Bantam Books, 1970. (2)

——, *The Third Wave,* Bantam Books, 1981. (2)

Tognoli, J., "Male Friendship and Intimacy Across the Lifespan," *Family Relations,* June 1980. (13)

Triandis, H. C., et al., "Social Status as a Determinant of Respect and Friendship," *Sociometry,* vol. 29, no. 4 (1966). (9)

Vaillant, G. E., *Adaptation to Life,* Little, Brown, 1977. (13)

Verbrugge, L. M., "A Research Note on Adult Friendship Contact: A Dyadic Perspective," *Social Forces,* vol. 62 (September 1983). (2, 16)

Wagner, R., and Schaffer, D., "Social Networks and Survival Strategies: An Exploratory Study of Mexican-American, Black and Anglo Family Heads in San Jose," in M. Melville, ed., *Twice a Minority,* Mosby, 1980. (10)

Walker, A., *The Color Purple,* Harcourt Brace Jovanovich, 1982. (8)

Walster, E. W., *Equity: Theory and Research,* Allyn & Bacon, 1978. (3)

Weiss, L., and Lowenthal, M., "Life Course Perspective on Friendship," in M. F. Lowenthal, M. Thurnher, and D. Chiriboga, eds., *Four Stages of Life,* Jossey-Bass, 1975. (13)

Weiss, R. S., "The Fund of Sociability," *Trans-Action,* vol. 6 (1969). (3)

——, *Marital Separation,* Basic Books, 1975. (6)

Weldon, F., *Female Friends,* Heinemann (London), 1975. (8)

Williams, D. G., "Gender, Masculinity-Femininity and Emotional Intimacy in Same Sex Friendship," *Sex Roles,* March 1985. (13)

Williams, J. G., and Solano, C. H., "The Social Reality of Feeling Lonely: Friendship and Reciprocation," *Personality and Social Psychology Bulletin,* June 1983. (4)

Williams, J. H., "Close Friendship Relations of Housewives Residing in an Urban Community," *Social Forces,* May 1958. (9)

Wolf, D. G., *The Lesbian Community,* University of California Press, 1979. (11)

Wolfe, L., "Friendship in the City," *New York,* July 18, 1983. (9)

Women and Disability Awareness Project, *Building Community: A Manual Exploring Issues of Women and Disability,* Educational Equity Concepts (114 East 32 Street, New York, N.Y. 10016), 1984. (11)

Wortman, C. B., and Dunkel-Schetter, C., "Interpersonal Relationships and Cancer," *Journal of Social Issues,* vol. 35, no. 1 (1979). (6)

Wright, P. H., and Keple, T. W., "Friends and Parents of a Sample of High School Juniors: An Exploratory Study of Relationship Intensity and Interpersonal Rewards," *Journal of Marriage and the Family,* August 1981. (13)

Young, W., "An Ecological Approach to Theories of Aging." Paper presented at the Speech Communication Association Conference on Communication and Gerontology, July 1981. (16)

Zimring, C. M., "Stress and the Designed Environment," *Journal of Social Issues,* vol. 37, no. 1 (1981). (12)

Index

Index